Fiscal Decentralization and the Challenge of Hard Budget Constraints

Fiscal Decentralization and the Challenge of Hard Budget Constraints

edited by Jonathan Rodden,
Gunnar S. Eskeland, and
Jennie Litvack

The MIT Press
Cambridge, Massachusetts
London, England

This book was set in Palatino by SNP Best-set Typesetter Ltd., Hong Kong.

Printed and bound in the United States of America.

Library of Congress Cataloging-in-Publication Data

Fiscal decentralization and the challenge of hard budget constraints / edited by Jonathan Rodden, Gunnar S. Eskeland, and Jennie Litvack.
    p.   cm.
   Includes bibliographical references and index.
   ISBN 0-262-18229-7 (hc. : alk. paper)
   1. Fiscal policy. 2. Intergovernmental fiscal relations. I. Rodden, Jonathan. II. Eskeland, Gunnar S. III. Litvack, Jennie I. (Jennie Ilene), 1963–
HJ192.5 .F567   2003
336.3—dc21   2002029553

10 9 8 7 6 5 4 3 2 1

Contents

Preface

This book is the product of a multicountry research project at the World Bank aimed at understanding the institutional settings in which decentralization may lead to large fiscal deficits and macroeconomic instability. The project was undertaken by the Decentralization Thematic Group, which found a significant gap in knowledge regarding the macroeconomic risks associated with decentralization. Not until there is a better understanding of how and why decentralization poses risks to macroeconomic stability can governments begin to design policies and institutions to safeguard against those risks.

The study develops an analytical framework for considering the issues related to soft budget constraints for state and local governments, including the institutions, history, and policies that drive expectations for bailouts among subnational governments. Four mechanisms for disciplining subnational governments—fiscal, financial, political, and land markets—are developed and applied to each of the eleven country case studies (Argentina, Brazil, Canada, China, Germany, Hungary, India, Norway, South Africa, Ukraine, and the United States).

While recent econometric studies and scattered case studies allude to the complexity of hard budget constraints, this is the first in-depth look at a wide range of institutions that individually and collectively affect subnational discipline. Including developed and developing countries in the same study is important since the latter provide a historical perspective unavailable in many newly decentralizing developing countries.

The policy implications of the study are very strong, playing directly into the long-standing debate (in which the World Bank, International Monetary Fund, and many academics have participated) between market and hierarchical mechanisms in the support of fiscal discipline under decentralization. The study concludes that this will often be a false dichotomy. In practice, most countries, and virtually all developing countries, will require both in order to maintain fiscal discipline and derive some efficiency gains. The cases provide ample examples of different combinations of mechanisms that have resulted in varying degrees of success. Expectations about extraordinary fiscal support from the central government are formed not only by whether there is a history of bailouts, but also by cues embedded in a variety of fiscal, political, and financial institutions. These institutions range from the basic architecture of government, like the separation of powers and the fiscal strength of the central government, to specific rules governing municipal bankruptcies and the distribution of intergovernmental transfers. Rather than portraying bailout episodes merely as regrettable failures, several of the cases suggest that if unavoidable bailouts are properly structured, they present opportunities to reform the underlying institutions that create bad incentives. The editors conclude that successful market discipline is not likely to appear instantly in newly decentralizing countries, but can emerge from a gradual evolutionary experience that starts with carefully crafted rules and oversight.

We are grateful to the World Bank, especially Shanta Devarajan and Cheryl Gray for their insights and support throughout the project. Robert Inman deserves special thanks for helping to give the study its direction and form. We appreciated helpful comments on the introduction and conclusion chapters from Amaresh Bagchi, Nirvikar Singh, Jürgen von Hagen, and the authors of the case studies. For useful comments on the entire manuscript, we thank four anonymous referees. We also thank John Covell for his help in bringing the volume to fruition at MIT Press. Finally, we are thankful to Humaira Qureshi for logistical support and Diana Rheault for editorial assistance.

Contributors

Junaid Ahmad, Lead Economist, Infrastructure and Urban Development Department, South Asia Region, World Bank

Richard M. Bird, Professor Emeritus and Director of International Tax Program, Rotman School of Management, University of Toronto, Canada

Gunnar S. Eskeland, Senior Economist, Development Research Group, World Bank

Robert Inman, Miller-Sherrerd Professor of Finance and Economics, Wharton School, University of Pennsylvania, Philadelphia

Jing Jin, SAIS, Johns Hopkins University, Washington, D.C.

Jennie Litvack, Senior Economist, Poverty Reduction and Economic Management Network, Public Sector Management Division, World Bank

William J. McCarten, Senior Economist, South Asia, Poverty Reduction and Economic Management Network, World Bank

Sean O'Connell, Securities Analyst, Columbus Circle Investors

Anita Papp, Economist, Poverty Reduction and Economic Management Network, World Bank (Sadly, Ms. Papp passed away in September of 2000.)

Jørn Rattsø, Professor, Department of Economics, Norwegian University of Science and Technology, Trondheim, Norway

Jonathan Rodden, Assistant Professor of Political Science, Massachusetts Institute of Technology, Cambridge

Almos Tassonyi, Senior Economist, Property Taxation Policy Branch, Ontario Ministry of Finance, Canada

Steven B. Webb, Senior Economist, Latin America and Caribbean Region, Economic Policy Sector

Deborah Wetzel, Lead Economist, Europe and Central Asia, Poverty Reduction and Economic Management Network, World Bank

Zou Heng-fu, Senior Economist, Development Economics and Chief Economist, World Bank, and Professor of Economics, Peking and Wuhan Universities, China

I

Introduction

1 Introduction and Overview

Jonathan Rodden,
Gunnar S. Eskeland, and
Jennie Litvack

1.1 The Context of Decentralization

The basic structure of government is undergoing a major transformation in countries around the world. In the past decade, demands for greater democracy and frustrations with the inability of central governments to deliver local services have provided politicians with incentives to decentralize power and resources to lower levels of government. Although many industrialized countries have had a long history with decentralized governance, developing countries—federal and unitary alike—have only recently begun to follow suit. Challenges facing industrialized countries are often magnified in developing countries, where the institutions necessary for successful decentralization are weaker.

This wave of decentralization is often driven by politics, yet its repercussions can be felt heavily in the economic sphere. And just as global experience with decentralization has accelerated, so too has research examining its economic impact on efficiency, equity, and macroeconomic stability. This has engendered a debate about the costs and benefits of decentralization.[1] On the one hand, economists have long posited that moving decision making to the lowest level possible—as long as externalities and economies of scale are tolerable—will lead to decisions that reflect local needs and preferences better and thus improve efficiency. On the other hand, it is becoming increasingly clear that decentralization can introduce new costs that undermine the benefits. In particular, the decentralization of fiscal and political authority creates incentives for opportunistic behavior among state and local officials. If the incentive framework is not well structured, the scope for microeconomic efficiency gains and even such goals as macroeconomic stability might be undermined.[2]

1.1.1 The Challenge of Fiscal Discipline

Maintenance of fiscal discipline, the subject of this study, is perhaps the most serious challenge for decentralizing countries. As discussed in greater length in this chapter and throughout the book, when budget constraints are soft, an entity can increase expenditures without eventually facing the full cost, and thus it will tend to overspend. Conversely, if budget constraints are hard, the entity understands that it will face undesirable consequences if it spends more than it can afford, and thus has incentives to manage its resources prudently. Decentralized countries are particularly susceptible to overspending in situations of soft budget constraints because subnational governments are likely to put their own interests (and those of their constituents) before those of the larger country. This is a simple collective action problem. If soft budget constraints exist and the subnational government can appeal to the central government for additional resources through channels such as intergovernmental fiscal transfers, state-owned enterprises, and banking, they are likely to overspend, under-tax, or overborrow. This behavior is not in the interest of the country at large, but it is in the interest of each subnational government.

Whether subnational governments face reasonably hard budget constraints depends, as this study shows, not only on formal policies and institutions, but also on more subtle determinants of expectations and behavior. There must be no doubt among all actors that subnational governments manage their own affairs and will receive a fixed, transparent sum from the central government to do so, while all additional resources must be raised locally or borrowed. Hard and soft budget constraints represent two end points on a scale. The question is not whether a particular country has a hard or soft budget constraint; rather, this study seeks out the weak spots that soften the budget constraint and alter the expectations and behavior of subnational governments.

This book uses case studies to explore the sources of soft budget constraints and unearth the mechanisms used to harden them. It identifies the main channels through which expectations are determined—for example, intergovernmental fiscal relations, financial sector regulations, and political systems—and analyzes these within different country settings in the developing and industrialized worlds. This exploration thus transcends more abstract debates about the merits of decentralization, showing how the relationship among decentralization, efficiency, and accountability to citizens depends critically on a country's background and institutions. Moving beyond the initial questions about whether decentralization is good or bad for macroeconomic management, we seek a practical assessment of how to improve management in decentralized settings.

1.1.2   A Brief Theoretical Background

Decentralization may be defined in many ways, but typically involves increased autonomy and responsibilities for lower-level entities in one dimension or another. For a country, as for a firm or any other organization, autonomy for a member entity raises the potential for opportunistic behavior, possibly with undesirable as well as desirable effects.

In public finance, one prominent tradition analyzes problems of governance from the perspective of a benevolent planner. For example, Samuelson (1954) takes this perspective when developing principles for optimal expenditure on public goods, as do Diamond and Mirrlees (1971) when developing principles for an optimal tax structure. Similarly, Musgrave (1959) offers the classic assignment of powers and responsibilities in a federal structure from the perspective of what level of government is best suited to handle the various tasks of government. These authors view the assumption of a benevolent planner as a useful analytical device rather than a realistic assumption.

Results from another literature on local public goods do not require a benevolent planner. This literature points to benefits of small jurisdictions. Tiebout (1956) shows that selfish governments (landowners, in fact) would—under stringent conditions including mobile residents (who "vote by their feet")—efficiently provide public goods. Using an assumption that government is restricted to implement policies uniformly, Oates (1972) shows that small jurisdictions are more efficient since decentralized government can then differentiate policies among jurisdictions. These simple models, as well as the more general family of decentralization results in economics,[3] can be interpreted as saying that decentralization of government, if done properly, can be a helpful step toward more responsive and efficient government.

In practice, as Musgrave recognized in his thorough treatment, local governments exist in a hierarchical setting, and local public goods exist along with public goods and externalities with regional or national benefits. The optimal structure aims not only to assign responsibilities to provide these goods and internalize the associated externalities, but must also take account of problems of redistribution and externalities that result from taxation and migration (Gordon 1998; Inman and Rubinfeld 1997).

Decentralization can undermine efficiency when each jurisdiction faces incentives that lead to uncorrected externalities among jurisdictions. The soft budget constraint problem—when the local government believes that the center ex post will accommodate and share in local excessive expenditures—is but one example of such externalities.[4] While traditionally many analysts have assumed such problems to be unimportant under government decentralization, more recent literature has been aware of these practical challenges, as well as others that arise in settings where mobility is limited and accountability mechanisms weak. These discussions have been more balanced in terms of the costs and benefits of decentralization.[5] These studies, of particular interest to international donors and policy advisers, focus on the conditions under which decentralization enhances or undermines efficiency and accountability, and emphasize the incentives resulting from political and other institutions.

Recent literature has begun to examine country-specific experiences to learn more about what works where and when. For example, it has become increasingly clear that decentralization cannot lead to more responsive allocative decisions (and efficiency gains) unless preconditions exist to enable widespread, informed participation in local decision making and unless decision makers are rewarded or punished for performance—in other words, unless there is meaningful accountability. If this does not exist, then decentralizing resources to local governments may simply lead to "local capture"—in stark terms, corruption.[6] As thinking on these issues evolves, it becomes increasingly apparent that the impact of decentralization on governance will depend on many country-specific social, cultural, political, and other institutional factors, including social capital (Isham and Kahkonen 1999), social and ethnic heterogeneity (Bardhan 2000, Gugerty and Miguel 2000), economic inequality (Khwaja 2001, Galasso and Ravallion 2001), electoral rules (Case and Besley 1993, Khemani 2000), and independence of the media (Azfar, Kahkonen, and Meagher 2001).[7]

Recent studies have also begun to look at the incentives driving decisions affecting economic management. Ter Minassian and Craig (1997) examine the influence of financial sector regulation on subnational fiscal behavior, and Dillinger and Webb (1999) expand this treatment to examine the important role of political systems in shaping incentives in Argentina and Brazil, while Rodden (2002), Treisman (2000), and Wibbels (2000) pursue this comprehensively worldwide.

This chapter provides a framework for assessing factors that influence the relative hardness of subnational budget constraints, and the rest of the book applies this framework to a range of OECD and developing countries with vastly different institutional settings. We believe the framework will be useful for analyzing other countries and drawing some tentative conclusions about types of vulnerabilities and ways of mitigating risk. This chapter introduces the goals and the architecture of the case studies, and thus foreshadows some of the arguments posed and conclusions derived in the final chapter.

Our analysis starts in the next section by defining and discussing the soft budget constraint problem in order to gain an understanding of soft budget constraints that goes well beyond describing them as unfortunate policy errors. Section 1.3 then explores how incentives can be inadequate in some institutional settings. Section 1.4 lays out several specific mechanisms that might harden the budget constraints for provincial and municipal governments, and the final section introduces the case studies that follow.

1.2   Soft Budget Constraints and Bailouts: Exploring the Commitment Problem

The term *soft budget constraint* describes the situation when an entity (say, a province) can manipulate its access to funds in undesirable ways. A soft budget constraint exists for a subnational government if there is not an ex ante fixed resource envelope within which it must function. Kornai (1992) introduced the term to describe how state-owned enterprises could rely on increased subsidies if they increased their losses. In recent literature, the problem of soft budget constraints has been addressed in the context of the relationship between firms and creditors (Dewatripont and Maskin 1995, Maskin 1996). This literature provides an appropriate definition: "A soft budget constraint arises whenever a funding source finds it impossible to keep an enterprise to a fixed budget, i.e., whenever the enterprise can extract ex post a bigger subsidy or loan than would have been considered efficient ex ante" (Maskin 1996, 125). The enterprise predicts it can position itself for the subsidy by taking certain actions (such as not having money to pay workers) and then undertakes those actions to manipulate the center. Keynes is credited with the statement, "There is no such thing as an unfunded deficit." When subnational budget constraints are soft, the national government eventually funds more of subnational expenditures than it intended, and this unintended cost sharing results in an externality that tilts governments toward excessive spending (or too little tax effort). In many cases, the open window is called borrowing.

Bailouts—the kind of ad hoc additional funding that is provided when an entity would otherwise be unable to service its obligations—do not necessarily represent soft budget constraints, but *expectations* of bailouts often do. Subnational entities are likely to expand their services to an inefficient extent when other entities are expected to pay part of the cost eventually.[8] The causes and the mechanics of this ex post cost sharing take many forms, so a simple identifier of soft budget constraints does not exist. The key may be subtle—hidden in expectations—or it may be more obvious—as when the central government's constitution and the courts obligate it to share costs. A simple cross-national measure of soft budget constraints is unavailable, though sustained subnational fiscal deficits often result. We return to this indicator when comparing country experiences in Chapter 13.

Softness of budget constraints comes about in various ways, but often there is a time lag and an implicit contractual relationship. The most obvious problem arises when a provincial government incurs liabilities that later may be passed on to (and accepted by) the national government. For example, the financial crisis of the late 1990s in Brazil was triggered, if not caused, by states' de facto defaulting on their debt. But direct borrowing is only one of the many subnational liabilities that may eventually become national liabilities. Others include the underfunding of public sector pensions, the underprovision of public goods, and debts owed to or by public and private enterprises.

1.2.1 Bailouts as a Sequential Game

The problem of bailout expectations boils down to a simple sequential game played between the central and local governments. A key feature of the game is that the local governments do not have complete information about the center's payoffs. The center may be one of two types—committed or not—and the subnational governments make assessments about the probability that it is the committed type. In the first stage of the game, the central government sets up its institutions and announces its cofinancing and regulatory policies regarding subnational governments. At this stage, the central government will announce that it is committed to a policy of *never* bailing out profligate subnational governments. The subnational government then examines the center's institutions, policies, and statements to assess the credibility of this commitment, making its move at the second stage of the game in light of these assessments. At this stage, it can either spend and borrow within reasonable limits, or attempt to shift costs onto others by borrowing to adopt an unaffordable policy that provides local benefits. If it chooses to spend within its means, the game ends. If it chooses the cost-shifting strategy, it then finds itself in fiscal difficulties and requests a special deficit-reduction grant or asks that the central government take over its obligations. The central government has the third move, and it must choose either to provide the bailout or refuse. If the costs to the central government of *not* providing additional funds exceed those of providing them, the government reveals itself to be noncommitted. If the subnational government has strong *beliefs* that the government is not committed at the first stage of the game, it has incentives to spend too much or refuse to adjust.[9] On the other hand, if the local government believes that the central government will be committed to a no-bailout policy when making its fiscal decisions at the first stage, it will spend within its means.

This game is formalized and expanded by Robert Inman in chapter 2, but the key questions of this study emerge directly from this simplified version. First, if such accommodation and cost sharing is costly and unproductive for the system as a whole, why would subnational politicians expect the central government to provide them? In other words, what underlies the central government's commitment problem? Second, can such expectations be altered once they have evolved? Third, if they cannot be altered, how can the costs of the resulting moral hazard problem be mitigated? In order to address these questions, it is necessary to understand the basic commitment problem, which we introduce with a simple analogy.

1.2.2   *The Commitment Problem: If You Own a Fire Truck . . .*

Consider the problem of a voluntary fire protection cooperative. Incentives to contribute voluntarily to a fire department would appear to be adequate if it established a policy of extinguishing fires only for contributing members. But a policy of refusing to put out the fires for nonmembers might not be credible. With a fire truck around, to put out any fire may be rather compelling, either because there is an externality (fires can spread) or simply because wasting fortunes and lives is senseless and unethical. But if people expect all fires to be put out, incentives to contribute voluntarily will be inadequate.

It could be, of course, that letting a house burn down despite the ability to stop it would be an excellent way to make people contribute voluntarily. However, to make such sacrifices to earn a reputation may be a costly way to improve incentives. It may also be infeasible due to commitment problems. In either case, voluntary fire services might be nonviable, even when there is a compelling economic case for them. The combined effect of the externality and the commitment problem can explain why governments provide fire protection through coercive taxation and enforce fire codes, even if these policy instruments are clumsy and bureaucratic relative to an idealized, incentive-compatible world.

1.2.3   Why Do Subnational Governments Expect Bailouts?

Now consider subnational fiscal problems, something less dramatic than burning houses. What if teachers cannot be paid and children are about to be sent home after a municipality spends its money on an extravagant project and the mayor throws up his hands? If the central government's standard policy is that jurisdictions must face the consequences of their decisions, is the policy still credible? Extraordinary transfers to keep children in school may look like a policy blunder if they destroy incentives for municipalities. But the lack of credibility might have been evident in advance. The municipality may have had a variety of reasons to surmise that the center would not be able to resist using its "fire truck."

First, as with houses on fire, externalities are an important part of the bailout story. Wildasin (1997) shows how the center may choose a bailout ex post if otherwise the failing entity would cause negative spillovers to other jurisdictions. This argument applies when large financial institutions may fail or there is a risk of a currency crisis. It also applies if financial markets fail to distinguish the promises of one province from another—so-called financial contagion. More directly, spillovers exist when the national government is viewed as having implicitly guaranteed the liabilities (see, for example, Bai and Wang 1999) and where its own reputation would be hurt by failing on those guarantees.

Spillovers are not the only cause of commitment problems, however, and, contrasting Wildasin's argument, in many countries, bailouts have gone to some of the smallest jurisdictions.[10] It is important to distinguish between an entity that is the subordinate part of a larger organization and one that is the creation of its citizens. If a local government is merely a branch of the central government, then punishing its citizens is useless at best. It is only as the municipality becomes a body on its own, a creature of its own citizens with powers to match its responsibilities, that the central government might credibly commit to let it face the consequences of "its" actions.

An additional commitment problem results from government's role in enforcing property rights, typically through the judiciary. A task springing out of this obligation is to adjudicate and help creditors receive payment. However, the national government and its institutions might be weak—lacking instruments or guts, or both—in its ability to enforce loan contracts against defaulting subnational governments. Approached by creditors to enforce their property rights, a weak national government may face the prospect of failing in this obligation and prefer to help creditors through a bailout. The case studies examined in this book will show that a key challenge is to have institutions that match responsibilities. A serious problem arises if the center has few enforcement options—or a faint heart—but is not absolved from heavy enforcement obligations.

1.2.4   Can Expectations Change?

Soft budget constraints result when expectations of bailouts or other forms of ex post cofinancing result in strategic cost-shifting moves by subnational entities. Inman's chapter builds on this problem and lays out a formal model expressing a range of conditions under which the center is likely to prefer bailouts. Most of the case studies demonstrate that basic commitment problems allow bailout expectations in some context. Since many of these problems are rooted in history and the organization of institutions, we also wish to ask whether changes in behavior and institutions can lead to changes in expectations. Can commitment develop over time? Can the center earn a reputation for resisting bailout demands? Some of the case studies discuss historical episodes in which some subnational governments learned through painful defaults that the central government would not provide bailouts. These same studies also emphasize institutional and situational factors that bolstered the central government's commitment. Other case studies examine recent institutional reforms that have explicitly aimed to increase the central government's ability to commit.

1.2.5   What If the Center Cannot Commit?

Although the case studies provide some encouraging examples of institutional reforms that improve the central government's commitment, we will argue in the concluding chapter that completely credible commitments are quite rare. In the vast majority of multitiered fiscal systems, the central government is a bit like the fire department that keeps its fire truck but promises not to use it.

A key proposition of this book is that *if* national government is vulnerable to subnational fiscal problems, like the fire department that cannot refuse to put out fires, then this should be acknowledged up front. Under decentralized government, the center's vulnerability to fiscal crises of subnational governments can have causes ranging from contagion and concern for the national financial system to an interest in keeping provincial schools open or teachers calm. This acknowledgment can lead to steps toward commitment—equivalent to locking away the fire truck—or to selective hierarchical instruments—strategies similar to fire codes and financing the truck with taxes as opposed to voluntary contributions.

If the central government is sufficiently disinterested in local performance or committed not to get involved, wide-ranging fiscal autonomy can be granted. But if such a distance or commitment cannot be established, then an expectation of assistance ex post will exist even without a history of such assistance, and borrowing restrictions and other measures—though counter to the purist idea of decentralization—can serve a useful purpose. This argument will be developed in greater detail in the final chapter.

1.2.6   The Importance of Institutions

The case studies will demonstrate that these commitment problems are built into the basic governance structure of many decentralized systems. Soft budget constraints need not follow from a history of bailouts, but rather from an understanding of the nature of the center, its powers, and its commitments. A consistent and sad history of bailouts may thus reflect stable but unfortunately structured institutions rather than a game in which past play determines future play.[11] Similarly, in a newly decentralizing country, even if a government with no history of bailouts makes verbal and parchment commitments not to help troubled subnational governments, the basic institutional structure might undermine their credibility. Consequently, normative policy prescriptions require an understanding of what drives expectations, what drives the bailout when it is given, and how this unfortunate equilibrium can be changed. The next section pursues this goal with a focus on fiscal and political institutions. Section 1.4 then builds on this analysis by identifying several mechanisms through which hard subnational budget constraints might be achieved.

1.3 Basic Fiscal and Political Institutions

The basic rules for the sequential game are given by fiscal and political institutions, and since these are different in each country, the game is also played differently. This section first discusses the vertical architecture of the intergovernmental fiscal system and the resulting incentives for voters and politicians, and then discusses the organization of the central government.

1.3.1 Intergovernmental Fiscal Institutions

Several aspects of intergovernmental fiscal relations play critical roles for hard budget constraints: (1) transparency and predictability of intergovernmental transfers, (2) the ability to respond to local needs by raising local revenues rather than relying heavily on central transfers ("transfer dependency"), and (3) assignment of expenditures to appropriate levels of government and adequate flexibility in determining local expenditures.

Intergovernmental Transfers
The traditional understanding of intergovernmental grants and tax sharing comes from welfare economics. It assumes that a benevolent, omniscient central government assigns expenditure and revenue authority according to efficiency criteria and that grants serve purposes of efficiency and redistribution (Oates 1972, Musgrave 1959). Indeed, the ability of the central government to use grants to overcome problems of externalities and inequality is central to any normative

conception of a multitiered government. In practice, central governments may be vulnerable to tendencies of political economy and rent seeking well known elsewhere, and systems of transfers and revenue sharing may thus cause inefficient responses that are not foreseen in textbooks.

Unless funding between governments is completely independent of the recipient jurisdiction's choices, it is likely to create moral hazard problems between the central and subcentral governments, just as it does between a funding source and a large firm or between a wealthy family head and a child in college. Subnational officials—and perhaps the whole jurisdiction—then face inadequate incentives since citizens of other jurisdictions will pay for part of their programs. Local officials are thereby led to expand programs and to raise or exaggerate their costs (see Borge and Rattso 1998, Inman, chap. 2, this volume).

The textbook solution is to let revenue-sharing and transfer programs depend on local choices only when this explicitly is the intention, as when a matching grant supports activities with positive externalities. As an example, transfers to make poor jurisdictions afford a certain provision of schooling would be based on the number of children or need rather than paying for actual educational expenditures. This goal may be important to strive for, but not fully attainable in practice. Subnational jurisdictions will try to play games to exploit the center (and thereby each other), and a key institutional design challenge is to contain the costs of these games.

Transfer Dependency and Local Revenue Raising
Consider a public sector in which subnational governments are boxed in by limited taxing powers, so that they are dependent on transfers and loans from the central government. Such governments have little flexibility to raise additional revenue when faced with adverse shocks. If the situation escalates into a fiscal crisis in which the subnational government is unable to pay workers or may default on loans, it can claim with some justification that it is not responsible for its fiscal woes. Then pressure from voters, employees, and creditors will likely be directed at the central government, which *can* resolve the current crisis. Knowing this, transfer-dependent governments face weak incentives to be fiscally responsible, since it is more rewarding to position themselves for a bailout.

In this case of transfer dependence and limited autonomy, subnational politicians will not be held responsible by voters or creditors for local fiscal outcomes. An important consideration in the case studies is therefore the level of vertical fiscal imbalance for subnational governments or intergovernmental transfers as a percentage of their revenue. However, attention is given also to the structure of intergovernmental grants and regulations in the fiscal system. We expect to see that if poorly defined criteria or political bargains determine the distribution of grants and revenue sharing, the resulting flexibility at the center harms the credibility of any no-bailout policy. In contrast, local voters and politicians are less likely to expect discretionary bailouts if intergovernmental transfers are tied to rules and criteria that are not easily manipulated. A separate difficulty is that the rules themselves might create soft budget constraints. More specifically, we shall see that some transfer systems designed to combat interjurisdictional inequality and absorb regional shocks create poor incentives for performance.

Expenditure Assignment and Local Autonomy
Another consideration is the assignment and regulation of expenditure responsibilities. The central government might be unable to resist bailout demands if local governments are failing in their responsibility to provide certain key services that have national constituencies, like welfare or pensions. This problem is exacerbated if national policies, such as minimum service standards, limit local autonomy. By the same token, cost shifting and deficit shifting should be less likely if the central government is not involved in the provision of purely local public goods.

Each case study also examines the incentive effects of attempts to regulate the fiscal activities of local governments. Like transfer dependence, central regulation of local fiscal affairs can send a strong signal to local politicians, voters, and creditors that the central government is ultimately responsible for local fiscal outcomes. In some countries, the tax bases or maximum tax rates of subnational governments are limited by regulation. In others, public sector employment and wages are regulated by the center.

Finally, the case studies examine the clarity of the distribution of expenditure and revenue authority. According to the subsidiarity principle, responsibilities should be assigned to the lowest level where scale economies are acceptable and externalities are internalized. And to strengthen accountability, responsibilities of central and subnational governments should be divided into well-defined, mutually exclusive categories. These ideals are not fully attainable in practice, as when the public goods in question naturally belong between levels, for example, when a metropolitan area needs infrastructure comprising several municipalities or provinces. The case studies will show that unclear or shared responsibilities have a cost in terms of accountability and incentives.

1.3.2   Central Government Political Institutions

In addition to the intergovernmental fiscal system, the beliefs of subnational governments about the credibility of the center's no-bailout commitment are also shaped by the political institutions supporting central government behavior. Subnational governments examine those incentives to take cues about likely behavior, including the prospects of bailouts. The case studies will show that a number of political factors might undermine the credibility of a policy not to provide bailouts. The horizontal organization of the central government plays an important role, and it is necessary to examine the incentives and constraints facing legislators, premiers, and presidents. For instance, the central government might choose to provide a bailout if it faces strong electoral incentives to favor bondholders or local taxpayers over national taxpayers. It is important to know who holds local debt, and how they are represented in the political process at the center (see Inman, chap. 2, this volume).

In addition, local governments might have strong reasons to believe that bailouts will be forthcoming if their interests are well represented in the central legislature, or if decisions in the legislature are made through regional logrolling. In several of the cases examined in this book, fiscally irresponsible governments obtained bailouts through their influence in the national legislature, trading votes with other legislators, or threatening to veto unrelated policy proposals. Some problems of horizontal bargaining are exacerbated if a few provinces are dominant in size. In many countries, a two-chambered legislature gives each region representation proportional to population in the lower chamber, with small regions relatively overrepresented in the upper chamber. In such systems, small states have disproportionate power, and their votes may be shifted cheaply in political bargaining.

In one particularly troubling scenario, the central government might appear to be little more than a loose coalition of logrolling regional interest groups. This danger is most pronounced in formally federal systems, which usually include direct representation and constitutional protections for the states. These features, along with others (e.g., the nomination process or in districting for national elections), can make national government beholden to subnational governments rather than to citizens, as when provincial governors are instrumental in who is represented in national parliament. This kind of regional logrolling has been a fact of life in Brazil and is becoming one in India. This problem might be mitigated in presidential systems if the president has a national constituency and the ability to mobilize majorities in the legislature (Fitts and Inman 1992). This has sometimes been the case in Argentina (Dillinger and Webb 1999, Webb chap. 6, this volume) and perhaps in Brazil under Cardoso (see Rodden, this volume). Fiscal discipline can also emanate from national parties if national party leaders have power—for instance, through the nomination process or the campaigns. Disciplined national political parties might also be helpful if subnational officials, hoping to build a career in federal politics, face incentives to avoid playing cost-shifting strategies. In the central legislature, party leaders with no control over backbenchers must buy cooperation at every juncture to manufacture a legislative majority, weakening any commitment to a no-bailout policy. Indirect elections at the local level may lead to greater party discipline, but less responsiveness to local needs and preferences and thus possibly lower efficiency gains.[12]

In short, the case studies often describe central government politics as a bargaining scenario in which short-term opportunism results in costly bailouts. By the same token, some of the case studies also lay out conditions under which such self-interested national politicians support positive reform efforts and affirm the hardness of budget constraints.

1.4   Additional Hard Budget Constraint Mechanisms

The previous section argued that the structure of basic fiscal and political institutions shapes the beliefs and incentives of central and local decision makers, and hence the hardness of budget constraints. Government fiscal behavior is also shaped by other actors who have a stake in local fiscal decisions, including creditors, voters, and factor owners. Under the right conditions, these actors might pressure governments to behave with fiscal prudence, creating marketlike hard budget constraint mechanisms. We first discuss the possibility that subnational governments can be disciplined by credit markets. Second, we examine the role of competition for votes and other forms of political support. Third, we discuss land markets and the role of workers and investors who own mobile factors.

The proper functioning of each of these mechanisms depends on features of the political and fiscal systems, and that they are highly dependent on each other. In some settings, spending and borrowing decisions will be unaffected or even perversely affected by the competition for capital, votes, and mobile factors. While some of the case studies (primarily the United States and Canada) point out instances where these mechanisms are reasonably successful, most of the case studies focus on the factors that undermine them. By delineating the conditions under which these market mechanisms fail, the case studies also point to conditions that invite hierarchical intervention by the central government.

1.4.1 Capital Markets

Capital markets perform the allocative function well only if capital owners and institutions have the right incentives to select good credit objects. When borrowers are subnational governments, it is not necessarily the case that lenders bear the consequences if a borrower cannot or will not service its loans. If the capital market mechanism works, subnational fiscal decisions are disciplined by the competition for credit, and poor fiscal performance will then lead to higher borrowing costs or constrained access. Credit ratings, summarizing these market responses, can also provide important signals to voters about their government's performance. The functionality of the credit market depends on the quality of information, and thus on regulations covering disclosure, accounting principles, auditing, and the like.[13]

A variety of additional preconditions must be present for capital markets to perform the function of constraining or guiding subnational fiscal activities (see Lane 1993). Most obviously, the capital markets themselves and the general supportive institutions must be sufficiently developed. In countries with limited capital markets, access to capital is predominantly through the central government—a development bank, housing bank, or on-lending mechanisms, for example. When this is the case, lending and the servicing of loans often become embroiled in politics, resulting in soft budget constraints (as when these intermediaries themselves expect to be bailed out) or other dysfunctional characteristics. Among our case studies, such institutions have played the most prominent roles in Argentina, Brazil, India, and Ukraine. In China, subnational governments obtain credit on favorable terms through their state-owned enterprises in a politicized process involving the central bank, line ministries, and on-lending institutions. Even if local governments borrow in competitive markets, the capital market mechanism may fail. If lenders perceive bailouts to be likely (or provokable), they may continue to lend to subnational governments in spite of poor fiscal and economic performance. Credit ratings, and the price and availability of loans, will then reflect the creditworthiness of the central government or the public sector as a whole and carry little useful information about individual local government.

When a subnational government's liabilities are not explicitly or implicitly backed by central government institutions, its effects may in the ultimate extreme be parallel to the textbook version of a limited liability corporation. Creditors know that they have nowhere else to go if the entity has borrowed too much, so they will watch fiscal performance and solvency carefully. But the resemblance of a limited liability corporation will be slight. Since a jurisdiction's revenue base does not represent the government's own assets (the revenue base is a combination of taxes levied on persons and property and grants), a bankruptcy procedure for subnational government must do more than simply apply the procedure for private defaults.[14] Importantly, if the impression exists that some third party with deep pockets will keep the entity afloat, the monitoring function of credit markets is eliminated, effectively leaving all responsibilities with the third party.

A final note on credit markets is that the feasibility of financial contracting depends to some extent on a government that can protect property rights and enforce contracts. Part of this role is to arbitrate and enforce a sharing of the burden when it happens that lenders are not getting what they are owed. In that capacity, government institutions act on behalf of creditors against the borrower, but they also give the borrower a limited protection against creditors. Limits in these functions arise in multitiered systems in two ways. First, and particularly in a federal context, the central government may have limited powers relative to member states, even in the enforcement of contracts (on the United States, see McConnell and Picker 1993, English 1996). Second, the central government may be weak when acting against a body that is seen as part of itself, as opposed to a separate entity.

These two are at the extremes of a line from sovereign to subservient, commanding different institutional approaches and giving different potential roles to the capital market mechanism. In the case of a sub-national sovereign (or a weak central government), credit markets can function, but only to the extent that credit can be sustained without or with very little collective enforcement.[15] In the case of a subservient government, the borrower will to a great extent be protected through burden sharing in the case of default. For this reason, in the latter case, supplementary interventions and institutions (such as hierar-chical controls, discussed below) typically play a role. The case studies demonstrate the range from subnational sovereigns (e.g., the U.S. states) to subservient governments (e.g., Norwegian local governments).

A task of each case study is to describe the nature of subnational bor-rowing and assess whether the credit market mechanism is allowed to operate. When public intermediaries are used, the case studies describe and assess the regulatory regimes under which they operate. In several of the cases, a good deal of attention is given to the issue of why the credit market does not serve this function of discipline or why it is an insufficient constraint on subnational borrowing.

1.4.2 Political Competition

The political realm also provides a potential form of market discipline for subnational officials: the competition for political power. Ideally, voters in democratic systems face incentives to punish fiscally irre-sponsible representatives—local as well as national—by voting them out of office. The key question is whether voters have the authority, incentives, and information necessary to do so. Free, fair elections with vigorous opposition and autonomous media might play an important role in constraining subnational fiscal decisions.

But many conditions must be satisfied for this mechanism to be effec-tive. Voters might not punish local politicians for large deficits and unsustainable debt levels if they believe the costs will eventually fall on future residents of other jurisdictions, or if it is difficult for voters to obtain information about local performance. For instance, local politicians might be able to shift blame upward when they are highly dependent on intergovernmental transfers or boxed in by central regulations or unfunded mandates. Similarly, budget constraints are soft if politicians can fund popular programs in part by running up liabilities that are less visible to voters, such as unfunded pension liabilities, or by providing infrastructure with substandard durability.

The case studies assess the strength of the political mechanism in hardening subnational budget constraints. This involves examinations of the mechanisms through which power is allocated and the career incentives facing public officials. In some of the cases, incentives may lead to fiscal discipline, but many of the studies also point out serious deficiencies in the structure of political incentives.

1.4.3 Land Markets and Factor Mobility

Tiebout (1956) showed how competition between local jurisdictions run by landowners can, under very strict theoretical conditions, support efficient provision of local public goods and corresponding taxation. But land markets also play a role in a more practical context, in particular for intertemporal incentives.[16] To the extent that residents are owners of tradable land (or housing), they have incentives to handle their local public affairs well, under the assumption that the net value of expected public services and tax payments (including debt service) is fully capitalized into current land prices.

An important assumption here is that those affected by the capitalization of local debts (and of public services) into land prices control the local political process. In a democracy, this works intuitively and directly to the extent that voters are landowners and vice versa, because ownership gives people a long-term stake in the community. But the mechanisms can also work in other ways. To give an example of the potential problems, undeveloped land is often held by a very few (it is by definition not occupied by residents). Its value can thus be under threat in a democratic political process. Nevertheless, interests can be represented in politics in many ways, depending on the institutions for policymaking. If many residents are renters rather than owners, they may have an insufficient financial stake in the future of the community, biasing politics toward borrowing and consumption and against investment.[17] Landowners might try to address this in part by buying influence directly, or if interests are concentrated, they may subsidize larger policy packages.

Land values and demand for land may also give local politicians important incentives directly as a revenue source. If the revenue base of local government in large part is property and land taxes (directly or indirectly), then this may give local politicians positive incentives to pursue policies that maximize property values, including sound fiscal policies.

Mobile factors (workers, financial capital, entrepreneurs) also play a role in determining the prices for immobile assets and by putting pressure on local officials directly through their mobility. Workers and residents thus exert pressure not only directly through voice but also by exit (Hirschman 1990, Tiebout 1956). If these exit threats are credible, local politicians are likely to respond to such demands in order to protect their tax base (Brennan and Buchanan 1980).

A critical assumption for this mechanism is that citizens and firms must be highly mobile. This is often not the case in developing and transition countries, especially those with large jurisdictions, heavy dependence on agriculture, and large state-owned enterprises, or in fragmented settings with important ethnic and linguistic cleavages across jurisdictions. Second, of course, competition has to be real. This requires that jurisdictions are of a relevant size and have relevant powers (not overregulated by the center) and that collusion is not too pervasive. Furthermore, the effect of mobility can be limited by intergovernmental transfers or revenue-sharing arrangements.

Land markets and factor mobility receive scant attention in the case studies. For the sake of completeness, it has been useful to discuss them here, especially since these market-driven forms of discipline are so central in the theoretical literature. But the assumptions driving these theories are simply too heroic for most real-world settings, especially in developing countries. That is not to say that theoretical accounts of market-driven fiscal discipline are irrelevant to analysts approaching case studies where, for example, land markets do not exist (e.g., South Africa) or barriers to mobility make exit threats noncredible (e.g., India). By categorizing the ways in which incentives for market discipline fall short, one understands why governments might seek out other nonmarket mechanisms to enforce fiscal discipline and harden budget constraints.

1.4.4 Hierarchical Mechanisms

As we have laid out above, an institutional setting can be envisaged in which creditors, home owners, and the local electorate provide a good incentive framework for subnational fiscal decisions. The no-bailout policy would then be credible to all of these actors, and subnational officials would face few incentives to seek bailouts. Above all, the costs and benefits of local spending and borrowing decisions would be borne locally. Should a jurisdiction borrow too much, the pain would fall on the jurisdiction, with some burden sharing by creditors in the more extreme cases, but no funds would come from the higher-level government. In this institutional setting, hierarchical restrictions on subnational spending and borrowing would be unnecessary, and indeed difficult to rationalize. They could clumsily and unnecessarily constrain credit, and even signal that the central government assumes responsibility.

Most of our case studies, however, are very different from such a setting. Central governments cannot firmly commit to a no-bailout policy, and local politicians, along with local voters, creditors, and asset holders, have reasons to play cost-shifting and deficit-shifting strategies. Thus, in many situations, an additional line of defense becomes attractive: hierarchical oversight and regulation by the central government. In fact, the case studies display a wide range of mechanisms aimed at imposing hard budget constraints from the center. The most direct and bluntest way to do this is simply to prohibit subnational governments from borrowing or to allocate all credit through the central government.

But central allocation of credit is often politicized or for other reasons ends up being quite inefficient. It also undermines even further the central government's attempt to commit to an apolitical, no-bailout policy. William McCarten's case study of India (chap. 8, this volume) makes this painfully clear. Several of the case studies demonstrate that difficulties abound in practice, but some mechanisms work better than others. There are also less blunt forms of regulation. In some cases, borrowing prohibitions are limited to foreign borrowing. In others, subnational governments can make their own decisions about borrowing initially, but with final approval subject to review by a central government agency.

In addition to direct central administrative oversight, a variety of mechanisms based on rules is also used around the world.[18] A common strategy is to place limitations on the use of debt at the local level—for instance, to limit long-term borrowing to capital projects. Another uses numerical limits—for example, limiting the aggregate stock of long-term debt to a fixed share of the local tax base. In addition, the case studies will examine a variety of balanced budget rules. For instance, some rules require submitting a balanced budget, and others limit actual expenditures and prohibit deficit carryovers into subsequent years. Some subnational governments own banks and borrow from them, or borrow through and receive funds from local public enterprises, making hierarchical controls more difficult to implement.

In some cases, a bailout has been difficult to avoid but has offered the central government an opportunity to strengthen hierarchical mechanisms. Conditions for debt relief can then attempt to reduce or eliminate the incentive problems that engendered the fiscal crisis in the first place. In this way, a properly structured bailout featuring institutional reform and new oversight can signal that the game to be played in the future will be a different one, rather than signaling that the central government's credibility is weak. Thus, some of the case studies view bailout episodes not as policy blunders, but ask whether they might be first steps on a path toward harder budget constraints.

Additionally, laws and other institutions can in general serve to clarify how subnational fiscal crises will be handled before they actually occur. Clear, well-crafted public bankruptcy laws can be very important in this regard and will likely have to give creditors limited powers if they are to forestall political intervention and bailouts. Some of the case studies describe such laws, their associated penalties, and methods of enforcement.

Finally, it is important to note that any of these hierarchical mechanisms—from borrowing restrictions to bankruptcy laws to conditional bailouts—are only as good as the strength and credibility of the institutions that must enforce them, and obviously the central government that may intervene to change or circumvent them. Thus, an important part of assessing the strength of the hierarchical mechanism is to return to the questions about incentives in national political institutions.

1.5   Introduction to the Case Studies

The rest of this book builds on the framework established in this chapter to lay out the conditions under which the soft budget constraint problem is most severe and the mechanisms that are most likely to mitigate it. Our ultimate goal is to understand better what factors, policies, and institutions make a country prone to soft budget constraints and begin to identify some realistic institutional reforms that can harden subnational budget constraints in practice. First, in each case study, we try to understand the basic pathologies discussed in section 1.2. Some of the case studies include detailed descriptions of the strategic interactions that culminate in subnational fiscal crises and, in some cases, bailouts. In other cases, however, fiscal crises have largely been avoided or bailouts denied, even if other forms of inefficiency persist.

Second, it is useful to examine the role of each of the mechanisms outlined in sections 1.3 and 1.4 in mitigating the problem. We seek to ascertain which mechanisms work under which conditions, which complement one another and which are antithetical, and, perhaps most important, which are most realistic as targets for reform.

Most of the case studies point out significant weaknesses in the basic underlying political and fiscal structures. An important lesson, also featured in Inman's theoretical treatment, is that when higher-level government cannot be committed to firmness ex post, hierarchical mechanisms can be an important defense. Many of the conditions discussed above and in the next chapter that underpin firm no-bailout commitments are simply not present in most of the countries under analysis. But in order to understand the hierarchical rules and the conditions under which they work, it is necessary to understand the larger institutional context in which they are embedded. Thus, the case studies try to strike a balance between addressing basic, overarching institutional design issues and examining specific rules pertaining to borrowing, bankruptcy, and the like.

The cases were chosen to represent the widest possible diversity in geography and experience with fiscal and political decentralization and also to provide a range of variation in the hardness of subnational budget constraints. Every continent except Australia is represented, and the countries range in size from Norway to China and include both highly centralized, top-down unitary systems and some of the world's most decentralized federations.[19] We include some countries, like the United States, where some subnational governments are older than the country itself, and others, like Hungary and South Africa, where new subnational entities are being created and their powers just beginning to evolve.

Chapter 2, by Robert Inman, serves as both a theory chapter and the first case study. It expands on and formalizes many of the issues raised in this chapter, building on the sequential bailout game to drive home lessons about the conditions under which central governments are likely to resist calls for bailouts and examining conditions under which hierarchical restrictions might be attractive. Inman then provides a segue into the case studies by applying these general concepts in one of the oldest and most frequently studied federations—the United States—pointing to the evolution of credible no-bailout commitments by the central governments and identifying the institutions that undergird them, even while also illuminating some weaknesses in the system.

Chapter 3, by Richard Bird and Almos Tassonyi, also makes important distinctions between the federated units and the municipal governments in a large, wealthy North American federation. As in Inman's discussion of the U.S. states, they argue that credible no-bailout commitments facilitate strong market discipline among the provinces, but fiscal discipline is achieved largely through hierarchical rules among Canadian municipalities. Chapter 4, by Jørn Rattsø on Norway, develops further some of the themes introduced in the discussion of the Canadian municipalities; in spite of some other inefficiencies, fiscal discipline can be maintained among constrained, highly regulated local governments by an array of strict hierarchical restrictions. Jonathan Rodden's chapter on the German states is alone among the OECD cases in describing a potentially serious soft budget constraint problem embedded in the basic institutional structure, though to date outright bailouts have been provided to only two of the smallest and most troubled states.

Chapters 6 through 8 consider large, developing federations with histories of fiscal decentralization and rather serious recent manifestations of the soft budget constraint problem. Stephen Webb's study of Argentina describes incentives that created soft budget constraints and bailout dynamics in the 1980s and 1990s, but also draws attention to recent reforms aimed at hardening provincial budget constraints. Similarly, Jonathan Rodden's examination of the Brazilian states points out political and fiscal institutions that have created a serious moral hazard problem and engendered a series of very costly recent bailout episodes, but also discusses prospects for reform. William McCarten's study of the Indian states describes both the accomplishments and (increasingly) the failures of a rather elaborate system of central regulation of state finances, emphasizing the complexities of administration and politics in a poor, diverse country undergoing significant political change.

Chapters 9 through 12 examine countries in which decentralization is unfolding in the context of major political and economic transitions. Jing Jin and Heng-fu Zou describe the complexities of China's oft-changing fiscal contracting system and the unique challenges of structuring a hard budget constraint when the subnational governments are heavily involved in operating state-owned enterprises and the center is in a poor position to monitor their activities. Junaid Ahmad's chapter illuminates the monumental task of structuring a hard budget constraint while building a workable new postapartheid system of fiscal and political federalism in a rapidly changing South Africa. Next, in analyzing the difficulties of decentralization in Ukraine, Sean O'Connell and Deborah Wetzel touch on a long list of pathologies and basic institutional issues that remain to be resolved in a fragile, complex post-Soviet environment. In the final case study, Wetzel and Anita Papp tell a much more encouraging story about the potential hardening of budget constraints in Hungary, where an evolving nexus of administrative rules and judicial enforcement mechanisms appears to have clarified expectations and improved incentives.

While the emphasis and most important lessons from each case are different, their contributions aggregate into a useful body of information. Taken together, the case studies create an impressive database with eleven observations. This database is used in the final chapter to make some broad assessments, general arguments, and specific recommendations.

Notes

1. For examples of this debate, see Prud'homme (1995) and McLure (1995).

2. Several empirical studies using pooled cross section and time-series techniques have suggested that fiscal decentralization may be harmful for efficiency and stability. Results indicate that fiscal decentralization has not been associated with faster economic growth (Davoodi and Zou 1998) and promotes fiscal imbalance (De Mello 2000). Yet these studies are highly controversial for the choice of decentralization variables used in the regressions. For example, Ebel and Yilmaz (2001) tested the others' results by using different, more precise variables and have produced different results.

3. Adam Smith (1776), not in general impressed by markets and the forces of political economy, coined decentralization results with the seductive phrase, "He is in this, as in many other cases, led by an invisible hand to promote an end which was no part of his intention."

4. Other examples include excessive vertical or horizontal tax competition and the local protectionism that arises when subnational politicians gain opportunities and incentives to obstruct the free flow of labor, goods, and services across jurisdictional boundaries.

5. See, e.g., Inman and Rubinfeld (1997), Litvack, Ahmad, and Bird (1998), Rodden and Rose-Ackerman (1997), Tanzi (1995), Qian and Weingast (1997), and Ter-Minassian (1997).

6. See Bardhan and Mookherjee (2000).

7. For general overviews, see Azfar et al. (2001a,b) and Rao (2001).

8. See figure 2.1.

9. This problem is called the time-consistency problem in the economics literature. An appropriate example in public finance may be that a bridge project is found worthwhile and funded under a certain cost estimate. A stated policy not to increase funding if the cost estimate is exceeded is not time consistent (i.e., not credible), given that it is still worthwhile to complete a half-built bridge when the new estimate arrives.

10. For example, bailouts in Germany have been concentrated in two of the smallest states: Bremen and Saarland. In Brazil, bailouts have gone not only to large, externality-producing states like São Paulo, but also to some of the smallest, most isolated states, like Tocantins.

11. Game-theoretic treatments (e.g., Bulow and Rogoff 1989 and the broader literature on repeated games) show that if economic agents try to calculate their opponents' best responses, in important settings there is no scope for changing expectations by playing in a certain way (there simply is no reputation effect).

12. In a system of pure proportional representation, elected members do not respond to geographically based constituents. Strong, disciplined political parties under proportional representation may have some disadvantages if they weaken the incentives of individual representatives to respond to the preferences of their constituents.

13. Hopes and ambitions should be modest, however. Most governments, high and low, rich and poor, if they can produce a list of explicit liabilities, cannot produce a list of assets, let alone a balance sheet. Furthermore, while credit markets react to the likelihood of default, they are silent about the optimal debt level being exceeded, as long as it is sustainable.

14. It may be argued that powerful creditors would cause political intervention (the system would not allow too much citizen suffering because of municipal mismanagement), and thus that municipal bankruptcy codes must give creditors quite limited powers to protect the enforcement machinery from political intervention. The U.S. municipal bankruptcy procedure can be interpreted this way. It protects from creditors those assets of the municipality that are crucial to its government functions. In practice, this has shielded almost all assets and powers to change taxes and expenditures from creditor influence (McConnell and Picker 993). Thus, actual institutions do not allow citizens to lose their school, for instance. Rather, it distributes all of the pain ex post to the creditors. This, in the absence of higher-level guarantees, constrains credit by limiting the harm to jurisdictions that borrow too much.

15. Bulow and Rogoff (1989) provide a good discussion of what sustains credit in the case of sovereigns.

16. See Oates (1972) generally and Sprunger and Wilson (1998) for an application to local borrowing.

17. For an analysis of differing incentives facing owners and renters, see Epple and Romer (1991).

18. For overviews, see Ter-Minassian and Craig (1997) and Inter-American Development Bank (1997). In our treatment, we do not consider self-imposed constraints, such as the balanced budget requirements of most U.S. states, as a hierarchical mechanism.

19. The term *federalism* is often used by economists simply to highlight a hierarchical structure of government, but among political scientists it describes more specifically a structure in which the lower level—constituent units in a federation—has powers that cannot easily be taken over or reduced by the higher level.

References

Azfar, Omar, Satu Kahkonen, Anthony Lanyi, Patrick Meagher, and Diana Rutherford. 2001b. "Decentralization, Governance and Public Services: The Impact of Institutional

Arrangements: A Review of the Literature" Mimeo., Development Research Group, World Bank.

Azfar, Omar, Satu Kahkonen, and Patrick Meagher. 2001a. "Conditions for Effective Decentralized Governance: A Synthesis of Research Findings." College Park, Md.: University of Maryland, Center for Institutional Reform and the Informal Sector.

Bai, Chong-En, and Yijiang Wang. 1999. "The Myth of the East Asian Miracle: The Macroeconomic Implications of Soft Budgets." *American Economic Review* 89(2):432–437.

Bardhan, Pranab. 2000. "Irrigation and Cooperation: An Empirical Analysis of 48 Irrigation Communities in South India." *Economic Development and Cultural Change*, 48(4):847–865.

Bardhan, Pranab, and Dilip Mookherjee. 2000. "Relative Capture of Local and Central Government: An Essay in the Political Economy of Decentralization." Berkeley, Department of Economics, University of California, Berkeley, and Boston: Department of Economics, Boston University.

Borge, Lars-Erik, and Jørn, Rattsø. 1998. "Local Government Grants and Income Tax Revenue: Redistributive Politics in Norway 1900–1990". *Public Choice* 92:181–197.

Brennan, Geoffrey, and James Buchanan. 1980. *The Power of Tax: Analytical Foundations of a Fiscal Constitution.* Cambridge: Cambridge University Press.

Bulow, Jeremy, and Kenneth Rogoff. 1989, "Sovereign Debt: Is to Forgive to Forget?" *American Economic Review* 79(1):43–50.

Case, Anne, and Timothy Besley. 1993. "Does Electoral Accountability Affect Economic Policy Choices? Evidence from Gubernatorial Term Limits". National Bureau of Economic Research working paper, no. 4575.

Davoodi, Hamid, and Heng-fu Zou. 1998. "Fiscal Decentralization and Economic Growth: A Cross-Country Study." *Journal of Urban Economics* 43:244–423.

De Mello, L. R. 2000. "Fiscal Decentralization and Intergovernmental Fiscal Relations: A Cross-Country Analysis". *World Development* 28(2):365–380.

Dewatripont, Mathias, and Eric Maskin. 1995. "Credit and Efficiency in Centralized and Decentralized Economics." *Review of Economic Studies* 62(4):541–556.

Diamond, Peter, and James Mirrlees. 1971. "Optimal Taxation and Public Production". *American Economic Review* 61(1):8–27, 61(3):261–278.

Dillinger, William, and Steven Webb. 1999. "Fiscal Management in Federal Democracies: Argentina and Brazil." Policy Research working paper 2121, World Bank, Washington, D.C.

Ebel, Robert D., and Serdar Yilmaz. 2001. *On the Measurement and Impact of Fiscal Decentralization.* Washington, D.C.: World Bank.

English, William. 1996. "Understanding the Costs of Sovereign Default: American State Debts in the 1840's." *American Economic Review* 86(1):259–275.

Epple, Dennis, and Thomas Romer. 1991. "Mobility and Redistribution." *Journal of Political Economy* 99(4):828–858.

Fitts, Michael, and Robert Inman. 1992. "Controlling Congress: Presidential Influence in Domestic Fiscal Policy." *Georgetown Law Journal* 80:1737–1785.

Fornasari, Francesca, Steven B. Webb, and Heng-fu Zou. 1999. "The Macroeconomic Impact of Decentralized Spending and Deficits: International Evidence." Working paper, World Bank.

Galasso, Emanuela, and Martin Ravallion. 2001. "Decentralized Targeting of an Anti-Poverty Program." Mimeo. Development Research Group, World Bank, Feb.

Gordon, Roger. 1998. "An Optimal Taxation Approach to Fiscal Federalism," In *The Economics of Fiscal Federalism and Local Finance*. Northampton, MA: Elgar Reference Collection.

Gugerty, Mary Kay, and Edward Miguel. 2000. "Community Participation and Social Sanctions in Kenyan Schools," Mimeo., Harvard University.

Hirschman, Albert. 1990. *Exit, Voice and Loyalty: Responses to Decline in Firms, Organizations and States.* Cambridge, Mass.: Harvard University Press.

Holmstrom, Bengt, and Paul Milgrom. 1994. "The Firm as an Incentive System." *American Economic Review* 84(4):972–991.

Inman, Robert, and Daniel Rubinfeld. 1997. "The Political Economy of Federalism," in Dennis Mueller, ed., *Perspectives on Public Choice: A Handbook.* Cambridge: Cambridge University Press, 73–105.

Inter-American Development Bank. 1997. "Can Decentralized Democracy Deliver Fiscal Stability?" In *The Institutional Dimension*, Washington, D.C.: Inter-American Development Bank.

Isham, Jonathan, and Satu Kahkonen. 1999. "Institutional Determinants of the Impact of Community-Based Water Services: Evidence from Sri Lanka and India." Working paper 236, IRIS Center, University of Maryland, Nov.

Khemani, Stuti. 2000. "Political Cycles in a Developing Economy: Effect of Elections in Indian States." Policy Research working paper no. 2454, World Bank.

Khwaja, Asim Ijaz. 2001. "Can Good Projects Succeed in Bad Communities? Collective Action in the Himalayas." Mimeo., Harvard University.

Kornai, János. 1992. *The Socialist System: The Political Economy of Communism*. Princeton, NJ: Princeton University Press.

Lane, Timothy. 1993. "Market Discipline." *Staff Papers* (International Monetary Fund) 40:53–88.

Litvack, Jennie, Junaid Ahmad, and Richard Bird. 1998. *Rethinking Decentralization in Developing Countries*. Washington, D.C.: World Bank.

Maskin, Eric. 1996. "Theories of the Soft Budget-Constraint." *Japan and the World Economy* 8(2):125–133.

McConnell, Michael, and Randal Picker. 1993. "When Cities Go Broke: A Conceptual Introduction to Municipal Bankruptcy." *University of Chicago Law Review* 60:425, 466, 474–476.

McLure, Charles, E. 1995. "Comment on Prud'homme." *World Bank Research Observer* 10(2):221–226.

Musgrave, Richard. 1959. *The Theory of Public Finance: A Study in Public Economy*. New York: McGraw-Hill.

Oates, Wallace. 1972. *Fiscal Federalism*. New York: Harcourt Brace Jovanovich.

Prud'homme, Remy. 1995. "The Dangers of Decentralization." *World Bank Research Observer* 10(2):201–220.

Qian, Yingyi, and Barry Weingast. 1997. "Federalism as a Commitment to Preserving Market Incentives." *Journal of Economic Perspectives* 11(4):83–92.

Rao, Vijayendra. 2001. "Community Driven Development: A Review of the Evidence." Mimeo., Development Research Group, World Bank.

Rodden, Jonathan. 2002. "The Dilemma of Fiscal Federalism: Grants and Fiscal Performance Around the World." *American Journal of Political Science* 46(3):670–687.

Rodden, Jonathan, and Susan Rose-Ackerman. 1997. "Does Federalism Preserve Markets?" *Virginia Law Review* 83(7):1521–1572.

Samuelson, Paul A. 1954. "The Pure Theory of Public Expenditures." *Review of Economics and Statistics*, Nov. 36(4):350–356.

Smith, Adam. 1776. *An Inquiry into the Nature and Causes of the Wealth of Nations*. Oxford: Clarendon Press.

Sprunger, Philip, and John Wilson. 1998. "Imperfectly Mobile Households and Durable Local Public Goods: Does the Capitalization Mechanism Work?" *Journal of Urban Economics* 44(3):468–492.

Stein, Ernesto. 1997. "Fiscal Decentralization and Government Size in Latin America." In K. Fukasaku and R. Hausmann, eds., *Democracy, Decentralization and Deficits in Latin America*, Washington, D.C.: IDB-OECD.

Tanzi, Vito. 1995. "Fiscal Decentralization." *Annual World Bank Conference on Development Economics 1994*. Washington D.C.: World Bank.

Ter-Minassian, Teresa. 1997. *Fiscal Federalism in Theory and Practice*. Washington, D.C.: International National Monetary Fund.

Ter-Minassian, Teresa, and Jon Craig. 1997. "Control of Subnational Government Borrowing." In Teresa Ter-Minassian, ed., *Fiscal Federalism in Theory and Practice: A Collection of Essays* Washington, D.C.: International National Monetary Fund.

Tiebout, Charles. 1956. "A Pure Theory of Local Expenditures." *Journal of Political Economy* 64:416–424.

Treisman, Daniel. 2000. "Decentralization and Inflation: Commitment, Collective Action, or Continuity?" *American Political Science Review* 94:837–858.

Wibbels, Erik. 2000. "Federalism and the Politics of Macroeconomic Policy and Performance." *American Journal of Political Science* 44:687–702.

Wildasin, David. 1997. "Externalities and Bailouts: Hard and Soft Budget Constraints in Intergovernmental Fiscal Relations." Working paper 1843, World Bank.

II   Decentralized OECD Countries

2 Transfers and Bailouts: Enforcing Local Fiscal Discipline with Lessons from U.S. Federalism

Robert P. Inman

The move toward fiscal decentralization among the world's public economies and the fear that these new local governments will yield to the temptation to shift local costs onto the national budget through transfers and bailouts has led public finance scholars and practitioners alike to search for structural safeguards to ensure local fiscal discipline in a federalist public economy. The recent financial crises in Argentina and Brazil, largely precipitated by excessive local government borrowing, are prominent recent examples of how a fiscally irresponsible local sector can impose significant economic costs on a national economy (see, e.g., Webb, chap. 6, this volume; Rodden, chap. 7, this volume). This chapter reviews the historical fiscal performance of the U.S. state and local public sector, generally regarded as an example of a well-managed federal fiscal system, with the goal of identifying those institutional features that promote responsible local budgeting.

To generalize from the U.S. record for other federal public economies, it is important to begin with an analytic framework within which to interpret the U.S. evidence; section 2.1 provides that framework. The analysis takes a general view of local fiscal discipline and considers not only excessive deficits bailouts but fiscal transfers generally as means by which local governments can shift current period budgetary costs onto nonresidents. Both bailouts and transfers soften the local government's budget constraint and may lead to economically inefficient local government resource allocations. The analysis assumes democratically elected central and local governments, each with constitutionally protected spending and taxing powers.[1] In such a setting, local fiscal discipline will emerge only when local taxpayers find it in their interests to be disciplined. Section 2.1 outlines how appropriately designed political and market institutions can provide that discipline. Section 2.2 then reviews the current and historical U.S. record, seeking to identify how each of the political and market institutions specified in section 2.1 might have contributed to the overall fiscal performance of the U.S. local public sector. Section 2.3 summarizes the lessons learned for other democratic federalist public economies.

2.1   Ensuring Local Fiscal Discipline

Efficient resource allocations by governments require that all benefits and all costs of the public action be fully internalized, that is, accounted for, by public officials when making their policy choices. The failure to account for all social benefits of a public action will typically mean that too little of that activity is provided. Conversely, the failure to account for all social costs will mean that too much of the chosen service or regulation is provided. Called benefit or cost spillovers, these failures can be significant for subnational governments in economies with mobile residents, workers, and capital. In some cases, these policy failures are an unavoidable consequence of using subnational governments to provide public services; for example, children educated in one community will provide benefits to other communities when they relocate as adults. In these instances, there are central government policies—typically, intergovernmental grants-in-aid—that can induce local and provincial governments to provide the efficient level of the affected service (see Inman 1999). Our concern here, however, is not with these resource, or allocative spillovers, but rather with what might be called fiscal spillovers, created when local or state governments shift the budgetary costs of their own expenditures onto nonresidents, current or future. Again, there will be a failure by subnational governments to account for all the social consequences of their fiscal choices. An economically inefficient provision of local services will result. Controlling the ability of subnational governments to shift the costs of their fiscal choices becomes important.

Cost shifting by local governments can occur in three ways. First, local governments, working on behalf of resident taxpayers, may shift the production costs of local services onto nonresidents through federally funded transfers or by tax exporting through local taxes whose burdens fall primarily on nonresidents. Second, local governments may borrow money for current-period expenditures through deficit financing and then refuse to repay those debts, thereby shifting costs onto current-period lenders if the debt defaults or onto current-period national taxpayers if the debts are covered by a central government bailout. Third, local governments again deficit-finance current-period expenditures, but now use deficit rollovers year after year until current local taxpayers have left the local jurisdiction, leaving future residents to finance aggregate debt repayment through higher future taxes. Each of these cost-shifting strategies, if successful, subsidizes the provision of current public services to current local residents with the subsidy paid by current nonresidents or by future residents and nonresidents.

What are the economic consequences of allowing local cost shifting? Figure 2.1 describes how a typical local government might set its local budget and illustrates the economic inefficiencies that may arise under each cost-shifting strategy. The MB curve measures the marginal benefits to a typical local resident from another unit of the local public service consumed in the current period; the local service provides no benefits outside the local jurisdiction. The MC curve measures the social marginal costs of producing each unit of the local service in the current period. Efficient local government allocations occur at point X_e where MB = MC; here local taxpayers receive area $[A + B + E]$ in benefits and pay area $[B + E]$ in costs earning a net fiscal surplus of area $[A]$. Successful local cost shifting breaks this equality at MB = MC by introducing a subsidy of $\Phi \cdot MC$ between social marginal costs, MC, and

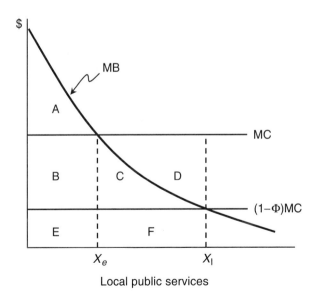

Figure 2.1
Local budgeting with cost shifting.

the marginal costs actually paid by local residents, $(1 - \Phi) \cdot MC$ (see figure 2.1). With tax exporting, Φ equals the fraction of social costs paid by taxing nonresidents. With transfers, Φ equals the fraction of social costs paid by the national government through monetary or in-kind grants. With deficit spending, Φ equals the fraction of current social costs paid by borrowing, later financed by defaults or bailouts or through the taxation of future residents. In each case, local residents now find it optimal to increase local spending until MB equals their after-subsidy local marginal costs: $MB = (1 - \Phi) \cdot MC$. Local residents now purchase X_1 in services, receiving area $[A + B + C + E + F]$ in taxpayer benefits, but now paying only area $[E + F]$ in local taxes, thereby earning a net fiscal surplus of area $[A + B + C]$ (see figure 2.1). Clearly, local taxpayers prefer the subsidy. National taxpayers, bondholders, or future taxpayers pay the cost of the subsidy—area $[B + C + D]$ in Figure 2.1. For the economy as whole, this is an inefficient outcome; subtracting national taxpayers' costs from local taxpayers' net benefits yields a measure of the full economy's aggregate net benefits equal to only area $[A - D]$, less than what economy as whole had earned—area $[A]$—when the local government bought services fully on its own. Area $[D]$ in Figure 2.1 measures the resulting economic inefficiency.[2] Local bailouts and transfers are privately preferred but, without significant extra-jurisdiction allocative spillovers, socially inefficient.

To control these inefficiencies from local cost shifting, Φ must equal 0; local taxpayers must be responsible for the full marginal costs of the local services they purchase. Yet Φ is itself endogenous and determined within the context of a wider federal system, a context within which local taxpayers may have important influence. If so, a richer institutional analysis than local choice alone (Figure 2.1) is required for an understanding of local fiscal discipline. Ensuring local fiscal discipline must be done with an understanding of the full political economy of local finance. The analysis that follows illustrates how narrow, local interests might come to undermine a national interest in an efficient local public sector. In the process, we learn what wider political and market institutions will be needed to check inefficient cost shifting by the local public sector.

2.1.1   Controlling Local Transfers and Tax Exporting

Both transfers from the central government and approval by the central government for local governments to tax nonresidents' income or consumption offer an implicit subsidy to the local sector for the purchase local public goods. Transfers may be paid as direct price subsidies (matching grants), as in-kind services such as federally financed infrastructure construction, or as targeted lump-sum grants for new services or activities (closed-end grants). Absent significant intergovernmental spillovers, each such transfer creates a wedge between the social marginal costs (MC) and benefits (MB) of local services; an inefficiency of area [D] results.[3] So too will allowing local governments to tax nonresidents, for example, through the taxation of firm capital, natural resources, or other export goods (see Inman and Rubinfeld 1996 for an overview). Both strategies require the cooperation of the central government, either directly through the payment of intergovernmental transfers or indirectly by allowing local governments to tax nonresident incomes and consumption. Why would national taxpayers, those who pay the subsidy, allow such inefficiencies to stand?

Exhibit 2.1 illustrates the core difficulty facing any democratically elected national government wishing to remove inefficient local transfers or the taxation of nonresidents. The problem arises when central government policies are set by a national legislature composed of independent representatives elected from each of the country's many local governments. In such a legislature, if local interests are to shift local costs, then cost shifting wins, despite a national interest in checking such behaviors. The problem, as exhibit 2.1 makes clear, is the prisoner's dilemma character of legislative politics dominated by independent local interests.[4] While all local representatives might agree that a national policy favoring local cost shifting is collectively inefficient— each local government gets its own subsidy but then must pay for the subsidies given to all other local governments—no single local representative can afford unilaterally to sacrifice his own government's subsidy for the benefits of improved national fiscal policy. In Figure 2.1, for example, all subnational governments would prefer allocation X_e to allocation X_l, but only if all other local governments joined a coalition and also supported the efficient outcome.[5]

To control local cost shifting, it is essential to control the prisoner's dilemma game played by these representatives when setting national policy. To do so, the incentives of the independent local legislators must be changed. Either penalties must be imposed when they vote for a local cost-shifting policy or extra rewards must be offered when they do not. Either way, the cooperative no-cost-shifting strategy must become the best choice for every locally elected representative no

Exhibit 2.1
The Central Legislature's Cost-Shifting Game

The central legislature's decision to allow cost shifting by local governments is an example of a prisoner's dilemma game in which the locally elected representative chooses either to support the legislative action σ ("shift"), which provides benefits to its citizens while shifting a fraction of the costs of those benefits to the citizens of all other subnational governments, or the legislative action γ ("no shift"), which provides the benefits without shifting any of the associated costs. The shifting strategy σ can be thought of as proposing and voting for a local tax on nonresident tax bases (tax exporting) or submitting a local subsidy for national financing (pork-barrel spending or deficit bailout). The no-shifting strategy γ can be thought of as not submitting a local subsidy for the national budget. If all local governments adopt the strategy of no shifting, then each of their citizens receives a payoff of $\Pi_{\gamma\gamma}$. (For simplicity, but without loss of generality, assume all governments are identical.) If, however, all local governments adopt the strategy of shifting, then the citizens of each of those governments receive a payoff of $\Pi_{\sigma\sigma}$. If one government adopts the strategy γ of no shifting, but all others choose σ and support to shift local costs, then the payoff to the citizens of the "honest" no-shifting government will be $\Pi_{\gamma\sigma}$, while the citizens in a typical government adopting the shifting strategy will receive $\Pi_{\sigma\gamma}$. Conversely, if one government adopts the shifting strategy σ, and all others adopt the honest no-shifting strategy γ, then the citizens of the shifting government receive $\Pi_{\sigma\gamma}$ and the citizens of a typical no-shifting government receive $\Pi_{\gamma\sigma}$. The game presents each subnational government with the following payoff matrix (with the local government's payoffs reported first):

	All other subnational governments	
	No shift (γ)	Shift (σ)
One local government — No shift (γ)	$\Pi_{\gamma\gamma}; \Pi_{\gamma\gamma}$	$\Pi_{\gamma\sigma}; \Pi_{\sigma\gamma}$
Shift (σ)	$\Pi_{\sigma\gamma}; \Pi_{\gamma\sigma}$	$\Pi_{\sigma\sigma}; \Pi_{\sigma\sigma}$

For the game to qualify as a prisoner's dilemma game, the payoffs for each local government must follow the sequence:

$\Pi_{\sigma\gamma} > \Pi_{\gamma\gamma} > \Pi_{\sigma\sigma} > \Pi_{\gamma\sigma}$.

The other payoffs in the matrix, $\Pi_{\sigma\gamma}$ and $\Pi_{\gamma\sigma}$, are the payoffs to other governments and are not relevant to each individual government's making its own choices. To rule out a randomized strategy as preferred, we also require that $\Pi_{\gamma\gamma} > [\Pi_{\sigma\gamma} + \Pi_{\gamma\sigma}]/2$. In words, each local government will most prefer to cost-shift (σ) and have all other local governments pay for their own services from own fiscal resources. If that outcome cannot occur, then all local governments' agreeing not to shift their costs is

Exhibit 2.1

(continued)

> preferred. Having all governments adopt the shifting strategy is each government's third best outcome. In last place is the outcome from the naive strategy of not cost shifting while all other governments do.
>
> With this ordering of outcomes, each local government prefers the cost-shifting strategy knowing that all other local governments also prefer that strategy. The outcome of the game is all governments' adopting the cost-shifting strategy and receiving the socially inefficient payoff of $\Pi_{\sigma\sigma}$.

matter what the other representatives do.[6] With appropriate penalties and rewards, the cooperative outcome can be enforced. The needed penalties and rewards must come from some organization or individual with sufficient extralegislative resources, however, and it must be an organization or individual rewarded for encouraging the nationally efficient—no local cost shifting—allocations. Within the structure of democratic politics, either of two commonly mentioned alternatives will meet these two conditions:

1. Nationally elected political parties with the ability to control the election prospects of local representatives (Wittman 1989), or nationally elected presidents with the ability to grant or deny favors valued by local representatives and their constituents (Fitts and Inman 1992, Chari, Jones, and Marimon 1997).

Paradoxically perhaps, to ensure efficient local government finance, we must first establish institutions to ensure a strong central government.

2.1.2 *Controlling Local Defaults and Central Bailouts*

However successful an economy might be in finding extralegislative institutions to check the inefficient prisoner's dilemma behaviors of local representatives in decentralized legislatures (exhibit 2.1), there remains a second route through which local governments can extract socially inefficient subsidies from the national government: demand and receive a bailout for a locally created fiscal crisis. Even strong central governments capable of resisting local demands for current period subsidies remain susceptible to this strategy. Here the local government spends borrowed money to subsidize current services.[7] The

Exhibit 2.2
The Default-Bailout Game

The default-bailout game is a special case of a sequential game in which the local or state government—more generally, the subordinate division in an organization's hierarchy—adopts an action Δ (unfunded deficit) that provides benefits to the local government of B^l (>0) and benefits to central government—more generally, the center in an organization's hierarchy—of B^c ($\geq$ or ≤ 0). Following the adoption of action Δ, the central government responds by adopting either an action β (bailout) or an action η (no bailout). If action β is chosen by the central government, it costs the center C^c_β (>0) and the local government C^l_β (≥ 0), while if action η is selected, then the central government bears a cost of C^c_η (>0) and the local government C^l_η (≥ 0). If the local government chooses not to adopt action Δ, then the status quo remains in place and the local and central governments receive the payoffs in the status quo, Q^l and Q^c, respectively.

The game has the following payoff structure:

	Local Government Adopts Action:			
CURRENT PERIOD:	Δ	OR		T
FUTURE PERIOD:	Center Adopts Action:			Center Adopts Action:
	β	OR	η	Status Quo
Center Payoff:	$B^c - C^c_\beta$		$B^c - C^c_\eta$	Q^c
Local Payoff:	$B^l - C^l_\beta$		$B^l - C^l_\eta$	Q^l

This sequential game becomes the default-bailout game when the local government prefers action Δ, the central government prefers action β given that the local government has chosen Δ, and together these actions reduce aggregate social welfare measured by the combined net benefits to the citizens of the local and central governments. For this to be the case, three restrictions on the values of benefits and costs must apply:

Condition 1: Central government prefers β, given Δ. That is,

$B_c - C^c_\beta > B^c - C^c_\eta$

or

$C^c_\eta > C^c_\beta$

Condition 2: Local government prefers Δ, given β, but would prefer the status quo, given η. That is,

Condition 2a: $B^l - C^l_\beta > Q^l$

Condition 2b: $B^l - C^l_\eta \leq Q^l$

Condition 3: Aggregate inefficiency. That is, $[B^c - C^c_\beta] + [B^l - C^l_\beta] < Q^c + Q^l$

In words, the local government (i.e., division) adopts an action Δ that is beneficial to its residents (i.e., employees) but prompts a second-best

Exhibit 2.1

(continued)

> β response from the central government (i.e., center), which is damaging to the country (i.e., organization) as a whole. The problem arises because the central government bears a large cost if it does not respond with β (condition 1), and knowing this, the local government prefers the privately beneficial (condition 2) but socially inefficient (condition 3) strategy Δ.

local government then declares a "fiscal crisis" and defaults on its local debts. The hope is that the central government will step in to cover the debt through a fiscal bailout. Will it?

Exhibit 2.2 illustrates when the central government might offer a fiscal bailout to a local government threatening default. The essential problem here is one of time inconsistency, or what has become known as the problem of the soft budget constraint: today's promises by the central government of no bailouts are not credible against tomorrow's circumstances (see Kornai 1986). First, the central government promises there will be no bailouts, perhaps because of a constitutional provision requiring balanced local budgets and no national government deficit relief. Second, the local government then decides how to finance its current local services, either by borrowing some or all of the needed resources (action Δ in exhibit 2.2) or, alternatively, by not borrowing and paying for services through local taxes only (action T in exhibit 2.2). If only local taxes are used to finance local services, then the efficient allocation at X_e in Figure 2.1 results. If the local government has borrowed Δ today, then tomorrow it declares default and asks the central government for a debt bailout. Third, the central government can decide to offer the bailout (action β in exhibit 2.2) or not (action η in exhibit 2.2). If no bailout is offered, then the burden of debt repayment is shifted back onto the local government, which either repays the debt from local taxes or defaults, shifting the final burden onto bondholders.

Which decisions are best for the local and central governments turns on the benefits and costs associated with each of the three possible outcomes in exhibit 2.2: the default-bailout (Δ,β) path, the default–no bailout (Δ,η) path, or the tax-financing path (T). If the local government has borrowed to finance local public services—either path (Δ,β) or

(Δ,η)—then a level of local public services will be chosen by the local government today, resulting in benefits for the central and local decision makers of B^c and B^l, respectively. If there are no spillovers from the local budget to citizens outside the community, then $B^c = 0$;[8] local services will be provided only if there are local benefits, so $B^l > 0$. Once the local government has chosen its service level, I also assume the resulting benefits are then fixed and not affected by the subsequent bailout decision of the central government.

The central government's bailout decision—either path (Δ,β) or (Δ,η)—does affect the costs for both levels of government, however. Because a bailout is a subsidy, a local government's net fiscal costs with bailouts (Δ,β) will always be less than its net costs without bailout (Δ,η)—that is, $C^l_\beta < C^l_\eta$. If it chooses bailouts, then the central government's costs may be larger, equal to, or smaller than its costs from choosing the no-bailout strategy: $C^c_\beta >, =, < C^c_\eta$. Bailouts will cost the central government national tax dollars, but not to bail-out a distressed local government may lead to costly financial or political crises. It will be the magnitude of the costs of not bailing out a "failing" local government that will prove decisive in this analysis. Finally, if the local government chooses the tax financing path (T), the central government accepts the resulting allocation, and net benefits are simply Q^c for the central government and Q^l for the local government. As (I assume) there are no national spillovers from the locally provided public services ($B^c = 0$), and no central government tax payments when T is chosen, $Q^c = 0$ as well.[9] Local government net benefits from tax-financing local services are assumed to be positive when the public service is provided; thus $Q^l > 0$.

For this default-bailout game to be a source of local government fiscal inefficiency, the local government must prefer action Δ, the central government must prefer action β given that the local government has chosen Δ, and together these actions must reduce aggregate social welfare measured by the combined net benefits to the citizens of the local and central government decisions. For this to be the case, three conditions must hold; they are listed in exhibit 2.2. First, the central government must prefer to use the bailout strategy. This occurs when the no-bailout choice is more costly than the bailout itself; thus, condition 1: $C^c_\eta > C^c_\beta$. Second, knowing this, the local government must prefer to use local debt for the financing of local services; thus, condition 2a: $B^l - C^l_\beta > Q^l$. To be sure that it is central government bailout policies that are really creating the economic inefficiencies, we also require that had the central government adopted the no-bailout strategy, then the local government would have preferred efficient local tax financing; thus, condition 2b: $B^1 - C_\eta^1 \leq Q^1$, with indifference favoring tax financing. Together, conditions 2a and 2b imply, and are implied by, the assumption that $C_\eta^1 > C_\beta^1$. Finally, the fiscal allocation with a central government bailout must be economically inefficient compared to the alternative of full local government tax financing; thus, condition 3, where $[B^c - C_\beta^c] + [B^1 - C_\beta^1] < Q^c + Q^1$.

Which decisions are made by local and central governments turns on the benefits and costs associated with each outcome of the sequential default-bailout game. The analysis here is for a typical local government as described by Figure 2.1, where now the area $[B + C + D]$ is interpreted as the unfunded deficit($= \Delta$). If the central government bears a significant cost from allowing the local government to default on its unfunded debt and this cost is larger than the cost to the central government of assuming the local debt (condition 1), then the central government will prefer the bailout strategy, β. In Figure 2.1, the present value cost to the central government of a local deficit will be area $[B + C + D]$. Thus, the bailout strategy will be preferred if $C_\eta^c > C_\beta^c = \Delta = $ area $[B + C + D]$; I specify the likely determinants of C_η^c below. For the moment, assume condition 1 holds. Knowing that they will be bailed out by the central government, local governments will prefer the unfunded deficit strategy, Δ, to a status quo balanced budget strategy when condition 2a holds; this is in fact the case for Figure 2.1.[10] Finally, if a central government bailout is preferred and, knowing this, local governments adopt the default strategy, then the bailout game produces an inefficient social outcome if aggregate social welfare is lower under deficit and bailout than if all local governments had adopted the status quo tax-financed budget or no-bailout strategy (condition 3). Again, this will be the case for the local governments of Figure 2.1.[11] Like the local transfer–tax exporting game of exhibit 2.1, the default-bailout game also yields the inefficient local budget of X_1 as an equilibrium; area $[D]$ in Figure 2.1 is again the measure of the resulting economic inefficiency.

The key assumption that forces an inefficient outcome in this default-bailout game is that the central government bears significant costs (C_η^c) if it allows the local government to default on its unfunded deficit. If the costs to the central government of not bailing out a defaulting local government, C_η^c, are small enough, then the default-bailout outcome can be avoided and efficiency will result.[12] There are two important categories of costs that the central government might bear from failing to bail out a particular local government in deficit distress. The first, called the *financial costs of no bailout* and denoted by F_i, occurs because the local default creates financial spillovers onto the rest of the economy, which in turn have real (economic) consequences for subsequent public and private sector investments outside the local community in default. The second, called the *distributional costs of no bailout* and denoted by V_i, represents the differential costs to the central government of having the debt burden of local government i borne directly by local taxpayers or by its bondholders rather than by national taxpayers. Together, these national financial and distributional costs equal the full costs of not bailing out a local government. Since F_i and V_i will be measured as costs per national taxpayer and will be compared to bailout costs measured as current period debt per local taxpayer, F_i and V_i must be measured in present value dollars and must be deflated by the share of the national population residing in the defaulting community $(= \rho_i)$: $C_n^c = [F_i + V_i]/\rho_i$. Importantly, F_i and V_i are specific for each local government and to the size of the local deficit; thus, some local governments might receive a bailout and others not.

The national financial costs (F_i) from a no-bailout decision will increase with the stock of uncovered debt per national resident $(= \Delta \cdot \rho_i,$ where Δ is debt per local resident and ρ_i is the portion of the national population residing in the defaulting community), the share of this debt, which is actually placed in default $(= \sigma)$, and the allocative inefficiencies, which each dollar of defaulted debt creates for the wider economy (Ψ_i): $F_i = \Psi_i \cdot \rho_i \cdot \sigma \cdot \Delta$.[13] The magnitude of these financial costs is likely to be larger, the less sophisticated are the nation's financial markets. First, an immature banking system with incomplete insurance for sudden losses of liquidity—for example, from a local government default of bonds held by banks—may lead to bank runs and the need to liquidate the bank's investment in productive long-term assets before their full returns are realized (see Allen and Gale 2000). The resulting loss in productive private investments may have adverse effects on overall country economic performance, in some instances causing and in other cases exacerbating recessions. When local defaults have the potential to precipitate a banking crisis, values of $\Psi_i \approx .10$ for developed countries and perhaps as high as .40 in developing economies are possible.[14] Second, countries with immature capital markets may exhibit a wedge between returns earned in the formal (i.e., national) and informal (i.e., local) capital markets. To the extent that municipal debt is funded by the formal capital market, defaults will move investment resources from the national to the local markets. If the national capital market offers higher average returns, then allocative inefficiencies will result by a failure to bail out municipal defaults; here, Ψ_i may be as large as .20.[15] In countries with weak banking systems and immature capital markets, defaults without bailouts may create allocative inefficiencies that together are as large are as .60 per dollar of defaulted local debt.

Distributional costs (V_i) to the national government of a no-bailout decision arise when local taxpayers or local bondholders are perceived by the national government as favored relative to national taxpayers. When a local government declares bankruptcy, either national taxpayers pay (under bailout), or bondholders pay (under no bailout and default), or local taxpayers pay (under no bailout and no default). A local debt of Δ imposes a nationwide burden of $\rho_i \cdot \Delta$, where again ρ_i is the portion of national citizens residing in the defaulting community. V_i is assumed to be proportional to this national burden of default and is measured as $V_i = (1 + v_i) \cdot \rho_i \cdot \Delta$, where $v_i = \sigma \cdot v_i^{bond} + (1 - \sigma) \cdot v_i^{tax}$ is the incremental weighted average distributional cost of $1 of the deficit burden borne by bondholders and local taxpayers, with σ defined as the share of local debt allowed to fall into default.[16] This distributional cost of a dollar of local deficit may be greater than, equal to, or less than the $1 cost to the national average taxpayer as the central government values the "weighted average" local taxpayer-bondholder incrementally more ($v_i > 0$), the same as ($v_i = 0$), or less than ($v_i < 0$) the average national taxpayer.[17] The distributional weight v_i is likely to be positive when holders of local government debt are also the national median voter (Aghion and Bolton 1990), when the city in default is the national capital (Ades and Glaeser 1995), or when local taxpayers are very poor and the services denied under any subsequent fiscal repayment are important "good Samaritan" services such as health care, income maintenance, or personal safety (Coate 1995). In addition, the distributional weight may be positive when local economic interests dominate a central government's decision making, as outlined in exhibit 2.1. Here, bailouts are just another form of transfer to politically decisive local governments, an example of where bailouts occur because these many local governments might now be seen as "too small to fail."[18]

When the financial or distributional costs to the national government of the no-bailout alternative ($C_\eta^c = [F_i + V_i]/\rho_i$) are large relative to the cost of bailout ($C_\beta^c = \Delta$), then condition 1 will hold, and inefficient local deficit financing will result. Condition 1 can now be specified as $C_\eta^c =$ $[F_i + V_i]/\rho_i = [\Psi_i \cdot \sigma_i \cdot \rho \cdot \Delta + (1 + v_i) \cdot \rho_i \cdot \Delta]/\rho_i > C_\beta^c = \Delta$, which reduces to $\Psi_i \cdot \sigma + v_i > 0$ or $v_i > -\Psi_i \cdot \sigma$. Central government bailouts will occur when the local taxpayers or bondholders (or both) are, on average, favored over national taxpayers ($v_i > 0$) even when there are no financial costs from failing to provide a bailout ($\Psi_i \cdot \sigma = 0$), or when local taxpayers or bondholders are not specially favored (or maybe even slightly disfavored, $v_i \leq 0$) but financial spillovers become important ($\Psi_i \cdot \sigma > 0$).

Controlling local bailouts therefore reduces to making both v_i and $\Psi_i \cdot \sigma$ equal to zero, or if $\Psi_i \cdot \sigma > 0$, electing a central government that is actively hostile to community i's taxpayers or bondholders so that $v_i \leq -\Psi_i \cdot \sigma < 0$. In either case, $v_i \leq -\Psi_i \cdot \sigma$, condition 1 does not hold, and the central government denies a bailout request. Knowing this, the local government will not borrow and threaten default, and the efficient local budget of X_e will result (see figure 2.1).

To reduce v_i, the central government should be granted a range of targeted commodity and income taxes and transfers so as to narrow the after-tax-and-transfer income differences between rich and poor, thereby reducing the need for the coarse redistributive tool of local government bailouts, one likely to benefit rich and poor simultaneously.[19] Thus:

2. Efficient central government redistribution policies are required.

To reduce Ψ_i:

3. A mature banking system with interbank markets in demand deposits and fully integrated national capital markets will be needed.

Lacking these institutional preconditions, the central government stands at risk of being exploited by the socially inefficient default-bailout strategy of local governments. If a local government knows with certainty that condition 1 holds for the central government, it will adopt an inefficient budget funded by Δ. Surprisingly perhaps, allowing just a small amount of uncertainty on the part of the local government as to the central government's true values of v_i, Ψ_i, or σ can deter inefficient deficit financing if only the central government and the local government interact over many budget periods (see Kreps and Wilson 1982).[20] With such uncertainty, a central government that is truly accommodating ($\Psi_i \cdot \sigma + v_i > 0$) may be able to adopt a tough no-bailout stance early in its relationship with the local government and fool the local government into believing that it is a truly tough central government, that is, one for which $\Psi_i \cdot \sigma + v_i \leq 0$. The most compelling source of local uncertainty over the central government's true type is likely to be the central government's distributional costs (v_i) of a no-bailout policy. Is the true value of v_i positive (bailout), or is it zero or perhaps even negative (no bailout)?

For an accommodating central government, it may pay to develop a tough reputation: first, to talk tough so as to suggest v_i may be negative and then, if a local government defaults, to act tough and deny the bailout. Unable to distinguish a central government's true type—tough or accommodating—the local government must confront the risk that its request for a bailout of Δ will be denied. If it is denied, local residents must then repay the debt and suffer an economic inefficiency equal to area $[D]$ in figure 2.1. The larger is area $[D]$ relative to the subsidy Δ or, equivalently, the more elastic are residents' demands for local government services, the less likely it will be that the local government will take a chance on a now uncertain bailout.[21] Fiscal competition between individual local governments or between all local governments and private or non profit providers will increase local residents' elasticity of demand for any individual local government's public services, thereby raising the local government's cost of choosing the now risky bailout strategy. With bailout uncertainty:

4. Competitive suppliers of local public services will help to control bailouts.[22]

Creating this bailout uncertainty is not free to a truly accommodating central government, however. For these governments, acting tough is costly when local governments are denied their bailout. (Truly tough central governments always prefer to deny the bailout; they enjoy saying no). Thus, for accommodating central governments, there must be a compensating benefit when they act tough. The benefit comes in the future budget periods when local governments are deterred from setting $\Delta > 0$ and nationally financed bailouts are avoided. To ensure that there are enough future saved bailouts to justify the costs of building the tough reputation, the accommodating central government must be:

5. A stable, long-lived central government.

Further, it is important here that the uncertainty be limited to the behavior of the central government. If we also observe uncertainty as to the source of the local deficit—is it a strategic deficit in search of a bailout, or a deficit resulting from some unobservable, exogenous fiscal disaster—then the resolve of the central government to be tough might be weakened. Thus there are two important complementary institutions for a central government seeking to control local deficit behaviors.

6. Clear and enforceable accounting standards to distinguish strategic deficits from truly exogenous local disasters.

7. A well-managed aggregate economy to limit the frequency of such disasters.

Finally, uncertainty as to the fiscal response of the central government to deficit or bailout requests will, with sophisticated bond markets, translate into higher local borrowing rates for local governments contemplating the deficit strategy.[23] This means a greater expected cost for those local governments that choose to run a deficit and seek a bailout; these greater expected costs will discourage local governments from pursuing the deficit-bailout strategy. Thus, to discourage inefficient local deficits, policies are needed that encourage

8. An informed and sophisticated municipal bond market.

2.1.3   Controlling Deficit Rollovers and Taxpayer Exit

Even if inefficient transfers and bailouts from the central government can be successfully controlled, local taxpayers retain a final strategy for shifting the costs of local services onto nonresidents: create an unfunded deficit of Δ, move out of town, and hope future taxpayers do not recognize the resulting liabilities at the moment they purchase a home or business in the community. Like transfers and bailouts, unfunded liabilities followed by the exit of current taxpayers provides these taxpayers with an implicit subsidy for the purchase of current period local public services—$\Phi > 0$ in figure 2.1.[24] Here, the subsidy comes from future taxpayers who now are required by a now credible no-bailout strategy of the central government to pay all past local deficits. Again, the result will be an inefficient local public sector budget (see figure 2.1). A successful counterstrategy would be to provide information of each community's Δ so that future taxpayers could demand a compensating reduction in the prices paid for homes or businesses when moving into the community. When the present value of the fall in asset values owned by current residents just equals Δ, full market capitalization of the unfunded deficits results. With full market capitalization, current residents pay Δ and thus the full costs of current services; thus $\Phi = 0$.[25]

Unfortunately, future residents cannot be counted on to provide the needed information about Δ on their own. Discovering the true value of Δ will be costly to any future resident. Once discovered, Δ plus its interest costs ($= (1 + R) \cdot \Delta$) will be deducted from the underlying market value of the home or business ($= A$); therefore, informed future residents bid only $A - (1 + R) \cdot \Delta$. If A is known, as it will be for all but one-of-a-kind properties, the informed bidder's offer automatically reveals the estimate of Δ. This is true for open oral auctions or, as is common in most real estate sales, for sealed-bid auctions in multi-property communities posting winning bids. Since Δ is the same for all properties within a community, each future resident can learn the value of Δ from the sales prices of other properties. Since learning Δ on one's own is costly but market prices reveal Δ for free, all future residents will prefer to use market prices. But then, no one invests in learning Δ on their own, and local deficits go undiscovered. The argument here is an application of Grossman and Stiglitz's (1980) more general analysis of the public good nature of costly market information. One solution is to provide these facts publicly—here the value of Δ. Thus:

9. Direct central government monitoring of Δ or central government accounting standards and a competitive accounting market provide the information needed for the full capitalization of local deficits into land prices.[26]

Knowing Δ, deficit shifting to future taxpayers will then be checked in the following situation:

10. Local land markets have enforced property rights and the market for property is competitive.

With these two additional institutions in place, the final route for local cost shifting will have been blocked.

2.1.4 Constitutional Regulation: A Final Safeguard

Exhibit 2.3 summarizes the ten institutional preconditions needed to ensure an efficient allocation of public resources through a decentralized, local public sector. Together they define the wider political and economic environment—a strong and stable central government and mature and competitive capital and land markets—necessary to control

Exhibit 2.3
Institutional Pre-conditions for Enforcing Local Fiscal Discipline

---

Precondition for Controlling Central Transfers and Local Tax Exporting

1. Nationally elected political parties with the ability to control the election prospects of local representatives, or nationally elected presidents with the ability to grant or deny favors valued by local representatives and/or their constituents.

A Constitutional Regulation When the Precondition Fails to Hold: Fiscal assignment limiting central transfers to demonstrable spillovers and local taxation to resident taxation.

Preconditions for Controlling Local Defaults and Central Bailouts

2. Efficient central government redistribution policies
3. A mature banking system and fully integrated national capital markets
4. Competitive suppliers of local public services
5. A stable, long-lived central government
6. Clear and enforceable accounting standards
7. A well-managed aggregate economy
8. An informed and sophisticated municipal bond market

A Constitutional Regulation When the Preconditions Fail to Hold: A no-bailout clause and a bankruptcy standard requiring local repayment of all local debts, enforced by a politically independent oversight board.

Preconditions for Controlling Deficit Rollovers

9. Direct central government monitoring of local deficits or centrally decided accounting standards for defining local deficits, relying on a competitive accounting market to provide efficient monitoring
10. Enforceable property rights and competitive land markets

A Constitutional Regulation When the Preconditions Fail to Hold: Balanced budget rule requiring tax financing of all current accounts spending.

cost shifting by democratically elected local governments. Lacking any one of these preconditions provides an opportunity for local governments to extract a transfer or a bailout from nonresidents, a transfer that leads to socially inefficient fiscal allocations. Creating a local public sector, even a Tiebout-competitive local public sector, is not by itself a guarantor of fiscal efficiency. It is perhaps no surprise, then, that recent empirical studies find that fiscal decentralization contributes to national economic growth, as one measure of economic efficiency, only in advanced capitalist democracies (see Davoodi and Zou 1998).

What can be done if one or more of these important institutional preconditions do not hold, as is likely the case in developing economies and newly emerging democracies? Apart from a decision to abandon democratic local governments altogether and return to the fully centralized fiscal state, the answer is to regulate local fiscal behaviors selectively through independently enforced constitutional regulations. Each missing political or market institution has an appropriate regulatory response (see exhibit 2.3). To control inefficient local transfers and tax exporting, the constitution should use its powers of local fiscal assignment to limit intergovernmental transfers to only those local activities with demonstrable intergovernmental spillovers and to limit local taxes to resident-based taxation only (see Inman and Rubinfeld 1996). To control defaults and bailouts, the constitution should contain a no-bailout clause (save for unforeseen local fiscal emergencies) and establish a national bankruptcy standard that requires all local debts to be repaid in full from local taxation (i.e., $\sigma = 0$; see McConnell and Picker 1993). To control local deficit rollovers and the accumulation of unfunded liabilities, the constitution should require current-accounts balanced budgets within each fiscal year—that is, local debt incurred for periods longer than one year must fund long-term capital investments only (see Bohn and Inman 1996).

Successful enforcement of these constitutional regulations will require politically independent courts or regulatory agencies, with the rules themselves grounded in a constitution requiring a supermajority to amend (see Inman 1997). Successful enforcement will also require the court to draw a bright line for each regulation between what is acceptable and unacceptable local financing: What is an intergovernmental spillover, a residential tax, an unforeseen fiscal emergency, a current-account expenditure? Drawing such distinctions is a subtle but manageable task (see, e.g., Merritt 1988 and Gillette and Baker 1999). To the extent such constitutional rules prove effective, local democratic choices will necessarily be constrained. Local policy choices that might be allowed when efficient market and political institutions are in place will be denied by these assignment (*no* business taxes for business services), bailout (*no* national sharing of local fiscal shocks), and balanced budget (*no* deficit financing for local tax-smoothing) rules. When stable, efficient central governments and competitive capital and land markets are in place, constitutional regulation is no longer necessary. In this instance, more local choice and greater fiscal efficiency result.

2.2 Fiscal Discipline in U.S. Federalism: Some Lessons Learned

The U.S. public economy is viewed by many as one federal system that has successfully established the principle of fiscal discipline for its local and state (provincial) governments. Although this impression is largely correct, there are examples from the historical and contemporary record that illustrate just how fragile the hard budget constraint can be. Missing one or more of the institutional preconditions in exhibit 2.3 opens the possibility for inefficient transfers or bailouts to the state and local public sector.

Lesson 1: Strong Executives and National Political Parties are Required for Efficiency

In locally elected national legislatures, local governments will seek to exploit the national treasury. To control central government transfers and local tax exporting, strong executives or strong political parties elected by national constituencies will be required to ensure fiscal efficiency. Exhibit 2.1 outlined the incentives of local representatives when given the chance to finance local services with national taxes. Paying only a small fraction of the costs but enjoying all the benefits, locally elected representatives overbuy nationally financed local public goods. Historical and current U.S. evidence strongly supports the three underlying tenets of this cost-shifting argument:

1. Locally elected representatives benefit from the passage of national policies that favor local economic interests (Levitt and Snyder 1997).

2. Locally elected representatives demand larger national programs for their constituents, the greater the share of program costs paid for by national taxes (Inman and Fitts 1990, DelRossi 1995, DelRossi and Inman 1999).

3. In undisciplined national legislatures, locally elected representatives form majority legislative coalitions, often nearly unanimous coalitions, to pass locally beneficial but nationally financed policies (Wilson 1986, Collie 1988).[27]

Evidence presented in Inman (1988) attributes much of the historical growth in U.S. national grants for state and local public services—grants other than for income and health care aid for low-income families—to just such a process. The alternative hypothesis—that industrialization creates significant economic spillovers between communities that are rationally financed through intergovernmental transfers—explains neither the growth nor the cross-community allocation of U.S. intergovernmental aid. What does explain the growth and distribution of federal transfers to the local public sector is the growing demand for local public services, the emergence of organized local government lobbies, and the decentralization of U.S. congressional decision making. The only significant downturn in the long history of growth in real aid per capita occurred during the first term of the presidency of Ronald Reagan as he leveraged his considerable national popularity into significant reductions in domestic program spending and personal taxes. As part of this broader fiscal reform, intergovernmental transfers were reduced from projected levels of $773 per capita to $602 per capita (1999 dollars). In the last years of Reagan's presidency, as his influence with members waned, Congress began to restore the cuts. Over the past twelve years, national grants spending has returned to its historic trend, returning to the pre-Reagan levels of funding by 1990. Today (2001) federal assistance for the state and local public sector for services other than income support totals $1071 per capita. The consequence of this weak structure for national budgeting has been an inefficiently too large local public sector, with one estimate of the average rate of economic inefficiency per dollar of federal intergovernmental aid—area $[D]$/area $[B + C + D]$ in figure 2.1—at $.17 per dollar of aid (Inman, 1988), though estimates of the inefficiencies in individual grants programs are often much higher, ranging from $.30 per dollar of federal assistance for water projects (DelRossi and Inman 1999) to $.85 per dollar of federal transportation aid (Knight 2001).

Nor have U.S. state and local governments been prohibited by the U.S. Constitution or federal law from accessing the taxable assets, income, or consumption of nonresidents. As a consequence, state and local governments have been free to use their local taxes to export the costs of local services. To the extent they are successful, as they may be when states or cities occupy economically unique locations and land is elastically supplied or owned by nonresidents, there will be an implicit subsidy to residents equal to the share of the nonresident-owned tax base in the aggregate local government tax base. This subsidy, often measured empirically by the share of commercial-industrial property in a government's property tax base, has been shown to have a significant positive effect on the demand for local public services (see the survey evidence in Bergstrom, Rubinfeld, and Shapiro 1982). For a commercial-industrial share of .40 and a price elasticity of demand for local public services of $-.50$, both plausibly within their ranges for U.S. state and local governments, the implied average rate of economic inefficiency will equal \$.10 $(= .5 \cdot \varepsilon_{px} \cdot \Phi = .5 \cdot .50 \cdot .40)$ per dollar of business taxes raised.[28]

Lesson 2: Constitutional Regulations Require Clean Guidelines to Acceptable Local Behaviors
Constitutional regulation of central government transfers and tax assignment is possible, but clear constitutional guidelines as to what constitutes a valid spillover for national policy or a valid tax base for local revenues must be provided. The U.S. Constitution fails to provide the needed guidelines; as a consequence, local governments have found it possible to extract significant transfers in the form of intergovernmental grants and nonresident taxation. Efforts by the U.S. Supreme Court to define a workable standard for what constitutes the valid domains of policy for national and local governments have proven ineffective given the limited constitutional guidance.[29] Clear and workable definitions of economic spillovers and residential taxation can be written and successfully enforced by courts or politically independent regulatory agencies. The recent experience of the European Union with the implementation of its new principle of subsidiarity provides direct evidence on the point (see Bermann 1994).[30]

Lesson 3: A Mature Banking System, Efficient Capital Markets, and a Well-Administered Fiscal System are Needed to Check Bailouts
Efficient central government redistribution policies, a mature national banking system, and an integrated national capital market provide the institutional preconditions necessary to remove the temptation for central government bailouts. The heart of lesson 3 was taught early in U.S. fiscal history and by all accounts learned well by U.S. state and local governments: bailouts will not be forthcoming from a central gov-

ernment (or for municipal defaults, a state government) whose constituents are economically unaffected by the default ($\Psi_i \approx 0$) and who are indifferent or actively hostile to the fate of citizens or bondholders of the defaulting government ($v_i \leq 0$). Whatever is the value of σ—see lesson 4 below—the necessary condition for a tough central government that $v_i \leq -\Psi_i \cdot \sigma$ will then apply. The U.S. fiscal history and its four significant periods of defaults by state and local governments reveal the importance of these institutional preconditions for local fiscal efficiency. Throughout U.S. history, there have been only two direct bailouts of a state or local government by a responsible higher government: the federal government bailout of Washington, D.C., in 1997, a case where $\Psi_i > 0$, and the current state bailout by New Jersey of its poorest city, Camden, a case where $v_i > 0$.

The first major wave of lower government defaults occurred during the 1840s, when eight states (Arkansas, Illinois, Indiana, Louisiana, Maryland, Michigan, Mississippi, and Pennsylvania) and the Territory of Florida defaulted. The federal government's response marked a historical turning point in its treatment of local fiscal crises.[31] Legislative efforts by the eight defaulting states led by Representative William Cost Johnson of Maryland to secure a federal government bailout of their debts, offered as a logroll to relieve all states' debts, was defeated in Congress. Johnson offered all the right arguments: default would stop the construction of important public works with significant interstate spillovers ($\Psi_i > 0$) while a bailout would relieve worthy state taxpayers of a heavy load of taxation ($v_i > 0$; Scott 1893). Opponents from the majority of fiscally sound states rejected both arguments, pointing out that the defaulted loans were for transportation projects or state banks providing only local economic benefits ($\Psi_i \approx 0$) and that the state taxes needed to repay the debts would come largely come from the wealthy (nonmedian) landowners through property taxation ($v_i \leq 0$; Scott 1893). The fact that almost 70 percent of the defaulted debt was held by sophisticated foreign investors ($v_i \leq 0$) and was not an important part of the portfolios of the large U.S. banks ($\Psi_i \approx 0$) cooled any temptation for a bailout (English 1996). Importantly, opponents of a bailout stressed the strategic implications of such a policy; bailouts would signal an accommodating central government and encourage future deficits, defaults, and ultimately inefficient local governments.[32] Congress said no, and there have been no state defaults since.

The no-bailout position also has been adopted by U.S. states when confronted with defaults by their municipal governments. With the single exception of New Jersey's current treatment of Camden, U.S.

states have also said no to bailouts. The first major test for the states came in the 1870s, and no states provided a bailout (Hillhouse 1936). Most of the defaulting local debts were for local infrastructure projects designed to attract real estate developers or a railroad spur, with planned repayment tied to increases in property taxes on adjacent lands. When the projects failed, and many did, the local governments assumed direct responsibility for debt repayment. Almost all of this municipal debt was held by foreigners or out-of-state residents, and again the bulk of local taxes necessary to repay the debt would come from upper-income households ($v_i \leq 0$). All of the defaulting local projects provided only narrow local benefits ($\Psi_i \approx 0$), in some instances extending no further than corrupt local politicians' back pockets (see Hillhouse 1936). Like their federal counterparts from the 1840s, state legislators also appreciated the incentive for future fiscal problems that a bailout would create. The 1870 no-bailout decision was a first step toward controlling local fiscal excesses. To add credibility to a state's future no-bailout position, all states passed regulations to limit the extent of local debt (usually to a fraction of local taxing capacity), and some states approved constitutional amendments prohibiting bailouts.[33]

The 1930s saw another wave of municipal defaults.[34] With the emergence of the automobile and the beginning of suburbanization in the 1920s came a new demand for public capital. The level of capital investment by U.S. local governments roughly doubled from 1920 to 1930. Virtually all of this investment was financed by general obligation bonds backed by the property tax base of the issuing communities. By 1932, debt service payments exceeded 15 percent of annual local spending in fourteen states; nineteen more states had debt service burdens over 10 percent of annual local spending. Any significant downturn in tax base would threaten the ability of high-debt communities to meet their interest and principal obligations. The downturn came with the Great Depression of 1932, which placed new spending burdens on this shrinking tax base, for local governments still had the primary fiscal responsibility for services to low-income households and unemployment relief. The result was an explosion of municipal defaults, rising from 678 local governments in default in 1932 to over 3,200 governments in default by December 1935. In dollar terms, $2.4 billion, or $.16 of every dollar of outstanding local debt, was in default (see Hempel 1971). In contrast to the 1840s and the 1870s, the 1930s defaults were not limited to a few governments nor were they the result of obvious fiscal mismanagement or corruption. The outstanding debt was now held by U.S. investors, and local taxes were being paid primarily by middle-income city residents. A state or federal bailout for the debt of these distressed municipalities must have been a tempting policy option.

There is no compelling evidence that a federal or state bailout was forthcoming. To be sure, from 1932 to 1940, federal and state assistance to the local public sector did increase above its historical trend, but the additional funds were never officially treated as a default relief program and, more important, were insufficient to make any contribution toward repaying the $2.4 billion in defaulted local debt. The depression reduced local property values by approximately 10 percent on average, leading to a fall in local tax revenues of $3.280 billion below their predepression trend over the period 1932–1940. Over those eight years, U.S. local governments managed to trim $1.409 billion from projected predepression service spending, but these cuts still left a shortfall of $1.817 billion in the local budgets. The increase in federal and state aid filled this current-accounts fiscal gap, but not completely. Additional aid above the 1932–1940 predepression trend totaled $1.890 billion, of which $.196 billion must be counted as federally required increases in local welfare spending. This left $1.694 billion in new federal and state aid to fill the $1.817 billion gap between local service spending and local taxes. Rather than providing new money to cover defaults, the increase in federal and state aid was not quite enough to close the local sector's budget gap; the remaining $.123 billion shortfall had to be covered by additional local borrowing. In the end, it seems more reasonable to view the depression-related increase in federal and state assistance as local revenue insurance in the face of an economic disaster rather than a fiscal bailout in response to strategic local deficits.[35]

The reluctance of the federal government to bail out local governments in deficit distress continues to this day, best symbolized by President Ford's response to New York City's request for federal assistance following its 1974–1975 default: "Ford to City: Drop Dead," said the *New York Daily News* headline.[36] In the most recent fiscal crises in Philadelphia (1990), Bridgeport (1991), Miami (1996), Orange County (1996), and Camden (2000), federal bailouts have never even been raised as options. There is no evidence of significant national spillovers from these (near) defaults ($\Psi_i \approx 0$),[37] and while Camden is a poor city with median household incomes approximately half the national median (the other distressed cities have median incomes near or greater than the national median), there are other equally poor U.S. cities not in fiscal distress. Further, Camden is located within one of the nation's richest states and, constitutionally at least, remains the fiscal responsibility of New Jersey. It is difficult to imagine how national redistribution politics might single out this one city for special federal relief; at the federal level, at least, $v_i \simeq 0$ seems reasonable.

The federal bailout of Washington, D.C. has been the one exception to the rule of no federal assistance. The reason for this bailout lies in the city's unique fiscal and political position as the nation's capital. First, without a supervising state, Washington has been given financial responsibility for the usual state functions of courts, prisons, transportation, and health care for the poor. These services entail significant public spillovers and are typically financed at the wider level of the state. In the case of Washington, D.C., however, local taxes provide most of the needed funding and do so in an economic environment where business and middle-class residential tax bases are highly mobile. The consequence has been a steady erosion of the city's tax base over time (see O'Cleireacain 1997). Second, as the nation's capital, Washington provides a unique national service as the political and historical center of the country. Local services such as crime control and sanitation provide national benefits as a significant number of city's "residents" are national or international visitors. While there is little redistributive reason to bail out either the taxpayers or the bondholders of Washington, D.C.—the city's median income equals the national median income (thus, $v_i \simeq 0$)—there are good spillover reasons that the federal government might offer such support ($\Psi_i > 0$). In effect, local politicians held hostage national politicians through their monopoly control over a unique, nationally valued local public good: safe, clean streets in our nation's capital. The city got a federal bailout estimated to be worth an additional $600 million per year in federal government assistance. Local politicians, however, lost policy control over important public services to a federally appointed control board.[38]

Today, U.S. state governments continue to follow a no-bailout policy when confronted with local defaults, again with only one important exception: Camden. For the New York City, Philadelphia, Bridgeport, Miami, and Orange County defaults, no new state monies were provided to repay bondholders or supplement local tax revenues. At the time of default, the debts of each locality were widely held, and city services provided only local benefits—thus, $\Psi_i \simeq 0$. The median-income household in New York City, Philadelphia, and Orange County earned as much as or more than the state's median household—thus, $v_i \approx 0$ for these cities. The typical resident of Bridgeport and Miami was poorer than their state's median household, but the earnings gap of 30 percent was apparently not sufficient to warrant significant state fiscal relief. What the states did offer were loan guarantees to allow the city access to short-term borrowing (New York, Philadelphia, Bridgeport, Miami), accelerated grants payments in return for lower future payments (New York City), or permission to spend already allocated state capital grants on current services (Orange County). New Jersey's bailout of Camden has been the one exception to the rule. The median Camden resident earns only the national poverty level for a family of four ($17,000), earnings that are about 40 percent of what the median New Jersey household earns. The city's crime rate is the highest in the state, and the public schools are the worst performing. Poor city residents cannot afford to exit to any neighboring community. The state has responded with new monies sufficient to fund fully the city's debts and most of city services for the foreseeable future, largely motivated by a desire to ensure minimal public services to the city's residents and children.[39]

A primary lesson from this fiscal history is that central governments can resist the political and economic need for local government bailouts if the appropriate market and fiscal institutions are in place to minimize economic spillovers ($\Psi_i \approx 0$) and adverse distributional consequences ($v_i \approx 0$) from a local government default. The required institutions include a mature national banking system or diversified holdings of local public debt, integrated national capital markets, and a system of centrally financed taxes and transfers targeted to deserving poor households. Only in the recent cases of Washington, D.C. and Camden is there any evidence of significant bailouts. Both bailouts can be rationalized as a failure to establish the needed market or fiscal institutions. In the case of Washington, D.C. local officials exploited their monopoly control over an important national public good: a safe, clean national capital. In the case of Camden, local officials successfully exploited the redistributive preferences of the state's relatively wealthy median income household. When appropriate market and fiscal institutions are in place, however, central government bailouts can be prevented.

Lesson 4: A Constitutional Bankruptcy Standard Requiring Local Debt Repayment is Essential

An explicit constitutional bankruptcy standard requiring local repayment of all local debts and enforced by an independent court or oversight board is essential to ensure debt repayment and thereby to discourage local defaults. The fiscal history of U.S. municipal defaults is informative on the point.[40] Despite the significant and often widespread episodes of state and local government defaults of the nineteenth century, the United States lacked any national guidelines for what should be done when local government debt fell into arrears. During this period, defaulted state and local debts were rarely repaid at more than $.50 on the dollar ($\sigma \geq .50$; see Hillhouse 1936). The New England states were the one exception to this historical pattern. These states introduced their own regulations requiring full repayment of local debts ($\sigma \simeq 0$) and even allowed the seizure of private property to repay municipal debt (see McConnell and Picker 1993). Perhaps more than coincidentally, the New England states also showed the lowest rates of local government defaults during this period (see Hillhouse 1936). Finally in 1937, in response to widespread municipal defaults during the Great Depression, the U.S. Congress passed, and the U.S. Supreme Court approved, a standard for debt repayment and a formal procedure for declaring municipal bankruptcy so that the standard might be enforced. The standard, defined as the "best interests of the creditors and is feasible," has been interpreted by the U.S. federal courts to mean full access to the state or local government's tax base to ensure debt repayment; the "New England rule" allowing the seizure of private property no longer applies.[41] Today, $\sigma \simeq 0$ is the working standard for U.S. municipal defaults.

Lesson 5: A Competitive Local Bond Market Disciplines Defaulting Local Governments and Discourages Strategic Borrowing
A competitive local government bond market with informed buyers and multiple sellers fully prices the risk of default by local government borrowers; disclosure rules and the enforcement of accepted accounting practices may be necessary for infrequent borrowers. Defaulting local governments that fail to receive a bailout bear a significant cost in higher future interest rates. Lending to local governments involves both the risk of default without full bailouts and the risk of an unexpected rise in future interest rates. The efficient pricing of local government debt should reflect both risks, with interest rates for new debt rising with fiscal weakness, limitations on access to taxation, the stock of outstanding debt and other contractual obligations, current yields on alternative investments, and the debt's years to maturity. U.S. evidence shows this to be the case, both historically and in today's

markets. Defaulting states from the 1840s were initially denied access to the bond market and regained entry only as they began to make at least some payments toward their early defaults. In all cases, new debt could be acquired only at borrowing rates often twice as high as the rates paid by nondefaulting states (see English 1996). Investors were sophisticated, even separately pricing debt from the same state (Louisiana) but issued by separate governmental affiliates with distinct default histories (English 1996). The bond market showed a similar ability to distinguish risky from secure debt, even when the debt was issued by local governments. During the 1870s, secure debt from the municipalities of New England traded at par during the decade, while debt issued by the defaulting local governments of the South and West traded well below par—as low as $.15 on the dollar in the states with the worst default records: Arkansas, South Carolina, and North Carolina (Scott 1893). Again, interest rate penalties on new debt were significant.[42]

The contemporary evidence tells the same story. For current U.S. local governments, borrowing costs are higher for state and local governments rated as riskier by Moody's and Standard and Poor's (higher outstanding debt, lower incomes), for revenue bonds limited to specific taxes or user fees, bonds of longer maturities, and bonds with call provisions allowing issuers to repay the debt if interest rates decline (see, e.g., Fairchild and Koch 1998). The bond market also recognizes the advantages for controlling default risk through constitutionally grounded balanced budget rules and expenditure limits, rewarding states with these rules with lower borrowing costs (see Bayoumi, Goldstein, and Woglom 1995, and Poterba and Rueben 1999).[43]

While the evidence is clear that the U.S. bond market prices the measured risks of local debt, and thus local defaults without bailouts pay a penalty, their remains the more fundamental question of whether the market knows all the risks that should be priced: Is the U.S. municipal bond market fully informed? This is a more difficult question to answer, but the evidence presented in Fairchild and Koch (1998) comparing the pricing of government debt from states with and without full disclosure laws is instructive. Governments in full disclosure states are required to meet the standards of the Government Finance Officers Association.[44] If the local government bond market is fully informed, then the presence or absence of disclosure laws should have no significant effect on the pricing of local debt. For debt issued by large and active borrowers, this is exactly what Fairchild and Koch find. In contrast, the pricing of government debt issued by smaller and infrequent borrowers is affected by the presence of disclosure rules; the average cost of borrowing for these governments is lower in disclosure states.[45] The implication of these results is that the local government bond market in the United States appears to price the debt of frequent borrowers efficiently, using detailed information about local finances and deficits to set local interest rates. It is only for smaller local governments or new borrowers that lender information may be imperfect; for these governments, disclosure rules requiring detailed fiscal data meeting accepted accounting standards may prove useful.

Lesson 6: With Appropriate Incentives, Local Governments will Borrow Efficiently
Confronted with the realities of the central government's no-bailout policy, a court policy that requires local taxpayers to repay all local debts, and a bond market that penalizes unfunded local deficits, U.S. local governments have, with only a few notable exceptions, not pursued the inefficient default-bailout strategy. The exceptions include the 1840s defaults by U.S. states, the 1870s defaults by local governments investing in land development and railroad expansions, the 1930s depression defaults, and the few large city defaults of the modern period. If these governments knew there would be no bailouts, why did they run excessive deficits and then default? The defaulting states in the 1840s in fact thought a central government bailout was very likely. Prior to 1840, no bailout request from a state or local government, or from any important private concern, had been denied by the federal government (Ratchford 1941). States had every reason to view themselves at the top of any priority list for federal assistance. Alexander Hamilton's successful efforts in 1790 to have the federal government assume all debts of the states following the approval of the new Union were based on the argument that the federal government must stand behind the creditworthiness of its member states if those states, and the federal government, were to have access to European capital; even Jefferson, who strongly opposed assumption of state debts, agreed.[46] Indeed, Hamilton saw assumption of state debts as more than just a guarantee of credit; it was also essential "to cement more closely this union of states" (McGrane 1935, 1). President George Washington was an active lobbyist on behalf of debt assumption (Ratchford 1941). Against this political backdrop, it is not surprising that states viewed a future bailout of their debts as a likely prospect.

In terms of the analytic framework of section 2.1, the value of Ψ_i (spillovers from no bailout) was assumed high.[47] Subsequent federal government behavior did nothing to disabuse the states of their presumption of favored fiscal status. State debts incurred during the War of 1812 were assumed by the federal government, as were the debts of Washington, D.C., in 1836. It is not surprising, then, that the states borrowed as they did during the three decades leading to the defaults of the 1840s. Nor is it surprising to learn how the debt proceeds were spent: recklessly. To be sure, some of the borrowed funds found their way into revenue-producing capital projects (e.g., the Erie Canal, though even New York State borrowed regularly for current accounts spending), but large sums were given to state banks to be spent on unproductive private ventures or to private transportation companies for canals, roadways, and railroads only partially, or sometimes never, built (Ratchford 1941). When the loans fell due and additional loans could not be obtained to repay past borrowing or complete the projects, the states defaulted. State efforts to secure a federal bailout were not successful (see lesson 3). This failure to bail out distressed states signaled clearly, and for the first time, that the federal government had reversed its guarantee of state and local debt.[48]

By 1870, it was clear that the federal government could not be counted for bailouts, but states had not yet been tested. The widespread local government defaults of the 1870s appear to have been the result of two facts. First, the courts at the time did not fully protect bondholder interests and require full debt repayment; values of $\sigma \geq .5$ were typical. Second, the local investments that backed local debt were often speculative investments in land development projects and railroad spurs; debt repayment depended on the future appreciation of local land values through special property tax assessments. If the probability of success of these investments was high enough and the shared penalty for failure $(1 - \sigma)$ low enough, local governments would still make the investments, even if there would be no national or state bailout if they failed. Without bailouts, local defaults would then occur at a rate equal to one minus the probability of project success. Given that many local governments found these risky investments attractive, it is not surprising that there were then widespread defaults.[49] States responded by saying no to bailouts (see lesson 3).

The 1930s depression defaults and the more recent defaults by a few large U.S. cities (except those of Camden and Washington, D.C.) are also best explained by reasons unrelated to default-bailout behaviors.

In contrast to the defaults in the 1840s and the 1870s, the local government debt defaulted in the 1930s was for capital outlays for local roads and new schools and was not spent to subsidize current-accounts spending or politically connected private ventures. Further, the debt was defaulted not to force a bailout from the national or state governments but because the local property tax base supporting the debt fell in value by an average of 10 percent during the depression. Most of the defaulted debt principal and interest was repaid in full by 1940.

Finally, the recent New York City, Philadelphia, Miami, Bridgeport, and Orange County fiscal crises also seem to have their origins not in the incentives of the default-bailout game but in other causes, most likely an attempt to shift current costs through the strategy of deficit rollovers and taxpayer exit. In each city, problems arose only when a long history of accumulated hidden deficits forced large interest, pension, and capital stock expenditures just when the local economy (or in the case of Orange County, the local governments' investment portfolio) suffered an economic downturn. Taxes could not be increased enough to meet all financial obligations (see Inman 1992). It does not appear that these cities were borrowing with expectations of a state bailout.[50]

Since 1840, only Camden and Washington, D.C., appear to have played the default-bailout game. They won. Importantly, their circumstances appear unique among U.S. cities.

Lesson 7: Land Markets May be a Less Effective Check on Inefficient Local Borrowing

Local land prices set by competitive markets do reflect the current period benefits and costs of local government service provision. Preliminary evidence suggests land markets are less successful in monitoring future benefits and costs—in particular, excessive local borrowing or undermaintained public capital. If so, local governments retain an important outlet for shifting current budgetary costs onto nonresidents. There is now compelling evidence that U.S. land markets do reflect the differential burdens of current-period local taxes and the differential benefits of current-period local services (see, e.g., Palmon and Smith 1998 and Bogart and Cromwell 1997). But are future-period taxes and benefits reflected in land prices? Epple and Schipper (1981) estimate a capitalization equation for small Pennsylvania communities regressing community home values on actuarial estimates of the town's level of underfunded pension liabilities—a source of deficit financing.

They find more than 100 percent capitalization but then argue that their estimates are likely to be too large because the actuarial estimates of unfunded liabilities systematically understate true liabilities. Unfortunately, the degree of reporting bias is unknown, and therefore so too is the rate of capitalization. Inman (1982) adopts an alternative approach in his study of large-city labor budgets. From the analysis in Figure 2.1, we see that deficit financing for current services will increase the demand for such services from X_e to X_1. With independent estimates of the price elasticity of demand for local services and knowledge of MC, X_e, and X_1, Inman is able to estimate the implied rate of subsidy for local services (Φ in figure 2.1) and from this estimate to compute the implied rate of deficit capitalization.[51] On balance, the cities in Inman's sample behave as if $\Phi > 0$—that is, as if full capitalization of local deficits does not hold. Local budgets will therefore be inefficiently too large ($X_1 > X_e$; figure 2.1), and Inman estimates the resulting inefficiencies to average .$20 for every dollar of local spending for his sample of the large U.S. cities. Together, the two studies provide at best only tentative evidence: perhaps full capitalization in small communities but less than full capitalization in large cities. This makes sense if deficit financing is easy to discover in small-city budgets but difficult to detect in large-city budgets. Local cost shifting through deficit financing must still be viewed as a potential source of fiscal inefficiency in U.S. local finance.

Lesson 8: Balanced Budget Rules Enforced by a Politically Independent Court Can Control Inefficient Local Borrowing

As a final line of defense against local defaults, the central government can establish balanced budget rules to regulate excessive current-accounts borrowing. To be effective, such rules must entail an end-of-fiscal-year review, be constitutionally grounded, and be enforced by a politically independent court or oversight agency. The historical experience of U.S. states provides a natural experiment for testing the effectiveness of balanced budget rules in controlling lower government fiscal deficits. Following the defaults of state debts during the 1840s, the European bond market was naturally reluctant to lend to U.S. states. The states responded by agreeing to debt repayment schedules for their outstanding debt and then by promising never to default again.[52]

The promise took the form of a constitutional or statutory commitment to run balanced budgets on the current accounts—that is, not to play the default-bailout game. The nondefaulting states and new states entering the Union after 1850 found it important to signal their commitment to balanced budgets; they too passed balanced budget rules. Today, all U.S. states—except Vermont, whose fiscal prudence is legendary—have either constitutional or statutory balanced budget rules aimed at constraining state and local deficit behaviors.

Have these balanced budget rules worked? Yes, but only when appropriately designed. Poterba (1994) and Bohn and Inman (1996), who examined the contemporary deficit decisions of state governments, identified five conditions sufficient for an effective balanced budget rule (see Inman 1997). First, the rule must require that deficits be balanced at the end, not just the beginning, of each fiscal year. To this end, not only must budgetary procedures be transparent, but budgetary accounting must conform to accepted principles of what constitutes current and capital spending. (For example, in the years prior to its 1975 default, New York City found it useful to treat expenditures for janitorial services as a capital outlay.) Second, the rule must be based on constitutional, not statutory, law with a supermajority required for constitutional amendments. A supermajority (say, two-thirds) protects the budgetary rule from being temporarily overturned for the convenience of a deficit-minded simple (50 percent) majority in the legislature. Third, if the balanced budget rule is violated, there must be a politically independent court or regulatory agency willing to enforce the rule. How best to ensure a politically independent court is an important question, but one not yet answered by the available U.S. evidence.[53] Fourth, when the rule is violated, access to the regulating court or agency must be open to all parties potentially harmed by the violation so that a case against the deficit can be heard and adjudicated. Finally, the court or agency must have a means of enforcement to correct the violation—most likely a court-appointed oversight board with the powers to set future budgets and to impose management and accounting reforms. The evidence in Poterba (1994) and Bohn and Inman (1996) shows that U.S. states with these rules and supporting institutions have significantly lower deficits, or higher rainy-day surpluses, than do states without the rules. For the period 1970–1991, states with effective rules have deficits (rainy-day surpluses) that are, on average, $158 per capita lower (higher) than states without effective rules (see Bohn and Inman 1996). This difference is about 11 percent of the average level of state spending for the period.

2.3 Conclusion

The growing importance of local and provincial governments as providers of public services and the importance of local services for the overall performance of the national economy have led to a careful reexamination of how public resources are allocated by decentralized governments (Oates 1999). The Tiebout (1956) proposition that local governments automatically guarantee efficient local taxation and service spending is true only in the special environment of mobile and informed taxpayers, no spillovers, and many competitive jurisdictions. While perhaps a valid characterization of local suburban governments in a large U.S. metropolitan area, it is not an accurate description of most local public sectors in most economies, ones dominated by a few large cities each surrounded by a few residential suburbs, all overseen by a still larger provincial government. There is no guarantee that this more realistic local public sector will efficiently allocate public services. This chapter has described the likely incentives of local governments in this more general institutional setting and then outlined those political and market institutions needed to encourage efficient resource allocations given those incentives. Three such institutions have been identified here:

1. A stable central government managed by nationally elected political parties or presidents capable of making (second-best) efficient interpersonal redistributions of income while at the same time denying inefficient intergovernmental transfers or access to nonresident taxation, or both

2. A mature banking system and fully integrated national capital markets capable of containing within the jurisdiction the economic consequences of a local government's failure to repay its debts

3. A network of local land markets with informed investors capable of evaluating local services and finances so as to shift back onto local residents the full economic consequences of inefficient local government fiscal choices

Efficient central governments, an efficient banking system, and efficient capital and land markets are seen here as necessary institutional preconditions for an efficient local public sector, even a Tiebout local public economy.

Lacking these efficient political and market institutions, regulatory policies will be necessary to hold local fiscal inefficiencies in check. Three such regulatory regimes were identified, each a replacement for a failed political or market institution:

1. To replace a weak central government, fiscal assignment limiting central transfers to demonstrable economic spillovers and local taxation to resident taxation

2. To replace an immature banking system and less than fully integrated capital markets, a no-bailout requirement for the central government and bankruptcy standards requiring full local repayment of all local debts

3. To replace missing local land markets, a balanced budget rule requiring tax financing of all current-accounts spending

These fiscal rules must be enforced by courts or agencies uninfluenced by local political pressures, and they must be constitutionally grounded, requiring a supermajority to overturn. To the extent such regulations are effective, they may constrain other useful local choices. If so, they must be considered second best to the efficient political and market institutions.

A review of the U.S. fiscal record spoke to the importance of these institutional preconditions. Lacking either strong political parties or a strong president to manage fiscal policies, U.S. local governments have succeeded in extracting inefficient intergovernmental transfers and obtaining access to inefficient taxation of nonresident incomes and assets. The U.S. performance in controlling bailouts of local defaults has been more successful. The economy's mature banking system at least since 1850, a nationally integrated capital market, and in more recent years local bankruptcy standards protecting creditors' interests have helped minimize the financial spillovers from a local government default; thus, the economic incentive for local government bailouts has been muted. Historically, poor households within the United States have been geographically dispersed, and U.S. governments have always used individually targeted transfer programs; thus, the distributive incentive for local bailouts has been held in check. Finally, while U.S. local land markets seem to be a weak check on inefficient local deficits, the U.S. regulatory regime of constitutionally based balanced budget rules has proven an effective substitute. On balance, U.S. local governments do face a mostly hard budget constraint. If there is room for improvement in enforcing local fiscal discipline in the U.S. public sector, it is in checking local influence over national fiscal policies.

Notes

1. The analysis here differs from the principal-agent approach to federalism as studied, for example, by Tirole (1994). That approach is appropriate for public economies run as administrative states where local officials have little or no independent policy or (perhaps most important) revenue discretion apart from that given to them directly by the central government's elected officials.

2. This inefficiency can be significant. Area D can be approximated by the formula: area $[D] = .5 \cdot \varepsilon_{px} \cdot (X \cdot MC) \cdot \Phi^2$, where ε_{px} is the absolute value of the price elasticity of demand for local government services (see Rosen 1999). The average rate of inefficiency per dollar of local government subsidy is therefore: area$[D]$/area$[B + C + D]$ = area$[D]/(\Phi \cdot X \cdot MC)$ = $.5 \cdot \varepsilon_{px} \cdot \Phi$. For small changes in the rate of subsidy, the marginal rate of inefficiency per incremental dollar of subsidy will be: ∂area$[D]/\partial(\Phi \cdot X \cdot MC) = \varepsilon_{px} \cdot \Phi$.

3. Matching grants and in-kind service provision provide direct subsidies at rate Φ. Closed-end matching grants, which give a lump-sum transfer greater than X_e, can create an "implicit price" subsidy of Φ. Only fully unconstrained lump-sum transfers, called general revenue sharing in the United States, will be efficiency neutral. Such grants have no role to play in a system of efficient intergovernmental transfers, however (see Inman 1999). Their only possibly valid role is income redistribution, a goal more efficiently pursued through individual, not governmental, transfers (see Bradford and Oates 1971).

4. See, for example, Weingast (1979), Weingast, Shepsle, and Johnsen (1981), and Chari, Jones, and Marimon (1997) for formal models of legislative voting with local interests.

5. From Exhibit 2.1, the cost-shifting game will be a prisoner's dilemma game if $\Pi_{\sigma\gamma} > \Pi_{\gamma\gamma} > \Pi_{\sigma\sigma} > \Pi_{\gamma\sigma}$. This is in fact the case for the cost-shifting game described in figure 2.1, where $\Pi_{\sigma\gamma}$ = area $[A + B + C] > \Pi_{\gamma\gamma}$ = area $[A] > \Pi_{\sigma\sigma}$ = area $[A - D] > \Pi_{\gamma\sigma}$ = area $[A - D - B - C]$.

6. That is, the payoffs in the legislative game of exhibit 2.1 must be changed so that the cooperative strategy (γ) becomes the dominant—"best no matter what"—strategy. This will occur when $\Pi_{\gamma\gamma} > \Pi_{\sigma\gamma}$ and when $\Pi_{\gamma\sigma} > \Pi_{\sigma\sigma}$. When local governments behave as shown in figure 2.1, these two conditions will be met when either (1) cooperators—legislators who vote against local cost shifting—are rewarded with a transfer for their constituents worth at least area $[B + C]$ in figure 2.1, or (2) noncooperators—legislators who vote for local cost shifting—are penalized by losing other valuable federal services worth at least area $[B + C]$ in figure 2.1. This result follows directly from the definitions of $\Pi_{\gamma\gamma}$, $\Pi_{\sigma\gamma}$, $\Pi_{\gamma\sigma}$, and $\Pi_{\sigma\sigma}$ in note 5. Note that area $[B + C]$ equals the maximal net gain to the local district when it acts noncooperatively rather than cooperatively; see figure 2.1. These rewards and penalties do not have to be paid to, or imposed on, every legislator, only enough legislators to repeal existing local cost-shifting legislation or to block new legislation (see Fitts and Inman 1992).

7. Local debt, whether accumulated through rollovers, underfunded pensions, or reallocated capital grants, operates as an implicit subsidy to the marginal costs of buying additional current public services, that is, $\Phi > 0$ in figure 2.1 (see Inman 1982).

8. I assume here that there are no national spillovers from the provision of the local public good so as to concentrate on bailouts created by financial market spillovers. Wildasin (1997) provides an analysis of bailouts when there are significant allocative spillovers from the provision of local public services. The Wildasin analysis may be appropriate for one U.S. bailout, however: the case of Washington, D.C., in 1997; see below.

9. If there were important positive spillovers ($B^c = Q^c > 0$), then the central government might indeed want to subsidize the provision of local public goods, but there are better ways to proceed (e.g., targeted matching grants) than fiscal bailouts (see Inman 1999).

10. Net benefits $B^1 - C_\beta^1$ to the citizens of the local government from the debt-shifting strategy will be area $[A + B + C]$. (I ignore the fact that these local net benefits are reduced slightly by the local government's own tax share of the national bailout: $(1/N) \cdot [B + C + D]$.) The net benefit from the status quo balanced budget strategy is only area $[A]$. Thus $B^1 - C_\beta^1$ = area $[A + B + C] > Q^1$ = area $[A]$, and condition 2a of exhibit 2.2 holds.

11. In figure 2.1, $B^c \equiv 0$, C_β^c = area $[B + C + D]$, $[B^1 - C_\beta^1]$ = area $[A + B + C]$, $Q^c \equiv 0$, and Q^1 = area $[A]$. Upon substitution, area $[A - D]$ < area $[A]$ as required by exhibit 2.2, condition 3.

12. If $C_\eta^c < C_\beta^c$, then the central government would choose the no-bailout strategy, η, even if the local government adopts the deficit strategy, Δ. Knowing this, the local government will then choose the status quo if $B^1 - C_\eta^1 < Q^1$ (condition 2b). For the local fiscal choice specification in figure 2.1, condition 2b holds. If no central government bailout occurs, then the local government must repay the local debt and cover the full costs of the initial X_1 allocation. In this case, the local government's net benefits equal area $[A + B + C + E + F]$ – area $[B + C + D + E + F]$ = area $[A - D]$, which is less than the status quo allocation of area $[A]$; thus $B^1 - C_\eta^1 < Q^1$ holds and condition 2b is met.

13. Note that the financial costs of no bailout (F_i) are larger for larger governments as measured by ρ_i, but this fact alone is not sufficient to justify the typically offered argument that large local governments are simply "too big to fail" and must be bailed out. What is relevant is the comparison of F_i to the cost of the local bailout to national taxpayers (= $\rho_i \cdot \Delta$), which also grows with ρ_i. What will be sufficient for a "too big to fail" argument is evidence that inefficiencies per dollar of defaulted debt increase with debt: $\Psi_i = \Psi(\rho_i \cdot \sigma \cdot \Delta)$, where $\Psi(\cdot)' > 0$.

14. The parameter Ψ_i is defined as the ratio of the dollar value of market inefficiency following default to each dollar of defaulted local debt. Estimates of Ψ_i following a default-induced banking crisis can be calculated using estimates by Bordo and Eichengreen (2000, table 9) of the economic consequences of a banking crisis. They estimate the lost output from banking crises to range from 3 percent of trend GDP for modern crises (1973–1998) to perhaps as much as 5 percent for historical and modern crises (1880–1998). Assuming the probability of a banking crisis following a local default equals the ratio of lost bank liquidity following default (dL) to all bank demand deposits per capita (M_0) and that lost bank liquidity equals defaulted local government debt multiplied by the local default's "contagion" or spillover effect (κ) affecting all bank liquidity (dL = $\kappa \cdot \rho_i \cdot \sigma \cdot \Delta$), then the expected present value loss per dollar of defaulted local debt from a banking crisis will equal:

$$\psi_i = (.03 \cdot \text{GDP}) \cdot (dL/M_0) \cdot (1/\rho_i \cdot \sigma \cdot \Delta) = (.03 \cdot \text{GDP}) \cdot (\kappa \cdot \rho_i \cdot \sigma \, \Delta/M_0) \cdot (1/\rho_i \cdot \sigma \cdot \Delta)$$

or

$$\psi_i = .03 \cdot (\text{GDP}/M_0) \cdot \kappa.$$

In economies with immature banking systems, the contagion effect κ is likely to be greater than 1 and to increase with the size of the local default: $\kappa_i = \kappa(\rho_i \cdot \sigma \cdot \Delta)$, where $\kappa'(\cdot) \geq 0$ (see Allen and Gale 2000). The (GDP/M_0) ratio ranges from 10 to 15 in developing economies (e.g., India, Chile, Brazil, South Africa) and typically equals 3 to 5 in advanced economies (see Diamond and Rajan 2000). For developing economies with $(GDP/M_0) \simeq 10$ and $\kappa \simeq 1.25$, a value of Ψ_i near .40 is likely and indeed may be a conservative estimate. In more developed economies where $(GDP/M_0) \simeq 3$ and $\kappa \simeq 1$, a value of Ψ_i closer to .10 seems appropriate.

15. The failure to bail out a municipal default will reallocate productive capital from the national capital market to the (potentially) less efficient local capital market. National lenders to the defaulting local government will lose $\rho_i \cdot \sigma \cdot \Delta$ in income because of the no-bailout decision, while local taxpayers in the defaulting community will gain an equal amount. (We ignore the fact that with no bailout, national lenders and local taxpayers will not pay their—likely small—share of national taxes needed to support a bailout.) The loss of income of $\rho_i \cdot \sigma \cdot \Delta$ will lead to less future capital returns of $r^n \cdot mps^n \cdot (\rho_i \cdot \sigma \cdot \Delta)$, where r^n is the annual rate of return foregone on national investments and mps^n is a national market lenders' marginal propensity to save. Similarly, the gain in income of $\rho_i \cdot \sigma \cdot \Delta$ to local taxpayers will lead to an increase in future capital returns of $r^l \cdot mps^l \cdot (\rho_i \cdot \sigma \cdot \Delta)$, where r^l is the annual rate of return now earned on local investments and mps^l is local taxpayers' marginal propensity to save. The net annual loss in capital income will equal $[r^n \cdot mps^n - r^l \cdot mps^l] \cdot (\rho_i \cdot \sigma \cdot \Delta)$. Discounting at r^n, the present value loss per dollar of defaulted local debt from capital market failures equals:

$$\psi_i = (1/r^n)[r^n \cdot mps^n - r^l \cdot mps^l] \cdot [(\rho_i \cdot \sigma \cdot \Delta)/(\rho_i \cdot \sigma \cdot \Delta)]$$

or

$$\psi_i = [mps^n - (r^l/r^n) \cdot mps^l].$$

When local taxpayers do not save, $\Psi_i = mps^n \simeq .20$; this seems a plausible upper limit to the consequences of default when capital markets are imperfect. In fully mature capital markets, where $r^l = r^n$, then $\Psi_i = [mps^n - mps^l]$, which may be close to zero in rich economies.

Note that the discussion here does not consider as an allocative inefficiency the effects that a no-bailout decision might have on municipal or national interest rates and subsequent public investment. Two comments are relevant here. First, in this initial, simple world where all the benefits and costs of the bailout decision are known by both the local and central governments, there will be no interest rate effect from the no-bailout choice. If the central government decides not to bailout the local government, then the local government will not create a deficit, and thus there can be no default risk. If the central government does offer bailouts, then local governments will run a deficit, but the subsequent default is covered by the central government—again, no bailout risk. Second, in a world where the central government's bailout decision is uncertain, there will be financial risk attached to the no-bailout decision, but sophisticated bond markets will have rationally anticipated the likelihood of that outcome and priced local debt accordingly. In this case, a central government's no-bailout choice will only confirm what the market had already anticipated. Only when a decision to deny a bailout actively changes the market's expectations of future bailouts will there be an interest rate effect. There are instances when this can occur, but I expect the effect to be of second-order importance and unlikely to affect any of the conclusions presented here.

16. The share of local debt borne by bondholders through default, σ, is assumed to be exogenous. A richer analysis would add the determination of σ to the default-bailout game as the outcome of a third-stage bargaining game between taxpayers and

bondholders, conditional on the local government's having first chosen Δ in the first stage and the central government's having chosen η in the second stage. For a general discussion of bargaining in bankruptcy, see Bebchuk and Chang (1992). For evidence on the outcomes of such bargains from the U.S. historical record, see p. 61–62 (lesson 4).

17. The analysis here assumes that Δ is small relative to the income of all participants so that v_i can be taken as constant for the purposes of selecting bailout strategies.

18. Formally, v_i is defined as the percentage difference in the politically weighted marginal utility of a dollar to person i (v_i) relative to the politically weighted marginal utility of a dollar ($v_.$) to some reference (e.g., median income) voter: $v_i = (v_i - v_.)/v_. = \Delta v/v_.$. Specifying ε_v as the elasticity of the marginal utility of income schedule for central government politicians, then $v_i = \varepsilon_v \cdot \Delta y/y_.$, where $\Delta y = y_i - y_.$, and y_i and $y_.$ are the incomes of the person i and the reference individual, respectively. For example, if ε_v = –1.5 (as estimated by Mera 1969 for U.S. tax policies), y_i = \$30,000 (median household income in a typical U.S. city) and $y_.$ = \$39,000 (median household income for the United States as a whole), then v_i = .34. For the very poorest U.S. cities, such as Camden, New Jersey, with a median household income of only \$17,000, v_i rises to .85.

19. For example, the pre-tax-and-transfer differences in median household income between a very poor U.S. city such as Camden, New Jersey (\$17,000) and the median U.S. household (\$39,000), or more directly relevant the median household income in New Jersey (\$49,000), ranges from \$22,000 (United States) to \$32,000 (New Jersey). The income difference in post-tax-and-transfer median incomes is significantly less, however—closer to \$12,000 (\$23,000 versus \$35,000) for the United States as a whole and \$20,000 (\$23,000 versus \$39,000) for New Jersey residents. This reduces the U.S. value of v_i from .85 before taxes and transfers to .35 after taxes and transfers, and the New Jersey value of v_i from .98 before taxes and transfers to .62; see note 18.

20. The analysis here follows from adapting the model of reputation building in the entry-deterrence game by Fudenberg, Kreps, and Wilson (Kreps and Wilson 1982, and Fudenberg and Kreps 1987) to reputation building in the default-bailout game studied here. A formalization of this extension is presented in a technical appendix to this chapter, available from the author on request.

21. More formally, local tax financing will be preferred to the deficit-bailout strategy when the *expected* benefits of tax financing are greater than those from the deficit-bailout choice. From figure 2.1, tax financing promises area [A] for sure. If p_i is local government i's assessment that the central government will be tough, then in the simple case with no shifting onto bondholders (σ = 0) the expected benefit from the deficit-bailout strategy will be $(1 - p_i) \cdot$ area [A + B + C] + $p_i \cdot$ area [A – D]. Tax financing will be preferred when area [A] $\geq (1 - p_i) \cdot$ area [A + B + C] + $p_i \cdot$ area [A – D], or when $p_i \geq$ area [B + C]/area [B + C + D]. Since area [B + C + D] measures the size of the bailout subsidy Δ, and since area [D] = Δ – area [B + C], tax financing will be preferred when $p_i \geq 1$ – area [D]/Δ. Thus, for a given perceived level of central government toughness (p_i), the deficit strategy is less likely the larger is area [D] relative to Δ.

22. Though the argument here is somewhat different, the conclusion that competition helps to harden a soft budget constraint is similar to that found in Dewartripont and Maskin (1995), Segal (1998), and Qian and Roland (1998).

23. Fully efficient pricing of local debt assumes that bondholders can accurately assess the risk of default, the probability of a central government bailout, and if there is no bailout, the probability that the courts will require repayment, and finally, the probabil-

ity that the local government can in fact repay. Perhaps the most difficult to assess is the fiscal capacity of the local government to repay. This requires knowledge of the local economy as well as the stock of all outstanding local government liabilities, not just the size of the current local borrowing being priced. Bond rating agencies and the under-writers of municipal debt seek to provide this important risk assessment service for investors.

24. See Inman (1983) for a summary of the variety of ways local governments can manip-ulate their budgets to disguise local borrowing. When cities use debt to pay a share Ω of current expenditures—for example, through underfunded public employee pensions or rolled-over short-term debt—then the marginal cost of each unit of new public services will be $(1 - \Omega)MC$. In this case, $\Phi = \Omega = \Delta/MC \cdot X$.

25. As above (note 24) $\Omega = \Delta/MC \cdot X$ defines the rate of subsidy from deficit financing. After-tax and after-capitalization income for local taxpayers (y) then equals: $y = I - (1 - \Omega) \cdot MC \cdot X - \delta \cdot \Delta$, where I is pretax income and δ is the share of debt that is capitalized into lower market prices for taxable assets located within the city. Setting $\Delta = \Omega \cdot MC \cdot X$ and rearranging the local taxpayers' budget constraint gives: $y = I - [1 - (1 - \delta) \cdot \Omega] \cdot MC \cdot X$. Now the implicit subsidy for the purchase of local public services becomes $\Phi = (1 - \delta) \cdot \Omega$. When there is full market capitalization then $\delta = 1$ and $\Phi = 0$. Less than full capitalization implies $\Phi = (1 - \delta) \cdot \Omega > 0$; $\delta = 0$ implies a full subsidy from deficit financing or $\Phi = \Omega$.

26. It is possible that the information collected to price municipal debt efficiently could be used to price local land efficiently. The bond market internalizes the cost of gathering information by insisting that the purchaser of the local government debt buy all the debt for a given (unique) issue. This removes the free-rider incentive and thus encourages investment in information gathering. Obviously there can be no such requirement to "buy all property" in a local land market. The question then remains whether the infor-mation revealed by the bond market is sufficient to price local land efficiently. There are two reasons to be doubtful. First, what the bond market reveals is only the interest rate and level of debt of each new issue; what land purchasers need to know are the interest rates and levels of debt of all outstanding obligations. Second, many important local deficits are never priced through the bond market—in particular, unfunded pension debt, inadequate maintenance of public capital, and the use of long-term debt to pay for current account spending. It is true that the investment bankers and rating agencies work hard to reveal that information for potential bondholders and each bond prospectus is freely available, but the information is only as current as the local government's latest bond issue.

27. These incentives have long been appreciated by U.S. local governments. Hillhouse (1936) relates the experience of Philadelphia when today's city was originally formed by the 1854 merger of eight previously independent local governments: "As soon as it was seen that consolidation was inevitable, the old districts immediately hastened to vote improvements and borrow money therefor(e), and to shift the responsibility to the larger corporate body. The new city thus found itself saddled with an debt of more than $17,000,000, one-fourth of which had been created within thirty days prior to consolida-tion" (69).

28. See note 2. This inefficiency is in addition to any inefficiencies that such taxes might create in the location of business activity (Wildasin 1989).

29. The U.S. Supreme Court's current efforts to draw a bright line between national and local activities began with the 1976 decision in *National League of Cities v. Usery*, 426 U.S. 833 (1976) when it applied the language of the Tenth Amendment—"the powers not delegated to the United States by the Constitution . . . are reserved to the States"—to protect state governments' "traditional governmental functions" from federal intrusion or regulation. Over the following nine years, the Court found it impossible to agree on a definition of a traditional governmental function and finally decided in *Garcia v. San Antonio Metropolitan Transit Authority*, 469 U.S. 528 (1985) to abandon the *Usery* approach. In a series of more recent cases the Court has adopted a new constitutional strategy to drawing the line around acceptable central government activities, a strategy grounded in an implied theory of participatory federalism. The Court's primary objective in its new approach seems to be to protect states as democratic governments so as to ensure that local interests can be heard and respected; see *New York v. United States*, 505 U.S. 144 (1992). In *New York v. United States*, the Court decided states are not bound by federal regulations that cannot be grounded in a valid federal purpose (e.g., protect interstate commerce). It is not yet clear that the Court would invalidate a federal regulation that came with federal funding, however, if such funding were sufficient to insulate the state—as a governmental entity—from any adverse effects of the regulation. For a critique of the constitutional foundation of the *New York* decision and its progeny, see Jackson (1998). It is clear that whatever the validity of this approach for protecting local political participation and control, it will not ensure efficient local public finance.

30. The European Union's principle of subsidiarity, which assigns a policy responsibility to the lowest level of government with the capacity to achieve the policy's objective, is an important step in the right direction. If desired, constitutional guidelines can be made even more precise; for example, see Rosen (1999, 85–87) for a working definition of an economic spillover and Inman and Rubinfeld (1996, 309) for a definition of a resident-based tax.

31. Prior to 1840, the U.S. government had always assumed the debts of troubled states or cities. As part of the compromise to form the Union and to set the national capital in Washington, D.C., the federal government assumed the revolutionary war debts of the states (see Ratchford 1941, chap. 2). In 1836, the federal government bailed out the District of Columbia from a debt of $1.5 million (see McGrane 1935, 37).

32. In the words of one commentator, "To establish the policy of federal assumption of State debts would undoubtedly encourage recklessness and extravagance in the States. Indeed, it would be equivalent to giving a State legislature the power to appropriate for its use moneys out of the federal treasury. Such a policy would be contrary to that fundamental principle of Republican government which places the power to appropriate money and the responsibility for its expenditures in the same hands" (Scott 1893, 253).

33. One delegate to the 1870 Illinois constitutional convention saw the incentive problem clearly when arguing for a no-bailout clause in the state's constitution: "I can see like a creeping shadow on the wall, the time approaching when a log-rolling scheme will be brought into some future legislature, to saddle the state of Illinois, the assumption of that $40 million (of local indebtedness) perhaps twice, aye! thrice fold. I regard this section of the intensest importance; as the ounce of prevention that some day will save more than a pound of cure" (Hillhouse 1936, 323).

34. The discussion that follows is based on Hillhouse (1936, chaps. 1, 11, and 12).

35. The numbers here can only be suggestive of the true motive for new federal and state government assistance. Regression analyses seeking to explain interstate variation in

federal aid to state and local governments show insurance motives (measured by lost economic base) rather than bailout motives (measured by predepression income levels, v_i, and predepression exposure of state banks to bank runs, ψ_i) provide a statistically more compelling explanation for federal assistance (results from the author available on request). Yet even as a local revenue insurance program, new federal and state assistance was modest at best. The local sector still paid a sizable fraction of its depression-induced revenue loss: the implied rate of local copayment was a bit less than 50 percent (= .49 = ($1.409 billion + $.123)/$3.208 billion).

36. By fiscal year 1974–75, the accumulated stock of New York City deficits financed by the rollover of short-term debt totaled $3.03 billion against an annual current-accounts expenditure of $11.78 billion (see Gramlich 1976). To these deficits must be added $5 billion in unfunded city pension liabilities. The federal government's contribution toward these liabilities was to provide $2.3 billion in short-term loans at 1 percent above the Treasury rate of 6 percent. The city's borrowing rate at the time was 13.2 percent. Thus, the federal government offered a subsidy of at most $142 million (= (.132 − .07)· $2.3 billion) (see Morris 1980, 234). This assistance did very little to help bondholders or taxpayers, however. To achieve fiscal balance and repay bondholders, city services were cut dramatically, city taxes and user fees were increased, and the bondholders themselves were forced to accept a three-year moratorium on principal repayment (subsequently declared unconstitutional) and to purchase long-term debt at short-term rates; again (see Morris 1980).

37. While the New York City banks held a significant position in New York City short-term debt, the bonds were held in individual trust accounts and not in the banks' own portfolios. The New York City default was an embarrassment, but it did not create a banking crisis. It was true that the city's default did have implications for the interest rates paid by other U.S. cities, but the adverse effect was short-lived once investors realized that the causes of the New York City crisis were not endemic to all U.S. cities (see Smith and Booth 1985). There is no evidence that the other contemporary defaults or near-defaults by U.S. cities have had any effect on local bank profitability or aggregate municipal interest rates.

38. For references to estimates of the monopoly "rents" extracted through public employee shirking and excessive staffing, see O'Cleireacain (1997). For details of the federal government's financial bailout plan, see D. Vise and C. Chandler, "Clinton Proposes U.S. Run Many D.C. Services," *Washington Post*, Jan. 14, 1997, p. A-1.

39. *New York Times*, Nov. 21, 2000, p. B-1. While financial support is now being provided, the state has not yet succeeded in taking control of how the money is spent. The state is proposing a strong city manager appointed by the state and local officials through mutual agreement. Current elected local officials have to date resisted the plan's implementation. Council President Gwendolyn Eaison said she "strongly favors the elements [of the plan] that involved spending money to help pay the city's debt and revitalize the economy, [b]ut dismisses the idea of a city manager with powers greater than those of elected officials" (*New York Times*, Nov. 21, 2000, B-5).

40. The discussion here summarizes the legal history as reported in McConnell and Picker (1993) and the fiscal history as reported in Hillhouse (1936).

41. For much the same reason that one wants to enforce limited liability for corporate stockholders. If private assets could be seized, rich families might never locate anywhere but in protected enclaves with similarly wealthy households.

42. And clearly viewed as a disciplinary device. During the 1870's defaults one Boston banker wrote to the editors of the *Nation*, a leading public affairs journal, seeking to establish a fund to pay for a standing one-page advertisement to "list . . . all counties and states that have in any way been false to their promises by failing to pay their obligations at maturity. . . . This course I trust will make it more difficult for them to negotiate new loans and thus do something towards the creation of a public sentiment that will prevent the spread and prevalence of a spirit and practice so ruinous to the whole country" (Hillhouse, 1936, 168–169).

43. Although U.S. courts seek to protect the interests of investors by setting $\sigma = 0$ (Lesson 4), there remains the risk that the local government cannot repay immediately. It is the "default" risk of delayed principal and interest payments and subsequently reduced market liquidity that the municipal market penalizes.

44. These guidelines require detailed reporting on the history of operating costs, revenues, and debt not only for the government's primary budget for all related agencies and pension plans. Historical trends in employment, unemployment, income, property values, population, and new construction are also required (see Fairchild and Koch 1998).

45. There is a selection bias here, but that is the point. If the market is uninformed about the riskiness of local bonds, then good-risk and poor-risk governments will pay the same interest rate reflecting the overall level of risk of buying bonds in this undifferentiated pool. When better information is provided, the good-risk bonds will sell at a lower interest rate than the poor-risk bonds. However, some of the poor-risk governments now facing a higher borrowing cost will decide to remove their issues from the market. Thus, the average cost of debt declines for governments in the disclosure states, since only the relatively good risks remain within the borrowing pool. This effect will be noticed only if disclosure rules provide the market with useful information. These results for the local government bond market are similar to the results found by Simon (1989) for the effect of disclosure rules in the corporate security markets.

46. Jefferson confessed to Monroe that he "realized the necessity of yielding to the cries of creditors . . . for the sake of the Union and to save it from the greatest calamities, the total extinction of our credit in Europe" (McGrane 1935, 1).

47. After 1836, another tie between federal and state governments arose that further encouraged a belief that ψ_i might be high. In 1836, the federal government succeeded in repaying all its debts, including the state debts assumed in 1790. Surplus federal tax revenues were then invested in state bonds for state banks and transportation companies. If these projects ever fell on hard times, which they did given that the funds were often wasted, states felt that more surplus federal funding would be there to repay loans and allow completion of stalled projects (Ratchford 1941).

48. Following his historical analysis of the 1840 defaults and the federal decision to reject bailouts, Ratchford (1941, 104) concludes: "Then, too, the tender solicitude which the Federal government has always displayed for the financial welfare of the states would normally have been enough to put [a bailout] measure through. But regardless of the causes, the result was fortunate, for a second assumption would almost certainly have converted a precedent into a habit, the results of which are not pleasant to contemplate."

49. Risk-neutral local governments will make an investment if the expected returns exceeds the expected costs. In this case, expected return will equal $(1 + \Pi) \cdot \Delta \cdot p$, where Δ is the level of debt invested in the risky project, p is the probability that the project will be successful, and Π is the internal rate of return from the project. The expected costs of

the project will equal $(1 + R) \cdot \Delta \cdot p + (1 + R) \cdot (1 - \sigma) \cdot \Delta \cdot (1 - p)$, where $(1 + R)$ are the principal and interest costs per dollar of local debt Δ which is fully paid if the project is successful while $(1 + R) \cdot (1 - \sigma)$ are the local government's share of principal and interest costs per dollar of debt when the project is unsuccessful. When $(1 + \Pi) \cdot \Delta \cdot p > (1 + R) \cdot \Delta \cdot p + (1 + R) \cdot (1 - \sigma) \cdot \Delta \cdot (1 - p)$ or when:

$p > [(1 + R)(1 - \sigma)]/[(1 + \Pi) - (1 + R)\sigma]$,

local governments will invest in the local project. As more of project costs are shifted onto bondholders ($\sigma\uparrow$), riskier projects become attractive ($p\downarrow$). Given plausible values of R and Π from the 1870s and assuming $\sigma = .5$, projects need only have had a probability of success of .38 to prove attractive to local governments. In fact, about 29 percent of local debt initially defaulted, suggesting a per dollar probability of success of at least .71 (Hillhouse 1936). It is easy to see why local governments invested, even without the promise of a state or federal bailout.

50. Though perhaps New York City officials thought a bailout might be possible. When asked to describe how the city's fiscal crisis could have happened, Budget Director David Grossman said: "I knew we were overextended, of course, and I expected the other shoe to drop. But I thought that would mean we would have to face up to service cuts if the economy or the *aid picture didn't improve sharply. I never expected a financing crisis*" (italics added: Morris 1980, 239).

A more complete analysis would formally test among the alternative explanations of local deficit behavior, allowing local deficits to be determined by measures of v_i, ψ_i, and σ from the default-bailout model and by δ from the rollover-exit model.

51. See note 24, where the rate of subsidy for current services through deficit financing (Φ) equals $(1 - \delta) \cdot \Omega$ with δ equal to the rate of deficit capitalization and Ω equal to the ratio of deficit to current spending. Inman (1982) specifies a range of plausible values for Ω, and knowing Φ from the demand curve estimation he can infer estimates for δ; estimates range from .10 to .90.

52. Of the original defaulting states, Illinois, Maryland, and Pennsylvania repaid all their debts; Indiana, Michigan, and Louisiana repaid virtually all of their debts; but Arkansas, Mississippi, and the Florida Territory defaulted on most of their debts. The defaulting states did not borrow again until after the Civil War, presumably having been denied access to the European bond markets because of their default behaviors. The defaulting states that did eventually repay their debts could reenter the bond market, but only by paying a significant interest rate premium until their creditworthiness had been restored (usually by the mid-1850s; English 1996).

53. Hanssen (2000) estimates the effect of appointed versus elected state supreme courts on the behavior of state regulatory regimes, hypothesizing that politically independent courts will be more likely to overrule agency decisions thus stimulating "protective" actions by the agencies. Such actions will require additional agency staff. Hanssen finds higher agency staff per capita in three regulatory agencies—insurance, utility, and education—where judges are appointed. Under his maintained hypothesis, the results suggest appointed judges will be more independent than elected judges. Bohn and Inman (1996) hypothesize that independent courts will be more likely to enforce constitutionally based balanced budget rules against legislative deficits. They find lower deficits in those states with constitutional rules and elected judges. Under their maintained hypothesis, these results suggest elected judges will be more independent than appointed judges.

References

Ades, A., and E. Glaeser. 1995. "Trade and Circuses: Explaining Urban Giants." *Quarterly Journal of Economics* 110:195–227.

Aghion, P., and P. Bolton. 1990. "Government Domestic Debt and Risk of Default: A Political-Economic Model of the Strategic Role of Debt." In R. Dornbusch and M. Draghi, eds., *Public Debt Management: Theory and Practice.* Cambridge: Cambridge University Press.

Allen, F., and D. Gale. 2000. "Financial Contagion." *Journal of Political Economy* 108:1–33.

Bayoumi, Tamim, Morris Goldstein, and Geoffrey Woglom. 1995. "Do Credit Markets Discipline Sovereign Borrowers? Evidence from the U.S. States." *Journal of Money, Credit, and Banking* 27(4):1046–1059.

Bebchuk, L., and H. Chang. 1992. "Bargaining and Division of Value in Corporate Reorganizations." *Journal of Law, Economics, and Organizations* 8:253–279.

Bergstrom, T., D. Rubinfeld, and P. Shapiro. 1982. "Micro-Based Estimates of Demand Functions for Local School Expenditures." *Econometrica* 50:1183–1206.

Bermann, G. A. 1994. "Taking Subsidiarity Seriously: Federalism in the European Community and the United States." *Columbia Law Review* 94:331–456.

Bogart, W., and B. Cromwell. 1997. "How Much More Is a Good School District Worth?" *National Tax Journal* 50:215–232.

Bohn, H., and R. P. Inman. 1996. "Balanced Budget Rules and Public Deficits: Evidence from the U.S. States." *Carnegie-Rochester Conference Series on Public Policy* 45:13–76.

Bordo, M., and B. Eichengreen. 2000. "Is the Crisis Problem Growing More Severe?" Paper presented at Riksbank Conference on Asset Markets and Monetary Policy.

Bradford, D., and W. Oates. 1971. "The Analysis of Revenue-Sharing in a New Approach to Collective Fiscal Decisions." *Quarterly Journal of Economics* 85:416–439.

Chari, V. V., L. Jones, and R. Marimon. 1997. "The Economics of Split-Ticket Voting in Representative Democracies." *American Economic Review* 87:957–976.

Coate, S. 1995. "Altruism, the Samaritan's Dilemma, and Government Transfer Policy." *American Economic Review* 85:46–57.

Collie, M. 1988. "Universalism and the Parties in the United States House of Representatives, 1921–80." *American Journal of Political Science* 32:865–883.

Davoodi, H., and H. Zou. 1998. "Fiscal Decentralization and Economic Growth: A Cross-Country Study." *Journal of Urban Economics* 43:244–257.

DelRossi, A. 1995. "The Politics and Economics of Pork Barrel Spending: The Case of Federal Financing of Water Resource Development." *Public Choice* 85:285–305.

DelRossi, A., and R. P. Inman. 1999. "Changing the Price of Pork: The Impact of Local Cost Sharing on Legislators' Demands for Distributive Public Goods." *Journal of Public Economics* 71:247–273.

Dewatripont, M., and E. Maskin. 1995. "Credit and Efficiency in Centralized and Decentralized Economies." *Review of Economic Studies* 62:841–855.

Diamond, D., and R. Rajan. 2002. "Aggregate Liquidity Shortages and Banking Crises." NBER Working Paper No. 8937, May 2002.

English, W. 1996. "Understanding the Costs of Sovereign Default: American State Debts in the 1840s." *American Economic Review* 86:259–275.

Epple, D., and K. Schipper. 1981. "Municipal Pension Funding: A Theory and Some Evidence." *Public Choice* 37:141–178.

Fairchild, L., and T. Koch. 1998. "The Impact of State Disclosure Requirements on Municipal Yields." *National Tax Journal* 51:733–752.

Fitts, M., and R. P. Inman. 1992. "Controlling Congress: Presidential Influence in Domestic Fiscal Policy." *Georgetown Law Journal* 80:1737–1785.

Fudenberg, D., and D. Kreps. 1987. "Reputation in the Simultaneous Play of Multiple Opponents." *Review of Economic Studies* 54:541–568.

Gillette, C., and L. Baker. 1999. *Local Government Law: Cases and Materials.* 2nd ed. New York: Aspen Law and Business.

Gramlich, E. 1976. "The New York City Fiscal Crisis: What Happened and What Is to Be Done?" *American Economic Review, Papers and Proceedings* 66:415–429.

Grossman, S., and J. Stiglitz. 1980. "On the Impossibility of Informationally Efficient Markets." *American Economic Review* 70:393–408.

Hanssen, A. 2000. "Independent Courts and Administrative Agencies: An Empirical Analysis of the States." *Journal of Law, Economics, and Organization* 16:534–571.

Hempel, G. 1971. *The Postwar Quality of State and Local Debt.* New York: Columbia University Press.

Hillhouse, A. M. 1936. *Municipal Bonds: A Century of Experience.* New York: Prentice-Hall.

Inman, R. P. 1982. "Public Employee Pensions and the Local Labor Budget." *Journal of Public Economics* 19:49–71.

Inman, R. P. 1983. "Anatomy of a Fiscal Crisis." *Business Review: Federal Reserve Bank of Philadelphia* Sept.–Oct., 15–22.

Inman, R. P. 1988. "Federal Assistance and Local Services in the United States: The Evolution of a New Federalist Fiscal Order." In H. Rosen, ed., *Fiscal Federalism: Quantitative Studies.* Chicago: University of Chicago Press, 33–75.

Inman, R. P. 1992. "Can Philadelphia Escape Its Fiscal Crisis with Another Tax Increase?" *Business Review of the Federal Reserve Bank of Philadelphia,* Sept.–Oct., 5–20.

Inman, R. P. 1997. "Do Balanced Budget Rules Work? U.S. Experience and Possible Lessons for the EMU." In Horst Siebert, ed., *Quo Vadis Europe?* Tubingen: J.C.B. Mohr (Paul Siebeck), 309–332.

Inman, R. P. 1999. "On the Design of Intergovernmental Transfers with an Application to the New South Africa." In R. Schwab, ed., *Essays in Honor of Wallace Oates.* London: Edgar Elgar.

Inman, R. P., and M. Fitts. 1990. "Political Institutions and Fiscal Policy: Evidence from the U.S. Historical Record." *Journal of Law, Economics, and Organization* 6:79–132.

Inman, R. P., and D. L. Rubinfeld. 1996. "Designing Tax Policy in Federalist Economies: An Overview." *Journal of Public Economics* 60:307–334.

Jackson, V. 1998. "Federalism and the Uses and Limits of Law: *Printz* and Principle?" *Harvard Law Review* 111:2180–2259.

Knight, B. 2001. "On the Advantages and Disadvantages of Centralized Provision of Public Goods: Evidence from Congressional Voting on Transportation Projects." Working paper, Board of Governors of the Federal Reserve System.

Kornai, J. 1986. "The Soft Budget Constraint." *Kyklos* 39:3–30.

Kreps, D., and R. Wilson. 1982. "Reputation and Imperfect Information." *Journal of Economic Theory* 27:253–279.

Levitt, S. D., and J. Snyder. 1997. "The Impact of Federal Spending on House Election Outcomes." *Journal of Political Economy* 105:30–53.

McConnell, M., and R. C. Picker. 1993. "When Cities Go Broke: A Conceptual Introduction to Municipal Bankruptcy." *University of Chicago Law Review* 60:425–496.

McGrane, R. 1935. *Foreign Bondholders and American State Debts.* New York: Macmillan.

Mera, K. 1969. "Experimental Determination of Relative Marginal Utilities." *Quarterly Journal of Economics* 83:464–477.

Merritt, D. 1988. "The Guarantee Clause and State Autonomy: Federalism for a Third Century." *Columbia Law Review* 88:1–78.

Morris, C. 1980. *The Costs of Good Intentions: New York City and the Liberal Experiment, 1960–1975.* New York: McGraw-Hill.

Oates, W. 1999. "An Essay on Fiscal Federalism." *Journal of Economic Literature* 37: 1120–1149.

O'Cleireacain, C. 1997. *The Orphaned Capital: Adopting the Right Revenues for the District of Columbia.* Washington, D.C.: Brookings Institution.

Palmon, O., and B. Smith. 1998. "New Evidence on Property Tax Capitalization." *Journal of Political Economy* 106:1099–1111.

Poterba, J. 1994. "State Responses to Fiscal Crises: The Effects of Budgetary Institutions and Politics." *Journal of Political Economy* 102:799–821.

Poterba, J. M., and K. S. Reuben. 1999. *Fiscal Rules and State Borrowing Costs: Evidence from California and Other States.* San Francisco: Public Policy Institute of California.

Qian, Y., and G. Roland. 1998. "Federalism and the Soft Budget Constraint." *American Economic Review* 88:1143–1162.

Ratchford, B. U. 1941. *American State Debts.* Durham, N.C.: Duke University Press.

Rosen, H. 1999. *Public Finance.* 5th ed. New York: Irwin McGraw-Hill.

Scott, W. A. 1893. *The Repudiation of State Debts: A Study in the Financial History.* Boston: Crowell.

Segal, I. 1998. "Monopoly and the Soft Budget Constraint." *RAND Journal of Economics* 29:596–609.

Simon, C. 1989. "The Effect of the 1933 Securities Act on Investor Information and the Performance of New Issues." *American Economic Review* 79:295–318.

Smith, R., and J. Booth. 1985. "The Risk Structure of Interest Rates and Interdependent Borrowing Costs: The Impact of Major Defaults." *Journal of Financial Research* 8:83–94.

Tiebout, C. 1956. "A Pure Theory of Local Expenditures." *Journal of Political Economy* 64:416–424.

Tirole, J. 1994. "The Internal Organization of Government." *Oxford Economic Papers* 46:1–29.

Weingast, B. 1979. "A Rational Choice Perspective on Congressional Norms." *American Journal of Political Science* 23:245–262.

Weingast, B., K. Shepsle, and C. Johnsen. 1981. "The Political Economy of Benefits and Costs: A Neoclassical Approach to Distributive Politics." *Journal of Political Economy* 89: 642–664.

Wildasin, D. 1997. "Externalities and Bailouts: Hard and Soft Budget Constraints in Intergovernmental Fiscal Relations." Working paper, Vanderbilt University.

Wilson, R. 1986. "An Empirical Test of Preferences for the Political Pork Barrel: District Level Appropriations for River and Harbor Legislation, 1889–1913." *American Journal of Political Science* 30:729–754.

Wittman, D. 1989. "Why Democracies Produce Efficient Results." *Journal of Political Economy* 97:1395–1424.

3   Constraining Subnational Fiscal Behavior in Canada: Different Approaches, Similar Results?

Richard M. Bird and
Almos Tassonyi

A common concern about fiscal decentralization has been that it may increase the risk of macroeconomic instability. Subnational governments newly endowed with both financial resources and the freedom to spend them will, some have said, tend to spend too much, tax too little, borrow excessively, and generally behave in a fiscally irresponsible fashion (Prud'homme 1995, Tanzi 1996). The consequences of such behavior for central governments are all bad. They may feel obligated to bail out, directly or indirectly, insolvent lower-tier governments. Even if bailouts are avoided, the drain on central finances imposed by the tax-sharing arrangements and intergovernmental transfers often associated with decentralization may be so large and rigid that central governments will lose control over the fiscal tools they need for macroeconomic management. Since well-publicized subnational fiscal disasters in some countries, notably Brazil and Argentina (Dillinger and Webb 1999a), appear to confirm such bleak scenarios, it is not surprising that considerable attention has been paid to the apparent need to impose strong constitutional or administrative constraints on subnational governments: to restrain their expenditures, encourage their fiscal efforts, and above all restrict their access to capital markets through the imposition of rigid ex ante controls by the central government on their borrowing (Ter-Minassian 1996).

Nonetheless, as argued in Chapter 1, if the basic political and economic incentives facing decision makers at all levels of government are correctly structured, there should be little or no need for such prior control (Bird 1999a). Indeed, in these circumstances, rather than restricting access to the capital market in the name of imposing a hard budget constraint on subnational governments, such access may itself constitute an essential part of the institutional structure restraining governments from unduly reckless fiscal actions (Ahmad 1999). Several recent analyses have attempted to characterize the combinations of political, economic, and administrative factors that may interact to produce better or worse outcomes from specific forms of decentralization in specific institutional settings (Rodden 2002, Dillinger, Perry, and Webb 1999).

Canadian experience is interesting with respect to these issues for several reasons. One is that Canada is one of the most decentralized countries in the world. Canadian provinces are responsible for most major social expenditures and have a virtually free hand in levying taxes. They face essentially no constitutional restraints on tax rates, bases, or collection systems and no requirement to harmonize with either each other or the federal government. All provinces receive large unconditional transfers from the federal government, and in some provinces such transfers are more important sources of revenue than their own taxes. Moreover, if provinces wish to borrow, they may do so as and from whom they wish, with no central review or control. These are all factors that might be expected to induce the worst kind of opportunistic behavior by provincial governments. In section 3.1, however, we argue that despite the occasional twinge, there is surprisingly little evidence of such behavior and that Canada has, on the whole, weathered the storms of time moderately well.

A second reason that Canada provides an interesting case is that at the same time as it offers a clear example of the strength of market and political budget constraints in the face of very soft—indeed, nonexistent—hierarchical constraints at the provincial level, it also offers an equally clear example of almost the opposite in the highly controlled and tightly constrained world of Canadian local government. Unlike Canadian provinces, Canadian municipalities are essentially agents of provincial governments and face explicit hierarchical budget constraints imposed largely by administrative fiat. As we argue in section 3.2, the very strength of these provincial controls in, so to speak, saving local governments from some of the possible consequences of opportunistic behavior may to some extent create the moral hazard such controls are intended to offset. On the whole, however, this hierarchical system has been at least as effective as the market-cum-political constraints operating at the provincial level. Although a few smaller municipal governments have occasionally encountered such severe fiscal difficulties that they have been put under financial supervision, on the whole the municipal system, like the provincial system, seems to have avoided serious problems.

Finally, in the concluding section, we draw together some of the main considerations emerging from the diverse Canadian experience at the federal-provincial and provincial-local levels. Both systems, we argue, were largely effective in coping with recent crises. One reason may perhaps be that the hardest budget constraint is one that is forged in the fires of experience rather than one imposed from above, or from outside.[1] Countries (or, more accurately, such institutional manifestations as political parties and governments) may, like individuals, learn from experience and gradually inculcate norms of behavior that constrain their actions even when none of the more obvious forms of hard budget constraint would seem to be applicable at the margin. This line of thought is explored further in the conclusion.

3.1   Hardening Soft Budget Constraints: The Provinces

"In the area of Canadian public finance, history is everything; an understanding of yesterday is absolutely essential to an understanding of today."
—Perry, Taxes, Tariffs and Subsidies: A History of Canadian Fiscal Development

Canada has ten provinces, ranging from tiny Prince Edward Island with little more than 100,000 people to huge Ontario with around 10 million.[2] In this section, we set out some key aspects of Canada's federal-provincial fiscal and political structure that may appear to establish a soft budget constraint—for example, large and unconditional federal-provincial fiscal transfers and a revenue equalization system—and then suggest some reasons that the disasters some would expect as a result have not occurred. We first review the evolution and current structure of federal-provincial fiscal relations and then sketch the political context before setting out briefly some of the relevant historical experience.

3.1.1   Federal-Provincial Fiscal Relations

Fiscal discussions in Canada have long been dominated by issues of federal-provincial relations. This complex subject is simplified here into three principal components. First, there is a revenue equalization system introduced in more or less its present form in 1967, under which the federal government makes transfers to the seven poorest provinces (see appendix 3A). These transfers are intended to bring provincial revenues up to the level they would have received had they levied the national average (provincial) tax rate on a share of the national tax base equal to their share of national population.

Second, there is a separate and larger transfer to all provinces. Despite its name—it is called the Canada Health and Social Transfer—it is basically unconditional in nature. This transfer was introduced recently to replace two previous transfers: a conditional transfer in support of social assistance and another basically unconditional transfer that had itself been introduced in 1977 to replace earlier conditional transfers supporting health and postsecondary education (Bird 1987). The total amount transferred is based on the amount of the transfers replaced in 1996–1997, escalated by a moving average of GDP growth. Only part of this transfer is actually made in cash. The rest is a notional transfer of what are called equalized tax points, that is, the estimated yield of federal tax room—the amount by which federal taxes are reduced to make room for increased provincial taxes without increasing the total tax burden—turned over to the provinces in earlier years.

Third, although provinces have almost complete freedom to choose their own tax bases and rates, in practice most provincial income taxes are collected by the federal government under tax collection agreements, under the condition that the same base is taxed as for the federal income tax. The federal government collects corporation income taxes for seven provinces and personal income taxes for nine provinces under such arrangements. Beginning in 1997, three provinces consolidated their sales taxes with the federal value-added tax (the goods and services tax, or GST) as a harmonized sales tax (HST), which is also collected by the federal government. On the other hand, in Québec, the provincial government collects the federal GST along with its own VAT. Five of the remaining six provinces continue to levy separate retail sales taxes.[3]

To sum up, although the federal and provincial governments essentially tax the same bases, the federal government collects more from its taxes than its direct spending. Therefore, for many years, it has transferred much of the surplus through the two large unconditional transfer programs to the provinces, which, under Canada's constitution, control all expenditure on education and health, as well as social assistance. (On the other hand, direct income maintenance programs for the elderly, children, and the unemployed are largely federal.)

3.1.2 *Taxation*

The federal-provincial fiscal system has evolved slowly, and with reversals at times, over the past fifty years (Perry 1997). With respect to taxation, for example, both federal and provincial governments now rely heavily on income and consumption taxes, although in both fields the provincial share has risen sharply over the postwar period. The result has been a marked rise in the importance of provincial taxation since 1960, in sharp contrast to the relative stability of both federal and municipal taxes as a share of GDP (figure 3.1).

From 1955 to 1995, for example, taxes in Canada grew from 22 percent of GDP to 36 percent. Over four-fifths of this growth was attributable to the increase of provincial taxes, and about two-thirds of this increase was in turn attributable to the marked rise of provincial personal income taxes (Bird, Perry, and Wilson 1998). Despite the considerable attention that has been paid to sales tax issues in recent years, the real story of federal-provincial taxation in the postwar era has been the personal income tax.

The division of taxing powers between the two levels of government reflects more the outcome of political bargaining than the application of any consistent normative principles. This is perhaps as it should be, since norms are influential only to the extent they are accepted, and it

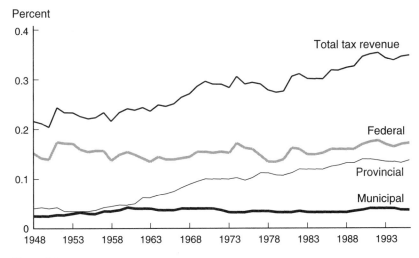

Figure 3.1
Tax revenue as a percentage of GDP, by level of government, 1948–1996.

is by no means clear that there is much agreement in Canada on the many contentious issues involved in tax assignment (Bird 1993). No doubt the economic costs of taxation may be somewhat higher when both levels of government tap most major tax bases. At least to some extent, however, such costs appear to be accepted as part of the necessary price of maintaining Canada's version of federalism, which presumably has its own rationale—or necessity—given Canada's history.

3.1.3 Transfers

Federal transfers to provinces increased sharply in the first half of the postwar period but have subsequently stabilized and, in recent years, declined (figure 3.2). Up to the early 1970s, the federal government reaped a revenue bonanza by maintaining an unindexed progressive income tax through the largest economic expansion in Canadian history. Rather than cut taxes, it chose to channel a substantial share of this revenue inflow to the provinces through several large transfer programs. The first big federal transfer was equalization, which was clearly unconditional.[4]

By far the biggest transfers, however, took the form of conditional shared-cost programs—essentially open-ended matching grants intended to foster provincial spending on the favored fields of

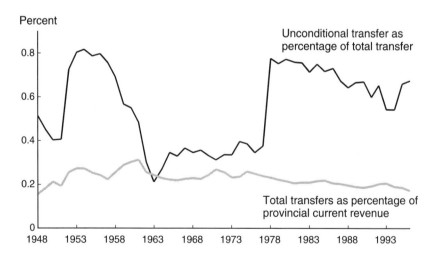

Figure 3.2
Federal transfers to provinces, 1948–1996.

postsecondary education, health, and welfare, all of which are, in terms of Canada's 1867 constitution, matters of provincial, not federal, competence. The result was both a rise in transfers (in the early part of the period) and, especially, a huge drop in the share of total federal-provincial transfers that were essentially unconditional (Bird 1987).

At first, this cornucopia of funds for politically popular expenditure was, unsurprisingly, welcomed by most provinces, although from the beginning, Québec was considerably less happy than the rest with this federal intrusion in provincial areas. Québec's objections were to some extent dealt with rather creatively by devising a system of opting out, under which, instead of receiving transfers, any province could choose instead to receive more tax room in the form of a lower federal income tax rate. Since only Québec chose this path, the result is that since 1966, Canadian federal finance has been clearly asymmetrical in the sense that the federal income tax rate levied in Québec is lower than in other provinces, while at the same time the transfers that Québec receives are lower by approximately the same amount.

Over time, however, as the era of rapid growth came to an end and the federal government slipped into a long series of annual deficits, it became increasingly eager to turn off the transfer tap. Initially, this goal was accomplished by changing the form of the largest transfers (for education and health) to a basically unconditional grant (the so-called established programs financing, or EPF transfer) in 1977, a move that was actually welcomed at the time by provinces such as Ontario as reducing the degree of federal interference in provincial functions. As figure 3.2 shows, the result was to restore the dominance of unconditional transfers (Bird 1987). This process was virtually completed in 1996 when the last major federal conditional grant program, the Canada Assistance Plan, was added to the existing EPF transfer and its name changed to Canada Health and Social Transfer (CHST). The relative size of federal transfers, especially to the better-off provinces (Ontario, Alberta, and British Columbia), had already been cut in several ways as the federal government in effect downloaded a significant part of its deficit to the provinces (Boothe and Johnston 1993). The further sharp cut in federal transfers accompanying the introduction of the CHST meant that the provinces as a whole received relatively less from the federal government than in earlier years, although they could now spend these funds virtually as they wished.

3.1.4   Borrowing

Provinces may borrow money for any purpose, whenever, wherever, and however they wish. There no federal controls at all over provincial borrowing, internal or external. Indeed, provinces do not even need to provide any information on their borrowing to the federal government. Although federal deficits were the driving force behind the rising public debt levels of the 1980s and early 1990s (figure 3.3), provincial debt also rose sharply in part as provinces attempted to maintain social expenditures in the face of declines in both own-source and transfer revenues.[5] As we note below, this pattern was essentially the same as had occurred in the 1930s. Moreover, while there has generally been a rough correspondence between borrowing and capital expenditure at the provincial level, this link was broken in the recession of the early 1990s as several large provinces, almost for the first time since the crisis of the 1930s, borrowed substantially more than they spent on investment (figure 3.4).

As some observers have noted, in principle this situation is not without potential dangers for sound monetary policy (Devereux 1993). On the other hand, so long as there is no express or implied federal guarantee for provincial debt, there may also be something to be said for letting the capital markets do the monitoring, a task that they seem to perform quite well.

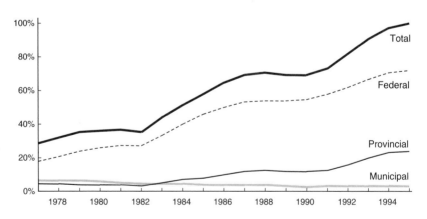

Figure 3.3
Net debt as percentage of GDP, by level of government, 1977–1995.

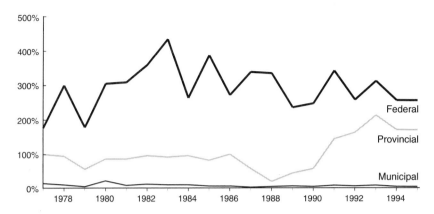

Figure 3.4
Government borrowing as percent of government capital expenditure, by level of government, 1977–1995.

3.1.5 The Political Context

Although constrained by economic realities, federal-provincial fiscal relations in Canada are essentially, and indeed almost exclusively, determined by political factors. As we have noted, the first half of the postwar period was dominated by the extent to which the federal government found so much money flowing in so easily that it could not, given its limited constitutional sphere of action, spend it all itself. Rather than give this pot of gold back to taxpayers, federal politicians decided to spend it through the provinces.[6] The second half of the period (after the mid-1970s) saw not only the reassertion of long-standing provincial and regional concerns about undue federal control but also the end of the revenue bonanza at the federal level. The upshot was increased provincial taxation and reduced (but less conditional) federal transfers, with an accompanying unsustainable blip in provincial non-investment-related borrowing in the early 1990s, which has now been virtually corrected. The recent return to a surplus position in the federal budget, in part by reducing transfers to the provinces, has led to renewed debate with respect to the appropriate role of different levels of governments in financing the politically popular, but costly, health system. We shall return to the question of how to deal with surpluses in section 3.3.

None of these developments can be fully understood without understanding the political context. Four factors deserve attention.

First, Canada appears to be unique among federations in the complete absence of any formal representation of provincial interests at the federal level (Watts 1996). Although there is a federal senate with regional representatives, it not only has virtually no legislative power, but its members are appointed by the federal government.[7]

Second, since Canada has a parliamentary system, with the government being formed by the majority party—and a "first-past-the-post" electoral system that usually produces a majority—there is seldom meaningful legislative opposition to government policy in the House of Commons.

Third, party discipline is extremely strong. Regional issues may perhaps be strongly represented behind the closed doors of the governing party's caucus, but they are never manifested in any public forum. Canadian parties almost invariably present a monolithic front on all policy issues, just as Canadian governments almost invariably get the legislation they want.

Finally, while the previous two characteristics also hold for the (unicameral) provincial governments, there is essentially no integration between provincial and federal parties. Canadians see nothing inconsistent with supporting one party at the provincial level and another at the federal level, and they frequently do so.[8] Moreover, there is very little crossover between the federal and provincial levels. With very few exceptions, provincial politicians and officials make their careers at the provincial level and federal politicians and officials at the federal level.

One result of these factors—exacerbated by the small number of provinces (ten) and the fact that only four of them (Ontario, Québec, Alberta, and British Columbia) really matter much—is that any policy issue with strong regional impacts sooner or later becomes a matter for dispute and negotiation between federal and provincial governments. Almost every major policy issue becomes a matter for what one author (Simeon 1972) has accurately labeled "federal-provincial diplomacy." At the federal-provincial level, the dominant political style has thus long been one of "negotiated accommodation" (Hettich and Winer 1999). Changes in either the political or the economic balance of the country have often been directly reflected in changes in the fiscal relations of levels of government to maintain political stability at the expense of allocative efficiency. Given the essentially distributive nature of this political process, it is not surprising that efficiency considerations sometimes fall to the wayside. There is no possibility of constraints from above—or even politically negotiated constraints—on provincial budgets. Canada's provinces thus afford an extreme test of the viability of market-constrained decentralization.

3.1.6 Budget Constraints in Practice

It is not surprising that provincial budget constraints in Canada have been considered to be relatively soft by some analysts (McKinnon 1997). Experience in the early years of the nineteenth century—for example, in the Province of Canada (now Ontario and Quebec) before Canada itself was created in 1867—indeed showed some of the expected outcomes. Provincial (and local) governments repeatedly ran into difficulties in financing infrastructure such as railways and canals, largely through foreign bond issues, and then engaged in various maneuvers to extricate themselves from the resulting problems (Piva 1992).

These early experiences, however, also revealed two perhaps surprising but prevalent tendencies in Canadian public finance. First, one important result of the repeatedly necessary efforts at damage control was a continuing improvement in subnational financial management. As Piva (1992) put it, "Financial administration . . . involved exercises in crisis management; as often as not it was an exercise in damage control. . . . Each crisis, however, led to a series of reform initiatives the final product of which was the creation of a relatively modern administrative system for managing government finance." Second, foreign bond markets proved to be very adept at interpreting the information available concerning what was going on in these far-away colonies, lagged and incomplete though it inevitably was in that era. Carlos and Lewis (1995), for example, demonstrate convincingly that the London market had little difficulty in pricing fairly accurately the ex ante positive probability that the Grand Trunk Railway, the largest single foreign bond issue of the 1850s, would be bailed out by the provincial government in the event of bankruptcy.[9] Both the adjustment of political and administrative practice in response to economic and financial problems and the discipline exerted by foreign capital markets continue to be equally evident a century and a half later.

After the formation of Canada, most provinces continued to encounter similar financial problems and corrective checks—for example, during the depression of 1875–1895 (Perry 1997). As in the pre-Confederation period, many provincial difficulties were occasioned by municipal indiscretions, with the result that many of the

corrective administrative measures were introduced at that level. For
example, in the early years of the twentieth century, Quebec dealt with
the bankruptcy of several small suburban municipalities by amalgamating them with Montreal (Poitras 1999).[10] The entanglement of
provincial and municipal finance continued to give rise to problems
even after World War I, owing in part to the involvement of both levels
of government in the provision of relief. Although the newer western
provinces—Alberta and Saskatchewan were created in 1905—had
begun to encounter debt problems even in the 1920s, the real crisis
came with the depression of the 1930s, which quickly doubled debt
service burdens even in some of the eastern provinces, which were, in
the words of one observer (Buck 1949, 291), already "conservative by
experience." As Forbes (1993) notes, such pressures were accentuated
in the poorer provinces, and especially the poorer municipalities in the
poorer provinces, by the uniform matching requirements of federal
debt relief.[11]

Perhaps the most striking result of the crisis of the 1930s was the first
and only default of provincial debt in Canadian history—that by
Alberta in 1936. Alberta, now Canada's richest province, was then one
of the poorest. It was experiencing drought as well as the general economic depression. Moreover, its newly elected government professed
a prairie populist version of an anti-(eastern) banking philosophy
called "social credit". The new provincial government proceeded to
put this philosophy into legislative form through a series of laws that
were either disallowed by the federal government[12] or ruled *ultra vires*
provincial authority.[13] The province's finances had been in a parlous
state to begin with, and the prolonged and exceedingly acrimonious
provincial-federal bickering that ensued did not help matters. The
province, for example, refused to participate in a proposed loans
council on the grounds that this would in effect cede control over
provincial borrowing to the federal government (Boothe 1995).

The upshot was that in 1936, the federal government flatly refused
to bail out Alberta, thus forcing it to default on approximately one-third
of its bonded debt (although it continued to pay a reduced rate of interest). That this decision was at least in part political has been suggested
to some (Boothe 1995) by the fact that almost simultaneously, the
neighboring province of Saskatchewan, whose finances were in a
similarly debilitated state, was rescued by federal funds and therefore
did not default.[14] Alberta actually stayed in default until 1945, when,
after prolonged negotiations, the federal government in effect bailed

the province out, explicitly in order to restore Canada's full credit-worthiness in foreign markets.[15] As the federal finance minister put it when explaining his action, "I would like the public to have complete assurance that when *any* Canadian government gives its promise to pay it will abide by its undertakings" (quoted in Buck 1949, 295, italics added).

On its face, this declaration and the federal action in bailing out (eventually) the provincial government seem to make it clear that the provinces indeed face a soft budget constraint and that the federal government had rendered itself implicitly liable for all provincial debt. Other postwar developments reinforce this conclusion. The explicit stabilization provision in the federal-provincial tax agreements (see appendix 3B) for instance, points in the same direction.

At a deeper level, however, other changes had taken place that had fundamentally changed the playing field. The advent of the war meant that no attention was explicitly paid to the recommendations of an important Royal Commission on Dominion-Provincial Relations (Rowell-Sirois 1938) that the federal government should take full responsibility for the relief expenditures that had, for the most part, been the precipitating factor in both the provincial and the municipal fiscal crises of the 1930s. Nonetheless, two important constitutional amendments in 1941 (unemployment insurance) and 1951 (old age pensions) had in effect largely accomplished this goal. Henceforth, it would be primarily the federal, and not the subnational, government that was primarily charged with interpersonal income distribution. In addition, the wartime creation of a highly productive personal income tax, which after 1947 became a major source of provincial as well as federal revenues, greatly improved provincial finances.[16]

With both provincial expenditures and revenues thus in much better shape, Canada entered a new era after World War II. Provincial education and health expenditure, financed by both their own revenues and large transfers financed from equally buoyant federal revenues, grew sharply until the revenue tide turned in the mid-1970s, resulting finally in the latest federal-provincial fiscal crisis. Once again, however, many of the same factors as already mentioned seem in the end to have largely offset the long-term detrimental macroeconomic consequences that some might have expected to result from Canada's extreme fiscal decentralization.

In contrast to earlier experiences, although the 1980s and early 1990s certainly saw a substantial increase in debt, especially federal debt (figure 3.3), despite the fears of some who seem to have confused transitional problems with deep-seated flaws (Bruce 1995, Devereux 1993), the system seems, after a lag of a few years, to have adjusted adequately to the changed realities (Kneebone and McKenzie 1999). Indeed, even before the federal government began to get its own fiscal house in order in the latter half of the decade, many provincial governments had already begun to deal with the fiscal problems arising not only from economic downturn but from the initial federal response of cutting transfers to the provinces (Boothe and Johnston 1993). Interestingly, neither political affiliation nor transfer dependence seems to have determined who did what and when. One of the most transfer-dependent provinces, although governed by socialists (Saskatchewan), was among the first to take remedial action, and one of the least transfer-dependent provinces, although controlled by conservatives (Ontario), was among the last. What seems to have been more important than transfer dependence or ideology in determining the timing and strength of provincial adjustment is the extent of the fiscal problem faced by the various provinces, with the weakest provinces (with the narrowest fiscal bases) reacting earlier and more strongly than the more diversified, richer, and much less transfer-dependent provinces.[17] The interaction of social norms, institutional modalities, political realities, and market forces that seems to have enabled Canada, and its provinces, largely to have escaped the macroeconomic trap sometimes thought to be inevitable in unconstrained decentralization evolved incrementally over time, in large part in response to previous crises. One part of the most recent corrective process, which has received some attention, has been the adoption, for the first time, of balanced budget rules by a number of provinces (see appendix 3C). The self-adopted nature of these rules and the general principle that no parliament can bind a future parliament suggests, however, that this development may have more symbolic than real significance.[18] As we note in section 3.3, the real lesson appears to be the flexibility of the Canadian political system and its ability and willingness to respond to market signals.

An additional point that deserves mention concerns the considerable importance of foreign borrowing at the provincial level. In contrast to the federal government, provincial governments have long been dependent on foreign capital markets, with about half of their borrowing in foreign currencies. Their debt costs are thus sensitive not only to interest rates but also fluctuations in exchange rates. Since the policies that affect both interest rates and exchange rates are in federal hands, provincial budgets are even more dependent on federal actions than might at first appear (Shah 1998). Nevertheless, given the importance of the provinces and their foreign borrowing, it also follows that provincial fiscal difficulties may affect exchange rates and hence federal budgets. Some have seen this as reason for federal concern about provincial budgetary policy (Harris 1993) and have concluded that a federal "nonbailout" policy is therefore inherently noncreditable (Bruce 1993).[19] This seems to go too far, however.

As Boothe (1993) notes, as debt levels increase, credit ratings decrease, thus increasing debt costs and, one assumes, reducing debt. If foreign capital markets at the end of the twentieth century are as good at reading Canadian political signals as they were in the middle of the nineteenth century (Carlos and Lewis 1995), it seems unlikely that anyone in Ottawa should lose too much sleep about the problem of provincial indebtedness. Profligate behavior by provincial decision makers will, it seems, be brought to their attention quite quickly enough by the capital market and reinforced by subsequent voter reaction.[20]

3.2 The "Second World" of Canadian Public Finance: The Municipalities

Taxes, transfers, borrowing—the picture is similar. The province proposes, and, on the whole, the province disposes.
—Bird and Chen 1998

Unlike Canadian provinces, Canadian municipalities face very explicit hard budget constraints imposed largely by administrative fiat. In the provincial-municipal world, in sharp contrast to the federal-provincial world, formal constraints on subnational fiscal actions abound (Bird and Chen 1998). As a rule, for example, local borrowing requires prior provincial approval and is severely limited (Amborski 1998). Moreover, both local revenue and expenditure decisions are tightly controlled, and the important transfers received by local governments from the provinces are generally highly conditional (figure 3.5). Many of the rules and regulations governing local fiscal decisions that originated in the 1930s remained virtually unchanged until very recently. Although occasionally some smaller municipal governments have encountered

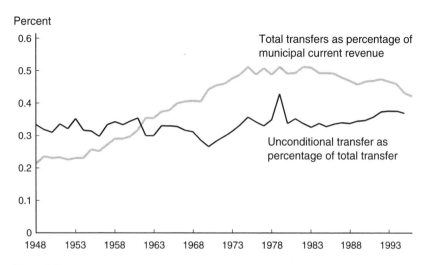

Percent

Figure 3.5
Provincial transfers to municipalities, 1948–1996.

such severe fiscal difficulties that they have been put under financial
supervision (with, in principle, all costs being charged locally), on the
whole this very different system also seems to have weathered the difficulties of the 1990s fairly satisfactorily. Indeed, one interesting, and
somewhat unexpected, effect of the recent crisis has been, if anything,
to liberalize rather than tighten provincial administrative control over
local borrowing.[21]

Of the three levels of government in Canada, the municipal level
is most visibly a provider of services to its inhabitants. The services
for which municipalities are responsible vary from those that require
considerable capital investment (water supply) to those that are
highly labor intensive (social services). Since most Canadians live in
cities, it is not surprising that provincial politicians, despite some
continuing rural bias in constituencies, often act in ways that imply a
strong implicit provincial guarantee of the services nominally financed
through local budgets.[22] Modern urban economies are especially
dependent on services that are highly capital intensive, such as water
supply, sewage treatment, and transportation. When municipal capacity to finance both capital and operating costs is threatened by either
the demands placed on the municipal fiscal system by competing
expenditure pressures to fund redistributive services, or the inability
of the existing political structure to cope with spillover effects among
adjacent municipalities, or simply to establish an adequate fiscal base,

a policy response from the province has generally been forthcoming. This situation is by no means new, however.

3.2.1 Early Experience

The early stages of local government development in Canada saw many local fiscal crises and subsequent provincial responses. For example, the original Municipal Corporations Act (1849) of the Province of Canada was intended in part to avoid further increases in the provincial debt by empowering local governments with the power to tax and borrow and finance local improvements. When municipalities turned out to be unable to raise money on their own credit, the Consolidated Municipal Loan Fund was created in 1852, from which municipalities could borrow to support transportation improvements. At least in official eyes, if not necessarily those of creditors, the debentures issued by this fund did not represent an increase in the public debt of the province since they were not secured by the Consolidated Revenue Fund (Piva 1992).

Most early local government legislation was intended more to prevent abuse than either to support or control local actions. In Québec, for example, which had perhaps the most extensive such legislation in place at the beginning of this century, the rules were not very restrictive. Municipalities were, however, required to inform the government when they wanted to borrow beyond the statutory limit (when interest and sinking-fund payments exceeded half the annual revenue of the municipality). Ontario's situation was broadly similar. Other provinces—New Brunswick, Nova Scotia and British Columbia—had almost no explicit legislation apart from some control over audit. Only the two new provinces, Alberta and Saskatchewan, had formal departments of municipal affairs with broad powers of supervision over finances, debt, and audit (Taylor 1991).

3.2.2 The Crisis of the 1930s

As the twentieth century unfolded, provincial legislative control over local governments became much more extensive, particularly as a result of the experience of the 1930s. Most provinces created departments of municipal affairs with extensive powers to supervise, influence, and pass money to local governments. Explicit provincial control was extended over a wide variety of local government functions (Buck

1949). In Ontario, for example, the severe effects of the depression on both provincial and municipal finances led the provincial government to modify drastically the existing framework for the regulation of borrowing and financial administration (Tassonyi 1994).[23]

Although a few western municipalities had defaulted after World War I, largely as a result of overly ambitious borrowing for infrastructure on the basis of inflated land values (Perry 1955), it was really the depression that led to a wave of local defaults amounting to about 10 percent of total municipal debt (Buck 1949). Nowhere was the situation more serious than in Ontario. By late 1934, over forty Ontario municipalities and school boards had defaulted on their obligations.[24] Most defaults occurred in 1932 and 1933, many of them in such one-industry company towns as Sturgeon Falls:

This northern Ontario company town of about 5,000 people was in a hopeless position after Abitibi Pulp and Paper, its only major employer, closed down operations near the end of 1930. Two years later, the town found itself saddled with $350,000 in debentured debt, three out of every four members of its population on relief, and a growing mountain of almost $56,000 each year in unpaid tax levies. Beginning in July 1932 the provincial and federal governments agreed to pay 85 per cent of town's relief bills to stave off municipal default, but Ontario officials soon became horrified at the way the community was spending the province's money. (Struthers 1991)

In response to such experiences, over the next few years Ontario established both a regulatory framework for municipal finance and the capacity to regulate, audit, investigate, and inspect municipal administration. In 1932, the province established the Ontario Municipal Board (OMB) and gave this body extensive power to validate the borrowing bylaws of municipalities and consider the nature of the undertaking, the financial position of the municipality, its existing set of obligations, and other matters.[25] A few years later, in 1935, the OMB was given power to control all municipal capital expenditures and limit local borrowing without OMB approval.[26] Previously, municipal debt had been limited in part by setting a mill rate limit on the amount that taxes could be increased to service debt, but municipalities had tended to increase their real property assessments artificially to avoid the limit.

The OMB was also given extensive powers of supervision over defaulting municipalities, exercisable either at the request of council or, when in default or with high probability of default, by creditors who represented not less than 20 percent of the indebtedness. The administration of the municipality could be turned over to the Committee of Supervisors, with authority to manage the financial affairs of the municipality: the collection of revenues, the making of expenditures, the establishment of the assessment rolls, the setting of tax rates, temporary borrowing, the disposal of assets, the consolidation of indebtedness, and the negotiation of new terms with creditors. Further borrowing could be done only with the approval of the OMB, which also retained extensive powers to review the decisions of supervisors.

The severity of the crisis in many communities provoked both creative responses from municipal officials and, and as suggested above with respect to Sturgeon Falls, provincial unease as to what was going on. In York Township, for example, an inquiry found that "in their desire to assist the unemployed and secure as large a payment as possible from the Governments of the Dominion and the Province, the officials undertook works that should not have been commenced at the time. They also claimed expenditures which were not properly within the scope of the agreement with the Province" (Commission to Enquire, 1933, 9).

By far the most serious crisis occurred in the Windsor area (on the U.S. border, opposite Detroit). In East Windsor, for example, in 1931, debt service represented 45 percent of expenditures. In 1934, no payments were made, and 40 percent of the total residential value of property in the municipalities of East Windsor, Windsor, Walkerville, and Sandwich was in arrears. Committees of Supervisors were established in all these municipalities. Among the principal problems identified were "the practices of budgeting on the basis of collecting 100 percent of the tax levy, and failing to pass the budget early in the year" (McPherson 1935, 330). Two other common problems were recourse to short-term borrowing based on the notion of the unlimited power of municipalities to raise taxes and the overstatement of the revenue base through the assessment process (Brittain 1934).

For each of the Windsor-area municipalities, refinancing schemes were suggested, generally to spread the retirement of the debt over forty years at rates between 3 and 3.5 percent, with only interest being payable for five years. The severity of the problem in the Windsor area led to the appointment of the Royal Commission, which reported in 1935. At that time, 29 percent of the population was receiving relief, and assessments had fallen by nearly 40 percent from their peak value in 1930. The Royal Commission (1935, 7) noted:

The situation existing in the Border Area today is giving rise to a condition by which something approaching total default is threatened. The present budgets are to some extent fictitious as the provision for maintenance in every department is entirely inadequate. . . . If the present scale of expenditure is continued, adequate maintenance resumed and a share of relief provided by the municipalities, there will be very little if anything, left to pay either principal or interest on the bulk of outstanding bonds. The consequence must be that the credit of the area, both public and private, will be destroyed.

In response to the continuing problems of the area, the province drastically altered the jurisdictional framework, amalgamating the cities of Windsor and East Windsor and the towns of Sandwich and Walkerville and establishing the Windsor Finance Commission to prepare a plan for funding and refunding the outstanding debts of the amalgamated municipalities to be recovered on the rateable properties of their former jurisdictions. This commission was provided authority similar to that granted to the Committees of Supervision.

In 1936, the provincial Department of Municipal Affairs, which had been established in 1934 to deal with the mounting local crisis throughout the province, replaced these committees. By 1939, the department had completed fifteen refunding plans, and six were in the process of being negotiated (Ontario 1939). These plans generally followed the pattern set in the Windsor situation and involved negotiations with bondholders and the municipalities to obtain feasible terms of repayment of accumulated indebtedness. As late as 1944, fifteen municipalities remained under supervision, although in most cases, supervision had been reduced to an approval of the annual budget and monitoring adherence.

3.2.3   Constraints on Municipal Fiscal Behavior

The traditional argument with respect to tax assignment in a multilevel government suggests two conclusions: first, most taxes should likely be assigned to the central government; second, so far as possible, different taxes should be assigned to different governments (Bird 1999b). At the federal-provincial level, Canada violates both these rules; at the provincial-local level, it largely satisfies them. Specifically, only the municipal level of government has a clearly separate tax source in most provinces: the property tax. Despite recent provincial encroachments on property tax revenues in a number of provinces (usually as part of a realignment of provincial-local responsibilities for education), this situation seems unlikely to change drastically in the near future. Nonetheless, even with respect to their "own" property tax, assessment—the determination of the tax base—is carried out by provinces,[27] and although local governments may generally set their own tax rates, even this freedom is often limited, for instance, with respect to the extent of variation in the structure of rates between residential and other properties.[28]

More generally, local governments in Canada are controlled by the provinces in all important fiscal respects; as a general rule, they cannot tax, charge, borrow, or spend without explicit provincial approval (Bird and Slack 1993). Although they can set property tax rates, municipalities on the whole get only the tax revenues that provinces let them have. In current fiscal circumstances, it is unlikely that any province will allow municipalities to tap such potential revenue sources as income and sales taxes, so the striking stability of local taxes shown in figure 3.1 seems likely to continue in the future.[29]

This local tax stability has been coupled with an inevitably greater role for local expenditures in an increasingly urbanized Canada largely by expanding the size (relative to GDP) of provincial transfers to municipalities. From 1955 to 1975, such transfers as a proportion of total local revenues almost doubled. Since then, this proportion has remained close to half (figure 3.5). At the same time, however, transfers to municipalities actually constituted a decreasing share of provincial revenues, reflecting the more rapid rise of the latter (Bird and Chen 1998).

Almost all of this huge stream of provincial-local transfers took the form of conditional transfers (figure 3.5). In striking contrast to the federal-provincial case, the importance of unconditional transfers has remained both low and constant as a share of total municipal revenues throughout the postwar period. Local governments received sufficient provincial funds through transfers to enable them to expand expenditures substantially. But most such funds came with restrictions and controls aimed at implementing provincial wishes at the local level.[30]

Most infrastructure expenditure in Canada, as in many other countries, is carried out at the local level. In 1993, for example, municipal governments accounted for 52 percent of total public sector expenditure on roads, bridges, water, and sewerage works and the like, with most of the balance being provincial expenditure (Slack 1996). Some of this expenditure (e.g., on water) may directly produce revenue through user fees. Other infrastructure expenditure (e.g., on roads) may add to productivity and hence improve local taxpaying capacity. Moreover, almost by definition, local investment in infrastructure will render services for years to come. For these reasons, it has often been argued that most local infrastructure expenditure can and should be financed by borrowing. One of the more striking features of Canadian local government, however, is how little local borrowing there is. Indeed, borrowing by municipal governments has actually exhibited a slight downward trend for several decades. Moreover, only a fraction of local capital expenditure has ever been financed by borrowing in any case (figure 3.4).

3.2.4   Why Don't Municipalities Borrow More?

One reason local borrowing has been little studied in Canada is perhaps that municipalities make so little use of the well-developed capital market. Why this is so is a bit of a puzzle. As noted earlier, it is true that municipalities are allowed to borrow only under strict provincial limits and controls: the type of debt they can incur, the time period for which they can borrow, and the use they can make of the funds are all strictly regulated. While the rules vary from province to province, all provinces have restrictive rules (Kitchen 1984, Amborski 1998). On the whole, local governments in Canada cannot incur any significant amount of long-term debt without the prior approval of the provincial government (and in some cases, of local taxpayers also). "An important advantage of this situation is that local governments in Canada . . . are most unlikely to go bankrupt. But this result is achieved only at the expense of severe restrictions on local autonomy" (Bird and Slack 1993, 105).

The specific characteristics of the provincial regulatory framework that governs municipal budgeting, borrowing, term, and supervision in cases of financial distress vary from province to province (Kitchen 1984). In Ontario, the legislative provisions pertaining to municipal supervision established in the 1930s have been maintained with little change. Both the Ontario Municipal Board and the Ministry of Municipal Affairs have a significant role in the process that regulates the level of indebtedness and the general financial affairs of municipalities. The statute allows for ministry or board appointees to take over the financial operations of the local government and charge back the costs to the local tax base. The most recent instance was with respect to the Ottawa-Carleton French Language School Board, from 1991 to 1998.

In every province, municipalities are required to budget for balanced operating budgets. In Ontario, for example, if a deficit is incurred for any reason, it must be financed in the next budget year. Approved auditors must be appointed, and generally accepted methods of accounting must be followed. Municipalities may borrow short term for only two reasons: to finance work in progress prior to the final sale of debentures or to meet short-term obligations prior to the collection of taxes and the receipts of revenue. Such borrowing cannot exceed 50 percent of total estimated revenues when borrowed between January 1 and September 30 or 25 percent from October 1 to December 31.[31] Any councillor who knowingly authorizes greater borrowings for temporary purposes may be disqualified from office for two years.

Long-term borrowing by municipalities is closely regulated in every province (Amborski 1998). In some provinces, special agencies borrow on behalf of municipalities.[32] Elsewhere, municipalities do the borrowing directly but are bound by provincially set rules and processes of approval directly administered by either a provincial ministry or agency. In Ontario until recently, the OMB had to approve all capital undertakings requiring the issuance of debt or future financing beyond the term in office of a local council. To issue debt, an enabling bylaw had to be adopted by the council. Commitments to commence the project and arrange the sale of debentures could be made only after approval was obtained to undertake a project at a specified cost. There was no retroactive approval authority. As noted below, these rules have been liberalized in some respects in recent years. Nonetheless, even local governments with good credit ratings do not borrow as much as they can.

Generally, the OMB process was sensitive to the considerable differences in municipal fiscal and administrative capacity in Ontario (see appendix 3D). Capital expenditure quotas were set annually for Metropolitan Toronto, the regional municipalities, and others that normally submitted applications, and on application for others, on the basis of information submitted by the municipalities. Municipalities were required to report other forms of long-term obligation to the board to be included in the calculation of expenditure quotas and debt limits. For example, lease agreements involving financing from current funds beyond the terms of council of a capital nature were capitalized for calculation purposes.[33]

Despite the generally deteriorating fiscal climate of the later 1980s and early 1990s, most Ontario municipalities maintained their bond ratings—in part perhaps owing to the continuing existence of the approvals framework and the limitations imposed on Ontario municipalities, combined with their conservative budgetary practices. Although there was no apparent impediment to the ability of Ontario municipalities to raise money domestically or in foreign bond markets, nonetheless, after the mid-1970s, their capital financing shifted away from the use of borrowed funds to pay-as-you-go policies, placing a heavier reliance on development charges and user fees to fund capital expenditures, as well as experimenting to a limited extent with public-private financing options. Although the economic efficiency of in effect replacing public borrowing with private borrowing may sometimes be questionable (Slack and Bird 1991), matters may look different from a municipal budgetary perspective. Local governments may perceive themselves as being crowded out with respect to their tax base, for example, and under great pressure to finance social services at the expense of maintaining and improving infrastructure.[34]

Increasingly pressed by fiscal exigencies arising from both the economic downturn and the cuts in federal transfers at the end of the 1980s, Ontario began to download some of its problems onto local governments. In particular, the province argued that municipalities could bear a greater share of the financial burden related to infrastructure funding as well as current operations (Ontario 1989). Both unconditional transfers and transfers for roads were frozen at existing levels. In effect, the conservative management of Ontario's municipal governments, all of whom were well within the existing guidelines on capital financing, was rewarded by funding cuts.

Another reward for conservative local financing practices was, perhaps surprisingly, a suggestion by the province that the pay-as-you-go policies of many municipalities (adopted in part as a reaction to the levels of interest rates prevailing for long term debt) meant that they had unused borrowing capacity and should therefore finance a larger share of growing infrastructure needs. Unsurprisingly, the municipalities were not happy to learn that "good guys" finished last, so to speak. Metropolitan Toronto, for example, argued that "unilateral actions by the Province, resulting in funding shortfalls, have weakened the financial partnership to the point that it is crumbling" (Municipality of Metropolitan Toronto 1989). Nevertheless, in 1992, in order to encourage local governments to borrow more, local government access to capital markets was liberalized, and municipalities were granted the ability to borrow and lend money in foreign currencies and to vary the type of instruments used. The process for undertaking long-term financial commitments was also streamlined.

The current limit for debt service is 25 percent of own-purpose revenues.[35] Since 1993, Ontario municipalities can borrow and undertake financial obligations that extend beyond the term of council without OMB approval as long as the prescribed debt limit is not exceeded. Borrowing above the limit still requires prior approval by the OMB. Ontario municipalities may borrow for capital purposes and issue debentures. Regional municipalities, counties, local municipalities in counties, and single-tier municipalities may borrow on their own behalf.[36] Interestingly, although local municipalities in a regional municipality are those charged with levying property taxes, they may not borrow on their own behalf. Instead, although municipal debentures are secured on the revenue base of the local government, and debt and debt service is an obligation of the lower tier, only the upper tier is allowed to borrow. Bonds may not be tied to the revenue generated by a specific project, but municipalities are permitted to use a variety of instruments, including retractable bond and sinking funds. They can also borrow in prescribed foreign currencies, although such borrowing must be hedged in Canadian funds.

On the whole, the recent fiscal record of Ontario municipalities suggests that the regulatory framework established in the depths of the depression withstood the recent fiscal difficulties. Ontario municipalities have a good reputation in both domestic and international capital markets. Still, the system is not without critics. Some argue that even the liberalized regulatory framework just described unduly hampers creative financing and the use of capital markets to their fullest. Others argue that the pay-as-you-go philosophy pursued by municipalities places an unwarranted burden on current ratepayers.

A more fundamental problem, however, is that municipal finance in Ontario remains heavily dependent on a narrow tax base while at the same time local governments are responsible for a significant share of social assistance expenditures. When times are hard, the combination of compulsory debt service and local responsibility for social assistance may substantially impinge on the ability of municipalities to maintain service levels in other categories. Policies such as those adopted recently to enhance the flexibility of municipal interaction with the capital market may be an improvement, but more appropriate placement of the financial responsibility for income redistributive services and perhaps some local access to more elastic revenue sources (such as the personal income tax) would clearly provide a more permanent solution to the problem.

Provincial authorities throughout Canada have begun to recognize the need for greater flexibility in the regulatory framework. While recent reforms in Ontario and Alberta simplified the regulatory process and presumably enhanced municipal ability to access innovations in the capital market, the system remains more complicated elsewhere (Amborski 1998). In British Columbia, where a provincial body borrows on behalf of municipalities (except for Vancouver), long-term borrowing requires both provincial approval and a two-thirds council majority (and possibly a referendum). In Québec, either voter approval or provincial approval is required for municipal borrowing except in Montreal and Quebec City, and all borrowing in foreign currency is controlled by the province. In Alberta until 1995, borrowing bylaws were reviewed by the Local Authorities Board. Although provincial oversight has now been removed, unless debt limits are exceeded, provincial regulation specifies the total indebtedness (1.5 times municipal revenue) and the level of debt service (25 percent of revenues) that is permissible.[37]

3.2.5 The Province Decides

In short, what local governments can do and how they can do it, and indeed what local governments exist and their boundaries, are largely in the hands of the provincial governments, which have not been reluctant to exercise these powers.[38] In Ontario, for example, most of the province's more urbanized areas were organized into two-tier regional governments in the 1970s. Neither the existing local governments nor local residents asked for this reorganization. Basically, someone decided it was a good idea, and a new structure was imposed from above. People who had lived for decades in village A suddenly found themselves residents of city B in region C, whether they liked it or not. Of course, if people are really unhappy, the channels of democratic politics are sufficiently open in Canada for their discontent to be registered. If strong enough, extended and pervasive local dissent may slow and even reverse the direction of policy. In part for this reason, reinforced by a series of review reports that found relatively few clear benefits from regionalization, the move to regional government in Ontario lost its momentum in the 1980s (Slack 1997). Nonetheless, as the recent imposition by the provincial government of an amalgamated government in Toronto demonstrates, those who have power sometimes seem driven to use it, even if the results seem unlikely to prove either economically or politically desirable.

Provinces can do as they will with municipalities at least in the short run, even if, in the long run, the political system may in practice establish some limits to their theoretically unfettered powers. Indeed, as suggested by recent events in the Toronto area (see appendix 3D), provincial dominance may have been increasing despite the diminished role of provincial transfers to municipalities and the partial loosening of the borrowing strings, in part as the result of the same forces that resulted in the cut in transfers. In any case, Canadian provinces clearly get the municipal governments they want and deserve. What they appear to want is, as a rule, to keep local governments under tight check. They do so by restricting their revenues, directing their expenditures, and in various ways controlling access to capital markets. If, nonetheless, local governments get into financial trouble, the province generally comes to the rescue in a variety of ways—adjusting municipal boundaries, taking over functions, and, in the extreme, taking control of finances. Paradoxically, therefore, the very existence of tight provincial control of local finances, as evidenced by the proliferation of rules and restraints to which local budgets are subjected, means that in effect, there is a strong implicit provincial guarantee that municipal obligations will, in the end, be met. Ex ante rules intended to harden budget constraints are thus offset to at least some extent by the ex post reality that the all-powerful and hence responsible province always, it seems, comes through. Since most costs under provincial supervision are borne locally, local citizens may still pay the cost of fiscal misbehavior by their local governments, but creditors, as a rule, do not.

3.3   Two Roads to Realism?

We have noted that recent events have, perhaps paradoxically, seen some apparent strengthening of hierarchical oversight mechanisms in the form of budget rules at the provincial level and some apparent softening of existing hierarchical constraints on local borrowing. In both instances, however, these formal changes, like the striking formal difference between the explicit rules in place at the two levels of subnational government in Canada, probably matter less than might at first be thought. In the end, both roads to fiscal discipline—the weak hierarchical and institutional constraints at the higher (federal-provincial) level and the strong formal constraints at the lower (provincial-municipal) level—seem to have produced essentially similar outcomes. All roads may not lead to Rome, but they do seem to have led, albeit sometimes after a short wander in the wilderness, to realism and generally prudent fiscal behaviour. The extent to which this conclusion may be generalized beyond the Canadian case, however, is by no means obvious.

Indeed, it may be that if Canada has any lesson in this respect, it is that what matters most may be not the method by which hardness is sought but the setting (or, if one will, culture) within which it is sought. Canada was founded as a country dedicated not to "life, liberty, and the pursuit of happiness" but rather to "peace and good government."[39] The symbolic image of Canada's frontier past is not the cowboy wild and free, but the mounted policeman bringing order. Even on a personal level, Canadians—at least outside Québec—have sometimes been characterized as people who will stand at an empty intersection on a cold winter's day waiting for the light to turn green before they venture to cross the road.[40] More directly related to our present topic, Canadian local governments do not even use the borrowing room they have, and they appear to pride themselves on their restraint. In the circumstances, although no doubt the point can easily be overdone, almost any set of rules (or nonrules) might, in the end, have produced an acceptable outcome in Canada.

In any event, Canadian experience suggests that a complete analysis of government behavior should take into account not only the political and market forces usually discussed as factors shaping the outcome of decentralization but also the important role that may be played in some circumstances by what are essentially social norms and conventions about appropriate behavior, themselves largely shaped by perceptions of shared historical experience. Specifically, what seems needed are not simply well-developed markets that in effect deliver strong and generally accurate signals to governments about the sustainability of their fiscal behavior but also a political system that, admittedly with lags, responds to these signals and, over time, adjusts its behavior accordingly. McCarten (1999) plausibly argues that for a capital market–imposed hard budget constraint to work, four conditions are essential: (1) borrowers should not have access to any pooling, (2) lenders should have full information on borrowers, (3) there should be a credible no-bailout rule, and (4) borrowers should respond to signals. Essentially the story we have told with respect to Canada is that while neither rule 1 nor, formally, rule 3 applies with respect to either level of government, rules 2 and 4 very much apply—and they seem to do the job.

Democracy *plus* markets, at least in a cold climate, thus works to overcome a number of institutional features that on their face might seem conducive to flagrant fiscal misbehavior by provincial governments. In Canada's constitutional and political situation, budget rules, whether self-imposed (some provinces) or imposed from above (municipalities), can be effective only through the working of the same forces—and if those forces work, it is not clear that much is gained by legislating such rules. In terms of the framework set out earlier in this book, although subject to no hierarchical constraints, and although many elements of the institutional structure—such as majority-rule strong provincial parties independent of federal parties and the partial underwriting of provincial revenues by the federal government through the equalization and stabilization agreements—also seem conducive to a soft budget constraint, in fact Canadian provinces have generally acted as though subject to the right economic incentives at the margin.[41] Three reasons seem to underlie this result. First, despite the words quoted earlier from a federal minister of finance fifty years ago, it seems to be accepted that there will be no federal bailout. Second, credit markets clearly exert effective discipline on Canadian public sector borrowers. And third, generally prudent fiscal behavior has become an institutionalized norm in Canada, in part because fiscal profligacy, while hardly unknown in election years (Kneebone and McKenzie 1999), has not proven an effective long-run electoral strategy.

On the other hand, municipalities are subject to formally hard hierarchical budget constraints, in part because the institutional incentives to behave well are less strong. Although local governments are also subject to credit market discipline, creditors can reasonably expect to be bailed out by the province. Local citizens may have to bear the cost of such bailouts, but the nonpartisan weak mayor systems general in Canada mean that local institutional incentives to behave are weaker than at the provincial level. While the generally prudent behaviour—"borrowing in a cold climate"—of Canadian municipalities is striking, at some level since provincial control of municipal action means that the province is ultimately responsible, these hierarchical constraints are somewhat offset. All in all, it seems that the very different approaches followed in the two worlds of Canadian public led to a rather similar destination.

While similar factors clearly affect the federal government also, it may well be that, as Shah (1998) argues, in the end it is the relative softness of the budget constraint at the federal level that really lies at the root of any problems the subnational finance system in Canada may have. The federal government's ability to run deficits for over two decades after revenues turned down in the early 1970s (Bird, Perry, and Wilson 1998) in effect financed undue provincial (and, indirectly, local) expansion over this period. It was not until the federal government finally began to cut back on provincial support, starting in the mid-1980s, that provincial deficits began to rise, and once they did, the provinces on the whole acted more quickly to bring their budgets back into control than had the federal government. No government can run deficits forever, but the federal government can clearly do so longer than the provinces. In the end, however, the day of reckoning always comes, and so far at least, Canada's political system has proved sufficiently resilient to meet the bill.

Virtually every government in Canada is now either in surplus or close to balance, so the real question is whether Canadian governments at all levels, though especially the federal level, will prove any better at managing surpluses than they were in the past. At least two aspects of surpluses appear to deserve consideration in the context of hard budgets. The first is perhaps peculiar to Canada: whatever the federal government does must be seen in the context of the federal-provincial system. If Canada is to have a future, it needs to maintain not only a sustainable economic balance but also a sustainable political equilibrium. The best way in principle to achieve the latter may be not to cut federal taxes or federal debt but rather, as in the heyday of the expansionary 1960s, to raise provincial expenditures and hence at least potentially to cut provincial taxes and provincial debts. Unfortunately, no one ever won a federal election by solving provincial problems—or, of course, vice versa—so it seems unlikely that anything very sensible will be done in the near future to work out these matters in a truly national context.

The second point is more general. In principle, both taxes and expenditures at all levels of government should presumably be set to maximize social welfare. If fiscal policy is optimal in this sense, the result may be large or small fiscal surpluses in the short run (for tax-smoothing or cyclical purposes) or even in the long run (e.g., to finance intergenerational transfers). If a surplus arose in such circumstances, however, a rational government would presumably not first consider how to "spend" it, whether by expanding expenditure or by lowering taxes. Instead, attention should presumably first be focused on the very different question of how to "save" it—for example, by retiring debt or, more daringly, perhaps acquiring higher-yielding foreign or domestic assets. Careful consideration of the optimal portfolio would thus appear to be an essential ingredient in any strategy of how to deal with the fiscal surplus. Although the emerging fiscal surplus at the federal (and to a lesser extent the provincial) level is not optimal in this sense, it is nonetheless surprising that despite the intensive discussion of this question in the early 1990s when debt ratios were rising precipitously (Harris 1993), no government in Canada appears to be thinking along these lines.

Contrary to what some have argued (Buchanan and Wagner 1977), democratic governments, at least in Canada, appear better able to manage deficits—largely, we suggest, because markets make them do so—than they are to manage surpluses. This is by no means a minor problem, since mismanaged surpluses build up problems, for instance, through the creation of unsustainable expenditure programs, when times turn bad. Hard budget constraints, it may be suggested, should thus cut both ways, restraining governments in good times as in bad. As we have argued, the fiscal perils of decentralization, to the extent they become reality, have, at least in the case of Canada, generated market and political reactions that led to the correction of the initial errors.[42] Unfortunately, entry into the paradise of surpluses does not similarly set up countervailing forces, and errors seem more likely to be made.

All is not roses even in deficit-land, however, largely because of the inappropriate entanglement of provincial and, in the case of Ontario, even municipal governments in the cyclically sensitive issue of poverty relief.[43] Although federal assumption of primary responsibility for unemployment insurance and old age pensions (including the parallel federal-provincial Canada and Quebec Pension Plans) means that a repetition of the 1930s relief crisis is unlikely, provinces are still somewhat vulnerable because their revenues are cyclically sensitive (Devereux 1993) and they continue to have primary responsibility for other social assistance.

The effects on the revenue side are somewhat muted through the pooling that in effect takes place through the equalization and stabilization agreements. Until 1996, similar risk sharing occurred on the expenditure side through the Canada Assistance Plan—broadly, an open-ended conditional grant under which the federal government paid 50 percent of provincial social assistance costs. Under the new CHST system, however, this link between provincial social expenditures and federal transfers has been severed, thus increasing the cyclical fiscal risk faced by provinces. Canada's federal-provincial transfer system commendably clearly puts the marginal impact of expenditure and (to a lesser extent) revenue decisions on provincial shoulders, thus largely obviating the problems some appear to consider inherent with large transfer programs.[44] There is simply no evidence in Canada, for example, to support the common suggestion (Rodden 2002) that the more "transfer-dependent" provinces are, for that reason alone, more prone to behave badly—indeed, since such provinces are more likely to be economically vulnerable, the evidence is, on the contrary, that they are less likely to run up large debts for long periods of time (Kneebone and McKenzie 1999).

3.4   Conclusion

To sum up the principal lessons we derive from this brief examination of Canadian experience, there are essentially no administrative or formal political constraints on budgetary behaviour at the provincial level. While the obvious potential for soft budget constraints has certainly been tested, in Canada as in most other democracies, by the growth of contingent liabilities (Alexander and Emes 1998), the other two main channels through which undue softness may manifest itself—nondelivery of services and accrual of unsustainable capital market liabilities—have, to the extent they occurred, quickly engendered political and market forces leading to their correction. In effect, through the combination of the electoral process and strong markets, there is a moderately strong ex post Wicksellian linkage between revenues and expenditures at the provincial level in Canada.[45] This linkage is, of course, much stronger at the local level, where it is essentially imposed ex ante by provincial fiat. Nonetheless, experience suggests that despite these controls (or perhaps to some extent because of them), the ills usually attributed to unduly soft budget constraints seem, if anything, more likely to manifest themselves at the local level, with the likely remedy being even stronger ex post provincial rules. In the end, however, history plus democracy plus markets seems on the whole to have kept Canada's subnational governments, different though their paths may have been, more clearly on the path of fiscal prudence than the federal government.

In terms of the mechanisms discussed in the opening chapters of this book, Canadian provinces are fundamentally politically and administratively independent of the federal government but have fairly clear responsibilities, and, on the whole, despite the fact that some of them are fairly transfer dependent, face sensible marginal incentives in part because there are no provincial interests represented in the federal legislature and little room for logrolling. Canadian municipalities, on the other hand, are fundamentally dependent on provincial governments, and although their responsibilities too are fairly well defined, they are much more transfer dependent and, on the whole, face less sensible incentives at the margin, a situation countered to a large extent by the imposition of fairly strict hierarchical controls on their activities. The softness inherent in some aspects of the federal-provincial system—notably the importance of unconditional and equalization transfers—is largely vitiated by the interaction of capital market discipline with political institutions, which makes it difficult for provinces to shift either costs or deficits upward. The softness inherent in municipal dependence on the provinces is, on the other hand, largely offset by administrative controls. Coupled with the lessons of history inculcating generally prudent fiscal behavior at both levels of government, each of these very different systems seems to have worked fairly well, at least so far, in constraining subnational fiscal behaviour in Canada.

Appendix 3A: Fiscal Equalization

Fiscal equalization is mandated by section 36 (2) of the Canadian Constitution, which states that "Parliament and the Government of Canada are committed to the principle of making equalization payments to ensure that provincial governments have sufficient revenues to provide reasonably comparable levels of public services at reasonably comparable levels of taxation." Although this provision was added to the Constitution in 1982, an equalization program has actually been in place since 1957, when it was introduced as part of a realignment of taxing powers following the extreme centralization that had evolved during the war years.

In 1967, the equalization system took what is essentially its present form with the adoption of the so-called representative tax system (RTS) approach, originally developed by the U.S. Advisory Commission on Intergovernmental Relations but not in fact used in the United States. Under the RTS approach, the fiscal capacity of each province is calculated each year (by the federal Department of Finance) as the difference between the sum of its per capita fiscal capacity for each separate revenue source and a standard capacity measure based on the average per capita fiscal capacity of the "middle" five provinces (excluding oil-rich Alberta and the four small and poor eastern provinces). The system works as follows:

1. Define and quantify all revenues with respect to which capacity is to be measured. There are over thirty separate revenue sources for which this calculation is made.

2. Define a tax base for each revenue source that reflects the tax base typically used in practice. In some instances, as with the personal income tax, where the base is essentially uniform across the country, this task is simple. In others, as with respect to property taxes, it may be very difficult to define and calculate a credibly comparable tax base.

3. Calculate a notional national average tax rate for each revenue source as the ratio of actual taxes collected by all provinces for the total standardized tax base.

4. Apply this average tax rate for each source to the standardized base for each province to estimate that province's capacity for that source.

5. Add up all the separate calculations to derive an estimate of total revenue capacity for each province.

6. Divide this total estimate by the population of the province to obtain per capita revenue capacity.

7. Compare these capacity estimates with the five-province standard. If a province's per capita capacity is below the standard, it receives an equalization payment sufficient to bring it up to that standard, which, on average, means to over 90 percent of the national average per capita capacity.

Four important aspects of this equalization system deserve emphasis. First, no attempt is made to measure differences in expenditure needs. This has been considered several times but has been rejected largely on the grounds that the data required to measure such differences are not very reliable. Second, although provinces below "standard" capacity receive equalization transfers, provinces with above-standard capacity are not penalized: equalization is paid entirely from federal revenues. Third, in principle, the total amount paid is determined by the calculations described above. In practice, however, total equalization entitlements are limited to 1.2 percent of GDP, and this limit has on several occasions resulted in a scaled reduction in the equalization payments generated by the formula. Finally, while Canada's extensive experience with this system is generally considered a success and seems to be well accepted by most relevant actors in the political process, substantial technical criticisms have been made of various aspects of the system, and it is not impossible that various changes may be made in the future—for example, to incorporate expenditure needs, move from the RTS to some other basis of capacity calculation, include other federal transfers in the sources for which equalization is calculated, or reduce the extent to which the system biases provincial tax policy choices.

Appendix 3B: Federal-Provincial Stabilization Agreement

Since 1957, a formal stabilization provision has constituted an integral part of federal-provincial fiscal arrangements in Canada (Perry 1997). The system dates from 1967, when the RTS equalization system (see appendix 3A) was introduced. Essentially, the legislation provided that any province whose revenues (from the sources equalized under the formula, and at the previous year's rates) fell below the previous year's revenues would receive a compensating stabilization payment. Although various changes were made in this provision over the years, notably to limit payments with respect to declines in natural resource revenues, it was not until 1987 that any province actually claimed a payment.

   In that year, Alberta claimed $539 million to compensate it for the sharp decline in its natural resource revenues. After some dispute about the amount, this claim was finally settled in 1991. With the recession in the early 1990s, a number of other claims were filed (for example, by Ontario), and by 1995, the federal government had paid out another $1.2 billion in stabilization payments. Perhaps unsurprisingly, as part of its new tighter fiscal policy in 1995, the federal government announced that henceforth it would make such payments only when provincial revenues fell below 95 percent of the previous year's revenue—a limit that had been in force during the 1967–1972 period.

The main argument for the stabilization arrangement made by the federal government is essentially one of fairness: to provide a cushion for the provinces that do not receive equalization (such as Alberta and Ontario) that is roughly comparable to that inherent in the equalization formula for recipient provinces, whose equalization payments automatically increase under the formula if their revenues decline relative to the average. As Perry (1997, 171–72) notes, however, the stabilization agreement, by putting a floor under provincial revenues, in effect provides a "letter of comfort" to prospective creditors by signaling an underlying federal guarantee of provincial debt-servicing capacity.

Appendix 3C: Provincial Budget Rules

Since 1993, several provinces have enacted some form of budget rule (Millar 1997). Alberta led the way with a 1993 law requiring the elimination of the deficit by 1997, followed in 1995 with another law requiring balanced budgets and the elimination of the provincial net debt over the next fifteen years. Manitoba similarly legislated balanced budgets in 1995, with the unusual provision that the salaries of cabinet members would be reduced if this commitment was not kept. Completing the sweep of the prairie provinces, Saskatchewan in the same year passed a somewhat milder Balanced Budget Act, which required a four-year balanced fiscal plan.

On the east coast, New Brunswick since 1993 has had the stated objective of balancing its operating budget, while Nova Scotia in 1994 established expenditure reduction targets and then in 1996 required budget appropriations not to exceed forecast revenues and actual expenditures not to exceed appropriations by more than 1 percent for any year. Finally, Québec legislated deficit reduction targets for the 1996–1999 period, with the budget to be balanced thereafter.

Four observations may be made about these laws. First, they clearly represent one component in the adjustment process discussed in the chapter. That is, these budget rules are perhaps better seen as symptoms of (or a response to) changing public preferences rather than as independent factors in themselves. Second, this interpretation is supported by the evidence that the adoption of such rules did not noticeably affect budgetary behavior (Millar 1997). Third, these rules are, by the standards found in other jurisdictions, such as New Zealand and the United States, quite mild. Some of them refer to "plans", "objectives", and "forecasts." Others have multiyear targets. Apart from Manitoba, none really has any penalties for breaches. Moreover, all the provincial budget rules make ample provision for "contingencies" and "unforeseen circumstances" to soften their application. Finally, and in many ways most important, these laws are simply laws and can be altered and abolished at any time. This last point is important. Canadian provinces do not have constitutions. No provincial legislature can formally bind any future provincial legislature. Budget rules such as those described above thus at most reflect either the ideology of the party in power or a response to perceived public pressure. The government that passes such rules may to some extent feel morally or politically bound by them, but no successor government is likely to be similarly constrained.

Appendix 3D: Ontario Muncipal Structure

Ontario's 10 million people live in over 540 municipalities, which vary significantly in population, responsibilities, administrative resources, and ability to raise revenue. The large number of small, sparsely populated municipalities contrasts sharply with a few very large municipalities, with the vast majority of the population concentrated in the area surrounding Toronto. Almost 75 percent of all lower-tier (local) municipalities in Ontario have fewer than 5,000 people and only 2 percent have populations of more than 100,000. Differences in resource endowments, access to transportation and markets, and balanced development versus single industry dependence are reflected in a variety of municipal structures to deliver services of a local nature, as well as those mandated by the provincial government. For example, in northern Ontario, with the exception of Sudbury, single-tier municipalities provide local services. Across southern Ontario, two levels exist with the exception of some twenty-three "separated cities and towns," which are not part of any upper-tier municipal structure. Rural areas in the south are organized in the county system, and urban areas are organized in the regional system.

The two-tier structure used to reorganize the municipalities in Toronto in 1954 became the model for the reorganization of municipalities elsewhere during the 1970s. The reorganization was a response to pressures to create entities fiscally strong enough to finance the infrastructure costs associated with rapid urban growth and large enough to enable services to be planned effectively and delivered efficiently.

Regions, counties, and (until recently) Metropolitan Toronto are termed upper-tier governments, while their constituent municipalities are generally known as lower-tier or area municipalities. Not all upper-tier municipalities have the same powers. Regional councils have considerable authority in such areas as policing, health services, social services, solid waste disposal, capital borrowing, and sewer and water treatment. Lower-tier municipalities tend to have responsibility for fire protection, recreation, municipal hydro services, public transit, tax collection, libraries, and licensing. Both levels share responsibility for such services as roads, planning, sewer and water services, and economic development.

The county structure has existed in Ontario since 1849. The powers potentially available to county governments are more limited than those of regions, and the powers that counties normally exercise are even more limited. County councils have responsibility for county roads, homes for the aged, and welfare. Counties also have the authority to provide policing, public utilities, parking, sewer and water services, and transit (although no county does). In some counties, some welfare is administered by lower-tier municipalities.

Other agencies and boards provide certain local services and draw on the local tax base for partial funding. In addition to school boards, of which there are now 168, such agencies include Childrens' Aid Societies, District Social Service and Homes for the Aged Boards in the North, and Conservation Authorities in southern Ontario.

In many ways, perhaps the most salient fact about local government structure in Ontario is that all relevant aspects of it are decided, virtually unilaterally, by the provincial government. The recent imposition of a so-called megacity (unified) structure in the Metropolitan Toronto area provides a clear instance. The change reflected more the vagaries of provincial politics than any considered economic or political restructuring of the metropolitan area. Indeed, prior to the imposition of the unified structure, two careful and detailed studies had recommended not the abolition of the lower-tier governments within Metropolitan Toronto but rather the elimination of Metropolitan Toronto (and the surrounding regional governments) and the creation of a new "Greater Toronto Authority," which would play much the same role in relation to the continuing municipal governments in an expanded territory as the Metropolitan government had originally played in its narrower geographical territory (Slack 1991). In Canada, what the province wants with respect to local government the province gets, whether the issue is boundary adjustments, expenditure functions, revenue authority, or borrowing limitations.

Acknowledgments

We are grateful to François Vaillancourt and Jonathan Rodden for helpful comments on an earlier draft. The views expressed here are entirely our personal responsibility, however.

Notes

1. Another case in which historical factors seem critical in explaining fiscal outcomes would appear to be Colombia, long an outlier in Latin America in terms of fiscally prudent behavior (Dillinger and Webb 1999b).

2. There are also now three territorial governments in the Arctic region. These areas, which are very sparsely populated and depend heavily on federal transfers, differ in many ways from the provinces (Slack 1991). They are not further discussed here.

3. The recent evolution of the sales tax system is discussed in Bird and Gendron (1998).

4. Indeed, it could even have been used to finance a tax reduction, although in Canada, as in every other country, what evidence there is demonstrates that the last thing most governments that receive transfers do is to reduce taxes—an illustration of what has been called the "flypaper effect": money sticks where it hits.

5. For a detailed analysis of the factors leading to provincial deficits over this period, see Kneebone and McKenzie (1999).

6. There has been extensive discussion in Canada about the legitimacy of this use of what is called the federal "spending power," but it clearly exists (Watts 1999).

7. Colomer (1999) suggests that an upper chamber facilitates intergovernmental cooperation only if it both has power and represents different parties from those that dominate the lower chamber. Neither condition holds in Canada.

8. In the last federal election, for example, the Liberals won all but one seat in the three Maritime Provinces. At the time, Liberal governments ruled in all these provinces. Now, all three have Conservative governments—indeed, in 2001 the Liberals were in power in only one province in the country, Newfoundland. An interesting question is whether provinces gain or lose if they are controlled by the same party as the federal government. The proposition can be argued both ways. The federal government may be nicer to its political friends than its enemies; as we note later, this is basically the argument of Boothe (1995) with respect to Alberta's 1936 default. Alternatively, as the neighboring province of Saskatchewan has often demonstrated, it may be argued that knowing that you have to be self-reliant—that you do not have a friend in Ottawa—may lead to more fiscally innovative and responsible policies. And, finally, as Québec has long known and shown, you can also sometimes do quite well out of being an enemy.

9. After many transmutations, this railway was indeed finally bailed out (by the federal government)—in 1920!

10. In this instance, there appears to be clear evidence of opportunistic behavior in that some local decision makers seem to have made deliberately imprudent infrastructure investment decisions precisely in order to go bankrupt and force an amalgamation with the larger neighboring tax base, thus shifting costs and preserving the value of their properties (Poitras 1999).

11. As Feldstein (1975) argues, matching grants, unless adjusted for "wealth" (tax base), invariably disadvantage poor areas.

12. In so acting, the federal government exercised a power granted it in the 1867 constitution for what turned out to be the last time in Canadian history. This power is now generally considered to be dormant, if not dead.

13. Such rulings were made by both the Supreme Court of Canada and the Judicial Committee of the Privy Council in London, which was, until 1982, the court of last resort on Canadian constitutional matters.

14. Saskatchewan was funded by the federal government's purchase, at favorable rates, of provincial treasury bills, the interest on which was paid by further issues of bills.

15. Some might consider this a federalist interpretation of events. In an interesting recent example of continuing "Western alienation," Boothe (1995) presents the 1945–1946 debt reorganization as an entirely provincial initiative, emphasizes the strong provincial efforts to reduce debt and raise revenues, and notes the federal payments in terms that make it clear they were less than Alberta was "owed." It is not surprising that his final words on the matter were that "Ottawa did not use its financial resources to prevent the province's default in 1936, although Saskatchewan, in a similar position, was rescued by federal aid" (109). This interpretation seems questionable. As Perry (1997, 19) points out, the two provinces were not really in a similar position because Alberta's problems were due more to the debt load it had accumulated in earlier years than to the relief payments that drove Saskatchewan into crisis. On the other hand, a recent study has suggested that the newly created Bank of Canada and the federal Ministry of Finance felt it was better to isolate Alberta and allow it to default in order to destroy the credibility of the Alberta administration and its "peculiar" ideas on debt relief and macroeconomic policy (Ascah 1998). A full comparative analysis of the situation of the two provinces in the 1930s may be found in Bates (1939).

16. Incidentally, the 1947 discovery of substantial oil and gas reserves in Alberta changed the fiscal base of that province from one of the weakest in the country to by far the strongest. One way or another, Alberta has always been the principal outlier in the Canadian fiscal scene.

17. See the detailed analysis by province in Kneebone and McKenzie (1999). As these authors show, ideological and electoral factors clearly affected the nature of fiscal adjustment—with, for example, more "left" governments being less inclined to cut expenditures than to raise taxes—but the clearest predictor of the strength and timing of the adjustment was the prior debt position, which largely reflected the strength of the regional economy relative to the national economy.

18. Such rules may perhaps make it more costly for future governments to breach them if, for example, doing so were to increase market perception of risk. As yet, however, the evidence does not suggest there has been any such effect (Millar 1997). These rules may also make it bit more difficult for future governments to follow an expansionary path, although again the evidence on this is not strong. British Columbia, for example, passed a so-called Taxpayer Protection Act in 1991 imposing both a spending limit (linked to

past GDP growth) and a five-year balanced budget requirement. This act was repealed the next year by a newly elected government.

19. Bruce (1995) adds the neat twist that the ease of interprovincial migration makes it easy for provinces to, as it were, "off-load" their debt burdens with a bit of a lag, although he offers no empirical evidence that any such effect is indeed perceptible. This proposition would appear to be testable, particularly in view of the much lower migration probability of the largely French-speaking population of Québec.

20. A more important problem in some ways for many years was the fact that, in effect, the payroll tax funding nominally collected to finance the Canada Pension Plan was used (on a derivation basis) to support provincial borrowing at favorable rates. As Perry (1989, 465) notes, "When the CPP appeared to be running out of money rather than call in some of the provincial borrowings revenues were increased by raising the contribution rates." This system has now been changed, however. While CPP funds may still be invested—now by an "independent" advisory board—in provincial securities, the provinces no longer have a captive market and will no longer be able to borrow at less than full market rates.

21. As Amborski (1998) notes, this liberalization has occurred even though the preexisting restrictions on local borrowing do not seem to have been perceived by municipal governments as unduly restrictive. We shall discuss this question further.

22. Although primary and secondary education is delivered at the local level in Canada, it is the responsibility not of municipal governments but of separately elected school boards. In most provinces, these boards may impose a tax on real property, which is collected for them by municipal governments, which have no role in determining the education rate. In Ontario and some other provinces, the provincial government in recent years has become the main player in both financing and controlling education. For further discussion of the complex system of education finance, see Auld and Kitchen (1995).

23. Much of the material in this section is taken from Tassonyi (1994, 1997).

24. Other important defaults occurred in the suburbs around cities such as Winnipeg, Montreal, and Vancouver that had expanded rapidly in the 1920s. Even Montreal itself defaulted in 1940, and its financial administration was taken over by the provincial government until 1944 (Dagenais 1992).

25. There had been earlier bodies such as the Ontario Railway and Municipal Board and the Bureau of Municipal Affairs with similar powers, but they were largely toothless.

26. Borrowing was limited to 70 percent of estimated revenues. The limit had previously been 80 percent for municipalities with populations greater than 100,000 and 90 percent for the others with no approval being required. No distinction was drawn between capital and short-term borrowing.

27. In consequence, municipalities have only very limited input into the process of assessment reform as inequities in the base arise.

28. In addition, at least in the case of Ontario, where only lower-tier municipal governments impose property taxes but where they must also impose such taxes on behalf not only of school boards but also of upper-tier (regional) governments, the "Wicksellian connection" (Breton 1996) between local responsibility for taxes and for expenditures is largely breached (Locke and Tassonyi 1993, Tassonyi and Locke 1993).

29. Although some provinces (e.g., Alberta and Ontario) have in recent years increasingly encroached on the property tax base, largely as part of the ongoing reform of educational finance, it might be argued that this may actually make it easier for municipal governments to raise their own property taxes as a result of the reduction in interlocal tax competition owing to the provincialization of education finance. This theme cannot be further explored here.

30. "Most provincial-municipal grants in Canada are conditional, closed-ended, matching grants that do not seem appropriate for achieving either allocative efficiency or fiscal equity. Provincial-municipal transfers in Canada thus appear to be designed to allow provincial governments to maintain a fair amount of control over the expenditure and taxing decisions of local governments while appearing to let local governments provide their own services. In effect, local governments in Canada, to a considerable extent, are really acting as agents, spending provincial funds on provincially designated activities" (Bird and Slack 1993, 138).

31. As part of a property tax reform, the 1998 limit was changed to 35 percent for the last quarter of the year and the 1999 limit was raised to 60 percent to deal with cash flow smoothing.

32. Gilbert and Pike (1999) demonstrate that such pooling may lower servicing costs.

33. Long-term agreements of an operating nature, involving a commitment of funds beyond the life of a council, also required OMB approval, although the present values of such agreements did not form part of the quota and limit calculation. These detailed reporting requirements contrast sharply with the situation at both the federal and provincial levels (Alexander and Emes 1998).

34. In Ontario, for example, Locke and Tassonyi (1993) and Tassonyi and Locke (1993) demonstrated the pressure on mill rate decisions created by the sharing of the tax base with school boards and various special-purpose bodies, while Kitchen and Slack (1993) suggested that the pressure to fund soft services reduced municipal expenditures on hard (infrastructure) services.

35. The previous OMB formula limited annual payments relating to debt and financial obligations to exceed 20 percent of revenue fund expenditures. Two significant limitations of this measure can be identified. First, the measure did not recognize that not all revenues are necessarily within a municipality's control. Provincial conditional grants, for example, are not available to meet the exigencies of debt service. Furthermore, an increase in expenditures automatically reduces the ratio of debt charges as a portion of the expenditures and consequently enhances the debt capacity measure. To emphasize the point, if social assistance expenses rise, debt capacity is improved in spite of the fact that it is likely that the own-source revenue base of the municipality may have been weakened. The change (in fiscal year 1995) to 25 percent of own-source revenues in part dealt with the first of these problems. In addition, however, in effect it reduced the limit for municipalities that rely on provincial grants for a relatively large portion of their annual revenues. The regions and larger cities, which do most of the borrowing, are not similarly constrained, however.

36. They may also borrow on behalf of school boards. As noted earlier, school board finance is an important factor in Canadian local finance but cannot be discussed in detail here.

37. The two large Alberta cities, Calgary and Edmonton, are granted special provisions: total indebtedness permissible is twice the municipal revenue, and the limit for debt service is 35 percent of revenues.

38. Incidentally, provinces do not welcome direct federal relations with local governments, as the federal government found out in the early 1970s when it attempted to establish a federal department of urban affairs and was soon told, in effect, to cease and desist from interfering in provincial business. It did.

39. The first quoted phrase comes from the American Declaration of Independence; the second phrase comes from a key section of Canada's 1867 Constitution.

40. That this statement, to the extent it conveys a truth, is much more applicable outside Québec is an interesting comment on the reality of the *deux nations* nature of Canada.

41. The more detailed study in Kneebone and McKenzie (1999) is consistent with the arguments here.

42. A somewhat similar point is made more generally by Haggard (1999).

43. All serious analyses of provincial-municipal finances in Ontario have concluded that the full financial responsibility for social assistance should be placed at the provincial level: see, for example, Ontario Ministry of Community and Social Services (1988). Nonetheless, the most recent reallocation of functions and finances continues, inappropriately, to place significant fiscal responsibility for these cyclically sensitive outlays on the decidedly nonsensitive local tax base (Slack 1997).

44. Contrary to McKinnon (1997), we would argue that the "Wicksellian connection" (Breton 1996) remains largely intact at the margin for provincial governments and since decisions are made at the margin, that is what matters. (Incidentally, we decidedly do not agree with the sweeping assertion of Dillinger, Perry, and Webb 1999 that when it comes to transfer programs, "marginal" can be considered equal to "average"—at least not in the case of Canada.)

45. Although we have not spelled out the role of land markets in this chapter, even a cursory view of Canadian fiscal history (Perry 1955, Gillespie 1991) demonstrates clearly the extreme sensitivity of Canadians—and hence of Canadian politicians at all levels—to changing land and natural resource prices. Contrary to U.S. experience (Inman 1999), the major consequences have tended to be not on location within metropolitan areas—although there have clearly been some such effects, they have been considerably muted by the overriding role of the provinces in shaping municipal finances (Bird and Slack 1993)—but rather at the provincial level, owing to the great importance of natural resource revenues in provincial finances. It is this factor, for example, that lies behind the earlier reference to Alberta's outlier status in Canada, as well as behind the characteristic Canadian obsession with the effects of fiscal differentials on interprovincial migration (Day and Winer 1991, Boadway and Flatters 1992). But further development of these points would demand another publication.

References

Ahmad, Junaid. 1999. "Decentralizing Borrowing Powers." In Jennie Litvack and Jessica Seddon, eds., *Decentralization Briefing Notes*. Washington, D.C.: World Bank Institute.

Alexander, Jared, and Joel Emes. 1998. *Canadian Government Debt*. Vancouver: Fraser Institute.

Amborski, David. 1998. *Review of the Regulatory Environment of Municipal Capital Borrowing*. Toronto: ICURR Press.

Ascah, Robert L. 1998. *Politics and Public Debt: The Dominion the Banks and Alberta's Social Credit*. Edmonton: University of Alberta Press.

Auld, Douglas, and Harry Kitchen. 1995. *Financing Education and Training in Canada*. Toronto: Canadian Tax Foundation.

Bates, Stewart. 1939. *Financial History of Canadian Governments*. A Study for the Royal Commission on Dominion-Provincial Relations. Ottawa.

Bird, Richard M. 1987. "Federal-Provincial Transfers in Canada: Retrospect and Prospect." *Canadian Tax Journal* 35:118–133.

Bird, Richard M. 1993. "Federal-Provincial Taxation in Turbulent Times." *Canadian Public Administration* 36:479–496.

Bird, Richard M. 1999a. "Intergovernmental Fiscal Relations in Latin America: Policy Design and Policy Outcomes." Inter-American Development Bank, Washington, D.C.

Bird, Richard M. 1999b. "Rethinking Tax Assignment: New Directions for Subnational Taxes." International Monetary Fund, Washington, D.C.

Bird, Richard M., and Duanjie Chen. 1998. "Federal Finance and Fiscal Federalism: The Two Worlds of Canadian Public Finance." *Canadian Public Administration* 41:51–74.

Bird, Richard M., and Pierre-Pascal Gendron. 1998. "Dual VATs and Cross-Border Trade: Two Problems, One Solution?" *International Tax and Public Finance* 5:429–442.

Bird, Richard M., David Perry, and Thomas A. Wilson. 1998. "Canada." In Ken Messere, ed., *The Tax System in Industrialized Countries*. Oxford: Oxford University Press.

Bird, Richard M., and Enid Slack. 1993. *Urban Public Finance in Canada*. 2nd ed. Toronto: Wiley.

Boothe, Paul. 1993. "Provincial Government Debt, Bond Ratings and the Availability of Credit." In Richard G. Harris, ed., *Deficits and Debt in the Canadian Economy*. Kingston: John Deutsch Institute for the Study of Economic Policy, 40–47.

Boothe, Paul. 1995. *The Growth of Government Spending in Alberta*. Toronto: Canadian Tax Foundation.

Boothe, Paul, and B. Johnston. 1993. *Stealing the Emperor's Clothes: Deficit Off-Loading and National Standards in Health Care*. Toronto: C.D. Howe Institute.

Bradshaw, T. 1935. "Maintenance of Public Credit." *Canadian Chartered Accountant*, Feb. 119–133.

Breton, Albert. 1996. *Competitive Governments*. Cambridge: Cambridge University Press.

Brittain, H. L. 1934. "Why Municipalities Go Wrong." *Canadian Chartered Accountant*, Nov. 387–392.

Bruce, Neil. 1993. "Provincial Budget Deficits and the Debt Crisis in Canada: Comments." In Richard G. Harris, ed., *Deficits and Debt in the Canadian Economy*. Kingston: John Deutsch Institute for the Study of Economic Policy, 85–96.

Bruce, Neil. 1995. "A Fiscal Federalism Analysis of Debt Policies by Sovereign Regional Governments." *Canadian Journal of Economics* 28:S195–S206.

Buchanan, James M., and Richard E. Wagner. 1977. *Democracy in Deficit*. New York: Academic Press.

Buck, A. E. 1949. *Financing Canadian Government*. Chicago: Public Administration Service.

Carlos, Ann M., and Frank D. Lewis. 1995. "The Creative Financing of an Unprofitable Enterprise: The Grand Trunk Railway of Canada, 1853–1881." *Explorations in Economic History* 32:273–301.

Colomer, Josep M. 1999. "Comment: Political Conditions of an Efficient Decentralization." Paper prepared for Annual World Bank Conference on Development in Latin America and the Caribbean, Valdivia, Chile, June.

Commission to Enquire into the Handling of the Unemployment Relief Fund in the Township of York. Toronto, King's Printer, 1933.

Dagenais, M. 1992. "Une bureaucratie en voie de formation: L'administration municipale de Montréal dans la première moitie du XXe siecle." *Revue d'histoire de l'Amerique française* 46:177–205.

Devereux, Michael B. 1993. Provincial Budget Deficits and the Debt Crisis in Canada." In Richard G. Harris, ed., *Deficits and Debt in the Canadian Economy*. Kingston: John Deutsch Institute for the Study of Economic Policy Harris, 59–84.

Dillinger, William, Guillermo Perry, and Steve B. Webb. 1999. "Macroeconomic Management in Decentralized Democracies." Paper prepared for Annual World Bank Conference on Development in Latin America and the Caribbean, Valdivia, Chile, June.

Dillinger, William, and Steve Webb. 1999a. "Fiscal Management in Federal Democracies: Argentina and Brazil." Washington, D.C.: World Bank.

Dillinger, William, and Steve Webb. 1999b. "Decentralization and Fiscal Management in Colombia." Washington, D.C.: World Bank.

Feldstein, Martin. 1975. "Wealth Neutrality and Local Choice in Public Education." *American Economic Review* 65:75–89.

Forbes, Ernest R. 1993. "Cutting the Pie into Smaller Pieces: Matching Grants and Relief in the Maritime Provinces During the 1930s." In Kris Inwood, ed., *Farm, Factory and Fortune: New Studies in the Economic History of the Maritime Provinces*. Fredericton: Acadiensis Press.

Gilbert, Mark, and Richard Pike. 1999. "Financing Local Government Debt in Canada: Pooled versus Stand-alone Issues—An Empirical Study." *Canadian Public Administration* 42:529–552.

Gillespie, W. Irwin. 1991. *Tax, Borrow and Spend: Financing Federal Spending in Canada 1867–1990*. Ottawa: Carleton University Press.

Haggard, Stephan. 1999. "The Politics of Decentralization in Latin America." Paper prepared for Annual World Bank Conference on Development in Latin America and the Caribbean, Valdivia, Chile, June.

Harris, Richard G., ed. 1993. *Deficits and Debt in the Canadian Economy*. Kingston: John Deutsch Insitute for the Study of Economic Policy.

Hettich, Walter, and Stanley L. Winer. 1999. *Democratic Choice and Taxation*. Cambridge: Cambridge University Press.

Inman, Robert P. 1999. "Local Fiscal Discipline in U.S. Federalism." Washington, D.C.: World Bank.

Kitchen, Harry M. 1984. *Local Government Finance in Canada*. Toronto: Canadian Tax Foundation.

Kitchen, Harry M., and Enid Slack. 1993. "Business Tax Reform." Government and Competitiveness discussion paper, School of Policy Studies, Queen's University, Kingston.

Kneebone, Ronald, and Kenneth McKenzie. 1999. *Past (In)Discretions: Canadian Federal and Provincial Fiscal Policy*. Toronto: University of Toronto Centre for Public Management.

Kulisek, L., and T. Price. 1988. "Ontario Municipal Policy Affecting Local Autonomy: A Case Study Involving Windsor and Toronto." *Urban History Review* 16:255–270.

Locke, Wade, and Almos Tassonyi. 1993. "Shared Tax Bases and Local Public Expenditure Decisions." *Canadian Tax Journal* 41:941–957.

McCarten, W. J. 1999 "Issues in Subnational Debt Control: International Evidence in Light of India's Needs—A Survey." Washington, D.C.: World Bank.

McKinnon, Ronald I. 1997. "Market-Preserving Fiscal Federalism in the American Monetary Union." In Mario I. Blejer and Teresa Ter-Minassian, eds., *Macroeconomic Dimensions of Public Finance* London: Routledge.

McPherson, L. G. 1935. "Some Aspects of the Municipal Problem." *Canadian Chartered Accountant*, May 325–392.

Millar, Jonathan. 1997. "The Effects of Budget Rules on Fiscal Performance and Macroeconomic Stabilization." Working paper 97–15, Bank of Canada, Ottawa.

Municipality of Metropolitan Toronto. 1989. *The Crumbling Financial Partnership: Metropolitan Toronto's Response to Provincial Retrenchment*, Toronto.

Ontario. 1939. *Budget Address Delivered by the Hon. Mitchell F. Hepburn*. Toronto: Queen's Printer.

Ontario. 1989. *Ontario Budget 1989*. Toronto: Queen's Printer.

Ontario Ministry of Community and Social Services. 1988. *Transitions: Report of the Social Assistance Review Committee*. Toronto: Queen's Printer.

Perry, David B. 1997. *Financing the Canadian Federation, 1867 to 1995*. Toronto: Canadian Tax Foundation.

Perry, J. Harvey. 1955. *Taxes, Tariffs and Subsidies: A History of Canadian Fiscal Development*. Toronto: University of Toronto Press.

Perry, J. Harvey. 1989. *A Fiscal History of Canada—The Postwar Years*. Toronto: Canadian Tax Foundation.

Piva, Michael J. 1992. *The Borrowing Process: Public Finance in the Province of Canada, 1840–1867*. Ottawa: University of Ottawa Press.

Poitras, Claire. 1999. "Construire les infrastructures d'approvisionment en eau en banlieue montrealaise au tournant du Xxe siecle: le cas de Saint-Louis." *Revue d'histoire de l'Amerique française*, 52:507–532.

Prud'homme, Remy. 1995. "The Dangers of Decentralization." *World Bank Research Observer* 10:201–220.

Rodden, Jonathan. 2002. "The Dilemma of Fiscal Federalism: Grants and Fiscal Performance Around the World." *American Journal of Political Science* 46(3):670–687.

Rowell-Sirois. 1938. *Report of Royal Commission on Dominion-Provincial Relations.* Ottawa: King's Printer.

Royal Commission on Border Cities Amalgamation. 1935. Toronto: King's Printer.

Shah, Anwar. 1998. "Fiscal Federalism and Macroeconomic Governance: For Better or Worse?" Washington, D.C.: World Bank.

Simeon, Richard. 1972. *Federal-Provincial Diplomacy.* Toronto: University of Toronto Press.

Slack, Enid. 1991. "Yukon and the Northwest Territories." In Melville McMillan, ed., *Provincial Public Finances: Provincial Surveys,* vol. 1. Toronto: Canadian Tax Foundation.

Slack, Enid. 1996. "Financing Infrastructure: Evaluation of Existing Research and Information Gaps." Report prepared for Canada Mortgage and Housing Corporation, Apr.

Slack, Enid. 1997. "The Harris Government and Municipalities: Who Does What and Who Pays for It?" Paper presented to the Centre for Study of State and Market, University of Toronto, Oct.

Slack, Enid, and Richard M. Bird. 1991. "Financing Urban Growth Through Development Charges." *Canadian Tax Journal* 39:1288–1304.

Struthers, J. 1991. "How Much Is Enough? Creating a Social Minimum in Ontario, 1930–1944," *Canadian Historical Review* 52:39–83.

Tanzi, Vito. 1996. "Fiscal Federalism and Decentralization: A Review of Some Efficiency and Macroeconomic Aspects." In Michael Bruno and Boris Pleskovic, eds., *Annual World Bank Conference on Development Economics.* Washington D.C.: World Bank.

Tassonyi, Almos. 1994. "Debt Limits and Supervision: An Issue in Provincial-Municipal Relationships in Times of Fiscal Crisis—A Comparison of the 1930s and the 1990s." Government and Competitiveness discussion paper, School of Policy Studies, Queen's University, Kingston.

Tassonyi, Almos. 1997. "Financing Municipal Infrastructure in Canada's City-Regions." In Paul A. R. Hobson and France St.-Hilaire, eds., *Urban Governance and Finance: A Question of Who Does What.* Montreal: IRPP, 171–205.

Tassonyi, Almos, and Wade Locke. 1993. "Accountability, Special Purpose Bodies and Local Public Expenditures." Paper presented at the Canadian Economics Association, Ottawa.

Taylor, John B. 1991. "Urban Autonomy in Canada: Its Evolution and Decline." In Gilbert A. Stelter and Alan F. J. Artibise, eds., *The Canadian City.* Ottawa: Carleton University Press, 478–500.

Ter-Minassian, Teresa. 1996. "Borrowing by Subnational Governments: Issues and Selected International Experiences." IMF Paper on Policy Analysis and Assessment PPAA/96/4, Washington, D.C.

Watts, Ronald. 1996. *Comparing Federal Systems in the 1990s*. Kingston: Institute of Inter-governmental Relations, Queen's University.

Watts, Ronald. 1999. *The Spending Power in Federal Systems: A Comparative Study*. Kingston: Institute of Intergovernmental Relations, Queen's University.

4   Vertical Imbalance and Fiscal Behavior in a Welfare State: Norway

Jørn Rattsø

In the unitary Scandinavian welfare states, central governments are in control of all public finances. Decentralized government is designed from the center, and local and county governments are an integrated part of the general public sector. They are an important part, however, since they provide the main public welfare services (schooling and health care). The design is better described as delegation rather than decentralization and can be called administrative federalism. Local and county governments are primarily agents of the central government. They have their own political systems based on elections to local and county councils, but the model allows little room for local democracy and accountability. As we will see, the local public sector certainly represents a challenge for central government control, but more in terms of broad spending pressure and cost control than strategic behavior.

Interestingly, the central government is vulnerable in this centralized environment. A major objective of the welfare state is to provide uniform welfare services across the country. Decentralized governments can exploit the national political concern for access to and the quality of the welfare services they provide. Centralized financing, mandating, and detailed service regulation combined with balanced budget requirement and loan controls impose fiscal discipline on the system.

The background of the challenge to central government control is the double common pool problem created by the redistributive welfare services and the vertical fiscal imbalance. The costs of the welfare services are not internalized at the individual level or the local government level, and spending pressure toward the center results. Local politics in this setting is about channeling individual demands for welfare services into local government demands for central government funds. Opportunistic behavior from individual local governments to exploit the weakness of the central government is not observed on a broad basis. The hierarchical controls and close oversight by the central government limit local fiscal imbalances and distorted service production and thereby any room for strategic behavior. In addition, given the availability of public information about economic conditions and performance, it is hard for any locality to break out of the pack. At the same time, centralized financing and control precludes any disciplining role for credit markets. Land and housing markets reflect regional imbalances in labor markets and are not seen as responsive to local public performance.

The key question of fiscal discipline is the functioning of the political system. Since the pressure is on the central government, national politicians must act loyal to the system to have it work. Politics can undermine the designed system of administrative delegation. Internalizing the costs of the welfare state is hard with the spending pressure resulting from the common pool problem (Weingast, Shepsle, and Johnsen 1981). This is certainly true under proportional regional representation, fragmented parliament, and minority and coalition governments. The parties, although many and weak, seem to have been able to collect their representatives to a national policy. Regional coalitions across party lines are seldom seen. The cooperation between the parties is the problem and the lack of ability to form stable majority coalitions. The strength of government is an important concept in this situation.

Overall fiscal imbalances have been avoided in both central and local governments. But other aspects of the performance are of concern. The local public sector has been the main growth sector of the economy (together with oil) and has taken an increasing share of the income and the labor force. The lack of local accountability in the system reduces the pressure to hold down costs and restructure services to changing demand. Productivity growth is slow, and competition and privatization in the service production are limited. These structural problems are the essence of the academic and public debate about the crisis of the welfare state.

Our broad evaluation is that the resulting budget constraints in general are hard and that individual strategic and distorted behavior from municipalities and counties, while present, is not important in practice. Moral hazard problems are more likely within local governments, where strong internal and external interest groups can take advantage of a weak local political system. Central regulations help keep the local budget constraints hard.

This chapter discusses the broader experiences with vertical fiscal imbalance in the welfare state. A broad outline of the Scandinavian type of administrative federalism is given in section 4.1, and the rest of the chapter concentrates on Norway. Hierarchical and political mechanisms of control are addressed in sections 4.2 and 4.3, and their consequences for fiscal balance are delineated in section 4.4. Section 4.5 discusses experiences of bailout and strategic behavior. The concluding section contemplates reform.

4.1   Scandinavian-Style Administrative Federalism

The understanding of decentralized government in the Musgrave-Oates-Tiebout tradition assumes local public goods, mobility, and benefit taxation. This model is far from the Scandinavian approach to fiscal federalism. First, the local public sector is responsible for welfare services with strong redistributive characteristics, and local public goods take only a small share of local spending. Second, mobility of the population is low and local jurisdictions are heterogeneous with respect to preferences for welfare services and local public goods. Third, financing is centralized and dominated by central government grants and regulated income tax revenue sharing. When local governments are agents rather than clubs, the working of the local public sector is very different from the standard theory model. Borge and Rattsø (1998) and Lotz (1998) express the frustration among Scandinavian economists that the guidelines from local public finance theory are of so limited relevance. Rattsø (2002) provides a discussion of Europe-U.S. differences in fiscal controls based on this perspective.

In particular, local public sector provision of welfare services raises new issues of decision making and distribution. The literature does not offer clear criteria for the handling of such "merit goods" (Musgrave 1959) or "redistributive services" (Foster, Jackman, and Perlmar 1980). A basic objective of the Scandinavian welfare states is to arrange equality and standardization of welfare services across the country, and national politicians are held accountable for its performance. Decentralization of the welfare state is consequently puzzling. This delegation must first be understood as a way to avoid an overburdened national bureaucracy. But the local public sector can also help adjust welfare services to local conditions. Redistributive welfare services have local characteristics that make local political choice important. The choice of school structure (size and location) is a case in point. Local and county governments may have informational advantages of preferences and costs and can better take into account local characteristics.

Decentralized government in the Scandinavian countries increased its importance in the economy with the expansion of the welfare state after World War II. Local and county governments now provide about two-thirds of all government service production—around 15 to 20 percent of GDP. Most of this spending is mandated and relates to welfare services, such as schools, primary health care and hospitals, and care for the elderly. The local public sector also provides more typical local public goods, such as infrastructure and planning.

While welfare spending is decentralized, the financing is strongly centralized. Centralized financing represents partly the instruments of macroeconomic control and partly the desire to equalize the provision of welfare services. Welfare services are to be distributed independent of the economic conditions of the households and the localities involved. Centralized financing also is the result of inadequate tax bases for local taxation. Property taxes and user charges barely account for the financing needed to cover 15 to 20 percent of GDP, and income tax revenue sharing adds necessary funds. Income tax is less suitable as a benefit tax, especially when it is shared among local, county, and central governments. Since income levels available for taxation are very different in urban and rural areas, a comprehensive tax equalization system delinks the relationship between local income tax rate and income tax revenue. Expenditure equalization grants, distributed partly as block grants and partly as matching grants, add to the centralized control. They compensate cost differences related to population size, age structure, and settlement pattern and are used to direct local service production.

This book seeks to elucidate the effects of this kind of vertical fiscal imbalance. Decentralized spending with centralized financing through grants and regulated tax revenue sharing implies that the population in each local government pays only a small share of the costs of the local service production at the margin. In Scandinavian countries, the problem is worsened since local governments can take advantage of the central government concern for welfare service levels across the country. Central government policies to deal with distribution under decentralization open up the possibility of a strategic game between the local and the national levels. Carlsen (1994, 1998) offers theoretical models to capture strategic interactions and arguments for regulations in this setting. The existing regulations of the local public sector can be seen as a way of avoiding bailout by limiting the room to maneuver to distort local decisions. It is also a way of responding to disadvantages of fiscal competition. Even competition between local governments can work badly with redistributive services, since new incentives are created to attract "cheap" taxpayers and discourage the entry of "costly" immigrants.

Interestingly, the political leadership of the Scandinavian countries and certainly the ministries of finance see centralized financing as a way of holding down public spending. Spending pressure is already there with redistributive welfare services, and they see the central government as better able than local governments to handle the pressure. The disadvantages of centralized financing are handled with strict hierarchical administrative controls. The design is consistent with recent international evaluations. Von Hagen and Eichengreen (1996) conclude that "fiscal restrictions do prevail in states characterized by a high degree of vertical fiscal imbalance." Qian and Weingast (1997) argue that regulations harden the local budget constraint and thus also preserve market incentives. In the international setting of this book, it is hard to argue that the Scandinavians have succeeded in holding down public spending, but they have succeeded in keeping fiscal balances.

4.2 Centralized Financing of Decentralized Spending: Hierarchical Controls

Norway is a small and rich welfare state of about 4.5 million people. The economy is based on raw materials (oil, fish). The public sector directly controls about 45 percent of GDP, including welfare state policies such as free health care and schooling and a comprehensive social security system. It is a unitary state, but with an economically important local public sector and with local political systems. The representative democracy is decentralized, and the 435 municipalities and 19 counties elect their own local and county councils with proportional representation and multiple (about eight) parties. The large number of locally elected politicians (about 16,000) in this small country implies that decentralized government is a forceful voice in national politics. Since about 20 percent of the labor force (about 450,000) works in the local public sector, with teachers and nurses as the dominant groups, it is a strong social institution also. The data are given in Table 4.1.

Centralized financing and financial controls are the key mechanisms of fiscal discipline. Since local and county governments are agents of the central government, they are not treated as independent sovereign entities at the financial markets as they implicitly have a central government guarantee. When mobility is low, land and housing markets are influenced by more permanent regional imbalances, and local fiscal performance is of little importance. The financial controls are related to the following main elements:

• Grants represent about 40 percent of revenues. Most of the grants are distributed as block grants based on objective criteria, but a variety of matching grants and funds for new political initiatives are in place to promote the detailed ambitions of national politicians. A residual discretionary grant is distributed annually to compensate for factors hard to include among the objective criteria and for "extraordinary factors," like flooding.

• About 45 percent of the revenue is based on income tax and wealth tax shared with the central government. Tax rules are determined in the national parliament, and local tax rates are limited to a narrow band. All local and county governments apply the maximum rate (since 1979), and in this situation the tax revenue works as a block grant, except that the local governments can influence the tax base over time.

Table 4.1
Fact sheet: Norway

Approximate numbers, 1998

Population size: 4.5 million

Gross national product per capita: $20,000

Local public sector spending share of GDP: 18%

Local public sector spending share of public sector total spending: 36%

Local public sector share of public sector service spending: 65%

Local public sector revenues: Local taxes, 46%; grants, 40%; user charges, 12%

Local taxes, compositions: Personal income tax, 90%; wealth tax, 7%; property tax, 3%

Local public sector investment: 10% of current local public sector revenues

Local public sector net debt: 30% of current local public sector revenues

Number of municipalities: 435

Number of counties: 19

• The property tax is not available to all local governments (in practice, 200 of 435 municipalities have property tax); it is restricted to urban areas and certain facilities (notably power stations). Those eligible for property taxation can choose whether to use this tax, and the rate then is limited to a narrow band.

• User charges are of increasing importance and are now approaching 15 percent of revenue. They are regulated by law and cannot exceed unit costs, but the share of costs covered and the cost levels do vary.

• The Local Government Act requires that operational budgets balance inclusive of interest payments and regular installment of debt. Investment level is decided locally, but total loan financing is approved by the central government. Recently, the loan control has been limited to local governments with potential financial imbalances. Actual deficits are allowed to be carried over but must be paid within two years.

Local revenue sources, local taxes and user charges amount to nearly 60 percent of total revenue. This figure is high compared to most other countries and may delude an external observer to think that the Norwegian system of financing is rather decentralized. To get a proper understanding of the system, the central regulations must be taken into account. In practice, county government revenues are determined by these regulations (given the income tax base); local governments have some discretion in property taxation and user charges. The regulations must be understood against the background of the serious horizontal income imbalance among the municipalities and the counties. The average share of local taxes in total revenues is about 46 percent, and the heterogeneity with respect to revenue bases is illustrated by the fact that this share varies from 11 to 75 percent across the municipalities and from 25 to 63 percent across the counties. The extremes are represented by small municipalities at the periphery that receive large regional grants and the larger cities that enjoy only small grants.

Formally, the local and county governments have the discretion to set the income tax rate within a narrow band, but they all use the maximum rate. The reason that they all use the maximum rate is strategic. If any local or county government reduces the income tax rate below the maximum, it expects to be punished by the central government for being "too rich." There is no announced policy of punishment, but the central government has discretionary grants and can also influence local revenues through matching grants and funds channeled to promote new services. If local governments are seen as sufficiently rich to reduce the income tax rate, they are in a weak position to gain from such marginal funds. The central government seems not to worry about this potential element of soft budget constraint and is happy to influence the marginal funding of every local and county government.

The important role of grants has been motivated by equalization and the desire to influence the local government service production. The wish to redistribute income has been taken care of by tax equalization and needs equalization schemes designed as block grants. Tax equalization attempts to raise the revenues of municipalities and counties with weak tax bases. The high ambitions of the system imply that few of them have much incentive to improve their tax base. Interestingly, the comprehensive grant system oriented toward equalization has created a new inequality. Since regional policy aspects are built into the criteria, the periphery, and in particular small municipalities, has been overcompensated. The result is a divide where urban areas are relatively rich in private income and poor in public services, while the periphery is relatively poor in private income and rich in public services. The effect is similar to Rodden's (2001) description of Germany, where "the last shall be the first." In addition to the complex equalization system, the services have been controlled by an array of matching grants, typically to promote new services and expand old services with central government priority. Matching under centralized financing first and for all influences the priority use of block grants and exogenous tax revenue.

The economic conditions of the local public sector are decided by the national parliament as part of the annual national budget and then related to macroeconomic stabilization policy. Prior to each fiscal year, the central government announces a desired growth of total local government revenue, and of tax revenue and block grants separately. The parliament sets maximum income tax rates and grants according to this overall revenue target. The distribution of block grants among local governments also is decided prior to the fiscal year. Given the nationally determined economic conditions, the local governments produce their own budgets. Local political decision making is organized around the budget process.

Local budgets are regulated by the Local Government Act, and the main requirement is a balanced operational budget. Current revenue must cover current expenditures, interest payments, and regular installment of debt. Loan financing of current spending is not allowed. The final budgets have been controlled and approved by the central government, but recently this procedure has been in effect only for municipalities and counties with potential fiscal imbalances. If the budget implies an operational deficit, it will not be approved and is sent back to the local government for revision. A balanced budget ex ante does not rule out an actual deficit when the account is settled. Income tax revenue during the year and expenditures linked to rules and rights (like social support) may deviate from the budget. Actual deficits are allowed to be carried over, but as a rule they must be "repaid" within two years. In understanding with the central government, the local council can extend the period to four years if faster repayment has dramatic consequences for local service provision.

The balanced budget rule is the key to sound finances and efficient resource use. The benefit principle with intertemporal efficiency is encouraged since investments are allowed to be financed by loans. The rule may reduce intertemporal flexibility, and service provision may be unstable when current spending is strongly linked to current revenues. However, central government smooths local government revenue over time, and local governments typically hold "rainy-day" funds to smooth out shifts in revenues, although this is not required. Local governments are expected to have a plan for future debt service. Of even more economic importance, investments typically start up new service production that requires future current spending for labor and materials.

Recent overviews by Dafflon (2002) and Owens and Norregaard (1991) show that central governments in most OECD economies control the level of local government loan financing and, in some countries, even the purposes for which loans can be raised. Compared to the OECD area, Norwegian local governments have large discretion in investment policy, given the constraint that interest payments and debt installment are included in the operational budget balance and that total loan financing is approved. The system is meant to encourage decentralized accountability and priority within a system of centralized financing with hard budget constraint.

In addition to the financial controls, the welfare services are regulated in detail by law. The regulations involve coverage (e.g., all children in primary school), standards (e.g., class size), and working conditions (e.g., children per employee in day care). Local governments must satisfy these demands, which are important in schooling and health care. Individual rights defined by national law (like that all youth shall have the opportunity of high school education) have grown more popular. The administrative regulations integrate local governments in national sectoral control systems that cut across the national-local divide. This leads to a segmentation of the system whereby education and health care, in particular, are quite autonomous sectors relative to local democratic control. The regulations can be said to modify the vertical imbalance. Even if local and county governments make spending decisions regarding 15 to 20 percent of GDP, the regulations imply a sort of centralized spending that matches the centralized financing. Centralized financing must be understood in this context of administrative regulation of welfare services.

The complex and comprehensive system of control does not allow a simple quantification of local fiscal autonomy. Broadly, the mandated welfare services represent 70 to 80 percent of the budgets of the local governments and more like 80 to 90 percent of the budgets of the counties, while the rest covers local public goods like infrastructure, cultural activities, and planning. But there are paradoxes of control. The welfare service prescribed in most detail is primary school. Nevertheless, the municipalities have the discretion to choose size and location of schools, probably the single decision with the largest economic consequence for the municipality. The dramatic variation in average spending per pupil in the municipalities, from NOK 40,000 (US$ 5,000) to well above NOK 100,000 (US$ 12,000) partly reflects this local decision. The discretion at the revenue side is limited to the 15 percent generated from property taxation and user charges, but in reality it is less, since user charges at most can cover costs. A strong and ambitious political leadership at the local level certainly can move around resources, but there is a strong status quo bias in the system, and many quietly wait for "fresh" money from the center to do anything new.

4.3   The Political Control Mechanism

Norway is a multiparty parliamentary system with proportional representation from twenty districts and with about eight major political parties with nationwide support. The parties nominate candidates for the national parliament in each of the districts, and elections are held every four years. The party composition of the parliament is the decisive factor of national policy, and the parliament is quite fragmented with respect to parties. The degree of fragmentation is important for the "strength of the government" (Borge and Rattsø 2002)—establishment of majority or minority government and whether the government is based on one party or a coalition. The parties are strong, and they seem to internalize the regional dimension of politics. Coalitions of representatives from regions across party lines are seldom observed in the national parliament. Still, regionalism is the key political battleground, with heated conflicts concerning the distribution of public resources, especially the grant system.

At the local level, the political system is a miniature of the national. Elected local and county councils are dominated by the national parties, and the election results to a large degree reflect national politics, although with geographic variation. Also, some nonparty groups are represented, typically in the periphery. The local and county councils do not work as a parliamentary system (except for the capital, Oslo). Instead, an executive board is elected among the members of the council, with proportional representation of the parties (and nonparty groups) in the council. The system of joint rule tends to facilitate consensual properties and allows for a more open struggle regarding political priorities. The mayor and the deputy mayor are elected by and from the council and are the leaders of the executive board. The constellation behind the political leadership will typically have a majority on the executive board and the local council.

Local political and administrative leaderships are monitored by the Ministry of Local Government, in practice by the regional commissioner (a central government representative in each county). This is a two-way communication, and the local governments have a national association promoting more funding from the ministry and the central government. It is very seldom that regional representatives in the national parliament are mobilized by a single local authority to lobby for more funds. Even when the same party controls the central and the specific local government, it is not considered acceptable to give special favors. (Exceptions from this situation are discussed in section 4.5.)

The centralized financing invites spending pressure from below, channeled through the association of local governments and often supported by opposition politicians and the media, which document inadequate welfare services. In analyzing how the national political system handles this spending pressure, Borge and Rattsø (1997, 2002) use a benchmark demand model of public services emphasizing price, income, and congestion effects. The demand model is modified to represent the common pool problem resulting from vertical fiscal imbalance. The benefits of decentralized government spending accrue to each municipality and county, while the costs are carried by general taxation and to a large extent financed by central government grants. The national political system must internalize the costs of local public services. In contrast to the standard universalistic model of the U.S. Congress, party fragmentation of the parliament and coalition politics in parliamentary democracies is important for the internalization of the costs. The econometric analysis confirms that political strength (measured by party fragmentation and coalition types) is important for decentralized spending growth. A minority coalition government implies 20 percent more decentralized spending than a one-party majority government in the long run.

In addition to political strength, the political ideology of the majority in parliament influences the size of government spending. A socialist majority drives up spending. Since strength has been associated with a socialist majority because of fragmentation on the nonsocialist side, voters have faced a trade-off between ideology and strength. Interestingly, the Borge and Rattsø estimates indicate that strength dominates over ideology in the sense that nonsocialist majorities, being more fragmented, have contributed to higher decentralized spending. Among the economic determinants of local public spending, strong support is given for Wagner's law. The share of the local public sector in the national economy increases as income per capita increases.

Spending pressure also is experienced by local politicians. The clients of the welfare services and their organizations are strong players in politics, together with trade unions representing public employees (like teacher unions). Political strength also has been investigated at the local level and has been operationalized as the political constellation (majority or not, one party or coalition) behind the mayor and deputy mayor by Kalseth and Rattsø (1998). They find that political strength keeps local administrative costs down. Falch and Rattsø (1999) show that political strength in the counties, measured by party fragmentation in the councils, has held down costs and allowed for large student enrollments in high schools. Their study includes a measure of local spending pressure. Municipalities campaign for high schools, and counties with many small municipalities are expected to exert more spending pressure. The econometric results confirm that reduced average population size of municipalities drives up school spending and that the effect is moderated by political strength.

The large redistribution programs of the welfare state mean that distributional conflict easily dominates the political agenda. Strong interest groups fight for more distribution, and the demand for welfare services is directed toward the local public sector. Fiscal federalism can be seen as a way of reducing the pressure on national politics. Local governments feel squeezed between the demand for welfare services from the public and the economic constraints determined by the central government. National regulations has avoided fiscal imbalances in this system.

4.4   Evaluation of Fiscal Performance

The design of the Norwegian system of local public finance attempts to establish a hard budget constraint for individual municipalities and counties. Given that the central government basically determines the balance between private and local public consumption in each locality, the decentralization is meant to encourage three types of efficiency: allocative efficiency among local public services, cost efficiency by the incentive to produce good services at low cost given the revenues, and intertemporal efficiency by allowing borrowing to finance investment spending. Fiscal discipline is meant to result from financial controls, including central government approval of new loans and the balanced budget requirement.

Local public investment amounts to about 50 percent of total public investment. The share is considerably lower than the local share of public employment, since local services are labor intensive. Fixed capital investment generally represents about 10 percent of current revenue and borrowing finances about 50 percent of investments on average and is long term. A positive operating surplus finances about 35 percent of investments, with the rest mobilized from internal funds. The average debt-revenue ratio is about 30 percent and has fluctuated between 20 percent and 40 percent since 1980, primarily due to cyclical revenues. Borge and Rattsø (2002) investigate the details of the borrowing regime, which seems to work well in terms of stability.

While the investment share of revenues strongly increased after World War II, it has been stagnating and even declining since about 1970. A similar experience has been named the infrastructure problem in the United States (Hulten and Peterson 1984). The stagnation of investment can be the result of myopic decision making or central controls. An analysis of aggregate local government investment throws some light on the intertemporal decisions taken. Rattsø (1999b) studied whether the recent stagnation of investment reflects a sensible response to future revenue growth and demographic shift or imperfections in the decision-making system. The analysis applies an intertemporal optimization model with rational expectations and concludes that unexpected changes of GDP and unemployment have been important determinants of investment. The stagnating GDP growth has reduced the growth in investment spending, even when the central government has kept the revenue growth of the local public sector high and stable. Stabilization of local revenue growth has not led to stable investment growth. The investment decisions of the local public sector emphasize the underlying economic development of the country more than the revenue growth of the sector. At the same time, greater macroeconomic volatility has led to fluctuations in local public investment. The results are not inconsistent with the forward-looking model.

In the context of financial controls, differences between localities are important. The share of investment financed by borrowing varies substantially across the local units. Ten percent of the municipalities had a borrowing rate above 70 percent. There is a strong positive correlation between per capita revenues and operating surplus. Large revenues mean that more internal funds are available for fixed capital investment. Furthermore, municipalities with above-average revenue and surplus invest more and borrow less. A low borrowing-revenue ratio is associated with high revenue levels.

The international literature about the empirical effects of balanced budget rules is limited. Poterba (1995) and Inman (1996) have surveyed the recent literature on U.S. states. The U.S. states form an interesting case because the shaping of the balanced budget rules varies widely across states. The study by Bohn and Inman (1996) is particularly interesting because it helps to identify exactly what attributes of the balanced budget rules are important for the deficit. The empirical analysis indicates that the most important attribute is whether the balanced budget requirement is imposed ex ante or ex post, that is, whether deficits are allowed to be carried over. Effective rules do not allow deficits to be carried over to the next fiscal year. Rules that require a balanced budget ex ante and allow deficits to be carried over seem to be less effective.

In Norway, regulation of revenue sources and rigid expenditure commitments (like employment contracts) do not allow much flexibility on the current account. It follows that the immediate effects of shocks on the current deficit can be relatively large. In addition, and according to Bohn and Inman, the budget balance rule is weak since actual deficits are allowed to be carried over. An econometric study of local government responses to shocks confirms that current expenditures and revenues are unaffected by deficit shocks (Rattsø 1999a). The investment level is the main shock absorber. When fiscal imbalances have not been important in practice, the limited size of the shocks is an obvious explanation. The shocks experienced are often related to changing central government policy. Also, the weak deficit rule is combined with the requirement that the deficit carried over must be paid down within two years (four years in exceptional cases). The strict application of this rule seems to be sufficient to keep the deficits under control.

Still, deficits are regularly experienced, even when the law requires balanced budgets. Deficits may reflect revenue and expenditure shocks during the fiscal year, turning a balanced budget into an actual deficit. Or the submitted budgets may be balanced by deliberate overestimation of revenues or underestimation of expenditures. It is hard to separate shocks from creative budgeting. If deficits are mainly the result of revenue shocks, one would expect revenues to be more volatile in municipalities that run deficits frequently. In evaluating this hypothesis, Borge (1996) distinguishes municipalities that did not have any deficits in the period 1981–1990 and municipalities that had a deficit in at least one year. It appears that the volatility of revenues, measured by the standard deviation of the revenue growth rate, is almost identical in the two groups. Moreover, the two groups did not differ with respect to revenue level per capita or average growth rate. Revenue shocks seem to be of little importance for violation of the balanced budget law, and although expenditure shocks are not analyzed, it is not unreasonable to conclude that creative budgeting in the form of overestimated revenues or underestimated expenditures may play a significant role.

In an econometric analysis of budget deficits, Borge (1996) shows that both economic and political determinants play a role. The effect of a short-run or transitory revenue increase is to reduce the budget deficit. Moreover, the impact of a permanent revenue increase is less than that of a transitory revenue increase. According to the estimates, the response to a transitory grant reduction is to reduce current spending by 60 percent of the revenue loss and increase the operating deficit by 40 percent of the loss. On the other hand, a transitory reduction in local taxes increases the operating deficit by 80 percent of the revenue loss. This difference is as expected because a change in local tax revenue is more of a surprise than a change in grants from the central government. However, the difficulty of predicting the growth of the local tax base cannot explain that the long-run effects differ. According to the estimates, a permanent reduction in local tax revenue increases the deficit by nearly 40 percent of the revenue loss, compared to around 20 percent for a permanent reduction in grants. Political characteristics add to the explanation of varying deficits. Municipalities with weak political leadership tend to have larger budget deficits.

Overall, the Norwegian local public sector has not experienced serious deficit and debt problems since World War II. The analyses referred to above indicate that the constraints built into the system are effective. The balanced budget rule is obeyed, and localities in general finance part of their investments with current surplus. Borrowing is restricted by the fact that interest payments and installment of debt must be financed within the balanced operating budget. The formal control of budget balance and borrowing forecloses spending sprees, usually in a dialogue between central and local governments and seldom with formal actions taken.

4.5   Strategic Behavior and Bailouts

The combination of vertical fiscal imbalance and decentralized welfare services is expected to generate strategic behavior from the local public sector. Local governments can exploit the national political concern for access to and quality of the welfare services across the country. It is hard for the central government to avoid blame when welfare problems anywhere in the country are publicized, even when they are under local government responsibility. At the same time, the central government has all the instruments needed to influence the economic situation in each municipality and county. If a locality neglects welfare services to specific groups, sets excessive fees, or accumulates high debt and then argues that it has been forced to do so by economic circumstances, the central government will be under strong political pressure to bail out the fiscally troubled jurisdiction. When information about local services and costs is limited, moral hazard may result.

Bailout in this context is understood as a transfer from the central government to a specific local government in response to a local economic problem resulting from local government behavior. Bailout consequently must be related to fiscal mismanagement. The transfer must not follow automatically from grant design or be permanent, and a key question is whether strategic behavior from the local government is involved. It is our contention that local units try to exploit the national concern for welfare services across the country, but that the adverse effects of strategic behavior are small in practice. There is permanent pressure for higher spending, but not typically combined with distorted resource allocation. The experiences are summarized under three headings: discretionary grants, categorical grants, and campaigns for extra funds.

4.5.1 Discretionary Grants

The case for rule-based block grants is that strategic behavior is avoided and local priorities are based on local preferences and costs. Many countries have had grant reforms implementing block grants and have worked hard to develop robust criteria in tax equalization and needs equalization schemes. There will typically be a conflict between finding exogenous and objective criteria and reaching the desired equalization goals, since many of the relevant criteria (i.e., unemployment) can be influenced by local governments. It follows that both types of schemes easily imply distorted economic incentives (tax base, cost factors, and social factors). The main economic disincentives in the Norwegian block grant system are the overcompensation of small municipalities, which delays necessary consolidation into larger units, the compensation of the high costs associated with decentralized settlement pattern, rewarding cost-inefficient locations, and tax base equalization, limiting the incentives for industrial growth. Tax base equalization rewards backwardness and may motivate lobbying for grants rather than stimulating entrepreneurship.

When grant formulas are designed or discussed, local governments will actively promote criteria that benefits them, and certainly in Norway, the establishment of tax and needs equalization has created great political controversy (see Borge and Rattsø 1998). In this sense, rule-based block grants are discretionary over time. Rules are developed and modified according to a national political process. While the determination of rules is controversial, we do not think that it creates strategic distorted behavior at the local level.

Even with a strong emphasis on rule-based grants, no country avoids having some discretionary grants. Since state-dependent contracts are hard to specify and implement, the central government needs some discretion to handle unexpected events such as flooding. Also, discretionary grants typically supplement the equalization schemes, since many relevant factors are hard to represent in the rule-based system.

In Norway, discretionary grants are small (1–2 percent of total grants), but very broad; they can be distributed to take into account all kinds on "injustices" between municipalities and counties. Even if discretionary grants are small, they can make a difference at the margin. Since discretionary grants are so broad, they may encourage strategic behavior to get a reward.

The only study available of the allocation of discretionary grants looks at data from the 1970s (Fevolden and Sørensen 1983). During the period investigated, investments were high to expand schooling and health care, and some municipalities experienced debt service problems. Fevolden and Sørensen find that high debt servicing costs (interest payments and installment) are rewarded by more discretionary grants. This element of debt bailout, however, involved limited amounts and generated closer control from the central government (through regional commissioners). The strengthened supervision of loans seems to have met the problem.

The allocation of discretionary grants throughout the 1990s shows extreme stability across municipalities and counties. This is surprising, given that discretionary grants should take into account exogenous shocks affecting the localities. Interviews with regional commissioners indicate that status quo bias explains the stability. Discretionary grants are understood as a correction of the equalization schemes of the block grants, and these corrections are seen as permanent in the municipalities. The regional commissioners need strong arguments about new and changed economic conditions to convince the municipalities that the distribution of the discretionary grants should be modified from year to year. Any change from the status quo will generate protest from the losers. The status quo seems hard to change, even when the status quo allocation is a result of historical circumstances. In this environment, strategic behavior is excluded.

4.5.2 Categorical Grants

The central government uses various categorical grants, often of the matching type, to promote new services. Recent examples include matching grants for new environmental projects in the transport sector in the counties and for more care for the elderly in the municipalities. Such grants are typically part of a policy package where the central government combines different initiatives to strengthen a priority welfare service. Such new funds for the local public sector are add-ons, not a regular part of the grant system. Ad hoc policy packages give much more political attention than modifications of a complex grant system. Since these policy initiatives are developed quite independently within the national political system, they do not create incentives for strategic behavior from individual municipalities or counties. But they represent an incentive problem at a larger scale that is of interest.

The strategic consequence of policy packages promoting new services is that localities should stick to "optimal backwardness." Counties that were in the front of implementing environmental projects in transportation suddenly found that they were punished when only new environmental projects could achieve central government funding. The effect of the new funds for new environmental projects was that established environmental projects were closed down, so that all projects could be presented as new. Interestingly, environmental projects were delayed because of the introduction of new matching categorical grants to promote them. Municipalities in the forefront of developing care for the elderly recently had the same experience. New matching grants were introduced to expand local capacity in care for the elderly. Again localities that already had created this capacity had to use their own funds, while localities that were lagging could have central government cofinancing to expand their supply. When new categorical grants for care for the elderly were discussed and introduced, local governments stopped constructing new homes for the elderly. Political initiatives at the national level can thus create perverse local effects. Currently, national politicians are discussing a new political initiative to stimulate renovation of school buildings. This has been a long time in the coming and probably has discouraged the rehabilitation of schools.

The worst example of strategic behavior in Norway is related to the financing of hospitals. Hospitals are few and visible and represent about half the budget of the counties. Health care is a major issue in national politics and is subject to serious problems of information and control. The central government recently strengthened its commitment to local performance in health care by establishing legal rights to medical treatment and waiting lists. Hospitals and counties have taken benefit of the central government's commitment. The introduction of the block grant system, which was meant to strengthen the discretion of the counties, has worsened the incentive problems. The grant reform aimed at breaking the link between county spending decisions and level of grants, so that the counties faced the full cost of their priorities. In this context, however, grant reform enabled the counties to exploit the national commitment to hospital services. Central government through the Ministry of Health Care was easily mobilized for support when counties shifted funds out of hospitals and waiting lists extended.

Carlsen (1995) presents a detailed account of the strategic behavior of one large regional hospital in one of the counties. The county studied was particularly active and engaged in new nonhospital activities to exhaust its financial capacity and stimulate supplementary funds. Central government repeatedly appropriated extra grants, but also introduced several new measures of control. The battle has not yet ended, and the county is bargaining with central government for the financing of a new hospital. This example seems to fit the "too big to fail" argument of Wildasin (1997). Disruptions at a regional hospital have large consequences, and the central government cannot neglect them. Nevertheless, the central government is aware of the problem and has revised the financing of hospitals. They are now financed by a combination of county block grant and matching grants related to hospital services. The ministry has also improved control systems and arranged reporting in order to compare the performance of hospitals. The government now has nationalized the hospitals, so they will no longer be a county government responsibility.

The existence of policy packages and supplementary grants to hospitals must be understood against the background of the national political system. The minister of health care certainly looks strong and active when she intervenes to "solve a problem" at a local hospital. National politicians taking the initiative to fund improvements in care for the elderly and environmental projects also may gain politically. The delegation of spending power to the local public sector in these areas seems not to stop them from taking this political advantage. They will typically argue that local governments have not been able to handle a serious welfare issue and therefore need help from the center. In general, reforms and innovations often seem to be imposed from the top. The centralized system takes the initiative away from the local governments, quite opposite from the desired "laboratory federalism" outlined by Oates (1999).

4.5.3 Campaigns for Extra Funds

The larger cities, and in particular the capital, Oslo, more or less permanently campaign for additional funds. They are active in the media and in political lobbying, and hire consultants to come up with arguments for their case. The general background here is that most European countries have problems arranging the local government structure in the capital and that the larger cities have special problems. Since they are different, their spending needs are hard to represent in the national equalization scheme. Social problems and immigrants tend to concentrate in the larger cities, and many users of the infrastructure live in neighboring municipalities. Given that the large cities are few, it is hard to separate out what part of their spending is involuntary cost disadvantages to be compensated and what is cost inefficiency. Since there are many central government transactions and projects of relevance for the capital, it is also hard to evaluate whether their campaign is successful. Oslo certainly has a high per capita revenue level and high spending in most service areas, but the service level generally is not considered above others. While strategic behavior with distorted spending probably is not part of the game, the permanent campaign may have a strongly adverse effect on fiscal discipline within the larger cities.

A few other individual municipalities have made strong attempts at getting extra funds from the central government. They are also different, but at the other end of the scale. They are all very well known in the public debate in Norway. In the mid-1980s, the "Lurøy action" hit the media. Lurøy is a very small municipality on the north coast with a large share of the population on islands. Its population size is in decline and aging. The mayor and the chief administrator presented their case for extra funds to the municipality in a public forum, claiming a difficult economic situation and inadequate services. Their presentation was well tailored to media attention. Unfortunately for Lurøy, many other municipalities quickly presented their case too. Lurøy no longer looked different from the rest of the periphery, and municipalities closer to urban areas could document even worse service levels. In the end, Lurøy did not achieve much. Lebesby represents a more successful case for additional funds. This is another small municipality on the coast, at the north end of the country. Fishing is the main industry, and the municipality has guaranteed loans for a number of local fishing companies. When fishing failed, many of the companies went bankrupt, and the guarantees required large amounts from the municipal funds. The municipality could not finance existing services and called on the central government. The central government provided additional funds, but also basically administered the municipality for a period. The conditions were sufficiently strict to discourage other municipalities affected by failed fishing to claim similar treatment.

Single municipalities now and then appear in the media with demands for special treatment. An interesting recent case is Grue, the home municipality of the minister of local government. Unsurprisingly, the mayor represented the main opposition party of the government. When the national budget, including the grant system, was discussed in fall 1998, Grue presented plans for large cuts in employment and demanded extra funds. The largest newspaper in Norway immediately sent a team to Grue to cover the case. Different from the regular "crisis" descriptions in the media, the journalists turned against the political and administrative leadership of the municipality, questioned the basis for their demands, and presented the leadership as "cheating with numbers" from the local accounts. The unfortunate media attention made this case easy to handle for the central government. Typically, such municipalities are convinced by regional commissioners and representatives from the ministry that their case is not unique.

Campaigns by individual municipalities have had limited success, except for Oslo. In general, the municipalities are "too small to worry" as opposed to "too big to fail". Since the many small municipalities have similar problems, the central government cannot accommodate their demands. Only when clear exogenous shocks have occurred has the central government been willing to give supplementary grants, and only when strict conditions are set that do not encourage others to emulate.

4.5.4   Overall Evaluation

Although centralized financing and decentralized welfare services invite strategic behavior, moral hazard and bailout are not serious problems in the Norwegian system. For the individual municipality and county, the budget constraint is hard. First, it is difficult for any municipality or county to break out of the pack. Central government and the local public sector itself are well informed about the economic conditions and the service performance of all local units. When local units appeal to the central government for help in handling a local crisis, the central government will know whether the locality has faced an exogenous shock or the problem is a result of its own behavior. Competing municipalities and counties will keep an eye on the situation, and rewarding bad behavior will not go unnoticed. Second, strategic behavior is risky in relation to the local political process. Political leaders that create a local crisis to get a bailout by central government and are not successful will have a hard time explaining their actions to the voters. Open information about local government behavior and performance and an open local political system are essential to secure hard budget constraints under centralized financing.

4.6   Reform

Decentralization is assumed to promote local democracy and economic efficiency, but neither local autonomy nor efficiency is a major goal of the welfare service production decentralized in Norway. The welfare state gives top priority to the provision of essential services to all parts of the population, geographically and socially. Allocative efficiency is less emphasized in this system, since providing services is seen as a basic welfare issue. Cost efficiency is difficult to evaluate, since service quality is closely linked to costs, as with the number of nurses overseeing a group of elderly. Low cost is easily presented as low quality. Local autonomy may create differences in welfare services between municipalities, which is in conflict with the goal of equality. Decentralization gains à la Oates are less clear in this system.

Norway's welfare services seem costly by international standards. Comparisons are hard to make, but indicators like spending per pupil and per patient treated are high. Partly, the high costs result from the desire for equalization combined with a decentralized settlement pattern along fjords and up mountain valleys. Partly they are associated with the welfare state service monopoly, with little competition and privatization. The supply side of the services looks more influential than the demand side. The broad challenge to the welfare state is to strengthen the demand side of welfare services against the producer interests dominating the existing monopoly model.

Studies evaluating the performance of this system are summarized by Rattsø and Sørensen (1998). They conclude that the welfare state model gives little scope for local democracy. The electorate is segmented into groups with different interests in welfare services, and they seem to be more active as special-interest consumers than as politically interested citizens. The party system is not well positioned to represent clear-cut alternatives in this situation. The decision-making problems have an impact on local economic performance. The shared responsibility of the welfare services with the central government distorts incentives for efficiency. Public sector efficiency is hard to achieve anyway, especially when service quality is closely linked to costs and monitoring is difficult. Interjurisdictional competition has been limited by low mobility, and local governments have refrained from market orientation, partly because of well-organized producer interests. The complicated decision-making system, the combination of local democracy and role as agency for the central government, influences the ability to hold costs down and restructure services to meet changing demands. In the public debate, local governments are typically seen as rigid and with weak cost controls.

Administrative federalism in Norway is characterized by frustration at both the local and the central levels. National politicians are blamed for welfare problems across the country, even when local governments are actually responsible for providing services. Local politicians are frustrated by the limited room to maneuver and a local democracy with little content. It may be, however, that the system of unclear responsibilities is favorable from the politicians' point of view. Local politicians can blame those above, since funding is determined at the center. National politicians can let local politicians take some of the heat of the permanent pressure for more welfare spending. This design creates the impression of fuzzy institutions and may threaten the legitimacy of the system over time.

Strong demands for reform in local government finance are expressed in the public debate, but there is no universal agreement on where to go. Further centralization is argued to give full responsibility of the services at the center and to get full control of the money. At the extreme, all revenues are distributed as grants, and ministries are given the power to regulate the supply of welfare services in each locality. It is seen as unacceptable that children shall have different quality and quantity of schooling across the country or that health care shall depend on each locality's financial situation and priorities. The recent decision to nationalize the hospitals, until now a county responsibility, is a step in this direction. But there are also attempts at further decentralization as a way of reducing the problem of unclear responsibilities. Decentralization also will increase local accountability and strengthen local democracy and local self-rule. The recent consolidation of block grants and a revision of the Local Government Act to give more freedom of organization at the local level are such attempts. A government commission has proposed a set of reforms, mainly in the direction of more decentralization (see Borge and Rattsø 1998). The main proposal involves local tax discretion for all municipalities in setting a broad property tax. As always, taxes seen as productive from an economic viewpoint are seldom popular. This reform process may end because of the unpopularity of the property tax.

There is a third way out. The deeper issue is the handling of the welfare services, which will determine the role of the local public sector in the future. Competition and choice, and possibly privatization, will change the financing and control of the welfare services. Then maybe local governments can concentrate on local public goods and operate closer to prescriptions in standard fiscal federalism theory.

Acknowledgments

Financing was received from the Norwegian Research Council and the World Bank. I have enjoyed discussions with Lars-Erik Borge, Fredrik Carlsen, Terje P. Hagen, Jørgen Lotz, Lars Søderstrøm, and Rune Sørensen and draw on joint work with some them. I appreciate comments on the first draft of this chapter from Gunnar Eskeland, Jonathan Rodden, and a reviewer.

References

Borge, L.-E. 1996. "The Political Economy of Budget Deficits: A Study of Norwegian Local Governments." Mimeo., Department of Economics, Norwegian University of Science and Technology.

Borge, L.-E., and J. Rattsø. 1997. "Local Government Grants and Income Tax Revenue: Redistributive Politics in Norway 1900–1990." *Public Choice* 92:181–197.

Borge, L.-E., and J. Rattsø. 1998. "Reforming a Centralized System of Local Government Financing: Norway." In J. Rattsø, ed., *Fiscal Federalism and State-Local Finance: The Scandinavian Approach*. Cheltenham: Edward Elgar.

Borge, L.-E., and J. Rattsø. 2002. "Spending Growth with Vertical Fiscal Imbalance: Decentralized Government Spending in Norway 1880–1990." *Economics and Politics*, 14(3):351–373.

Borge, L.-E., and J. Rattsø. 2002. "Local Government Budgeting and Borrowing: Norway." In B. Dafflon, ed., *Local Public Finance in Europe: Balancing the Budget and Controlling Debt*. Cheltenham: Edward Elgar.

Bohn, H., and R. P. Inman. 1996. "Balanced Budget Rules and Public Deficits: Evidence from the U.S. States." Working paper 5533, National Bureau of Economic Research.

Carlsen, F. 1994. "Central Regulation of Local Government Borrowing: A Game-Theoretical Approach." *Environment and Planning C: Government and Policy* 12:213–224.

Carlsen, F. 1995. "Why Is Central Regulation of Local Spending Decisions So Pervasive? Evidence from a Case Study." *Public Budgeting and Finance* 15:43–57.

Carlsen, F. 1998. "Central Regulation of Local Authorities." *Public Finance Review* 26(4):304–326.

Dafflon, B., ed. 2002. *Local Public Finance in Europe: Balancing the Budget and Controlling Debt.* Cheltenham: Edward Elgar.

Falch, T., and J. Rattsø. 1999. "Local Public Choice of School Spending: Disaggregating the Demand Function for Educational Services." *Economics of Education Review* 18:361–373.

Fevolden, T., and R. J. Sørensen. 1983. "Spillet om skatteutjevningen (The tax equalization game, in Norwegian)." *Tidsskrift for Sammfunnsforskning* 24:59–76.

Foster, C., R. Jackman, and M. Perlman. 1980. *Local Government Finance in a Unitary State.* London: George Allen & Unwin.

Hulten, C., and G. Peterson. 1984. "The Public Capital Stock: Needs, Trends and Performance." *American Economic Review* 74(2):166–173.

Inman, R. P. 1996. "Do Balanced Budget Rules Work? U.S. Experience and Possible Lessons for the EMU." Working paper 5838, National Bureau of Economic Research.

Kalseth, J., and J. Rattsø. 1998. "The Political Control of Administrative spending: The Case of Local Governments in Norway." *Economics and Politics* 10(1):63–83.

Lotz, J. 1998. "Local Government Reforms in the Nordic Countries, Theory and Practice." In J. Rattsø, ed., *Fiscal Federalism and State-Local Finance: The Scandinavian Approach.* Cheltenham: Edward Elgar.

Musgrave, R. 1959. *The Theory of Public Finance.* New York: McGraw-Hill.

Oates, W. 1999. "An Essay on Fiscal Federalism." *Journal of Economic Literature* 37:1120–1149.

Owens, J., and J. Norregaard. 1991. "The Role of Lower Levels of Government: The Experience of Selected OECD Countries." In J. Owens and G. Panella, eds., *Local Government: An International Perspective.* Amsterdam: North-Holland.

Poterba, J. M. 1995. "Balanced Budget Rules and Fiscal Policy: Evidence from the States." *National Tax Journal* 48:329–336.

Qian Y., and B. Weingast. 1997. "Federalism as a Commitment to Preserving Market Incentives." *Journal of Economic Perspectives* 11(4):83–92.

Rattsø, J., ed. 1998. *Fiscal Federalism and State-Local Finance: The Scandinavian Approach.* Cheltenham: Edward Elgar.

Rattsø, J. 1999a. "Fiscal Adjustment with Vertical Fiscal Imbalance: Empirical Evaluation of Administrative Fiscal Federalism in Norway." Report 57, Economic Research Programme on Taxation, Norwegian Research Council.

Rattsø, J. 1999b. "Aggregate Local Public Sector Investment and Shocks: Norway 1946–1990." *Applied Economics* 31:577–584.

Rattsø, J. 2002. "Fiscal Controls in Europe: A Summary." In B. Dafflon, ed., *Local Public Finance in Europe: Balancing the Budget and Controlling Debt.* Cheltenham: Edward Elgar.

Rattsø, J., and R. Sørensen. 1998. "Local Governments Integrated in a Welfare State: A Review of Norwegian Local Government Performance." In J. Rattsø, ed., *Fiscal Federalism and State-Local Finance: The Scandinavian Approach*. Cheltenham: Edward Elgar.

Rodden, Jonathan. 2001. "And the Last Shall Be First: Federalism and Fiscal Performance in Germany." Unpublished paper, MIT.

Weingast, B., K. Shepsle, and C. Johnsen. 1981. "The Political Economy of Benefits and Costs: A Neoclassical Approach to Distributive Politics." *Journal of Political Economy* 89:642–664.

Von Hagen, J., and B. Eichengreen. 1996. "Federalism, Fiscal Restraints, and European Union." *American Economic Review* 86(2):134–138.

Wildasin, D. 1997. "Externalities and Bailouts; Hard and Soft Budget Constraints in Intergovernmental Fiscal Relations." World Bank Policy Research working paper 1843.

5 Soft Budget Constraints and German Federalism

Jonathan Rodden

At first glance, the Federal Republic of Germany appears to have one of the most decentralized public sectors in the world. Together, the *Länder* (federal states) and the *Gemeinden* (local communities) are responsible for over 60 percent of total government spending. Yet the German public sector is not a paragon of the virtues of fiscal decentralization. On the contrary, the rising cost of German-style fiscal federalism has become a critical impediment to improved efficiency in the German public sector. Although the German federal government is famous for its prudent monetary and fiscal policies, the fiscal performance of the subnational sector has been far less admirable. Scholarly criticism of Germany's unique style of fiscal federalism has a long history, but the costs of German unification and implications of recent Constitutional Court decisions have pushed debates about the future of fiscal federalism into the arena of electoral politics. In spite of increasing scholarly and public attention, however, serious reform has been elusive.

The most obvious manifestation of the problem with fiscal federalism in Germany is the persistence of subnational deficits and public debt. Figure 5.1 provides a recent snapshot comparing the aggregate fiscal outcomes of the central, state, and local governments.

Most of the borrowing in the German federation—and most of the costs of unification—have been borne by the federal government, but the Länder, and to a lesser extent the Gemeinden, regularly run deficits and undertake significant short- and long-term borrowing. While stopping well short of the disastrous experiences with provincial borrowing in Brazil and Argentina, the borrowing activities of the German states have created a nagging problem. This chapter seeks to explain the institutional and political causes of soft budget constraints and bailouts among the German Länder in the 1990s. In contrast to many

Deficit as percentage of revenue

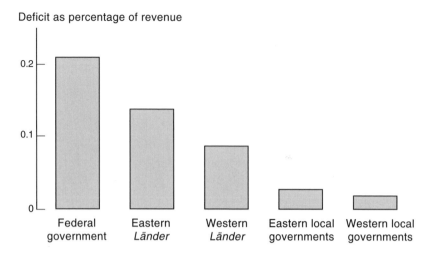

Figure 5.1
Deficit as percent of revenue at each level of government, Germany 1996. *Source*: Sachverständigenrat (1997, 120) and author's calculations.

of the other stories of soft budget constraints and bailouts described in
the book, incentives for fiscal indiscipline in Germany have been concentrated in a minority of the federated states. Prior to unification, the
problem was limited to two small states that were faced with rapidly
declining macroeconomic circumstances: Bremen and Saarland. These
states have consistently run large deficits in recent decades, refusing to
cut spending despite unsustainable debt levels (see figures 5.2 and 5.3).
Following a controversial court decision, the federal government may
have exacerbated the moral hazard problem for other jurisdictions by
extending large debt relief bailouts to Bremen and Saarland. The problems of perverse incentives, persistent deficits, and dangerous debt
burdens are now serious in the new eastern Länder as well.[1]

Starting from zero debt in 1990, by 1998 the per capita debts of the
eastern Länder have surpassed those of their western counterparts
(Seitz 1999). As this volume goes to press, a fiscal crisis in the city-state
of Berlin appears to be heading down a now-familiar path toward
federal bailouts (Seitz 2001). Soft budget constraints at the *Land* level
could threaten Germany's ability to stay within the general government deficit limit imposed under the terms of the Stability and Growth
Pact of EMU. If the Länder run excessive deficits under present conditions, the *Bund* (federal government) would have to bear the fines for
noncompliance under EU regulations (OECD 1998).

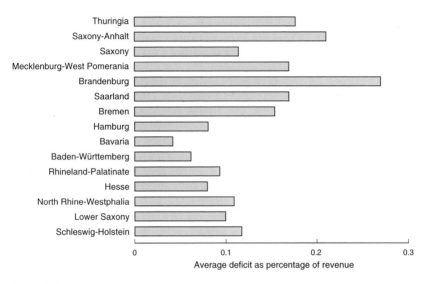

Figure 5.2
Average deficit as share of revenue in the German Länder, selected years. *Note*: 1975–1995 for the western Länder; 1992–1995 for the eastern Länder. *Source*: Statistisches Bundesamt and author's calculations.

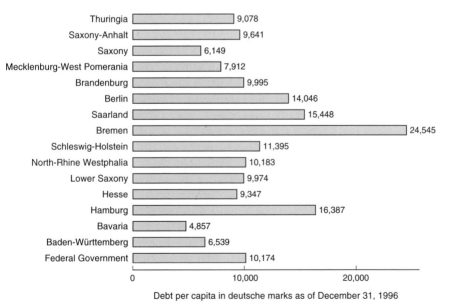

Figure 5.3
Per capita debt, German fereral government and Länder, 1996. *Source*: Sachverständigenrat (1997, 195).

Undoubtedly some of the fiscal problems of Saarland and Bremen are related to the challenges of governing small states with high personnel costs and high levels of unemployment, and deficits in Berlin and the eastern Länder reflect to some extent the need to combat massive unemployment and invest heavily in infrastructure. Nevertheless, this chapter argues that the recent crisis of fiscal federalism in Germany is best understood as a manifestation of underlying structural weaknesses in the German federal system that have been present throughout the postwar period. Specifically, the collaborative intergovernmental system of revenue legislation, collection, and distribution breaks the link between taxing and spending decisions that is critical for effective government provision of goods and services. While the Länder have wide-ranging expenditure responsibilities, they possess very little autonomy over the tax base or rates. While most spending and policy implementation occurs at the Land or Gemeinde level, most revenue decisions are made at the Bund level. As a result, voters cannot identify which level of government taxes or spends for which goods and services, and they have neither the ability nor the incentives to monitor or discipline the fiscal decisions of state or local governments. The leitmotiv of this chapter is that Germany's complex, interdependent, collaborative style of federalism tends to dilute fiscal accountability and soften budget constraints.

The basic constitutional structure of German federalism undermines the hierarchical oversight mechanism as well. Often called administrative federalism, the German system is characterized in most policy areas by central legislation and state implementation. The *Grundgesetz* (Constitution) requires that the "equivalence of living conditions" be maintained throughout the federation through a complex system of fiscal equalization. As explained below, aspects of the equalization system create perverse incentives in some of the states by rewarding fiscal profligacy. Most recently, in response to debt servicing crises in Bremen and Saarland, the Federal Constitutional Court has ruled that the "equivalence of living conditions" clause obligates the federal government to provide these Länder with special bailout transfers.

The remainder of this chapter examines the strengths and weaknesses of the German Länder in maintaining fiscal discipline through each of the channels discussed in chapter 1. First, it describes in greater detail the basic architecture of the German federal system and assesses the institutional incentive structures faced by Land-level politicians. Section 5.2 then considers additional political incentive structures.

Section 5.3 explains the role of the capital market and its regulation. The penultimate section discusses the bailout episodes in Bremen and Saarland and the growing difficulties of the new Länder. The final section concludes and discusses the prospects for reform.

5.1 Hierarchical Structure and Intergovernmental Fiscal Relations

Most of the theoretical literature on federalism in economics and political science assumes that central and subnational governments are responsible for the provision of distinct, nonoverlapping goods and services. According to normative theory, the central and subnational governments should raise their own revenue, and transfers from the central government to the subnational units should be used primarily to internalize externalities produced by the subunits. The German system of federalism is deeply at odds with this vision of dual federalism. Although some tasks, like national defense, are clearly allocated to the Bund alone, legislation and implementation in Germany is in most policy areas a complex, cooperative process between the highly interdependent Bund and Länder. Unlike the states in most other modern federations, the German Länder have few exclusive areas of legislative competence, and federal law generally overrides state law.

The Länder are nevertheless important players in the German policy process. This is not because they possess an autonomous role in legislation within a constitutionally protected set of responsibilities, but rather because they are key players in the formulation of policy at the federal level and in its implementation at the Land level. Unlike the states in most other federal systems, the governments of the Länder are directly represented in the Bundesrat, the federal upper house of parliament. Every law that affects the interests of the states must be approved by the Bundesrat, which gives the states a very important role as veto players in the federal policymaking process. Additionally, in contrast to most other federations, the German central government has a very limited bureaucratic apparatus under its own control; it relies on the Länder and Gemeinden to implement most federal policy. Given this structural interdependence of Bund and Länder, it is very difficult for either level of government to achieve its goals without bargaining, cajoling, or cooperating with the other level.

Multilateral bargaining between the interdependent Bund and Länder is also the modus operandi in the collection and distribution of revenue. All of the most important taxes accrue to the federal and state governments jointly. Most decisions about tax base and rates are made by the federal government (subject to the approval of the Bundesrat). While some taxes are collected by the Bund, most are administered by the revenue authorities of the Länder, which act as agents of the federation. The fiscal equalization system goes to great lengths to redistribute revenue from the wealthy to the poor Länder, and the parameters of this system are renegotiated periodically between the Länder and the central government.

5.1.1 Expenditures

The Constitution explicitly assigns a number of responsibilities to the federal government: foreign affairs, defense, monetary policy, citizenship, customs, rail and air transport, the postal system, and telecommunications. The states are responsible for such areas as culture, education, law and order, health, environmental protection, and regional economic policy. The municipalities are responsible for local health facilities, sports and recreation, the construction of schools, roads, and public housing, and other community services (Laufer 1994). Despite the Constitution's attempt to divide authority among the governmental units, however, it is difficult to identify a policy area in which only one level of government is involved. The Länder are responsible for implementing the vast majority of the federal government's policies and delegate a variety of tasks to the Gemeinden. As a result, neither the Constitution nor outlays by level of government reflect very accurately the actual distribution of authority or spending.

   Even in policy areas that had previously been the exclusive competence of the Länder, the activities and finances of the Bund and Länder have gradually become intertwined. The most important step away from dual federalism was the 1969 renegotiation of the Basic Law, which established the so-called joint tasks. The Länder agreed to give up their exclusive authority in several policy fields in exchange for complex forms of multilevel cooperation in policymaking and funding. These policy fields include university construction, regional industrial policy, and agricultural structural policy (Article 91a, Basic Law); housing, urban renewal, urban transportation, and hospitals (Article 104a IV, Basic Law); and secondary education and research financing (Article 91b, Basic Law).[2] Since the introduction of the joint tasks in 1969, the importance of intergovernmental planning and cofinancing of public activities has grown. Between the end of the 1970s and unification, federal outlays devoted to the joint tasks increased by 15 percent in real terms (OECD 1998).

The discretion of the Länder in spending is limited in most areas by uniform federal law. Nevertheless, the Länder enjoy relatively wide autonomy in practice. The federal government does not give specific instructions to the Länder in the execution of most federal law, and it has no powers of supervision or specific approval of administrative practices. The Länder have full autonomy over their budgets, and in many fields they can vary the amount of support they give to programs required by federal law and remain free to supplement services prescribed by federal statute.

The Länder are the largest public sector employers in Germany. In this capacity they also enjoy a good deal of discretion, again within federally imposed legal constraints. Länder make their own personnel decisions, but they must abide by national public service laws, which rigorously define the qualifications necessary for each position. The result is a very homogeneous bureaucracy in each sector across the Länder. Public sector wages are determined by a coordinated bargaining process involving the major public sector unions and representatives of the federal government, the Länder, and the Gemeinden.

5.1.2 Revenue

Like expenditure decisions, the responsibility for revenue legislation and administration is also intertwined between the Bund and the Länder. The Constitution specifies in great detail the assignment of revenue to the Bund and Länder, and major revisions in federal financial arrangements can be made only by amending the Constitution, which requires a two-thirds majority in both the Bundestag and the Bundesrat. The flow of revenue laid out in the German Constitution is far removed from the principles laid out in fiscal federalism textbooks. Instead of assigning specific taxes to the layers of government and matching them with specific expenditure responsibilities, the provisions of the German Constitution stipulate that all of the most important revenue sources are shared in Germany. The significance of taxes assigned directly to the layers of government is low. The income tax, corporation tax, and value-added tax (VAT), which yield almost three-quarters of total tax revenue, are shared.[3] Legislation regarding tax base and rates is the domain of the federal government, although administration is carried out by the revenue authorities of the Länder. In the administration of the shared taxes, the state authorities act as agents of the federation and are subject to uniform federal administrative guidelines.

The vertical distribution of the shared taxes between Bund and Länder is very stable over time because the actual percentage shares are laid out in the Constitution and can be changed only by amendment. In order to ensure that the Länder receive sufficient funds to fulfill their federally mandated responsibilities in the face of changing fiscal circumstances, the vertical distribution of the VAT is frequently renegotiated between the Bund and the Länder. The resulting bargain must be approved by the Länder in the Bundesrat. The VAT is the only aspect of the vertical distribution of resources that is flexible, and although the renegotiation is often contentious, it can be used to make adjustments in the vertical allocation of funds when made necessary by new policy programs or exogenous shocks (Renzsch 1991).

5.1.3   Equalization and Transfers

The German Länder actually spend more money than the federal government (figure 5.4), but they have very little independent authority over taxation. By far the most important sources of funding for the Länder are the shared taxes (figure 5.5). First, the primary system of tax sharing distributes the proceeds of the major shared taxes to the states as follows: income tax revenue is apportioned to the states according to the derivation principle, corporate tax revenue is divided according to a formula based on plant location, and a portion of the VAT is distributed to the states on a per capita basis. Next, the secondary system of revenue equalization proceeds in three stages. The first two states are horizontal, while the third involves vertical transfers from the Bund.

In the first stage, around 75 percent of the VAT is distributed by population, and up to 25 percent of the VAT is redistributed to the Länder with the lowest revenue after the primary tax-sharing receipts are calculated. Currently, this part of the equalization process benefits only the new Länder. Spahn (2001) points out that the redistributive effect of the VAT sharing is substantial; the eastern states receive roughly twice as much VAT revenue per capita as the western states. After this stage, the financial endowment (*Finanzkraft*) of each state is calculated and compared with its financial needs (*Finanzbedarf*). Then at the second stage of equalization (*Länderfinanzausgleich im engeren Sinne*),

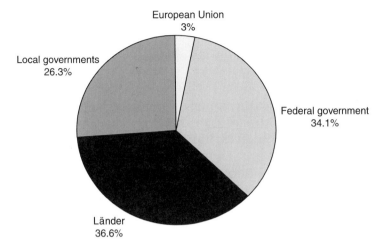

Figure 5.4
Public expenditure by level of government in Germany. *Sources*: Federal Ministry of Finance (1996, 328); Spahn and Föttinger (1997, 228).

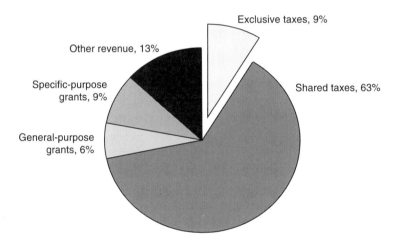

Figure 5.5
Sources of revenue in the German Länder, 1995 (percent of total land revenue). *Sources*: Federal Ministry of Finance (1996); Spahn and Föttinger (1997, 321).

revenue is redistributed from states whose endowments exceed their needs, to those for which the opposite is true. The concept of need is based on the per capita tax income for the entire country.[4] After this stage, the weaker (*Finanzschwach*) states reach 95 percent of the average national tax capacity.

In the third stage of the equalization system, the federal government steps in to lift the recipient states up to at least 99.5 percent of average fiscal capacity. It does this with supplementary grants (*Bundesergänzungszuweisungen*). These can be understood essentially as gap-filling transfers. At this stage, the Bund also bestows additional supplementary grants on some states to compensate them for "special burdens." Currently, these grants are most beneficial to the new Länder. Nine of sixteen states receive federal grants to relieve the costs of political management. As discussed in greater detail below, the Bundesergänzungszuweisungen are also being used to provide bailouts to Bremen and Saarland, and perhaps soon Berlin, because of their debt servicing obligations.

Finally, in addition to the vertical transfers associated with the final stage of equalization, the Bund funds specific activities and capital investments in the Länder through the mechanisms laid out in the 1969 renegotiation of the Basic Law. Policymaking on the so-called joint tasks is made by a plethora of sector-specific administrative planning committees in which the federal government and the states are represented. In order for a project to be funded, it must be approved by the federal government and a majority of the states. The central government plays an important role in determining priorities in these areas, not only because it is represented on the planning committee but because it can threaten to withdraw federal cofinancing. In 1999 spending on the joint tasks amounted to 7.3 billion deutsche marks (Huber 2001).

5.1.4   Intergovernmental Budgeting System

The budgeting and fiscal management processes of the Bund and the Länder are constitutionally autonomous and independent. Nevertheless, the Länder are obliged by the Constitution and federal legislation to follow uniform principles that apply to all public sector bodies. The Länder must follow a variety of general provisions and specific rules regarding the preparation of the budget, accounting, auditing, and transparency. They are also required to engage in multiyear financial planning and exchange budget-related information.[5] The Bund, Länder, and Gemeinden participate in the Financial Planning Council, which meets periodically to coordinate general budgetary policy and is designed to provide the central government with the information it needs to ensure macroeconomic stability. Although it helps coordinate long-term budgetary planning between the levels of government, the Financial Planning Council does not make binding decisions. Despite the high level of coordination and information sharing between the Bund and Länder, in the end neither can force the other to do anything, and when difficult sacrifices must be made in order to improve overall public sector fiscal balance, compromise can be very difficult to achieve.

5.1.5 Borrowing

The Financial Planning Council is complemented by the Committee on Public Borrowing, which attempts to coordinate public borrowing between the Bund, Länder, and Gemeinden. Its decisions are also nonbinding, however, and the central government has no power to place numeric restrictions on the borrowing activities of the Länder. Nor must the borrowing decisions of the Länder be approved or reviewed by the Bund. Like the federal government, however, the Länder have their own constitutional and statutory provisions that restrict them from borrowing more than the outlays for investment purposes projected in the budget. These so-called golden rule provisions at the Land level, however, have a number of well-known loopholes. First, "investment purposes" is an extremely slippery concept, and it is not difficult to recast a variety of expenditures as investment outlays. Second, financing arrangements associated with the contracting out of local public infrastructure projects provide an additional way around the "golden rule" provisions. Private investors are given guarantees and asked to build and prefinance infrastructure projects. On completion of the work, the government redeems the building costs over a certain period (Spahn and Föttinger 1997). In addition to the problem of loopholes, some states have chosen to ignore their constitutions, as explained in section 5.5 on Saarland and Bremen.

It is important to note that while most of the federal government's debt is in the form of bonds, the Länder and Gemeinden rely primarily on direct bank loans to finance their deficits. The Länder indirectly control a network of commercial banks—the *Landesbanken*, which make loans (*Schuldscheine*) to the municipalities and the Länder. The officials of the Landesbanks generally have excellent political connections at the Land level. Land politicians frequently accept lucrative stints on their Landesbank's supervisory board, and though proof is difficult to obtain, some suggest that the Landesbanks are used to channel cheap credit to politically favored businesses.[6] At the municipal level, the mayor of a commune is often also chairman of the supervisory board of the local savings bank (Spahn and Föttinger 1997).

5.1.6   Implications for Soft Budget Constraints in the Länder

In many respects, the unique structure of German administrative federalism has served it well throughout the postwar period. The German interjurisdictional market is perhaps more complete than that of any other federation. German-style cooperative federalism has facilitated mutual recognition and other agreements that facilitate the free flow of goods and services across jurisdictional boundaries. Since the Länder have a good deal of discretion in implementing federal law, they may be able to tailor implementation to suit local conditions. Yet the system also ensures a good deal of uniformity of service provision throughout the federation, and federal standards ensure that the Land bureaucracies are highly competent.

The disadvantage of German-style cooperative federalism is that it destroys the link between taxes and benefits and distorts accountability. The system creates a variety of bad incentives at the Land level, which have softened budget constraints. First, the expenditure responsibilities of the Bund and Länder overlap in almost every policy area, and they have only become more intertwined since the introduction of the joint tasks in 1969. Moreover, the Länder rely heavily on tax sharing and grants, and their tax autonomy has declined over time. As a result, it is almost impossible for voters to know whom to hold responsible for which activities. The equalization system provides few incentives for the Länder to raise their own economic performance and tax base. For individual states, an additional 1 million deutsche marks in income tax receipts—personal or corporate—is estimated to generate only between 80,000 and 290,000 deutsche marks in extra tax income (OECD 1998, Huber and Lichtblau 1998). After equalization, the Länder with the lowest initial per capita fiscal capacity—Bremen, Saarland, and the eastern Länder—end up with the highest fiscal capacity per capita. Meanwhile, the Länder with the highest initial fiscal capacity—

Hamburg, Hesse, and Baden-Württemberg—end up with the lowest capacity after transfers.

As a result, the Länder have relatively weak incentives to be concerned with low rates of revenue collection. Empirical analysis by Von Hagen and Hepp (2000) demonstrates a declining correlation of state tax revenues with state GDP over time, which they interpret as evidence of weakening state tax efforts in response to the incentive effects of equalization. This incentive structure contributes to what the German Council of Economic Advisors has identified as one of the most important problems in German public finance: falling rates of revenue collection despite increasing tax burdens (Sachverständigenrat 1997). Since the Länder bear most of the costs of tax administration, and only a small fraction of additional tax revenues accrue to them, they face weak incentives to strengthen audits and improve revenue collection. This problem is especially severe in the most dependent Länder, which receive almost no benefit from increasing tax collection efforts (OECD 1998). A recent report estimates that the cost of lost revenue resulting from tax evasion and avoidance is around 125 billion deutsche marks, or around 15 percent of GDP.[7]

While all of these features of Germany's complex, intertwined federalism conspire to weaken the incentives of Land leaders to be fiscally responsible, one feature of the equalization system may explicitly encourage irresponsibility: the supplementary transfers described above. These gap-filling transfers explicitly reward states whose fiscal performance has been poor in the past. As discussed in greater detail below, these transfers have recently been used as explicit bailouts for Saarland and Bremen. Econometric analysis shows that increasing dependence on such transfers among the Länder is associated with slower adjustment to negative revenue shocks (Rodden 2001a) and larger long-term deficits (Rodden 2001b).

The Basic Law and its interpretation by the courts require far-reaching efforts to achieve interstate equality, but at the same time, they impose important restraints on the hierarchical oversight and control mechanisms available to the central government. In spite of bad incentives, the current structure provides the central government with no authority to limit or regulate borrowing by the states. Significant changes to the incentive structure would require the consent of the Länder, and since many of them benefit from the current setup, they are reluctant to agree.

5.2 The Political Mechanism

The unique German system of administrative fiscal federalism is accompanied by a highly integrated yet unmistakably federal political system. This system creates incentives for voters and politicians that have a direct effect on state-level fiscal behavior. Some of the structural weaknesses of German federalism extend to the principal-agent relationship between voters and public officials at the Land level and undermine the electoral oversight mechanism. Voters at the Land level have the authority to vote fiscally irresponsible officials out of office, but they sometimes lack the information and the incentives to do so. However, the highly integrated nature of the German party system might discourage the dramatic, systemic deficit-shifting scenarios described in the chapters in this book on Brazil and Argentina.

Most German pundits believe that Land-level elections are primarily referenda on the popularity of the federal chancellor and his government rather than independent assessments of the performance of Land-level politicians. This supposition is borne out by empirical analysis of election returns. The reelection chances of Land-level politicians are strongly affected by the success of their partisan colleagues at the Bund level.[8] This is not surprising, since the Bundesrat possesses the power to veto, delay, or rewrite most federal legislation, and Land elections determine the makeup of the Bundesrat. As a result, the media, voters, and Land politicians themselves have come to interpret Land elections as something like nonsimultaneous midterm federal elections (Abromeit 1982).

Second, given the complex interdependence of the German federal system, it is very difficult for citizens to obtain and interpret information about the competence and performance of their representatives at the Land level. Since they have no autonomous control over local tax rates, most policy decisions are made through cooperative intergovernmental processes, and most of their expenditures are for the implementation of federal programs, Land-level officials can always credibly claim that the blame for local policy failures or revenue shortfalls lies elsewhere, even though this is not always true. Voters simply have no way of accurately sorting out credit and blame for outcomes. Thus, it makes sense for information-economizing voters to assess the performance of the governing coalition in Bonn and punish or reward the same parties at each level of government.

As a result, electoral incentives for sound fiscal policy at the Land level are sometimes diluted; it is relatively easy for Land-level officials to escape electoral sanction for imprudent fiscal policies. Such blame avoidance might be even easier in Länder controlled by the opposition party.[9] Moreover, under some conditions, Land-level leaders may actually face electoral incentives to spend beyond their means and run deficits. The equalization system ensures that the costs of public goods in several of the recipient Länder are externalized onto the paying Länder. Recent events have made it clear that excessive deficits might be rewarded with bailouts, so voters may face few incentives to punish fiscal irresponsibility if they believe it will lead to larger transfers in the future. If the state's debt burden becomes unbearable, voters are more likely to lobby the central government for a bailout than to put political pressure on state-level representatives to make costly spending cuts.

However, political incentives for indiscipline should not be exaggerated. Indeed, the integration of the party system places a countervailing limitation on the incentives of Land officials to self-consciously overfish the common revenue pool. Intentionally overborrowing in order to provoke a federal bailout, especially in a large, important, or relatively prosperous state, would surely be a self-defeating career move for an ambitious Land politician. Conversely, a reputation as a prudent fiscal manager is an asset for an aspiring finance minister or *Bundeskanzler*. While the growing debt burden in the 1980s and 1990s seems not to have been a political liability at the time for the governments of Bremen and Saarland, the bailouts were ultimately politically embarrassing for the leaders in power when the bailouts were distributed. Moreover, the assessment of blame for the burgeoning debt crisis in Berlin has been the most hotly contested political issue among parties competing in upcoming elections.

5.3   The Capital Market and Its Regulation

This section turns to the role of the credit market in enforcing fiscal discipline in the German Länder. The need to borrow in well-functioning capital markets might force subnational leaders to make prudent fiscal decisions. Above all, credit ratings and interest rates can provide voters with important signals of government performance. If the costs of high interest rates resulting from imprudent fiscal decisions must be paid by local citizens in the form of increased taxes or lower property values, they are more likely to vote incumbents out of office. Such incentives have not been present at the Land level in Germany. For the most part, Länder need not worry about credit ratings, and the cost of capital has traditionally been roughly the same for all Länder. This system may be changing, though, as some of the Länder and their Landesbanken seek new forms of credit. This section provides an overview of Land-level connected borrowing throughout the postwar period and assesses recent developments that may enhance credit market discipline in the future.

The Länder have fulfilled their borrowing needs throughout the postwar period in the domestic bond and *Schuldschein* markets. They are barred from issuing debt in currencies other than the deutsche mark. The Länder occasionally issue deutsche mark bonds, Länderan-leihen, which are typically managed by the state's Landesbank. Bonds have been an insignificant part of Land-level borrowing, however, because of the attractiveness of the Schuldschein market. Schuld-scheine are not securities. *Schuldscheindarlehen* are credits that are documented by negotiable promissory notes called *Schuldscheine*. They are not quoted on any exchange but can be transferred to third parties by way of a written assignment. This issue method is popular because of its low cost, flexibility, and discretion with which the terms can be agreed.[10] In most cases these are negotiated with the state's Landes-bank. Most state and municipal borrowing is made up of Schuld-scheine. In 1993, for example, state Schuldschein issues amounted to 489.2 billion deutsche marks, while state bond issues totaled only 104.1 billion deutsche marks.[11] A disadvantage of this method is that the Länder have not been forced to use credit ratings and respond to the rigors of more competitive, transparent international bond markets.

In the mid-1990s, some of the Länder started to make use of a wider range of instruments as their overall debt requirements grew and as barriers between domestic and offshore markets came down. Although the Länder are allowed to make only deutsche mark issues, there are no restrictions that prevent them from borrowing in international markets. Some Länder have recently structured new forms of debt securities to attract international investors. In late 1993, there was a spate of long-dated deutsche mark issues by several of the Länder, led by foreign investment banks. Although these deals have not performed well, it seems likely that the Länder will continue to seek international investors in the future. If this trend continues, the Länder will eventually be forced to go through a rigorous rating process. According to

Standard and Poor's, "As volume mounts, investors will be less prepared to accept these issues solely on the basis of the German 'Land' label. They will seek different yields based on differences in credit quality."[12]

Another source of burgeoning credit market discipline may come from the Landesbanken. Not only are the Länder starting to raise funds outside domestic markets, the Landesbanks are beginning to look to international sources of capital as well. Some of the larger Landesbanks are beginning to issue Eurobonds and hold substantial capital in foreign currencies. The Landesbanks are considered semisovereign debtors, and investors are attracted to them because they are guaranteed by their respective Länder. For this reason, each Landesbank has at least one triple A rating—from Ibca (London)—and several have the same from Moody's and Standard and Poor's. (See Table 5.1.) Note that there is very little variation across Länder; no Landesbank is rated below Aa1 by Moody's or below AA+ by Standard & Poor's. This is in spite of the fact that the Landesbanks clearly do not perform as well as conventional triple-A rated institutions and in spite of the fact that there are large variations from one Landesbank to another.

The logic behind Ibca's uniform triple-A rating is the argument that if any Landesbank gets into trouble, the Land government would support it, and if this support would lead to a financial crisis in the

Table 5.1
Landesbank credit ratings, 1997

Landesbank	Moody's	Standard & Poor's	Ibca	Moody's Bank Financial Strength Rating
Bayerische LB	Aaa	AAA	AAA	C+
Bremer LB[a]	Aa1	—	AAA	C
DSL-Bank	Aaa	—	AAA	D+
Helaba	Aaa	AAA	AAA	C+
L-Bank Berlin	Aaa	—	AAA	B
LB Rheinland-Pfalz[b]	Aa1	AA+	AAA	C+
LB Schleswig-Holstein[b]	Aa1	—	AAA	C
LKB	Aaa	AAA	AAA	C+
NordLB	Aa1	—	AAA	C+
SudwestLB	Aaa	AAA	AAA	C+
WestLB	Aa1	AA+	AAA	C

[a]Supported by NordLB and therefore indirectly guaranteed by Lower Saxony.
[b]Supported by WestLB and therefore indirectly guaranteed by North Rhine—Westphalia.

Land, the federal government would step in. Standard & Poor's, on the other hand, has been less convinced that federal bailouts would be forthcoming and thus does not automatically award triple A ratings. According to Standard & Poor's, a rating is concerned with the timely payment of interest and capital, and even if the federal bailouts are forthcoming in the event of a crisis, the time lag between crisis and bailout could prove costly.[13] Thus, it considers the economy and fiscal performance of the Land when deciding on ratings. The credit rating of West LB, the largest of the Landesbanks, has recently been threatened with downgrade by Standard & Poor's because of the public finances of Nordrhein Westfallen. Nord LB has had a difficult time achieving triple A status because of the finances of Lower Saxony. In such cases, the Land governments may indeed feel indirect pressure, via the Landesbanks, to improve their public finances. Moody's has recently responded to pressure from international investors to create a more realistic rating system for the Länder. This Bank Financial Strength Rating shows more variation than previous ratings systems, ranging from B to D+ (see table 5.1). As Landesbanks continue to diversify and attempt to attract global capital, credit ratings will continue to become more important to them, and the pressure on Land governments to improve their finances will increase.

Finally, the entire system of connected borrowing from the Landesbanks may not last much longer. Not only are credit-rating agencies beginning to pressure the Landesbanks with more realistic credit ratings, but the key pillar of their strength, public guarantee of debts, is being threatened by the European Commission. In addition, some cash-strapped Länder have started to sell off stakes in their Landesbanks. For example, Bremen now owns only 7.5 percent of Bremer Landesbank. Landesbank Berlin has been partially privatized through a transfer of 75 percent of its shares to the publicly listed Bankgesellschaft Berlin (BGB), while the Land government, as the majority shareholder in BGB, maintains its explicit guarantee. Most analysts agree that the pressure for privatization of the Landesbanks is likely to grow stronger. In any case, the introduction of the euro and increasing international competition have the potential to push the Länder further in the direction of credit market discipline.

5.4   Deficits and Bailouts in Saarland and Bremen

The previous sections have argued that while German federalism may have a number of strengths, its most important weakness lies in the fact that it may facilitate fiscal indiscipline and soft budget constraints in the Länder. Many of the problems described have been visible in the recent crises and responses in Bremen and Saarland.[14] Although Saarland has always been a receiving Land in the equalization process, Bremen was a contributor prior to the 1970s. Both Länder have faced major economic downturns and had to deal with vexing unemployment problems in recent decades. Thus, it is not surprising that both have faced significant pressure on their public finances. Given their lack of revenue autonomy and small size, they were poorly situated to bear the costs of adjustment alone.

In fact, they have not been forced to bear the costs of adjustment alone. Prior to unification, they became the largest beneficiaries of the equalization process. In recent years, Saarland and Bremen have generally been ranked number one and two among all the Länder in fiscal capacity per capita after equalization. Despite constantly increasing dependence on equalization payments and associated transfers, both continued to increase spending, run large deficits, and rely heavily on debt to fund current expenditures throughout the 1980s and 1990s (see figure 5.6).

The Land governments simply had no hierarchical, political, or market incentives to cut spending. The Bund and the other Länder grew frustrated with their refusal to cut spending and balance their

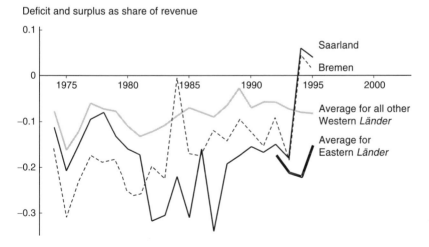

Figure 5.6
Fiscal outcomes in the German länder, 1974–1995. *Source*: Statistisches Bundesamt and author's calculations.

budgets, but they had no mechanisms with which to influence the decisions of Bremen and Saarland. Given their high level of fiscal dependence on other Länder and the Bund, the governments of Bremen and
Saarland were able to explain to their voters that they were not responsible for growing deficits and debt burdens; on the contrary, they
argued that the rest of the federation was not adequately fulfilling its
constitutional obligation to support them during their time of need.
Despite growing debt levels, the governments of Saarland and Bremen
had no trouble securing credit from their Landesbanks.

Saarland's constitution contains a golden rule provision that public
debt must not exceed investment spending. The government simply
ignored this provision, despite the fact that the highest court in the state
repeatedly declared that its budgets contradicted the state's constitution. Rather than suffering public embarrassment, the government of
Saarland used the "unconstitutional" nature of its deficits as further
proof that the rest of the federation was not fulfilling its obligations.

In the mid-1980s it became clear that the accumulated debt levels in
Bremen and Saarland were unsustainable, and both Länder declared
that they faced fiscal emergencies, calling on the federation and the
other Länder to provide special funds to pay down some of their debt.
Bremen eventually requested that the Bund explicitly take over its
obligations. The 1980s saw a variety of complaints by the Länder to
the Constitutional Court over the details of the fiscal constitution, and
Saarland and Bremen took their case for bailouts to the courts. A 1986
decision found that the federal supplementary transfers can be used to
bail out fiscally troubled Länder. This gave the governments of Bremen
and Saarland hope that they would eventually receive special federal
funds, and through the rest of the 1980s they had no incentives to
improve their finances. They continued to bring complaints to the
Constitutional Court in order to secure these funds, and in May 1992,
the Court declared that the "solidarity" obligation contained in the
Grundgesetz required that the Bund, as part of the renegotiation of the
equalization system in 1993, begin using the supplementary transfers
to provide Bremen and Saarland with bailouts amounting to 17 billion
deutsche marks.[15]

Bremen and Saarland started receiving the special funds in 1994.
Bremen has been receiving an extra 1.8 billion deutsche marks per year
and Saarland an extra 1.6 billion. In contrast to some of the bailouts
described elsewhere in this book, Bremen and Saarland are under no
obligation to make repayments. The bailout deals have involved con-

tracts between the central government and the states, whereby the states have agreed to limits on expenditure growth and have promised to use the extra funds only for the reduction of public debt and only to use savings on interest for further debt reduction or additional infrastructure investment. The bailouts have been sufficient to balance current budgets (note the sharp improvement in figure 5.6). Nevertheless, the Bund still has no carrots or sticks with which to punish or reward changes in spending or progress in reducing debt, and the progress of both Länder in reducing debt has fallen far short of expectations. Empirical analysis by Seitz (1998) shows that primary expenditure growth in Bremen and Saarland continued to outpace some of the other states after the bailout agreements. In fact, both Länder have since argued that the bailouts were insufficient, and they explain their inability to reduce debt by pointing out that they have experienced unexpected revenue shortfalls.[16]

Perhaps the most dangerous aspect of the crises is the demonstration effect for other fiscally troubled Länder, especially in the light of the court's interpretation of the federal government's obligations. The governments of Bremen and Saarland were able to use their status as small, transfer-dependent subnational units to their advantage. The nature of the federal system led them to believe that it was unlikely in the long term that the costs for their spending and borrowing decisions would be borne locally. They believed that the Constitution necessitated an eventual bailout, and now that the Constitutional Court has affirmed this, a concern is that other highly transfer-dependent Länder will have weaker incentives to worry about deficits and debt burdens in the future. Given the level of transfer dependence in the eastern Länder, the moral hazard problem may loom large. An important question is whether the limitations on budgetary autonomy and expenditure growth in the bailout agreements, along with the costs of political embarrassment, will dissuade Länder in the future from following the lead of Bremen and Saarland.

5.5 Conclusions and Prospects for Reform

Perhaps the most important source of soft Land-level budget constraints in Germany is the Constitution itself. By simultaneously creating wide-ranging Land-level administrative autonomy, guaranteeing the equivalence of living conditions, and entrenching strong representation of the Länder in the federal policymaking process, the

Constitution creates hurdles for the proper functioning of several fiscal discipline mechanisms. The constitutional structure divides taxing and spending decisions, carving out a good deal of spending autonomy for the Länder while giving them very little tax autonomy. Because of the equalization system, the Land governments face weak incentives to make prudent fiscal decisions. Because of blurred accountability and the possibility of bailouts, citizens and creditors have had neither the information nor the incentives to punish and reward Land representatives based on their fiscal decisions.

The Constitution provides the federal government and the wealthier Länder with no hierarchical mechanisms with which to constrain the spending or borrowing decisions of the dependent Länder. The lack of any such mechanism has always been an annoyance in the cases of Saarland, Bremen, and occasionally a few other western Länder, but the costs of redistribution and fiscal indiscipline are becoming a source of frustration that is beginning to undermine the solidarity and cooperation that have characterized the operation of the German federal system. Bavaria and Baden-Württemberg, two of the wealthiest Länder, have aggressively challenged the equalization system in the courts and in the political process. The Bund has had to shoulder most of the costs of unification and has been forced to fund the bailouts of Bremen and Saarland as well, and it is demanding that the Länder take on a larger share of the burden.

In response to numerous court challenges, the Constitutional Court issued a major ruling on November 11, 1999, obligating the Bund and Länder to renegotiate the system of equalization by the end of 2002, and it issued a set of guiding principles.[17] Among other things, the decision criticized the criteria used for the distribution of supplementary transfers and the extreme redistributiveness of the equalization system, and it advocated a more competitive form of federalism that preserved the identities and autonomy of the states while affirming the basic principles of solidarity and equivalent living conditions outlined in the Basic Law. This led to intensive intergovernmental negotiations and a wealth of reform proposals. The wealthier Länder have demanded greater tax autonomy and a complete overhaul of the equalization system.[18] The Bund is especially interested in reforming the system, since it is obliged under the terms of the Stability and Growth Pact to observe a general government deficit limit and to accept sanctions including fines in the event of noncompliance. The federal government argues that despite the fact that it has no mechanism to control the borrowing of the Länder, irresponsible Land-level borrowing decisions could cause the German public sector to run afoul of the Maastricht deficit limit, and the federal government would be forced to pay the fines.

As a result, the federal government is seeking to establish an internal equivalent of the Stability and Growth Pact (OECD 1998; Sachverständigenrat 1996). The government has proposed to determine legally binding allocations of the Maastricht deficit limit both vertically between the Bund and the Länder and horizontally across the Länder. These caps would come into play only in the event of an excessive deficit for Germany as defined by the Maastricht criteria. The idea is to allocate the EU fines among the Bund and Länder. Of course, this has led to a good deal of conflict over the fraction of the overall deficit that should be allocated to the Bund and Länder and how fines should be allocated horizontally across the Länder. However, it is not clear how the idea of penalizing particular Länder for deficits squares with the equalization system or with the Constitutional Court's interpretation of the Basic Law.

In June 2001, the Bund and Länder agreed to a new equalization law, to take effect in 2005. The basic structure of the old three-stage system remains unchanged, but the wealthy states agreed to the new system because it allows them to keep a larger share of the taxes they collect.[19] But the agreement will not reduce the receipts of the relatively poor Länder. This apparent win-win scenario was possible because the central government agreed to make up the difference by committing billions of additional deutsche marks to the system. In other words, the central government will be replacing some of the horizontal redistribution between the Länder with direct, vertical redistribution from the Bund to the Länder and transfer dependence among the poorest Länder will only grow. It is not yet clear whether the agreement will pass constitutional muster. Some of the thorniest issues raised in the negotiations, like reforming the joint tasks and instituting hierarchical Maastricht-style debt restrictions on the Länder, have been left unresolved.

Thus, it is quite difficult to see the agreement as a major departure from the status quo. In fact, any serious departure would require a constitutional change that calls for the approval of two-thirds of the Länder, meaning that several of the beneficiaries of equalization would have to approve. The wealthy and poor Länder have coalesced into distinct groups with clear objectives, and it may be very difficult to bring them to a compromise. The Länder have also shown that they are able to coalesce against the Bund to protect their interests.[20]

In the past, renegotiations of the system of fiscal federalism have been possible in spite of the entrenched interests of certain Länder because of cross-cutting partisan cleavages (Renzsch 1995). However, partisan cleavages are beginning to match up with the cleavages of fiscal federalism; the Social Democrats are strongest in the weaker, more dependent Länder, and the Christian Democrats are strongest in the wealthiest Länder that pay into the equalization system. In addition, the PDS (the former Communist party in East Germany) has become a regional party that effectively represents the interests of the eastern Länder. Attempts to improve the efficiency of the public sector in Germany often fail because of the difficulty of bringing together a reform coalition in a system with so many effective veto players. For these reasons, battles over fiscal federalism will continue to be a key feature of the German political landscape in the years ahead.

Notes

1. The new Länder are Brandenburg, Saxony, Saxony-Anhalt, Thuringia, and Mecklenburg–West Pomerania.

2. For critical analysis of the joint tasks, see Scharpf Reissert, and Schnabel 1976, Scharpf 1988, and Huber (2001).

3. For additional details, see Spahn and Föttinger (1997).

4. The benchmark for determining differentials in tax capacities is, roughly, the average tax revenue per capita multiplied by the population for each state. However, the procedure is complicated by a weighting that favors city states. For details, see Spahn (2001).

5. For additional details, see Spahn and Föttinger (1997).

6. "German Banking: Can Dachshunds be Whippets?" *Economist*, Jan. 4, 1997, 70.

7. Report of the *Institut der deutschen Wirtschaft (IW)*, cited in Peter Norman, "The Taxpayers Are Revolting," *Financial Times*, Nov. 3, 1997.

8. See Fabritius (1978), Lohmann, Brady, and Rivers (1997), and Rodden (2001c).

9. For instance, federal Finance Minister Oskar Lafontaine clearly did not have to pay an electoral price for repeatedly running massive deficits while serving as minister-president of Saarland during the Kohl era. Likewise, Gerhard Schröder's legacy of budget problems and massive debt in Lower Saxony was no impediment to his ascent in federal politics. Instead, he was able to use his state's economic and public finance difficulties as the basis for attacks on the Kohl government.

10. "Germany: Euroweek Supplement on Top Credits—Länder Look to New Horizons," *Euroweek*, Nov. 30, 1994.

11. Ibid.

12. Cited in "Germany: Euroweek."

13. Laura Covill, "Germany: When the Bankers Go Cap-in-Hand," *Euromoney*, Dec. 28, 1994.

14. For a more detailed account of the bailout episode, see Seitz (1998).

15. "Bund fordert Länder zur Mitfinanzierung auf," *Handelsblatt*, Mar. 3, 1998.

16. "Streit um Hilfen für das Saarland und Bremen," *Frankfurter Allgemeine Zeitung*, Feb. 25, 1998.

17. BverG, 2 BvF 2/98, Nos. 1–347.

18. Baden Württemberg's minister-president, Erwin Teufel, was the most vocal. See "Eigene Steuern für die Länder," *Focus*, Feb. 23, 1998, and "Attacke der Reichen," *Focus*, Feb. 23, 1998. See also "Letzter Einigungsversuch zum Finanzausgleich," *Frankfurter Allgemeine Zeitung*, Mar. 2, 1998. For overviews of academic reform proposals, see OECD (1998), Renzsch (1999a, 1999b), and Huber and Lichtblau (1998).

19. There will be a ceiling on the amount that a Land must contribute to equalization—no more than 72.5 percent of the amount of its tax income that is above the national average. Länder will also be able to keep 12.5 percent of the amount of any yearly increase in tax receipts that surpasses the national average increase.

20. Most of the fiscal burden associated with unification, the inclusion of the new Länder in the federal fiscal system, and the bailouts of Saarland and Bremen have fallen on the Bund because the Länder were able to cooperate against the federal government in the negotiations leading up to the 1993 "solidarity pact."

References

Abromeit, Heidrun. 1982. "Die Funktion des Bundesrates und der Streit um seine Politisierung." *Zeitschrift für Parlamentsfragen* 13:467–471.

Fabritius, Georg. 1978. *Weckselwirkungen zwischen Landtagswahlen und Bundespolitik.* Meisenheim am Glan: Verlag Anton Hain.

Federal Ministry of Finance. 1996. *Finanzbericht 1997.* Bonn.

Huber, Bernd. 2001. "Die Mischfinanzierungen im deutschen Föderalismus: Ökonomische Probleme und Reformmöglichkeiten." *Arbeitspapier* 48. Konrad-Adenauer-Stiftung e.V. Sankt Augustin.

Huber, Bernd, and Karl Lichtblau. 1998. "Konfiskatorischer Finanzausgleich verlangt eine Reform." *Wirtschaftsdienst* 3:31–52.

Laufer, Heinz. 1994. "The Principles and Organisational Structures of a Federative Constitution." In *The Example of Federalism in the Federal Republic of Germany: A Reader.* Sankt Augustin: Konrad-Adenauer-Stiftung.

Lohmann, Susanne, David Brady, and Douglas Rivers. 1997. "Party Identification, Retrospective Voting, and Moderating Elections in a Federal System: West Germany, 1961–1989." *Comparative Political Studies* 30(4):420–449.

Organization for Economic Cooperation and Development. 1998. *OECD Economic Surveys, 1997–1998: Germany*. Paris: OECD.

Renzsch, Wolfgang. 1991. *Finanzverfassung und Finanzausgleich*. Bonn: Dietz.

Renzsch, Wolfgang. 1995. "Konfliktlösung im parlamentarischen Bundesstaat." In Rüdiger Voigt, ed., *Der Kooperative Staat: Krisenbewältigung durch Verhandlung?* Baden-Baden: Nomos.

Renzsch, Wolfgang. 1999a. "Modernisierung der Finanzverfassung: Möglichkeiten und Grenzen." Unpublished paper, Otto-von-Guericke Universität Magdeburg.

Renzsch, Wolfgang. 1999b. "Reform der Finanzverfassung: Zwischen Ökonomischer Effizienz, bundesstaatlicher Funktionalität und politischer Legitimität." Paper presented at the conference "Finanzverfassung und Föderalismus," Zentrum für Europäische Wirtschaftforschung, Mannheim, Apr. 14–15, 1999.

Rodden, Jonathan. 2001a. "Breaking the Golden Rule: Fiscal Behavior with Rational Bailout Expectations in the German States." Unpublished paper, MIT.

Rodden, Jonathan. 2001b. "And the Last Shall Be First: The Political Economy of Federalism and Deficits in Germany." Unpublished paper, MIT.

Rodden, Jonathan. 2001c. "Creating a More Perfect Union: Electoral Incentives and the Reform of Federal Systems." Unpublished paper, MIT.

Sachverständigenrat. 1996. *Reformen Voranbringen: Jahresgutachten 1996/1997*. Stuttgart: Metzler-Poeschel.

Sachverständigenrat. 1997. *Wachstum, Beschäftigung, Währungsunion- Orientierung für die Zukunft: Jahresgutachten 1997/1998*. Stuttgart: Metzler-Poeschel.

Scharpf, Fritz. 1988. "The Joint-Decision Trap: Lessons from German Federalism and European Integration." *Public Administration* 66:239–278.

Scharpf, Fritz, Bernd Reissert, and Fritz Schnabel. 1976. *Politikverflechtung: Theorie und Empirie des kooperativen Föderalismus in der Bundesrepublik*. Kronberg: Scriptor.

Seitz, Helmut. 1998. "Subnational Government Bailouts in Germany." Unpublished paper, Center for European Integration Studies, Bonn.

Seitz, Helmut. 1999. "Where Have All the Flowers Gone? Die öffentlichen Finanzen in den neuen Ländern." Prepared for presentation at the University of Magdeburg, Oct. 1999.

Seitz, Helmut. 2001. "Haushaltsnotlage in Berlin?" Unpublished paper, Europa-Universität Viadrina.

Spahn, Paul Bernd. 2001. "Maintaining Fiscal Equilibrium in a Federation: Germany." Unpublished paper, University of Frankfurt.

Spahn, Paul Bernd, and Wolfgang Föttinger. 1997. "Germany." In Teresa Ter-Minassian, ed., *Fiscal Federalism in Theory and Practice*. Washington, D.C.: International Monetary Fund.

Von Hagen, Jürgen, and Ralf Hepp. 2000. "Regional Risk Sharing and Redistribution in the German Federation." Unpublished paper, Center for European Integration Research, Bonn.

III

Developing Countries
with Histories of
Federalism and
Fiscal Decentralization

6

Argentina: Hardening the Provincial Budget Constraint

Steven B. Webb

In setting hard budget constraints on subnational finances, Argentina went from being one of the worst countries in the 1980s to being one of the more promising in the 1990s among middle-income countries that have democratically elected subnational governments. The constraints developed in the 1990s represented a major improvement but were still vulnerable. The national economic difficulties since 1999 exposed the weaknesses and prompted the federal government to move to a more flexible and broader strategy. This strategy ran into trouble in the context of the country's overall fiscal and macroeconomic problems in 2001, which is beyond the period covered here.

Argentine provinces in the mid-1980s faced exceptionally soft budget constraints and, as one would therefore expect, had high deficits that were about half of the overall public sector deficit. Then, in a series of steps over the next ten years, policy changes, particularly at the federal level, tightened the constraints and filled various gaps. This raises three questions: Why was there a soft budget constraint in the 1980s? What measures hardened it thereafter? What weakness remained at the end of the 1990s?

The length of the process seems unavoidable. The reforms have proceeded stepwise, with progress coming as federal-level reforms opened opportunities and created incentives for provincial reforms and then individual provinces responded to those incentives. These are historic developments, and history takes time for institutions to build and establish their reputations. To understand the evolution of provincial budget constraints over time, it is important to know the macroeconomic and political-constitutional backdrops of the drama.

6.1 Macroeconomic Background

In the 1980s, Argentina went through its worst hyperinflation, peaking in 1989 and bringing the economy and society to what was widely seen as the brink of collapse. The new administration of Carlos Menem then had a mandate to take drastic measures to stabilize the economy. After a few months of indecision and miscues, Menem brought in Domingo Cavallo as minister of economy, who engineered a successful stabilization and fiscal adjustment of the whole public sector. Provincial fiscal adjustment contributed to the overall public sector reform, and Menem gained political support for being part of it. (See table 6.1.)

From the point of view of intergovernmental finances, the most important fiscal development associated with the stabilization was the rapid growth of tax revenues that were shared with the provinces. This was partly a direct result of new policies, particularly some improvements to tax collection and enforcement, and partly an endogenous result of the stabilization. Without high inflation, there was no longer the massive erosion of the real value of tax revenue resulting from the delays in payment. Such delays had been particularly costly to the provinces, because their own taxes and the taxes shared with the federal government were levied on domestic currency flows. (The exclusively federal taxes were on trade and therefore levied in foreign exchange.)

Table 6.1
Growth, inflation, and fiscal Balances in Argentina, 1983–2000 (percent)

	1983–1987	1988–1990	1991–1994	1995–1997	1998–2000
Real growth (annual average)	1.77	–3.43	8.89	2.69	–2.4
Inflation (annual average)	370	1,910	53	1.3	–0.34
Overall balance (% of GDP)					
Central	–5.11	–0.87	0.27	–1.32	–1.86
Subnational	–4.90	–1.99	–1.33	–0.88	–1.1
Primary balance (% of GDP)					
Central	–3.44	–0.07	1.40	0.28	–1.13
Subnational	–4.84	–1.76	–1.16	–0.56	–0.6
Public enterprises			0.73	0.02	

Source: Ministry of Economy, Argentina; International Monetary Fund *GFS* and staff estimates; authors' estimates.

Without adequate tax revenues during hyperinflation, the provinces came to depend on the inflation tax, as did the federal government. They borrowed from their provincial banks, which then discounted the debt at the central bank, effectively giving the provinces a share in the seignorage from inflation.

6.2 Constitutional and Political Framework

Argentina has a long history as a federal country, now with twenty-three provinces plus the city of Buenos Aires. It is a presidential system, as everywhere else in Latin America, with considerable power vested in the office of the president. Congress in normal times must approve his main fiscal policy initiatives, but he has substantial patronage and party discipline with which to convince them, and executive emergency powers are extensive and—at least prior to the 1994 constitution—were frequently used. Two additional features deserve special attention.

First, the executive or the military has suspended the normal constitutional process frequently. The military has taken over the national government twice since 1950, most recently from 1976 through 1982. Under both civilian and military rule, the national government has frequently taken over provincial governments, often dismissing elected governors. At least three provinces had such interventions in the 1990s, and Córdoba had federal interventions for twenty-four of the past fifty years (Nicolini et al. 1999, Cordoba 1997). The constitutional and practical autonomy of provinces face limits that would not permit serious flaunting of the rules. In contrast, the Brazilian states have not faced such strong limits in the past, and as a result, they have been able to ignore or circumvent central rules.

Second, political geography makes the Argentine federation very asymmetric in practice, although the constitution does not prescribe special treatment for any province. Buenos Aires province has 38 percent of the nation's population—48 percent when combined with Buenos Aires city—and together they generate well over half of the national GDP. This gives them a strong position in the lower house of Congress and a dominant position in the economy and public finances. Indeed, as the main source of tax revenue and the locus of the majority of the cost of any macroeconomic instability, Buenos Aires's gains from prudent macro-fiscal policy make it worthwhile for them to pay a substantial part of the cost, in contrast to the usual pattern in federal systems pointed out in chapter 1, where every state has incentives to refuse to contribute to national fiscal prudence in hopes of free-riding. At the other end of the size spectrum of provinces, all of the smaller-than-average provinces get above-average representation per capita in the Senate, and the minimum of five representatives per provinces gives ten of them substantially more representation than a one-person, one-vote system. Consequently, if it costs a certain amount of resources per voter to win the support of any province, buying support of a low-population province will cost less than support of a high-population province.

6.3   Historical Evolution of Fiscal Federal Relations

Although the 1853 constitution limited the federal government's taxing power on foreign trade, it granted the power to impose domestic direct taxes "for a determined time period" and subsequently allowed the federal government to impose domestic indirect taxes concurrently with the provinces (Murphy 1995). During the 1930s, in response to a drop in foreign trade taxes, the federal government introduced national income and sales taxes that replaced most existing provincial taxes. To compensate provinces for lost revenue, it established a system of revenue sharing (known as coparticipation). Revenue sharing has become more complex but remains the backbone of provincial revenues. Despite the historical origins that give provinces rights to share in the revenues, the national government makes all the decisions on the tax rates for the shared taxes.

Because of its historic origins, the allocation of *coparticipaciones* is made by a *ley de convenio*, a type of superlaw that requires the approval not only of both houses of Congress and the president but also of each of the governors. While the military government (1976–1983) used intervention and coercion to bypass these rules, they brought about deadlock in the mid-1980s after democracy was restored. The Radicals had the presidency and weak control of the lower chamber of Congress, while Justicialistas (Peronists) controlled a slim majority of provincial governments and thereby also the indirectly elected Senate. The divided government could not reach an agreement on distribution of *participaciones*, so they were all distributed by executive discretion, as *aportes del tersoro nacional* (ATNs) (World Bank 1990, Willis, Garman, and Haggard 1997). ATNs had existed for years, and continue to exist, but they became the main channel for transfers to provinces from the federal budget. While there was presumably some capriciousness by the executive in the distribution of these funds, the main problem seems to have been provinces' getting additional funds as conditions for political support needed by the weak president. In tandem with central bank funding, this situation in the mid-1980s represented the epitome of soft budget constraints for provinces.

In 1987, the Justicialistas took control of the lower chamber of Congress and expanded their control of provinces and the Senate. This broke the deadlock and led to the 1988 *Ley de Coparticipaciones*. This law remains in effect, although it was substantially altered by two fiscal pacts in the early 1990s and is overdue for a complete revision. As one would expect, the Justicialistas wanted to shift resources to the provinces as a group and passed a relatively generous formula for allocation of transfers to provinces, higher than in the early 1980s and equal in real terms to the formula transfers of the late 1970s. The law specifies that allocation by formula of 99 percent of the revenues from shared taxes, leaving 1 percent to be distributed by ATNs.[1] Most of the ATNs have gone to small provinces since 1988, which has softened the budget constraints of these provinces. By the same token, the executive has effectively no discretion in distributing meaningful resources to the large states. The law does set a firm limit on transfers to the large states and thus to the majority of provincial spending, so it has been a success for improving fiscal stability. The formula does not, however, return to a province most of any extra revenues generated there, meaning that it provides very weak incentives for provincial fiscal effort and is ultimately fiscally inefficient (World Bank 1999). Also, it is weak in improving equity, for the distribution is only weakly correlated with poverty indicators or (negatively) per capita income.

The most important determinants of the per capita distribution of transfers are the per capita representation in Congress, the inverse of population density (which also translates into more political clout per capita), and being the home province of the president (Porto and Sanguinetti 1998, Jones, Saguinetti, and Tommasi 1997, Kraemer 1997). Although almost everyone agrees that current transfer formulas have serious problems, the multiplicity of veto gates has made it difficult to get a revision in the democratic setting of Argentina with the 1994 constitution (Saiegh and Tommasi 1999).

In the late 1980s and 1990, poor tax collection and high inflation eroded considerably the real value of resources that provinces got from the *coparticipaciones* and other tax sources. Indeed, inflation hurt provincial revenue more than federal because the shared taxes were domestic and collected with longer lags, while the exclusively federal trade taxes were denominated in foreign exchange. The provincial as well as federal governments thus came to depend on seigniorage and the inflation tax. The availability of discretionary transfers to provinces, the softness of the federal government's own budget constraint, and the access that provinces had to monetary financing (given in part because the federal government could not deliver regular budgetary resources reliably) contributed significantly to the softness of the provinces' budget constraints.

In Argentina prior to 1991, provinces borrowed a lot, much of it from their own provincial banks, which then discounted the loans to the central bank, effectively giving provinces a share in the seigniorage and inflation tax. There were over twenty provincial banks, including two each in Mendoza and Córdoba. In 1990, they provided more than 60 percent of the credit needs of provincial governments at low or zero interest rates, and the central bank lent massive amounts through redis-counts to prevent the collapse of several provincial banks, due to poor loan recovery and overstaffing. By 1989, subsidies to subnational governments and others were estimated at about $8 billion, more than 5 percent of GDP and close to half of the overall public sector deficit. This was the worst kind of hole in the budget constraint, for it encouraged provinces to overspend their budgets, and it hid the cost, mixing it in with the cost of inflation from other sources.

In the late 1980s, macroeconomic instability reached the point of hyperinflation, following a long series of failed economic stabilization programs. Their main failure was the inability to reduce the public sector's deficit. On the eve of elections in 1989, real wages dropped precipitously. Inflation in one week reached 17 percent, and a banking crisis was imminent. The government was virtually bankrupt due to its inability to collect taxes (Peralta-Ramos 1992).

Macroeconomic instability had become closely, and correctly, associ-ated in people's minds with the overall decline of the economy since the first half of the century. When hyperinflation in 1989–1990 threat-ened to push the country further into underdevelopment, people grew desperate and were ready for strong policy measures. President Menem and his new economics minister, Domingo Cavallo, were able to muster political support for radical solutions. The keystone was the convertibility plan, introduced in April 1991. This fixed the exchange rate of the Argentine currency (renamed the peso) to the dollar and required that the monetary base not exceed the dollar value of international reserves. This in effect transformed the central bank into a currency board by mandating a 100 percent reserve requirement for the issue of high-power money (later, the law allowed up to one-third backing by federal government bonds). It also removed the power to devalue from the Ministry of Economy and placed it with Congress, where the need to obtain majorities made changing the law relatively difficult, especially in a federal presidential system. This helped harden budget constraint on the overall public sector, which gave the national government a strong incentive to set a hard budget constraint in its relations with the provinces. Other national governments, lacking such a hard budget constraint on themselves, have been less likely to enforce it on the other levels of government (Dillinger, Perry, and Webb 1999).

With the imposition of peso convertibility, inflation slowed to 3 percent in 1992, 0 percent in 1993, and 6 percent in 1994. Due to strong collection efforts, reverse-Tanzi-Oliveira effects, and economic growth, tax revenues increased dramatically, especially from shared taxes. This was reflected at the provincial level, where revenue jumped over 25 percent in real terms between 1991 and 1992, and over a percentage point in GDP, which was itself recovering strongly. (See table 6.2.)

Difficult fiscal adjustment was necessary at the federal level, especially reducing public employment and privatizing state-owned enterprises (World Bank 1996c). Extensive public relations explained how structural adjustment was necessary to prevent a revival of inflation, and in backroom political deals, the executive took advantage of

Table 6.2
Trends in provincial revenues and expenditures, 1991–2000 (percent of GDP)

Type of Revenue	1991	1994	1997	2000
Current revenues	8.19	9.45	9.52	10.9
Provincial taxes	2.59	3.42	3.21	3.9
Provincial nontax revenue	0.40	0.62	0.77	0.8
National transfers (*aportes*)	5.20	5.42	5.55	6.2
Current expenditures	7.77	9.10	8.25	11.5
Capital expenditures	1.21	1.40	1.55	1.2
Primary surplus (deficit)	(1.34)	(1.34)	0.11	(0.15)
Overall surplus (deficit)	(1.48)	(1.55)	(0.29)	(1.15)

Sources: For 1991–1994, World Bank (1996c); for 1997 and 2000, Republic of Argentina, *Informe Económico Regional.*

the federal system of representation. A winning set of provinces in both houses could consist of Buenos Aires province for its weight in the Chamber of Deputies and the low-population provinces for their weight in the senate. The *Fondo Conurbano* helped to obtain the support of Buenos Aires province, which ran a surplus the first couple of years after the stabilization and then kept spending from outstripping the growth of revenues.[2] For the small provinces, the flow of per capita coparticipation revenue, plus discretionary transfers in a few cases, was very high relative to their size but not in the aggregate (Nicolini et al. 1999). Because of their low population and high representation per capita, small provinces were inexpensive places to buy support in the House and especially the Senate (Gibson 1997).

By the time of stabilization in 1991, hyperinflation had greatly eroded the real value of domestic debt for governments at all levels, although external debts remained substantial. In 1991–1992, the federal government renegotiated its outstanding debts with the provinces. Each side had claims against the other. Provincial governments were in default on long-standing loans from the federal government, which in turn was in default on payments owed to the provinces. The exact value of these mutual obligations was subject to dispute, particularly since the hyperinflation of 1989 had distorted their value in real terms. The federal government emerged from the negotiations as the net debtor; the provinces emerged with virtually no debt to the federal government. This outcome proved advantageous not only for the provinces but also for the federal government in the future. Because the provinces had virtually no debt to the federal government on which they might default—they were just getting transfers—the center had a stronger hand to pressure them to adjust in response to subsequent fiscal shocks. From 1991 to 1999, total provincial debt grew little in pesos (or dollars) and declined as a share of GDP and of provincial revenues. Most of the debt is owed to the private sector, domestic and foreign, and has been serviced, at least until the national fiscal crisis in 2001.

From 1993, through the rest of the 1990s, a Ministry of Economy resolution explicitly prohibited any federal agency from using its resources to pay a creditor on behalf of a province. The Banco de la Nacion also, without hesitation, deducted debt service from the coparticipation transfers in cases where those transfers were used as collateral for provincial borrowing. This discouraged provinces from excessive borrowing (eventually, after 1995), but it made creditors more willing to lend.

To reinforce its autonomy, the central bank's charter was revised in September 1992, establishing an independent board of directors ratified by Congress, with fixed terms of tenure. Two provisions in the charter had important implications for provinces. First, the charter dictated that the central bank could not take any new domestic assets. This meant that provinces could no longer go to the central bank to rediscount loans by provincial banks to provincial governments, ending their access to seigniorage and the inflation tax. Second, the charter prohibited the central bank from guaranteeing bank deposits. Then provincial banks had to rely on depositor confidence to maintain liquidity. Both measures reduced the central bank's role as lender of last resort and hardened the financial budget constraint on provinces, limiting their ability to borrow from banks and eliminating access to central bank financing. At first, these constraints were not binding on provincial finances because of the rapid growth of tax revenues. However, it proved to be important that the limits were entrenched in the midst of the postconvertibility boom, because they were firmly in place when the boom came to an end and pressure for deficit financing increased.

Taking advantage of the provinces' rapid and unexpected increase in revenues, the federal government negotiated a series of fiscal agreements from 1992 to 1994. *Pacto Fiscal I* (August 1992) diverted coparticipation funds to the national social security system, which was poorly funded and required large subsidies. Under the agreement, provinces allowed 15 percent of the total taxes subject to coparticipation to be diverted to finance the transition costs of national social security reform. To close the pact, the federal government guaranteed a floor of $8.7 billion annually in coparticipation payments, expressed in terms of fixed amounts of pesos per month. In expressing the guarantee in terms of pesos, the federal government bet that revenues would grow (and that the regular formula for transfers would exceed the guaranteed amount). Over the next three years, the government won the bet, and the provinces did not collect on their insurance. Although they did collect in 1995 and early 1996, the national executive paid a modest price in exchange for important structural reforms.

As additional quid pro quo, the government established a *Fondo de Desequilibrio Fiscal* for small, poor provinces. Because the political power of the small provinces is disproportionate to their population due to their overrepresentation in both houses of Congress, the fund bought political support at relatively low cost. Government also called in political obligations from the delegation of Buenos Aires province, demanding support for the fiscal pact as a reward for the recently enacted *Fondo Conurbano*.[3]

Pacto Fiscal I followed soon after the transfer of federal health and secondary school programs, including 284,000 federal employees, to the provinces. In the *Pacto*, the federal government guaranteed payment equal to its expenditures in each province in 1992. The payment was financed not from central government revenues but from the provinces' share of coparticipation taxes. This allowed the federal government to exit from a major area of expenditure without any increase in transfers to the provinces.[4]

In August 1993, the federal government negotiated *Pacto Fiscal II*, which reformed provincial pension funds. Prior to the reforms, each province maintained a separate pension fund for its employees. Benefit payments were funded with earmarked salary deductions, plus subsidies from general treasury revenues. The scale of treasury subsidies was under 0.5 percent of GDP for the sixteen provinces expected to transfer their pensions to the federal government, but actuarial projections indicated that most provincial pensions were financially unsustainable. Although the pensions were legally a concern of individual provinces, the Ministry of Economy feared that a major collapse would ultimately redound on the federal government itself, especially since some of the personnel had been inherited from the federal level.

Under the second fiscal pact, the federal government agreed to take over the pension system of any province that passed a law authorizing it to do so. Once transferred, the federal pension system would eventually confer on federal and provincial civil servants the same retirement eligibility conditions, contributions, and benefits that were available to the private sector. Provinces were slow to implement the reforms, however. Because the transfer would reduce the benefits of active employees, it was opposed by public employee unions. Not all provinces would benefit from the transfer in any case. Although federalizing a provincial pension plan would eliminate the need to subsidize pensions from the general treasury, it would also increase employer contributions in some cases. The small provinces and Córdoba would be the primary beneficiaries (World Bank 1996b, 1996c). The provinces of Buenos Aires and Santa Fe would not benefit, because savings from the elimination of subsidies would be more than offset by increases in direct payments (from employers) into the national system.[5] In return for signing the second fiscal pact, the federal government offered to raise the guaranteed minimum of coparticipation funds. During the same period, the government also offered to finance the privatization of provincial banks, but prior to 1995 only four small provinces (Corrientes, La Rioja, Chaco, and Entre Ríos) had done so. While the takeover of the pension funds could be considered a bailout in that it reduced the obligations of the provinces (Sanguinetti et al. 1999), it was a fixed-value offer related to obligations usually predating the current governors, and the terms removed any possibility for provinces to get the transfer again in the future. Thus, it can be considered part of the process of hardening the budget constraint.

While provincial revenues increased rapidly in the 1991–1994 period, expenditures increased at the same rate or faster in some provinces. Between 1991 and 1994, revenues increased by 1.4 percentage points of GDP and expenditures by 1.5 points. Personnel costs accounted for about half the increase in expenditures. Growth in transfers to social security, private schools, and municipalities accounted for another 16 percent, and growth in capital spending for 13 percent. Interest costs remained small, about 2 percent of total outlays. Provinces with precarious finances at the start of the postconvertibility boom continued to have precarious finances despite dramatic increases in revenue. Smaller provinces, along with Córdoba and Buenos Aires city, were in greatest jeopardy. In other words, many provinces were behaving as though they had a soft budget constraint, although the rules on the books implied a hard one. The rules still lacked credibility due to the long history in Argentina of circumventing budget constraints.

In December 1994, an international and domestic debt crisis in Mexico (the Tequila crisis) caused a shock to financial market confidence in Latin America and ended the postconvertibility revenue boom. Argentina was particularly vulnerable to a financial crisis due to its heavy reliance on foreign capital inflows, the inflexibility of its exchange rate regime, and the need for a strong financial system under the convertibility plan. GDP fell 4 percent in real terms in 1995, and provincial revenues dropped 8 percent. The Tequila crisis also prompted a run on most provincial banks, except the Bank of the Province of Buenos Aires. With the prospect of central bank assistance closed off by the convertibility law and the central bank's new charter, provinces were forced to use their own resources to prevent provincial banks from failing and to recapitalize them. Through a project financed by the World Bank and the Inter-American Development Bank, the federal government refinanced the liabilities of the provincial banks taken over by provincial governments, but it made the assistance conditional on privatization of the banks.

The Tequila crisis tested the nascent hard budget constraint implied by the convertibility law and the new central bank charter. Initially, the provinces responded to the fall in revenues by borrowing—either directly from the treasury or from their provincial banks—or by obtaining emergency grants from the federal government. As a result, provincial debt expanded dramatically, totaling $17.3 billion by mid-1996, more than two-thirds of which had been run up since 1991. (See table 6.3.) They used mainly three sources. First, they ran up arrears to suppliers and personnel. Second, after exhausting the tolerance for delayed payment, they resorted to forced lending, paying staff and suppliers with bonds. These bonds could be converted to cash at a discount at provincial banks and then used to pay taxes. These two kinds of forced lending accounted for more than half of the debt incurred in the first year and a half of the crisis. Third, despite their financial difficulties, the provinces were able to continue borrowing from private banks, pledging their coparticipation transfers as guarantee. The federal government was a party to this arrangement in that Banco de la Nación would deduct the debt service from federal tax receipts and transfer only the remainder to the provinces. Even after the Tequila crisis, the government adhered to this practice. This sharply

Table 6.3
Provincial debt in Argentina, 1996–2000

	1995	1996	1997	1998	1999	2000
Total provincial debt	15,393	17,292	16,249	13,164	16,565	21,227
Banks[a]		5,771	4,382	5,315	6,459	7,599
National government[b]		768	473	233	235	158
International organizations		1,525	1,997	3,071	3,736	2,677
Provincial bonds	1,124	2,248	3,640	3,825	4,911	7,079
Consolidated debt[c]		5,142	5,582	628	1,222	1,090

Source: For 1996, Ministerio de Economía IEFE; for 1997, Republic of Argentina, *Informe económico regional*, December 1997, November 1998, February 2001.
[a]Including private and provincial banks. Bank debt and thus total debt declined from 1996 to 1997 largely because Buenos Aireo province renegotiated some of its debt with its provincial bank.
[b]Loans to provinces under BOTE 10 and BOCEP.
[c]Debt contracted with federal fiduciary fund to finance privatization of commercial banks and bonds issued to suppliers and other debtors in lieu of payment and bands issued to refinance such debt.

reduced net transfers to provinces with high levels of bank debt, taking as much as one-third of coparticipation to pay creditors. This experience increased the credibility of the rules. Although the rules were occasionally bent, these partial exceptions still required painful fiscal adjustment on the part of the provinces and indeed made it sustainable.

The timing of adjustment differed among provinces. Buenos Aires province adjusted substantially in the early 1990s and therefore had less need to adjust in the economic crisis. While the province began the postconvertibility period with an overall deficit of 10 percent of revenues, subsequent increases in expenditures, although large, were less than the increase in revenues between 1991 and 1994. With the help of the *Fondo Conurbano*, created in 1992, the province achieved an overall surplus in 1992. When the Tequila crisis caused a 3 percent drop in real revenues, the province responded by reducing capital expenditures, which sufficed to maintain the overall deficit at its 1994 level, 4 percent of current revenue. Total debt was still less than one-third of revenues in 1997, and more than half of this was a long-term zero-coupon bond.

The city of Buenos Aires was an administrative arm of the national government until 1996. When the convertibility law went into effect, the city's overall deficit was 12 percent of revenue. Partial adjustment in the early 1990s and in the Tequila crisis brought the deficit down to 8 percent of revenue in 1994 and thereafter, mostly financed by arrears that were later converted to bonds. Real adjustment did not occur until the city got self-government and the first elected mayor in 1996. The new administration (Radical) took major adjustment measures, which attained a surplus in 1997, and refinanced its debt with long-term bonds.

Córdoba is the classic case of post-Tequila adjustment. In 1991, it had an overall deficit of 16 percent of revenue, which widened further in the boom years, largely due to higher spending on personnel. A new administration in 1995 implemented drastic measures. It reduced work hours and salaries 30 percent temporarily, cut capital spending 40 percent, dismissed more than 6,000 nonstatutory staff, and transferred 1,500 health workers to the municipalities without compensation. In the next two years, the province's overall balance improved: a deficit of only 3 percent of revenues in 1996 and a surplus of 2 percent in 1997. Arrears were converted to short-term debt and then refinanced with longer-term debt to private banks. The Banco de la Provincia has been restructured, and the government has agreed to privatize it.

Other provinces followed a pattern of fiscal restraint where the provincial government was of the same party as the national president. Indeed, this pattern seems to go back to the 1980s as well (Jones, Sanguinetti, and Tommasi 1997). Next to the province of Buenos Aires, Santa Fe was the most important case of a Justicialista province adjusting promptly after the start of stabilization. Getting those two to adjust before the 1995 crisis provided a critical mass of fiscally sound provinces and allowed the central government to take a hard line in forcing the other provinces to adjust in the 1990s.

The success of the Menem-Cavallo team in coaxing and coercing the provinces to go along with the national adjustment program resulted from an unusual conjuncture of historical opportunities. To some extent, the establishment of sound rules and the precedent of upholding them in the face of political pressure institutionalized hard budget constraints. But the capital markets and political circumstances would test them again.

Since 1999, Argentina has suffered a recession because of international shocks like the decline of commodities prices, the rise of interest rates, and the real depreciation of its major trading partner, Brazil, relative to the dollar and the peso and because of domestic difficulties like bad weather and electoral uncertainties. Provincial finances everywhere have suffered; their overall fiscal balances worsened from zero in 1997 to a deficit of 11 percent of total revenues in 1999. Debt stocks jumped from an average of 61 percent of revenue in 1997 to 75 percent at the end of 1999.

The new federal government, taking office on December 10, 1999, responded with a program of debt relief or rescheduling, conditional on fiscal adjustment. The Federal Agreement for Growth and Fiscal Discipline, which all but one province signed, provided the context for the individual contracts and also included agreements for broader reforms of the fiscal pact and revenue sharing. For the smaller provinces, the federal government has created a new agency, the Provincial Development Fiduciary Fund, which will offer longer terms and lower rate financing to those that adopt qualified fiscal adjustment programs. By March 2000, nine provinces had signed onto the program, and others have joined since then. The larger provinces were expected to approach the international financial institutions for assistance. For both groups, the financing was made available only in tranches, contingent on continuation of the agreed reform programs. And for both, the federal government explicitly guaranteed the provincial debt.

To the extent that the federal government was taking over the provincial debt, it appeared similar to the initial pattern in Brazil, which ended with states repeatedly defaulting on their debt that the federal government and central bank had taken over (Dillinger and Webb 1999). Also, the politically divided government system in Argentina of 2000—a coalition government at the national level and the opposition party having most governorships—was a move away from the dominance by a single party (*Justicialista*) in the 1990s, although still a long way from the chaos of Brazil's party system.

There were important institutional and policy differences from the Brazilian experience, however. First, the Argentine federal government faced a hard budget constraint, at least until it started paying its bills with debt in 2001, and it could not access central bank financing because of the convertibility law. Second, the deduction of debt service from revenue-sharing transfers was firmly institutionalized through Banco de la Nación and established in people's expectations. Thus, any resources for a bailout required explicit legislative decisions at the national level.

6.4   Evolution of Budget Constraints

The historical overview shows that the budget constraints of the provinces must operate in several dimensions in order to ensure a sustainable fiscal posture that does not result in bankruptcy or otherwise require a federal bailout. Table 6.4 shows the three main fiscal policy dimensions: revenue, expenditure, and borrowing. To the extent that the political control from the center is weakened, an inevitable result of competitive democracy in a federal setting, the fiscal institutions must hold more strongly. The evolution of Argentine intergovernmental fiscal relations since the 1980s along the three dimensions indicates how far the country has come in the past decade and shows where further progress is needed.

6.4.1   *Revenues and Transfers*

Most transfers from the center to the provinces are based on rules, in contrast to the 1984–1987 situation. The remaining problem is that the transfers are so preponderant in financing the provinces. In 1994, shared revenues accounted for 64 percent of total provincial revenues. General revenue sharing (coparticipation) is the largest single transfer,

Table 6.4
Evolution of hard budget constraints on provinces

	1985	1995	2000
Revenue and transfers			
Rule-based transfers from the center	No	Yes	Yes
Ability of provinces to increase revenues	No	Yes	Yes
Expenditure			
Firm allocation of spending responsibilities	No	Yes	Yes
Provinces to control spending and costs	No	Yes	Yes
Borrowing			
Ex ante constraints			
From the center	No	No	Yes
Self-imposed	No	Not strict	Not strict
Ex post consequences and resulting incentives			
Enforcing payment by SNG	No	Yes	Yes
Enforcing losses on banks with bad loans to uncreditworthy SNGs—bank regulation	No	Yes	Yes
Autonomous central bank to enforce budget constraints on overall public sector	No	Yes	Yes

accounting for the bulk of transfers: 72 percent in 1991 and 57 percent in 1997 and 2000. The importance of revenue sharing varies among provinces, but it has at least some importance to all of them. In Buenos Aires city, it is only 9 percent of total revenue; in large provinces, it accounts for about half: Buenos Aires, 46 percent; Córdoba, 51 percent; Santa Fe, 57 percent; and Mendoza, 58 percent. In small provinces, the transfers typically account for more than 75 percent of revenues, reaching 95 percent in La Rioja and Tierra del Fuego.

Dependence on federal revenue sharing did not weaken provincial power. The provincial share of revenues is theirs by law, and there is little explicit federal discretion in determining the amount or distribution of transferred funds.[6] In the vast majority of transfers, the volume of funds subject to sharing is determined as either a fixed share of specified taxes or a fixed amount in pesos. The distribution of funds among provinces is determined largely by formula, with coefficients fixed in the 1988 coparticipation law. Nevertheless, the dependence on intergovernmental transfers gives the federal government some leverage over the provinces. Because transfers can be created or altered through legislation, new transfers can be offered as a quid pro quo for provincial compliance with federal initiatives, for instance, with the series of fiscal agreements in 1991–1994, discussed above. Transfers also pro-

vided commercial banks with instruments to ensure that debt service
was paid, because debt service could be deducted from transfers at
the source. This diminished their caution in lending, however, which
proved a disadvantage from the systemic viewpoint, as provinces
acquired too much debt going into the macroeconomic crises of 1996
and 1999–2001.

In the early 1990s and again in 2000, the federal government promised minimum floors on coparticipaciones in order to induce the
provinces to sign agreements that were advantageous to the federal
government. While the floors from the early 1990s never cost the
federal government, those from 2000 became extremely binding in the
subsequent recession and contributed a part (though less than half) to
the national fiscal crisis in 2001 (Gonzalez, Rosenblatt, and Webb 2002).

The provinces generate about 40 percent of revenue from self-
administered taxes. Four taxes—on gross receipts, property, automo-
biles, and stamps—account for the majority of tax revenue. Of this total,
the tax on gross receipts accounts for about 60 percent. Provincial taxes
are largely the purview of large provinces. In 1996, the city and
province of Buenos Aires accounted for two-thirds of total provincial
tax collection, and the five large provinces (including Buenos Aires city)
accounted for 87 percent of the total. Argentina does not meet the
condition of revenue independence of provinces, but it does meet the
condition of an aggregate limit on transfers.

6.4.2 Expenditure and Service Delivery Responsibilities

The decentralization law and the fiscal pacts with the provinces in the
early 1990s clarified which functions, such as primary and secondary
education, the states and municipalities had to take on. They also clarified which responsibilities could not be pushed back onto the federal
level. The provinces had authority to cut their costs, although the usual
politics and rules governing public employment did not make it easy.
Also, teacher protests at the national level in 1998 led the federal government to intervene, putting a special tax on autos to pay for teacher
wage increases.

6.4.3 Borrowing

Through the 1990s, as in the pre-1990 situation, there were no effective
ex ante limitations on provincial borrowing from commercial banks.

The effective limits in the 1990s came from market forces and provincial self-restraint. The critical steps from the federal government were a variety of measures that largely eliminated the provincial banks as sources of credit to the provinces. The 1991 convertibility law ended the ability of provincial banks to rely on the central government as a lender of last resort, forcing them to pursue delinquent loans vigorously (including loans to provinces), go out of business, or get capital infusions from the provincial government. Provincial governments that still owned banks usually had to pay in additional capital to meet the required ratios. The central bank could no longer discount any loans from provincial banks, and they had only limited deposit insurance, fully funded by the banks themselves. Since 1996, banks have monitored each other through the requirement for each bank to issue subordinated debt that other banks are willing to hold. Tight regulations limit the lending of a bank to any one borrower, including a province, and require banks to implement provisions against loans not being serviced.

Provincial bonds and some provincial loans are subject to ex ante federal government controls. Bonds have to be reviewed and registered by the Ministry of Economy. Until the Fiscal Responsibility Law, the ministry exercised this role with a light touch, and some bond issues even went on the international market without prior review, such as some Province of Buenos Aires bonds (Eggers 1999). This hands-off attitude had the advantage of forestalling the expectation that the federal government would take responsibility for the quality of provincial debt and might provide an eventual bailout.

The borrowing control in the 1990s centered on the provinces' arrangements to collateralize their debt. Usually this involved a pledge of coparticipaciones as collateral, generally handled by the Banco de la Nacion, a semiautonomous federal agency that, among other functions, distributes the coparticipaciones to the provinces. The provinces have an interest in keeping the agency free from political interference in order to keep the federal government from trying to delay distribution of the provinces' share in national tax collection. From the creditors' viewpoint, the same autonomy makes collateralization with Banco de la Nación an attractive enhancement of creditworthiness. Provinces with a weak credit position have to give an irrevocable instruction for Banco de la Nación to deduct the debt-service payments up front from their coparticipaciones. Provinces with a stronger credit rating are able to satisfy their creditors with a less onerous pledge: the creditor can collect from Banco de la Nación only if there is a default in payment. In either case, for each loan or bond issue, the province and creditor negotiate a percentage limit—the *cupo*—on the share of the daily flow of coparticipaciones that can be taken for service of that loan. The *cupo* is typically set at a level sufficient to pay the regular debt service even with coparticipaciones flowing at the low end of the expected range. The *cupos* sum to much less than 100 percent, of course, so that the province knows that it will have at least a minimum flow of copartic- ipaciones left for other uses. In case of a default and a subsequent accel- eration of claims, not all creditors get their money on schedule, with the length of delay for each creditor depending on its place in the queue and the size of its *cupo*. The sum and seniority of the *cupos* are known to all creditors; they calculate how long it will take to get their money back under various scenarios and negotiate the price and other terms of the loans accordingly. Entities with the strongest creditworthiness, including the province and the city of Buenos Aires, were able to borrow without pledging their coparticipaciones.

The success of this market-driven subnational credit system made borrowers and lenders too bold. The test of the mid-1990s seemed to prove the central government's willingness to enforce ex post conse- quences on the provinces, although mitigated enough so the conse- quences were not fatal. That success spurred more lending in the later 1990s, making Argentina more vulnerable to the longer, harder reces- sion after 1999. Furthermore, the province of Buenos Aires and the federal government were no longer copartisans, ending that political channel for central government influence. Indeed, when Buenos Aires became the nations' biggest fiscal problem, it greatly complicated the task of assembling a critical mass of reform-minded provinces.

6.5   Lessons from the 1990s

There seems no doubt that Argentine provinces faced a harder budget constraint at the end of the 1990s than at the beginning; many addi- tional challenges remain too. Evaluating the hardness of the regime since the stabilization requires a clear definition of bailout. Provinces in the early 1990s were coming out of a soft budget constraint regime and obviously pushing the limits, often spending and borrowing un- sustainably, or carrying obligations for debt and pensions that were unsustainable in a stable price setting, while inflation might have saved them before. The mere fact of a financial resolution, which had to come somehow at some time, does not indicate a bailout and soft budget constraint. What matters is whether the resolution occurred in a way that allowed or encouraged a repetition, by making the overspenders better off than they would have been with prudent behavior. By this standard, bailouts of provinces have become smaller in Argentina since the stabilization, although not eliminated.

First, the requirement for restructuring often eliminated future opportunities for imprudence: privatizing provincial banks and turning over pension systems to the federal government. In both cases, the provinces had been building up liabilities that could eventually threaten the nation's financial and fiscal systems, and the federal government was prudent to intervene.

Second, there were political costs to the extravagant provinces, most obviously in the cases of political intervention, when the governor lost office. Paying the debt service out of coparticipaciones was also politically painful when provinces had to cut their wage bills and other expenses. The adjustment process seems to have been politically unpleasant, because the provinces typically delayed accepting the programs until forced to do so by strong fiscal pressure and because few had to repeat the adjustment process, at least prior to the crisis of 2001.

For most provinces, the federal government succeeded in hardening budget constraints. Since provinces still depend heavily on transfers, however, the resource allocation is more rigid than in countries where local governments self-finance more. This rigidity and the accompanying inefficiency and inequity weakened the system.

The various measures to harden the provincial budget constraints succeeded in the 1990s because they were set in the context of a broader adjustment program that was perceived, correctly, as essential for the rescue of the overall economy. As this motive for imposing and accepting budget constraints waned, the institutional structure became more important. The institutional reforms of the 1990s improved incentives and closed some important loopholes; in most dimensions, notably the convertibility law and the prohibition against federal lending to the provinces, it would take congressional action to relax the constraint.

The economic crisis of 1999–2001 affected all states and contributed to a political consensus for federally sponsored debt rescheduling, conditional on substantial and continuing fiscal adjustment. While the new Federal Agreement for Growth and Fiscal Discipline represented a partial retreat from the principle of always imposing the consequences of excess borrowing, it also included ex ante restrictions on borrowing, based on the national and local fiscal situation. These were needed for restraining the excess borrowing, such as occurred in the 1990s despite the imposition of repayment. Ex post consequences in isolation had proven insufficient, so the new strategy tried to combine them with ex ante constraints. It remains to be seen whether and how this lesson, and the federal agreement, will be incorporated in the national fiscal system to be built in 2002 and thereafter.

Acknowledgments

The views here are those of the author and are not necessarily the position of the World Bank. This chapter draws heavily on Dillinger and Webb (1999). Christian Gonzalez provided valuable research assistance. This chapter benefited from comments by Jonathan Rodden, David Rosenblatt, Francisco Eggers, and Gunnar Eskeland, who bear no responsibility for any shortcomings.

Notes

1. The pool of taxes subject to coparticipation consists of the federal income, valued-added, excise, and asset taxes—all the major federal domestic taxes except those on fuel and social security. Before the transfer, several deductions are made from the provinces' share and are given to the national social security system and to several special funds for the provinces. Of those destined for special provincial funds, the largest deduction is to compensate for the costs of education and health services transferred to provinces (introduced in 1992) and for the *Fondo Conurbano*, which ostensibly assists Buenos Aires province in providing basic services in the suburbs of Buenos Aires city. Deductions from the pool before coparticipation are also made to finance transfers to provinces in financial difficulty, but such transfers are limited to a small percentage of the pool. In addition to coparticipation, the federal government shares its fuel tax revenues, allocating fixed shares to finance housing and provincial road and infrastructure projects. Oil-producing provinces receive directly a share of the royalties from oil companies.

2. The *Fondo Conurbano* was a special fund targeted to Buenos Aires. Although it is an ad hoc fund, outside the regular coparticipation system, its funding is legislated as a fixed transfer, not at executive discretion.

3. Based on an interview with Luis Antonio Zapata.

4. Provinces later claimed to have been blindsided by this agreement. In the 1994 revisions to the constitution, they insisted on adding a clause prohibiting the transfer of federal programs without adequate compensation.

5. Absorbing the net losers would cost the federal government, however. The federal government would have to pick up the provincial subsidy and also pay more because the contribution rate to the federal pension system is lower than in provincial plans. Thus, the amount of contributions coming in will fall. Because benefits paid to existing retirees will remain unchanged, the gap between contributions and pension payments

will widen. Over time, the net cost to the federal government is likely to fall, however. This is partly because pensioners retiring after the transfer will receive the national benefit regime, which is less generous than the provincial plans. In addition, the number of retirees will fall because the minimum retirement age is higher in the national system than in the provinces. Finally, once transferred to the federal scheme, pensions will be subject to the Solidarity Law of 1995, which eliminated automatic wage indexation for pensioners and imposed ceilings on the size of the monthly pension.

6. The main problem with subnational transfers in 2001 was that the federal government could not pay the level of transfers it had promised, particularly the minimum guarantees given to extract other concessions from the provinces.

References

The word *processed* in some of the following entries describes informally reproduced works that may not be commonly available through library systems.

Córdoba, Province of. 1997. *Gobernadores y legisladores de Córdoba 1820–1996*. Córdoba.

Dillinger, William, Guillermo Perry, and Steven B. Webb. 1999. "Macroeconomic Management in Decentralized Democracies: The Quest for Hard Budget Constraints in Latin America." World Bank, Washington, D.C. Processed.

Dillinger, William, and Steven B. Webb. 1999. *Fiscal Management in Federal Democracies: Argentina and Brazil*. Policy research working paper 2121. Washington, D.C.: World Bank.

Eggers, Francisco. 1999. "Control sobre el endeudamiento subnacional: las experiencias de Argentina y Brasil en los '90." Processed.

Fornasari, Francesca, Steven B. Webb, and Heng-Fu Zou. 1998. "Decentralized Spending and Central Government Deficits: International Evidence." LCSPR/DECRG World Bank, Washington, D.C. Processed.

Gibson, Edward L. 1997. "Federalism and Electoral Coalitions: Making Market Reform Politically Viable in Argentina." Department of Political Science, Northwestern University, Evanston, IL. Processed.

Gonzalez, Christian, David Rosenblatt, and Steven B. Webb. 2002. "Stabilizing Intergovernmental Transfers in Latin America: A Complement to National/Subnational Fiscal Rules?" World Bank Policy Research Paper.

Jones, Mark P., Pablo Sanguinetti, and Mariano Tommasi. 1997. "Politics, Institutions, and Public Sector Spending in the Argentine Provinces." In James Poterba and Juergen von Hagen, eds., *Budget Institutions and Fiscal Outcomes*. Chicago: National Bureau of Economic Research and the University of Chicago Press.

Kraemer, Moritz. 1997. "Intergovernmental Transfers and Political Representation: Empirical Evidence from Argentina, Brazil, and Mexico." Inter-American Development Bank, Washington, D.C. Processed.

Murphy, Ricardo. 1995. *Fiscal Decentralization in Latin America*. Baltimore, Md.: Johns Hopkins University Press for the Inter-American Development Bank.

Nicolini, Juan Pablo, Juan Sanguinetti, Pablo Sanguinetti, and Mariano Tommasi. 1999. "Decentralization, Fiscal Discipline in Sub-National Governments, and the Bailout

Problem: The Argentina Case." Inter-American Development Bank, Washington, D.C. Processed.

Peralta-Ramos, Monica. 1992. *The Political Economy of Argentina*. Boulder, Colo.: Westview Press.

Porto, Alberto, and Pablo Sanguinetti. 1998. "Political Determinants of Intergovernmental Grants: Evidence from Argentina". Mimeo. Torcuato Di Tella University, Buenos Aires.

Rudolph, James. 1985. *Argentina: A Country Study*. Washington, D.C.: U.S. Government Printing Office.

Saiegh, Sebastián, and Mariano Tommasi. 1999. "Why Is Argentina's Fiscal Federalism So Inefficient? Entering the Labyrinth." *Journal of Applied Economics* 2 (1): 169–209.

Tanzi, Vito. 1995. "Fiscal Decentralization." *Annual Bank Conference on Development Economics 1994*. Washington, D.C.: World Bank.

Ter-Minassian, Teresa, and Jon Craig. 1997. "Control of Subnational Government Borrowing." In Teresa Ter-Minassian, ed., *Fiscal Federalism in Theory and Practice: A Collection of Essays*. Washington, D.C.: International Monetary Fund.

Tiebout, Charles. 1956. "A Pure Theory of Local Expenditures." *Journal of Political Economy* 64: 416–424.

Treisman, Daniel. 1998. "Decentralization and Inflation in Developed and Developing Countries." Department of Economics, University of California, Los Angeles. Processed.

Wildasin, David E. 1997. "Fiscal Aspects of Evolving Federations: Issues for Policy and Research." Policy research working paper 1884. Policy Research Department, World Bank, Washington, D.C. Processed.

Willis, Eliza, Christopher Garman, and Stephan Haggard. 1997. "The Politics of Decentralization in Latin America." Department of Political Science, University of California—San Diego, La Jolla. Processed.

World Bank. 1990. *Argentina: Provincial Government Finances*. Washington D.C.: World Bank.

World Bank. 1996b. *Argentina: Córdoba Public Sector Assessment: Proposals for Reform*. Washington, D.C.: World Bank.

World Bank. 1996c. *Argentina: Provincial Finances Study*. Washington, D.C.: World Bank.

7 Federalism and Bailouts in Brazil

Jonathan Rodden

Brazil is the most decentralized country in the developing world. It has a long history of federalism and decentralization and has become considerably more decentralized over the past two decades. In comparison with states or provinces in other developing countries, the Brazilian states raise a good deal of revenue through taxation. On average over the 1990s, the states and municipalities were responsible for over one-third of all revenue collection, close to half of all public consumption, and almost 40 percent of the public sector's net debt stock (Ministry of Finance). Political and fiscal decentralization were key components of Brazil's transition to democracy in the 1980s. An examination of Brazil's experiences since then demonstrates the severity of the challenges for macroeconomic management posed by fiscal decentralization in the context of inequality, political fragmentation, and robust federalism. Above all, Brazil has been forced to deal with one of the most serious and persistent subnational debt problems in the world.

Brazil has experienced three major state-level debt crises since the late 1980s. In each of the crisis episodes thus far, the states—already facing precarious fiscal situations with high levels of spending on personnel and dangerous levels of borrowing—were pushed into debt servicing crises by unexpected exogenous shocks. In each case, their first reaction was to demand bailouts from the central government, and in each case the federal government responded by taking measures to federalize state debts.

This case study examines the political and economic underpinnings of soft subnational budget constraints among the Brazilian states in the 1980s and 1990s. It argues that the constitution and the basic structure of intergovernmental relations have undermined the most important mechanisms that enforce subnational fiscal discipline. Voters have not been provided with the incentives or the information they need to use the electoral mechanism effectively. The credit market did not adequately discipline state administrations because creditors were allowed to believe that state debt was backed up by the central government. Perhaps the most important problem underlies the others: in spite of its proclamations, the central government could not credibly commit to refrain from bailing out the troubled states during times of crisis. This commitment was undermined above all by the fact that the states have been able to influence all relevant central government decisions regarding subnational finance because of their strong representation in the legislature. Moreover, efforts to improve hierarchical oversight of subnational spending and borrowing in the wake of debt crises have fallen flat for the same reason.

Section 7.1 examines the structure of the Brazilian intergovernmental system and assesses the central government's ability to impose hierarchical control over subnational spending and borrowing decisions. Sections 7.2 and 7.3 examine the electoral and credit market discipline mechanisms. Section 7.4 analyzes the crisis episodes in greater detail. The final section describes a concerted effort by the Cardoso administration to change some basic rules of the game described in this chapter with a highly controversial, far-reaching reform program that envisions the transformation of a decentralized federation into a tightly controlled hierarchical regime. It is too early to assess or even prognosticate about the success of these efforts.

7.1   Hierarchical Structure

The hierarchical structure of Brazil's system of federalism is laid out in the 1988 constitution: the Union, twenty-six states plus the Federal District (Brasilia), and a constantly growing number of municipalities that by the year 2000 reached 5,559. Brazil is a presidential democracy, and the lower chamber of Congress (Chamber of Deputies) consists of 513 members. The Senate comprises three senators from each state, elected for eight-year terms with no limits. While the overrepresentation of small states in the upper legislative chamber is a central feature of most federal democracies, this asymmetry is especially severe in Brazil and applies to both chambers (Stepan 1999, Samuels and Snyder 2001). In comparative perspective, party discipline is extremely weak in Brazil, and both the Chamber of Deputies and especially the Senate are responsive to strong regional groups. The state governors exert a great deal of influence over the deputies and senators from their states.

Thus, state-based interest groups have a strong influence over most decisions made at the central level, and major reforms require extensive negotiation with, and ultimately concessions to, the governors and regional interest groups.

Not only are the states well represented in the Senate, but the political autonomy of the states and municipal governments is protected by the constitution. The central government is permitted to use federal troops to intervene in the affairs of the states only in the event of a foreign invasion. Moreover, the states preside over large, powerful militias that counterbalance the threat of federal intervention. The states and municipalities are responsible for a wide and expanding range of activities, and the states raise significant amounts of revenue themselves. Constitutional revenue-sharing provisions ensure massive revenue flows from the center to the states and municipalities, but subnational governments have wide-ranging budgetary autonomy. Despite numerous federal attempts to restrict their borrowing activities the Brazilian states and municipalities had access to credit through a wide range of sources and instruments, throughout the 1980s and 1990s. The remainder of this section lays out some of the most important constitutional and informal characteristics of the Brazilian intergovernmental system.

7.1.1 Expenditure

Surely no federal constitution is a perfect guide to the distribution of spending and governmental authority between levels of government, but Brazil's 1988 constitution is even less helpful than most others. The National constituent Assembly leading to the constitution ceded large amounts of revenue through devolved tax authority and guaranteed transfers, and ensured a high degree of fiscal and budgetary autonomy for the states. However, it did very little to specify new expenditure responsibilities. The constitution does carefully outline some exclusive areas of federal competence. These include most of the responsibilities that are generally allocated to the central government in normative fiscal federalism theory: defense, common currency, interstate commerce, and national highways. The constitution also explicitly lays out some spending activities for the municipalities: intracity public transportation, preschool and elementary education, preventive health care, land use, and historical and culture preservation. However, it does not itemize any exclusive responsibilities for the states. Rather, it lists a variety of concurrent, or joint, responsibilities of the federal and state governments. This list includes a variety of important spending areas, including health, education, environmental protection, agriculture, housing, welfare, and police. In these concurrent policy areas, the constitution stipulates that the federal government is to set standards, and the state governments are to deliver services. The constitution also stipulates that the states are free to legislate in all nonenumerated policy areas.

In practice, most policy areas are jointly occupied by two and sometimes three levels of government. Decentralization since 1988 has been a disorderly process in which the federal government, facing fiscal pressures because of the devolution of revenues, gradually discontinues programs. In the areas of education, health, urban transportation, recreation and culture, child and old age care, and social assistance, all three levels act in an uncoordinated fashion, which sometimes leads to "confusion and chaos in service delivery" (Shah 1991, 5). For example, in the area of education, the constitution envisions the role of the federal government as limited to setting norms and guidelines, leaving actual provision to the state and municipal levels. In reality, the federal government has continued its involvement in direct delivery of education services at every level.

The constitution does little to place specific restrictions on the spending activities of the states, and they are involved in a wide variety of policy areas. The states prioritize their spending according to their own agendas and even try to induce the central government to provide funds for their preferred programs through negotiated transfers in the areas of shared responsibility. Throughout the 1980s and 1990s, the constitution significantly restricted state autonomy in the area of public sector personnel management. According to the 1988 constitution, states cannot dismiss redundant civil servants or reduce salaries in nominal terms. During the 1990s, retiring state employees had the right to a pension equal to their exit salary plus any subsequent increases granted to their previous position. These constitutional provisions seriously restricted states' ability to control personnel costs, and given the importance of these costs in state revenue, it was very difficult for the states to make adjustments when fiscal conditions required spending cuts.

7.1.2   Revenue

One of the most distinctive characteristics of Brazil's federal system is the important role of the states in raising their own revenue, which is unique among non-OECD federations. Throughout the twentieth century, the Brazilian states funded a relatively large share of their spending through autonomous taxation, first through the export tax and then since the 1930s through a turnover tax. This was replaced in the 1960s with a value-added tax, now known as the ICMS (Imposto Sobre Circulaçao de Mercadorias e Serviços). Additionally, they have access to motor vehicle, estate, and gift taxes, and the federal government allows the states to levy supplementary rates up to 5 percent on the federal bases for personal and corporate incomes. The federal government assumes exclusive responsibility for the taxes on personal income, corporate income, payroll, wealth, foreign trade, banking, finance and insurance, rural properties, hydroelectricity, and mineral products. The federal government also administers a type of value-added tax, the IPI (Imposto Sobre Produtos Industrializados). All federal government revenue from income taxes, rural properties, and IPI must be shared with the state and local governments.[1] Finally, the municipalities levy taxes on services (the ISS—Imposto Sobre Serviços), urban properties, retail sales of fuels, property transfers, and special assessments.

The ICMS is a particularly important and unusual source of revenue. The Brazilian states, along with the Canadian provinces, are the only subnational units that administer their own value-added tax. The ICMS is Brazil's chief tax, accounting for 23 percent of the total tax burden and 84 percent of tax collection by the states (Mora and Varsano 2001). The ICMS is generally viewed as a poorly conceived tax characterized by a number of inefficiencies. Above all, collection of the ICMS is based on origin rather than destination, which makes it difficult for under-developed states (where consumption generally outpaces production) to raise revenue. This system makes it possible for states to export their tax burdens onto others (see World Bank 2001). Moreover, states compete vigorously, and technically illegally, for mobile investors with lower tax rates and exemptions for producers, leading some critics to complain that a "fiscal war" between the states shrinks the tax base of the states, burdens interstate commerce, complicates tax administration, and exacerbates interstate income disparities.[2] As is the case with spending authority, overlap in the distribution of taxing authority contradicts the basic principles of fiscal federalism and leads to confusion and inefficiency. In particular, the bases for the federal government's IPI, the states' ICMS, and the local governments' ISS overlap, and administration is extremely complicated.

7.1.3 Intergovernmental Transfers

Although the Brazilian states have access to an important broad-based tax and some of the wealthier states fund a large portion of their spending activities through locally raised revenue, intergovernmental transfers are an extremely important facet of the Brazilian federal system. Although overall levels of vertical fiscal imbalance are low for the state sector as a whole when compared to other developing federations, dependence on transfers varies dramatically from one state to another.

The far right-hand column of table 7.1 displays average levels of transfer dependence over the 1990s for all of the states. During this period, on average São Paulo depended on the federal government for only 7 percent of its revenue; for Acre, the figure was 75 percent. Unlike most of the states, the municipalities are all extremely transfer dependent; over 75 percent of municipal expenditures is funded by transfers from the central government and the states (Oliveira 1998), and some municipalities raise as little as 2 percent of revenue from their own sources.[3] Revenue is transferred to the states and municipalities by constitutionally mandated tax revenue-sharing arrangements and nonconstitutional specific-purpose transfers.

Revenue-sharing arrangements are specified in great detail in the Brazilian constitution. The constitution provides strict criteria for the allocation of revenue to the states and municipalities but does little to stipulate the final use of the funds, other than the requirement that states and municipalities must spend at least 25 percent of all tax revenues on education. The most important fund for the states is the State Participation Fund (FPE), funded with 21.5 percent of the net revenues of the three main federal taxes: the personal (IRPF) and corporate (IRPJ) income taxes and the VAT (IPI). The distribution of funds among the states is fixed by Act 104-A of 1989, which determines a participation coefficient for each state based mainly on regional redistributive criteria. The coefficients range between 9.4 percent for the state of Bahia and 1 percent for São Paulo. The fund sets aside 85 percent of the total for poorer regions: the North, Northeast, and Center-West.

Table 7.1
Key fiscal and demographic data, Brazilian states, 1990–2000 Averages

	Population	Poverty index	Real GDP per capita (1995 R)	Real state expenditure per capita (1995 R)	State deficit as share of revenue	Transfers as share of state revenue
Acre	468,867	30.66	2,066.34	890.76	−0.098	0.753
Alagoas	2,636,603	51.40	1,680.58	277.73	0.030	0.463
Amapá	355,923	37.19	3,206.24	1,229.55	−0.017	0.706
Amazonas	2,337,339	32.83	4,849.87	565.16	0.009	0.249
Bahia	12,480,193	51.12	2,252.30	332.57	−0.018	0.273
Ceará	6,731,876	54.11	1,832.65	307.42	0.022	0.311
Distrito Federal	1,774,824	12.98	7,836.46	1,714.53	−0.007	0.551
Espírito Santo	2,773,477	28.24	4,234.46	645.81	−0.088	0.198
Goiás	4,405,601	24.45	2,740.13	456.99	−0.139	0.139
Maranhão	5,187,500	64.20	1,024.06	207.57	0.056	0.557
Mato Grosso	2,227,149	25.83	2,994.60	600.56	−0.125	0.239
Mato Grosso do Sul	1,905,740	23.48	3,542.96	573.29	−0.131	0.188
Minas Gerais	16,517,107	27.64	3,824.05	504.97	−0.043	0.158
Paraná	8,867,247	21.59	4,417.68	450.72	−0.011	0.147
Paraíba	3,300,224	47.48	1,589.76	288.81	−0.086	0.536
Pará	5,425,679	38.34	2,367.17	276.29	0.004	0.385
Pernambuco	7,375,282	46.84	2,373.88	311.16	0.002	0.280
Piauí	2,673,439	60.59	1,137.13	271.97	−0.038	0.555
Rio Grande do Norte	2,545,940	44.32	1,924.42	365.71	−0.086	0.482
Rio Grande do Sul	9,560,723	18.65	5,604.92	675.65	−0.032	0.118
Rio de Janeiro	13,305,537	14.40	5,580.57	642.50	−0.070	0.125
Rondônia	1,243,090	22.90	2,469.33	530.27	−0.140	0.452
Roraima	246,824	10.65	2,212.90	1,334.00	−0.070	0.703
Santa Catarina	4,824,261	15.27	4,951.90	552.24	−0.070	0.151
Sergipe	1,603,101	46.24	2,395.81	506.83	−0.013	0.437
São Paulo	33,704,209	9.89	6,850.41	893.38	−0.080	0.069
Tocantins	1,023,999	51.57	1,192.50	588.80	−0.135	0.630

Sources: IBGE, Ministerio da Fazenda, and author's calculations.

This fund has not been successful in combating interstate inequalities in private income or public spending. Figure 7.1 illustrates these inequalities by plotting average real GDP per capita on the horizontal axis and average real expenditures per capita on the vertical axis. The wealthiest states have per capita incomes that are five times those of the poorest cluster of states, and there are corresponding interstate differences in public expenditures. These relationships have been quite stable over the past decade.[4] Figure 7.1 displays what are among the

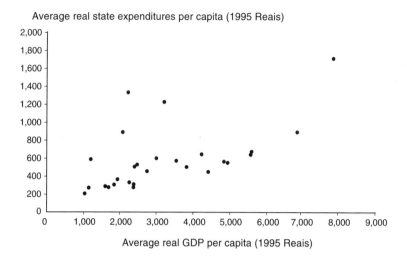

Figure 7.1
GDP per capita and state expenditure per capita, Brazilian states 1990–2000. *Sources*:
IBGE, Ministerio da Fazenda, and author's calculations.

largest regional income inequalities of any country in the world, and
revenue sharing has had little effect (Shankar and Shah 2000).

The constitution establishes a similar fund for the municipalities: the
Municipal Participation Fund (Fundo de Participacao dos Municipios,
FPM). The FPM is funded with 22.5 percent of the net revenues of the
income taxes and the IPI. The distribution of funds is determined by a
formula that is less redistributive and more population based than that
of the FPE. It also favors state capitals and large metropolitan governments. Municipalities also receive a variety of other general-purpose
transfers. First, they receive 50 percent of the net revenue of the rural
property tax collected by the federal government (ITR) in proportion
to the value of real estate properties located in their jurisdictions.
Second, they receive 100 percent of payroll deductions of income taxes
of municipal employees. In addition, they accrue 70 percent of taxes
levied on gold, distributed by origin, and 2.3 percent of revenues from
crude oil based on the value of production, and 50 percent of hydroelectricity and mineral taxes based on the sales value of the mineral
by origin. Finally, the states are required to transfer 25 percent of
their revenue from the ICMS to the municipalities, and the constitution
stipulates that 75 percent of these transfers should be distributed
among the municipalities on a pure derivation basis. The remaining 25

percent is distributed according to criteria determined by the individual states.

In addition to these general-purpose revenue-sharing arrangements, the federal government makes grants to the states and municipalities for a variety of specific purposes. First, a variety of grants have been instituted to comply with laws other than the constitution. States and local governments also undertake investment projects on behalf of the federal government, which funds them through the General Revenue Fund as well as the Social Investment Fund. In addition, a variety of transfers are made to state and local governments through specific central government agencies.

A large portion of the funds transferred to the states outside the revenue-sharing arrangement has traditionally been made through "voluntary" or "negotiated" transfers. These are not regulated by law and are based solely on negotiations between the federal and state (or municipal) governments individually. These provide support for a variety of activities, including regional development, agriculture, education, health, and housing. In most cases, funds are transferred to the state and local governments to undertake spending in areas constitutionally assigned to the federal government. The president and his administration enjoy wide-ranging discretion in the distribution of these grants. Ames (2001) demonstrates that each Brazilian president has used these grants to favor the states of his political allies. For example, in 1988, President Sarney's home state of Maranhão received more money through negotiated transfers than all of the other state governments in the northern region as a whole (Shah 1991). Although the transfers have become less discretionary in recent years, Arretche and Rodden (2001) show that voluntary transfers during the Cardoso administration have favored the states of members of the president's legislative coalition in the Chamber of Deputies. These transfers often accrue disproportionately to the most politically powerful, and often the wealthiest, states and thus often work at cross-purposes with the redistributive goals of the tax-sharing mechanism.

7.1.4 Borrowing

In the 1990s, the Brazilian states borrowed from a variety of sources, including the domestic private sector, the external private sector, federal financial institutions, and a variety of informal mechanisms. They borrowed from private domestic banks primarily for short-term cash management purposes and medium-term financing. An important form of short-term borrowing has been the revenue anticipation loan (ARO), a means of managing cash flow. States also floated bonds on the domestic capital market. Prior to a recent wave of privatizations, twenty of the states owned at least one public bank, all of which facilitated state borrowing by underwriting state bond issues. Like public enterprises, these banks also carried off-budget liabilities. Their lending activities were highly politicized; the directors were short-lived political appointees, bank personnel were hired for political purposes, and loans were directed to political allies (Werlang and Fraga Neto 1992). Many of the banks were insolvent by the mid-1990s. The state of São Paulo borrowed directly from its commercial bank, BANESPA. States also borrowed from international private sector institutions, most often in the form of medium-term contractual debt. Some states and their enterprises successfully floated Eurobonds in the 1990s (Dillinger 1997).

Second, states borrowed from federal financial institutions. Since the 1960s, long-term financing has been provided to the states by the Federal Housing and Savings Bank (CEF) and the Federal Economic and Social Development Bank (BNDES). In addition, the federal government mobilized savings through its deposit-taking commercial banks, above all, the Banco do Brasil, which were lent to the states (Dillinger 1997). The federal treasury and the central bank have also become important creditors to the states as a result of recent bailout agreements. The evolving distribution of subnational debt is displayed in table 7.2.

Finally, states borrowed through a variety of informal mechanisms. Short-term state deficits were frequently financed with arrears on payments to suppliers and state employees. In addition, states sometimes used time lags in the judicial process to facilitate a unique form of borrowing: cost-cutting measures, like land expropriation, that are likely to be overturned by the courts, but until a judgment is reached, states can avoid payment. Even when an unfavorable judgment is issued, the states can sometimes finance payment through special bonds called *precatorios* (Dillinger 1997).

The federal government took a variety of measures to control state borrowing in the 1990s, and at first glance it would appear to have had access to an impressive array of hierarchical control mechanisms through the constitution, additional federal legislation, and the central bank.[5] Most of these mechanisms have been undermined, however, by loopholes or bad incentives that discourage adequate enforcement.

Table 7.2
Subnational net debt (percentage of GDP)

	1987	1988	1989	1990	1991	1992	1993	1994	1995	1996	1997	1998
Total net debt	6.82	5.57	6.15	8.87	7.50	9.50	9.30	9.50	10.40	11.90	13.00	14.30
Domestic debt	5.23	4.18	5.18	7.67	6.40	8.40	8.30	9.20	10.10	11.50	12.50	13.70
Bonded domestic net debt	1.81	1.53	2.49	2.46	2.30	3.10	3.60	4.60	5.40	6.40	4.30	2.40
Banks	3.41	2.65	2.69	4.45	3.20	4.30	3.90	3.30	3.60	4.10	2.60	1.80
Federal government renegotiations								1.10	1.10	1.10	5.50	9.50
Other	0.01	0.00	0.00	0.76	0.90	1.00	0.80	0.20	0.00	-0.10	0.10	0.00
External debt	1.60	1.40	0.97	1.20	1.20	1.10	1.00	0.30	0.30	0.40	0.50	0.70

Source: Bevilaqua (2000).
a Excludes public enterprises.

This section describes the regime in place during the 1990s; more recent (post-1997) reforms are discussed in the final section.

The constitution stipulates that the Senate has the authority to regulate all state borrowing. The Senate placed numerical restrictions on new borrowing on the basis of two factors: debt service coverage and growth of the total stock of debt. These resolutions were merely guidelines, however, and the Senate was free to grant exceptions, which it did frequently (Dillinger and Webb 1999). Given that the Senate is dominated by the interests of the states, it is a very poor overseer of state borrowing. As section 7.4 describes in greater detail, the recent history of state debt crises shows that placing the Brazilian senators in the position of overseeing state-level borrowing and enforcing hard budget constraints is akin to asking the fox to guard the henhouse.

In addition to the Senate, additional constitutional provisions and federal regulations restrict domestic borrowing in theory. Federal laws stipulate that revenue anticipation loans (AROs) must be repaid within thirty days after the end of the budget year in which they are contracted. The issuance of domestic bonds is controlled by the constitution, which since 1993 has prohibited new state bond issues. The states were nevertheless allowed to issue precatorios to finance court judgments and roll over the principal and capitalized interest on their existing bonds. State external borrowing was exempt from these federal regulations, although most international lenders (including the World Bank) require a federal guarantee, which may be granted or denied by the Ministry of Finance. State borrowing from donor agencies was controlled by a multiministerial council (COFIEX). An office in the Federal Ministry of Finance also monitored the finances of the subnational entities and made recommendations to the Senate and the central bank.

The central bank is involved in the oversight of state borrowing in its capacity as overseer of borrowing in the domestic banking sector. Under several recent central bank resolutions, private banks were prohibited from increasing their holdings of state debt other than bonds, but "the complexity of these regulations and their subsequent adjustments has not enhanced their credibility" (Dillinger and Webb 1999, 12). Central bank regulations also prohibit states from borrowing from their own commercial banks. This regulation has been evaded with great success, sometimes subtly and sometimes blatantly. The most common trick is to allow a contractor on a state project to borrow from a state bank and then default, by prior agreement, leaving the bank with a bad loan that is then assumed by the state government (Dillinger 1997).

7.1.5   Implications for Soft Budget Constraints

The system described made hierarchical control of state borrowing in the 1990s difficult for two interlocking reasons: the constitution seriously restricts the ability of the central government to influence the fiscal decisions of the states, and the central government failed to take advantage of the authority it does have because it is itself at times little more than a loose coalition of regional interests. The hierarchical control mechanisms available in the constitution restricted the spending activities of the states in counterproductive ways. Above all, the states have until very recently been able to interpret the constitution as preventing them from changing levels of public employment in response to fiscal emergencies. Conditions attached to specific-purpose transfers have traditionally done very little to encourage fiscal discipline. On the contrary, these grants have been ad hoc windfalls negotiated according to a political logic.

Perhaps the most useful mechanism available to central governments in hierarchical intergovernmental systems is the ability to put effective restrictions on subnational borrowing. Owing largely to the politics of federalism, the Brazilian federal government has had weak or inadequate tools with which to curb the borrowing activities of the states. Perhaps the most serious stumbling block has been the central government's inability (until the Cardoso administration) to regulate the state-owned commercial banks.

7.2   The Political Mechanism

The most important reason for the central government's inability to gain control over state borrowing has not been a paucity of constitutional authority. Rather, it is the fact that both the Chamber of Deputies and the Senate are so easily influenced by governors and state-based interest groups. Given the low level of party loyalty and the frequency with which legislators change parties in the Chamber of Deputies, representatives generally cannot advance their careers by concentrating on national or even statewide issues, but rather on maximizing pork-barrel public works projects and other benefits for selected municipalities within their state (Ames 1995). In order to build a winning

coalition on any policy issue, it is necessary to make a large, complicated set of regional payoffs (Oliviera 1998). In many federal systems,
like the United States and Germany, national party labels play an
important role in state elections, and state-level candidates coalesce
around the party dynamics of federal-level presidential or parliamentary elections. The evidence in Brazil, however, suggests the opposite
pattern: Brazilian congressional candidates tend to coalesce around
gubernatorial candidates and organize their campaigns around state-
based rather than national issues and candidates (Samuels 2000). As a
result, the central government, often little more than a loose collection
of regional interests, is poorly suited to regulate state borrowing. The
Senate has the formal authority to restrict borrowing in a number of
ways, and it has been the primary overseer of recent debt renegotiations. It is difficult to expect the Senate to hold the line against the
states, however, when the senators' interests are so often driven by
those of state governors. On average, three-quarters of the senators are
former or future governors (Dillinger and Webb 1999). Mainwaring
and Samuels (2001) provide a wealth of examples, from the Sarney to
Cardoso administrations, of situations in which presidents attempted
through various means to restrain state spending or debts but ran into
opposition from influential governors. In each case, the governors had
important allies in the Senate or Chamber of Deputies whose votes the
president needed, and each time the president was forced to water
down or abandon the proposal.

The incentives created by the Brazilian political and fiscal systems
might undermine not only hierarchical mechanisms but market mechanisms as well. Voters in the Brazilian states receive very few cues to
suggest that state governments should be held responsible for their
own fiscal health. Voters have a perception, one that is at least partially
correct, that state-level deficits and debt are not the fault of governors
or other state-level officials. This perception is often reinforced by the
media and even members of Congress (Souza 1996). This may have its
roots in the role of the states prior to the democratic constitution, when
they borrowed large amounts on behalf of the central government.
Starting in the late 1980s, democratically elected governors in the states
could claim quite reasonably that their inherited burdens were actually
federal burdens. Moreover, the constitution gave the states very little
control over personnel decisions, even though payroll accounted for
well over 60 percent of expenditures in most states. Moreover, the
overlap of expenditure responsibilities between all three levels of gov-

ernment makes electoral accountability for service provision extremely difficult. On the revenue side, the ICMS does not provide incentives for large, encompassing coalitions of voters to lobby for preferred levels of taxes and public services or overall efficiency in the state public sector; rather, it encourages small sector-specific groups of constituents with high stakes to lobby for special favors.[6]

In some of the poorest states and all of the municipalities, most revenue comes from general-purpose transfers. In the case of the transfer-dependent states, the fact that most local expenditures are being funded by other jurisdictions may discourage careful oversight. According to Afonso and de Mello, "Rigidities in revenue sharing arrangements contributed to delaying subnational fiscal adjustment, since federal government efforts to increase revenues have also led to an increase in total subnational revenues via revenue sharing" (2000). Even in the large, relatively wealthy and fiscally "autonomous" states, voters might not face incentives to punish officials for rising expenditures and deficits and unsustainable debt levels. Although not favored in the distribution of constitutional transfers, these politically powerful states have been particularly adept at attracting voluntary transfers. Voters in these states have come to reward their governors primarily for their ability to attract spending projects that are in effect subsidized by the rest of the federation.

The most important disincentive to electoral oversight awaits more careful analysis in section 7.5: as Brazil's state fiscal crises unfolded, the federal government repeatedly confirmed the public's suspicion that it implicitly backs up the debt of the states. Most of the states' foreign debt has always been explicitly backed up by the central government, and during the first major fiscal crisis in 1989, the federal treasury assumed these obligations. The perception of implicit federal responsibility was reaffirmed throughout the 1990s as the federal government assumed other forms of debt, even temporarily taking over some of the state commercial banks. Given the likelihood of federal bailouts, voters face limited incentives to punish local officials for deficits. On the contrary, they may wish to reward local officials for externalizing the costs of current local expenditures on future generations in other jurisdictions.

It is also useful to examine more carefully the electoral and career incentives for public officials. One of the most common assessments of the Brazilian political system is that at every level of government, the most reliable route to career advancement is not through parties, but through the provision of particularistic goods to specific groups of constituents (Ames 1995; Mainwaring 1991, 1992). Brazil's open-list proportional representation electoral system perpetuates extreme political individualism and guarantees that parties play a limited role in mobilizing electoral and legislative coalitions at both levels of government.[7] Between two and four candidates run for governor in each state, and these candidates attempt to attract as many politicians as possible, regardless of party, to their camp. Each of these coalitions makes agreements about divisions of cabinet spoils and electoral lists for state and federal deputy elections (Samuels 2000). Thus, even gubernatorial candidates face few incentives to make statewide appeals to large groups of voters. "In each state, these processes involve personalistic negotiations, and downplay partisan or policy differences" (Samuels 2000, 5).[8]

Term limits have provided elected officials with short time horizons. Without reelection incentives, most politicians strive to build support networks that will allow them to move to a different level of government: city councilmen aspire to be state deputies, state deputies to be federal deputies, federal deputies to be state governors, and governors to be senators. Executive jobs are preferred to legislative positions because they provide power over money and patronage (Dillinger and Webb 1999). Mayors of large cities are some of the most important political figures in Brazil. This constant shifting of individuals without meaningful party labels makes electoral accountability, especially for fiscal outcomes, extremely difficult (Samuels 2002). Moreover, outgoing administrations frequently run up large deficits that must be dealt with by the next coalition. For example, in order to bolster their campaigns for new offices, outgoing governors have traditionally granted large salary increases to public employees.

7.3 The Credit Market Mechanism

The Brazilian constitution provides the central government with a wide array of tools with which to oversee, restrict, and even deny subnational access to credit, but most of these have been unsuccessful in curbing deficits and excessive borrowing in the states. Precisely because the central government is so heavily involved in financing, lending to, and (unsuccessfully) regulating the states, it creates expectations among voters and creditors alike that state debt is implicitly backed up by the central government. This expectation not only weakens voters' incentives and undermines the electoral oversight mechanism, but destroys the discipline of the credit market as well. Although the Brazilian states have undertaken significant borrowing from private banks, their spending and borrowing activities are not adequately disciplined by the need to attract investment capital on the private market. While most international investors require an explicit federal guarantee, domestic lenders appear to have assumed an implicit guarantee. This assumption proved to be correct time and again in the 1980s and 1990s.

Fifteen states and two municipalities have issued bonds, while all of the states borrowed in the 1990s through AROs. Bonds have traditionally been underwritten by the states' commercial banks and sold to private banks and investors. Although they bore five-year maturities, the bonds were generally rolled over at maturity (Dillinger 1997). As state finances became precarious in the late 1980s, the credit market began to put pressure on the states; interest rates demanded by private banks rose and maturities shortened. Eventually, private investors refused to hold state debt at any price. As the next section describes in greater detail, this credit market pressure was quickly transformed into political pressure on the federal government, which ultimately was forced to take on the debt of the states when they defaulted. In 1989, the federal government agreed with the states to transform the outstanding stock of federally guaranteed external debt into a long-term debt to the federal treasury. This move confirmed the implicit assumption of ultimate federal responsibility for state debts, which was subsequently reaffirmed several times. One of the important lessons of the Brazilian case is that even when subnational governments do a substantial amount of borrowing in the private market, the capital market will not discipline local governments if creditors have reason to believe that local government debt is backed up by the federal government.

7.4   State-Level Fiscal Crises and Bailouts

The Brazilian states have been through three distinct debt crises in the past decade. This section briefly discusses the first two crises and then provides a more in-depth analytic chronology of the most recent crisis.[9] In the mid-1960s, the debt of all subnational governments accounted for nearly 1 percent of GDP; by 1998, it reached over 14 percent (see table 7.2).

The rapid growth in state-level debt came about through a series of crises, each precipitated by events somewhat beyond the control of the states. Each incident ultimately accelerated and transformed into a systemic crisis, however, because of the moral hazard problems described above. In each case, when faced with growing, unsustainable debt levels, the states refused to bear the costs of adjustment and demanded that the federal government assume their debts in some way. In each case, the credibility of the states' demands for bailouts was enhanced by their professed (and in many cases real) inability to respond adequately to the crisis alone. Moreover, in each case, the credibility of the federal government's commitment not to assume subnational debt was undermined by its history of bailouts and the strong representation of the states in Congress and the executive.

7.4.1 Background

The first crisis, which arose during the international debt crisis of the 1980s, originated in loans made by the private sector. State bonds and AROs were held by private banks. Unable to roll over external debt and faced with foreign exchange constraints, states were unable to service their foreign debt. Throughout the 1980s, the federal government honored the states' federally guaranteed obligations to their respective creditors. In 1989, after lengthy negotiations the federal government agreed to transform the accumulated state arrears and remaining principal into a single debt to the federal treasury. The second crisis involved debt owed by the states to the federal financial intermediaries, principally the Federal Housing and Savings Bank (CEF). In 1993, this debt was also transferred to the federal treasury.

In both of these deals, the refinanced debt was rescheduled for twenty years at interest rates based on those specified in the original contracts, with a grace period for payment of principal. The federal government had difficulty securing the agreement of the states to the second deal, and in order to close on the arrangement, it conceded an escape clause: if the ratio of state debt service obligations to revenue rose above a threshold fixed by the Senate, the excess could be deferred. The states would be allowed to capitalize deferred debt service into the stock of debt, which would have to be repaid only when debt service fell below the threshold.

This capitulation by the federal government to the interests of the states created a new set of perverse incentives. The agreements drastically reduced states' immediate debt service obligations in cash terms and prompted considerable expansion in the stock of state debt. With the new debt service ceiling, states were able to capitalize existing debt service into the stock of debt, which would then expand at a rate that would accelerate whenever real interest rates increased. For the most indebted states, the debt service ceilings drastically reduced the expected future cost of current borrowing and interest capitalization. Moreover, the new incentive structure made it possible for current administrations to reduce debt service burdens, continue to borrow, and leave the fiscal consequences to future administrations. The agreements reinforced the perception that state debt was in the end backed up by the federal government.

7.4.2   The Most Recent Crisis

These new perverse incentives, combined with those inherent in the Brazilian intergovernmental system, precipitated another debt crisis in the mid-1990s. Debt burdens continued to grow during the 1990s, not primarily because of new borrowing, but because of the capitalization of interest on existing debt. Despite the previous crises and bailouts— or perhaps because of them—the states continued to increase spending, especially during and immediately after election campaigns. Figure 7.2 presents the average total expenditure per capita in the Brazilian states over the entire period, displaying severe spikes for the

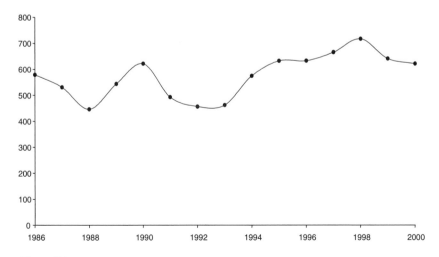

Figure 7.2
Average real expenditures per capita (R$ 1995), Brazilian states. *Sources*: IBGE, Ministerio da Fazenda, and author's calculations.

election years 1986, 1990, 1994, and 1998, and rapid growth from 1993, the year of the federal bailout, to 1998.

This expenditure growth was sustainable as long as inflation remained high. With high inflation rates, states could reduce payroll costs in real terms by simply holding nominal salaries constant. With the success of inflation-fighting efforts of the mid-1990s (the Plano Real), however, dramatically falling inflation rates reduced the states' ability to avoid real salary and pension increases by inflation. Recall that the states' hands have been tied to an extent by the constitution, and they could claim that they were unable to fire workers or reduce wages. As a result, real state salary outlays skyrocketed. The states also faced exogenous challenges because of interest rates; much of their debt was vulnerable to short-term interest rate fluctuations. The tight monetary policy of the Plano Real resulted in continued high interest rates. Faced with growing personnel costs and overwhelming debt service obligations, the states' response was to default. The states defaulted in a variety of ways: the further capitalization of interest on bonds, the collapse of state banks, and defaults on revenue anticipation loans and arrears (Dillinger 1997). The most severe problem was with state bonds, particularly in four of the states: São Paulo, Rio de Janeiro, Minas Gerais, and Rio Grande do Sul.

The states began to have difficulty marketing bonds in the late 1980s. Unable to liquidate the bond debt, they sought relief from the federal government. It was clear that if the federal government refused to act, the states would be forced to default. The federal government was concerned that such defaults would undermine the stability of the entire domestic capital market and responded by offering them the so-called *troca* arrangement, under which the federal government authorized the states to exchange their bonds for federal bonds. Under the terms of the agreement, state bonds would be held in the portfolio of the central bank, which would float a corresponding amount of central bank bonds, transferring them to the states. The Senate was authorized to determine the proportion of the bonds that would have to be liquidated at maturity. Not surprisingly, the most indebted states were able to achieve their desired outcome in the Senate in the initial years: 100 percent rollovers. In addition, the Senate allowed the states to capitalize the accumulated interest due on the bonds into the outstanding stock of bond debt at each rollover. Thus, the Senate allowed the states technically to avoid defaults, even while they avoided any cash obligations to service their bonds. Interest charges on the exchanged bonds were based on the rate for federal bonds, which remained high. As the interest was capitalized, the total stock of state debt grew at an explosive rate.

Some states also defaulted on debt to their state-owned banks. By far the largest problem was São Paulo and its debt to BANESPA. Throughout the 1980s, the government of São Paulo was able to skirt central regulations and run up massive debts to BANESPA. It did this with loans contracted directly by BANESPA from foreign banks, with short-term revenue anticipation bonds that were transformed into long-term debt and with loans to state-owned enterprises. São Paulo began to default on this debt during the early 1990s and by 1994 had ceased servicing the debt altogether. By the end of 1996, the state's debt to BANESPA had reached $21 billion and was the bank's principal "asset" (Dillinger 1997). By the mid-1990s, BANESPA had to meet its cash obligations by borrowing from the central bank. Several other state banks suffered heavy operating losses and stayed in business by borrowing from the central bank during this period as well. Because of the importance of BANESPA and São Paulo to the national economy, the central government viewed them as "too big to fail." The Ministry of Finance feared that the failure of BANESPA would prompt a liquidity crisis and a run on deposits, which would undermine confidence in the banking system as a whole. In 1995, the central bank assumed control of BANESPA and the state-owned bank of Rio de Janeiro with the goal of privatizing them, but it ultimately infused them with cash and returned them a year later, unreformed. According to Abrucio (1998), this was a direct response to pressure from the governor of São Paulo and its congressional delegation. By briefly assuming control of these two state banks and continuing to give liquidity support to them and other state-owned banks, the central bank not only permitted them to remain in operation and continue to capitalize the unpaid interest owed by borrowers, but it also bolstered the perception that the banks' liabilities carry an implicit federal guarantee.

States also defaulted on short-term cash management debt in the 1990s. As the state fiscal crisis deepened, states lacked the funds to liquidate their short-term debt and appealed to their creditors to roll it over. The states also began to run up arrears to suppliers and personnel. The state administrations blamed the central government as they failed to make payments to contractors and employees, and the political pressure on the central government increased. In November 1995, the federal government responded by establishing the Program for

State Restructuring and Fiscal Adjustment, which provided two lines of credit to the states: one to pay off arrears to employees and contractors and the other to refinance their revenue anticipation loans. Under the terms of the loans, the states agreed in theory to a series of reform measures dealing with personnel management, state enterprises, tax administration, debt reduction, and overall expenditure control (Dillinger 1997, Bevilaqua 2000). The federal government, however, had very little power to enforce these conditions, and funds were disbursed before any of the conditions could actually be imposed (Dillinger 1997).

The actions of the federal government with respect to each of these forms of de facto state default effectively federalized the state debt. Bonds that had previously been held by private banks are now held by the central bank. While the debt to BANESPA had previously been the concern of its shareholders and depositors, it was implicitly assumed by the central bank. While the revenue anticipation loans and arrears had been owed to private banks and individuals, the restructured debt is now owed to the federal treasury.

7.4.3 Intergovernmental Debt Negotiations

The central government and the states now face a monumental economic and political challenge as they attempt to work out long-term arrangements for the reduction of this debt. As has long been the case in India and more recently Argentina, state debt is now primarily a matter between the states and the central government rather than the states and their private sector creditors. As of September 2001, 84 percent of state debt was held by the national treasury (Banco Central 2001). Thus the reduction of state debt and the improvement of state fiscal health is now a matter of political bargaining between the representatives of the central government—Congress and the executive—and the governors. In the late 1990s, the structure of the Brazilian federal system introduced several roadblocks to successful reform. Executive agencies like the Ministry of Finance, the only actors with any claim to a national constituency, are reluctant to grant explicit debt reductions, fearing the exacerbation of the moral hazard dilemma. The major debtor states of Rio de Janeiro, Rio Grande do Sul, Minas Gerais, and São Paulo (see figure 7.3) have had few incentives to make concessions in negotiations. As a result of the deals described above, their debt service burdens are quite low, and the governors have no incen-

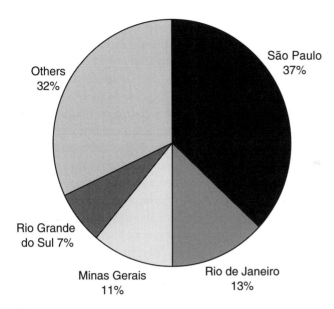

Figure 7.3
Distribution of subnational debt, September 2001. *Source*: Banco Central do Brasil.

tive to sign any agreement that would increase those burdens, particularly while they are still in office. The major debtor states are the most
fiscally autonomous states; they are financed primarily through VAT
revenue, over which the federal government has little control. Thus,
federal threats to withhold intergovernmental transfers, while important, can go only so far.

The most important roadblock to satisfactory debt renegotiation and
reform has been the Senate. Governors have pushed hard collectively
for the principle that all state debt negotiations should take place in the
Senate. Each state has three Senate seats, which means that the major
debtor states control only twelve of the eighty-one seats. Instead of coa-
lescing against the minority debtor states, however, the senators from
the other states took advantage of the situation and demanded pro-
portionate benefits for their own states in exchange for their votes to
protect the interests of the largest debtors. This is a classic example of
the Senate's norm of "universalism," whereby all of the senators agree
not to stand in the way of one another's spending projects and debt
relief.[10] Given the weakness of party discipline in Brazil, the president
was unable to use national partisan ties to convince representatives
to favor a national agenda over their regional interests. All of the

senators faced incentives to prolong the debt repayment process (Gomez 2000), and deadlines for agreements came and went while the stock of debt continued to grow from 1995 to 1997.

Eventually, Cardoso succeeded in his plan to pursue separate deals with individual states. In December 1997, the federal government signed its first agreement with a major debtor state, São Paulo. Under this arrangement, the federal government agreed to assume all of São Paulo's bond debt and debt to BANESPA. A large chunk (around 80 percent of the total) was refinanced as a loan to the state government with thirty years to maturity and a real interest rate of 6 percent, well below the prevailing domestic rate. Another chunk (12.5 percent) was to be amortized through the transfer of stock in state enterprises. The remainder was forgiven by the federal government. The agreement also created a debt service ceiling covering not only the newly refinanced debt, but also the debt refinanced under the two previous reschedulings (Dillinger 1998). For São Paulo, this amounted to virtually no increase in actual cash debt service, and it allowed the majority of debt service to be deferred indefinitely.

After São Paulo, Minas Gerais and Rio Grande do Sul signed similar agreements. In the course of the legislative debate, Congress chose to offer the refinancing terms to all the remaining states in Brazil. Although these agreements will lower the interest rates paid by the states, the federal government will continue to be the states' creditor and continue to pay the overnight rate as the marginal cost of borrowing funds. Moreover, the states will not be prevented from continuing to capitalize interest on debt owed to the federal government, and state debt will continue to grow. As a result, the aggregate interest costs for the public sector will not decline. The costs have merely been shifted explicitly to the federal treasury.

Furthermore, obtaining favorable debt workouts continues to be a high priority for most senators, and demands for further delays in repayment are likely to grow stronger. In a well-publicized incident in 1999, the governor of Minas Gerais, former president Itamar Franco, bitterly criticized the agreed fiscal targets and debt repayment schedule, threatening to cease all debt payments to the federal government. In fact, the governors and senators often appear to stand on reasonably firm ground when making their case. For instance, some governors have argued that as a result of the Kandir Law's reform of the ICMS, they face revenue constraints in addition to high real interest rates and social security expenditures, which make the debt repayment agreements excessively burdensome. In fact, however, ICMS revenue growth has been quite strong in recent years. It has become perhaps even more difficult than ever before for potential creditors, investors, or voters—even scholars and journalists—to distinguish between self-imposed and exogenous fiscal problems among the states.

7.5 Reform Efforts

In the wake of the most recent bailouts and debt negotiations, the prospects for effective market discipline among the Brazilian states seem more distant than ever before. The center has taken on most of the states' debts, and in order to induce repayment, it must now rely on bargains, threats, and, increasingly, administrative rules enforced by the judiciary. As part of its fiscal adjustment efforts, the Cardoso administration has attempted to transform one of the world's most decentralized federations into a tightly managed, hierarchical regime not unlike some of the unitary systems described elsewhere in this book. According to Afonso and de Mello (2000, 29):

The recent changes in legislation have laid the foundation for a rules-based system of decentralized federalism that leaves little room for discretionary policymaking at the subnational level. It has been motivated by the recognition that market control over subnational finances should be replaced, or strengthened, by fiscal rules as well as appropriate legal constraints and sanctions for noncompliance at all levels of government. More importantly, top-down coordination in intergovernmental fiscal relations has been preferred to more horizontal, collegial forms of multi-level fiscal policymaking.

It is too early to assess the success of these reforms. Rather, this section seeks to explain their origin and place them in context.

An evaluation of the Cardoso administration must cast considerable doubt on the popular characterization of the Brazilian presidency as a weak, ineffective victim of constantly shifting coalition politics. Although some difficulties in bargaining with legislators and governors have been described above, Cardoso's government was committed to stabilization and put together a legislative coalition that guided key reforms through the legislature (Melo 2000). Importantly, some governors belonging to the president's party have been able to advance their careers by associating themselves with the successful reduction of inflation. Thus, the president had a rare opportunity to take advantage of incentives for cooperation among some of the governors and within the legislature. Through a combination of bilateral bargaining attached to debt renegotiation, executive action, and federal legislation, the administration has obtained a number of concessions from the states.

First, as a condition for debt relief, each state agreed to a package of adjustment targets. Law 9496 of 1997 spelled out these targets, including scheduled declines in debt-revenue ratios, increases in primary balance, limits on personnel spending, growth in own-source revenues, ceilings on investments, and lists of state enterprises to be privatized. Particular attention was given to resolving the problem of rigidity in state personnel expenditures. Above all, states and municipalities are limited to a ceiling of 60 percent of tax revenue for payroll expenditures. In addition, the new legislation establishes a set of measures aimed at increasing the ability of all levels of government to control such expenditures, including prohibitions on wage increases and new hiring. The legislation stipulates that failure to meet expenditure targets will result in decreased transfers. Furthermore, the central government has the authority to charge interest rate penalties to non-complying states.

The banking sector has been one of the most important targets of the administration's reform efforts. Since 1994, a variety of new banking regulations have been implemented, and some moves have been made toward increasing the autonomy of the National Monetary Council and central bank (Faria 1996, Sola, Garman, and Marques 2000). Above all, after several long struggles, most of the state banks, including the most troubled banks, have finally been privatized. This is a major achievement that could go a long way toward hardening the budget constraints of the states. The Cardoso administration has also pushed with some success for the privatization of state-owned public enterprises.

The central government has implemented an array of new hierarchical mechanisms aimed at limiting states' access to credit in the future. Senate Resolution 78 (September 1998) resolves to put further restrictions on borrowing from state banks, imposes new borrowing ceilings, restricts new bond issues, and forbids the issuance of promissory notes to contractors (World Bank 2001). It also proscribes borrowing by jurisdictions that have not demonstrated a positive primary balance in the previous twelve months.

New discretion and autonomy have been given to the National Monetary Council to prohibit lending to states that are in violation of the resolution. The National Monetary Council, through resolution

2653, authorizes the central bank to control lending by domestic banks to subnational governments. Outstanding loans to the public sector (including public enterprises) are capped at 45 percent of any private bank's equity. If enforced, this will make borrowing by the states extremely difficult. The national savings bank, an important remaining source of long-term credit for the states, is already close to this limit (World Bank 2001).

Finally, the Fiscal Responsibility Law (Supplementary Law 101, approved in May 2000) and the Penal Law for Fiscal Crimes (approved in October 2000) may be the most important changes to the Brazilian intergovernmental system since the 1988 constitution.[11] The legislation attempts to improve the transparency of the central bank's operations dramatically. Moreover, the central bank is now prohibited from exchanging the debt securities of the states for federal public debt securities, one of the key bailout mechanisms. In several ways, the legislation attempts to enhance the credibility of the central government's no-bailout commitment by closing several avenues of federal intervention.

At the same time, the central government has become much more involved in regulating and monitoring the fiscal activities of the states. The Fiscal Responsibility Law gives the president a new obligation to set yearly debt limits for all levels of the public sector and stipulates that violating subnational governments will be prohibited from all internal and external credit operations and placed on a list of violators. The law attempts to enhance credit market oversight by seriously penalizing any financial institutions that attempt to lend to violators. The states and municipalities are required to submit multiyear plans and reports on the use of resources from privatization, social security funds, and contingent liabilities. The law also includes a golden rule provision stipulating that credit operations may not exceed capital expenditures. Additionally, it clarifies the legal authority of the federal government to withhold constitutional transfers from states that fail to repay debts to the federal treasury. Furthermore, all future revenue anticipation loans will be made through an electronic bidding process overseen by the central bank.

The law seeks to address the severe election-year expenditure spikes depicted in figure 7.2. Personnel expenditures may not be increased less than 180 days before the end of the executive's tenure in office. In order to undertake any financial obligation during an election year, the executive must prove that sufficient cash resources are available to repay in the same year, and credit operations based on anticipated revenues are prohibited during election years.

Borrowing from fiscal responsibility laws in other countries, the legislation imposes new uniform accounting, planning, and transparency requirements on all levels of government. Governments will be required to publish explicit justifications for revenue targets and detailed information about revenue sources and tax breaks. Each level of government will be required to make bimonthly comparisons of expected and actual revenues and adjust within thirty days to revenue shortfalls. Reports must be filed each year on the achievement of targets, evaluations of fiscal risks, and the compatibility of state fiscal policies with federal monetary, credit, and foreign exchange policies. The law creates a fiscal management council with the mandate of adopting procedures for the dissemination of information about fiscal accounts. The Ministry of Planning, Budget, and Administration and the BNDES have already made an impressive array of information, including up-to-date monthly data for states and municipalities, available through their Internet sites. The legislation is clearly aimed at enhancing citizen oversight by requiring the dissemination of information, publishing lists of noncomplying governments, and requiring public discussions of fiscal targets in the legislature.

One of the most striking aspects of the new legislation is the increased role given to the judiciary and the penal system in the enforcement of certain of its provisions. The law includes prison sentences for illegal efforts to issue public bonds. It also stipulates that the executive mandate of a mayor or governor may be stripped if debt limits or personnel expenditure ratios are exceeded. Even the omission of an expenditure item in a budget or a misrepresentation in a revenue forecast is subject to penal prosecution (Almeida 2000).

Finally, Article 35 of the Fiscal Responsibility Law prohibits the central government from bailing out any member of the federation. This provision attempts to make a clean break with the past by announcing that the central government will no longer be in the business of financing or refinancing subnational debts in the future. As a whole, the legislation seems to be a rather serious attempt to convince subnational voters, officials, and creditors that the rules of the game have changed and the central government will be resolute in the future if pressed for bailouts.

Unfortunately, it may not be possible to change expectations with the stroke of a pen. The legislation may be viewed as simply the most recent in a long line of legislative pronouncements and debt limits that ultimately proved to be cheap talk. Above all, the recent legislation makes it very clear that the federal government has explicitly accepted responsibility for subnational finance, which makes the no-bailout clause perhaps the least noteworthy facet of the legislation.

Figure 7.4 plots the aggregate state fiscal surplus (as a share of state revenue) from 1986 to 2000. Aggregate deficits were severe throughout the late 1980s and early 1990s, with pronounced election-year spikes, most notably in 1994. However, the state sector was actually in surplus in 1997 and after another major election-year spending spree in 1998 returned to positive territory in 1999 and 2000. It is tempting to interpret this dramatic improvement as evidence that the Fiscal Responsibility Law has been effective.[12] This is a rather difficult case to make, however, since the LRF was not passed until spring 2000. Most of the debt rescheduling agreements were not signed until 1998, and the Senate and National Monetary Council resolutions described above are from 1998 and 1999. There are a number of competing explanations for the increase. First, economic growth and improved tax administration have combined to boost ICMS revenue growth to an all-time high. Furthermore, the privatization of state-owned enterprises has given some

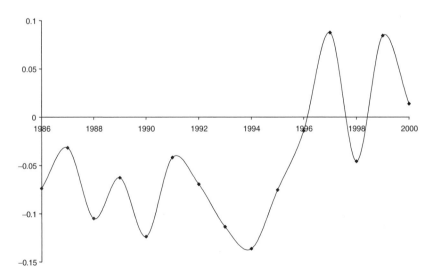

Figure 7.4
Aggregate surplus/revenue of Brazilian states. *Sources*: IBGE, Ministerio da Fazenda, and author's calculations.

states sudden, large infusions of cash. Furthermore, the state fiscal data displayed in figure 7.4 do not fully reflect interest obligations on state bonds. However, the change over time is remarkable, and states have been making significant cuts in personnel and capital expenditures. The fact that privatization and ICMS windfalls have not been spent on new projects does seem to suggest a new pattern of behavior.

It is too early to evaluate the success of these reforms and difficult to assess their long-term impact. It certainly would appear that borrowing by state governments has become much more difficult, and there are a number of new disincentives to overborrowing ranging from fines to impeachment. In addition to altering the incentives and tying the hands of governors and mayors, the reforms restrict the central bank and domestic banks and attempt to close a number of the loopholes described in the chapter. On paper, the fiscal discretion of the Brazilian states appears to have been severely limited, and significant borrowing seems impossible unless approved and essentially undertaken by the central government.

Of course, this does little to resolve the challenge of repaying existing debt, which remains serious. Furthermore, unfunded pension liabilities loom as a major unresolved problem (World Bank 2001). Above all, it remains to be seen whether the recent reforms amount to cheap talk, or whether they will be accompanied by costly action. These reforms clearly make an effort to address the commitment problem by delegating new enforcement activities to the National Monetary Council, the central bank, and the judiciary. Although the delegation of authority from the Senate to independent agencies is a step in the right direction, it is doubtful that the enforcement of these new restrictions has truly been placed out of the reach of ambitious senators (Gomez 2000). Governors have developed expectations that such restrictions can always be undone or circumvented in the Senate. Rather than distancing itself from state government finances, the central government has implicated itself more heavily in state-level fiscal affairs, and in spite of legislative pronouncements, debt repayment is clearly a political bargaining game, and the governors and senators are key players. As a result, the central government's basic commitment problem remains serious: state governments and their voters still believe that the central government can ultimately be held responsible politically and morally for state-level outcomes, perhaps now more than ever before. Thus, the central government's commitment to fiscal discipline will continue to be shaped by politics.

The most important concern is whether the provisions of the new legislation can be enforced. The legislation will place a huge administrative burden on virtually every arm of government, including the executive, the legislature, and especially the judiciary, given its heavy enforcement obligations. Central government agencies are now responsible for tracking and approving all subnational borrowing ranging from cash management to suppliers' credits to long-term lending. The ambition of the Fiscal Responsibility Law is probably unprecedented among large, diverse, democratic federations. It also remains to be seen whether the judiciary will follow through with some of the particularly harsh enforcement mechanisms. The most important concern, however, is that the central government's commitment to enforce the laws may recede, as in the past, under less auspicious circumstances.

7.6 Conclusions

The primary goal of this chapter was to describe and analyze the institutional weaknesses underlying the disastrous bailout episodes of the late 1980s and 1990s among the Brazilian states. Each debt crisis had a proximate exogenous cause: an unexpected drop in inflation, high interest rates, or foreign exchange constraints. The states were able to claim to their voters and their creditors that they were not responsible for dealing with the fiscal consequences, even though they had placed themselves at risk by overborrowing. The episodes only taught the governors that a pattern of overborrowing and demanding bailouts is an effective way to maximize outlays from the central government. The experiences of the Brazilian states over the past two decades demonstrate how hierarchical and market-based oversight mechanisms can fail. The Brazilian constitution and the structure of intergovernmental relations provided voters with neither the information nor the incentives they needed to hold state governments accountable for their fiscal activities. Creditors were led to believe that state debt was backed up by the federal government. Thus, when faced with an unexpected external shock, state governments faced no incentives to adjust; rather, the logical course of action was to demand a bailout. Abrucio (1998) refers to this pattern of behavior as "predatory federalism," in which the states prey on the vulnerability of the central government.

It is important to understand the sources of the center's vulnerability. Part of the problem in Brazil is that it is common knowledge that some states like São Paulo are too big to fail. In addition, since even before the promulgation of the 1988 constitution, the structure of the intergovernmental system has provided a number of cues to suggest that the center is ultimately responsible for the fiscal health of the states. The most important reason for the center's vulnerability, however, is the fact that the center itself is often little more than a loose coalition of state-based interest groups. The motivational commitment not to bail out subnational governments during a debt crisis is seriously constrained when the relevant decisions are made by vote-trading coalitions of politicians whose career advancement is based primarily on pleasing state-based interest groups. Above all, it is impossible to expect the Senate to hold the line against state demands when it reflects so directly the interests of the state governments.

The most recent administration has been rather successful in using the resources available to the executive to overcome political obstacles to reform. It has attempted to enhance future commitment by delegating authority to the central bank and judiciary, but these commitment mechanisms have not yet been put to the test. In addition, the central government has recognized the asymmetry between its perceived obligation for state and local fiscal outcomes, on the one hand, and its regulatory powers, on the other. As a result, it has undertaken a major reform effort aimed at strengthening its authority to regulate subnational fiscal decisions. This is a rather bold experiment in micromanagement for a federation with an ongoing history of pronounced political and fiscal decentralization. The reforms, of course, do nothing to reduce the political power of mayors and governors or change the incentives of legislators. For those who are attached on normative grounds to the ideals of federalism and markets, there is much to criticize. Indeed, these reforms seem to have all but given up on the possibility of market discipline.

However, if future administrations manage to disentangle the finances of the center and the states, a less controversial aspect of the new legislation may ultimately help strengthen market discipline: its emphasis on transparency, information access, and accountability. It is impossible to predict whether the central government can follow through with this new experiment in hierarchical federalism or be forced to retreat. In either case, the best hope for self-enforcing subnational fiscal discipline in the future lies with voters who have learned from the events described and possess the information and the incentives to reward politicians at all levels for prudent fiscal management.

Acknowledgments

Thanks to Mansueto Almeida, Gunnar Eskeland, Eduardo Gomez, Jennie Litvack, João Oliviera, and Stephen Webb for helpful comments, and José Roberto Afonso and Sergio Ferreira for help in locating resources.

Notes

1. One key problem with the Brazilian tax system is that because of its obligation to share such large portions of these taxes, the federal government seeks to overexpand several inefficient, cascading taxes that are not subject to sharing (Mora and Varsano 2000).

2. The so-called Kandir Law of 1996 substantially altered the ICMS by exonerating exports and investment goods and allowing taxpayers to compensate with their liabilities taxes previously paid on all their inputs. For more details, critical views of ICMS tax competition, and reform proposals, see Varsano (2001), BNDES (2000), and Mora and Varsano (2000).

3. Serious efforts are being made by the federal government to improve municipal tax administration and encourage municipalities to exploit their tax base more fully. For a review of these efforts, see Afonso and de Mello (2000).

4. The interstate Gini coefficient for real GDP per capita (calculated by the author) has been steady at around .30 from 1986 to 1998, while the coefficient for real expenditures per capita has declined from .36 to .30 over the same period.

5. For a comprehensive review of central government attempts to regulate subnational borrowing going back to the 1970s, see Bevilaqua (2000).

6. For a more general discussion of this problem, see Rodden and Rose-Ackerman (1997).

7. Voters can vote directly for an individual candidate or for a party's entire label. From the candidate's perspective, this creates a strong incentive to make individual appeals to voters through patronage and pork. The party's total list vote equals the sum of the party's candidates' votes plus its party-label votes. The candidates with the most individual votes get the highest priority in distributing the party's seats, so each candidate prefers a vote for himself or herself over a party-label vote (Samuels 2000).

8. Recent studies (e.g., Figueiredo and Limongi 2000) reveal that the accepted wisdom about partisan fragmentation and the impotence of legislative coalitions has probably been exaggerated. Presidents do in fact preside over stable legislative coalitions that often vote together, and parties play an important role. Nevertheless, the system is quite fragmented when placed in comparative perspective (Carey and Reinhardt 2001).

9. Much of the historical information presented in this section has been adapted from previous World Bank studies: Dillinger (1997), Dillinger and Webb (1999), Oliviera (1998), and World Bank (2001). Additional descriptive accounts include Bevilaqua (2000) and Rigolon and Giambiagi (1998).

10. On federalism and the norm of universalism in the legislature, see Inman and Rubinfeld (1997) and Inman (chap. 2, this volume). On the Brazilian Senate, see Mainwaring and Samuels (2001).

11. It is possible here to give only a broad outline of what is an extremely detailed, far-reaching legislative package. For details on the Fiscal Responsibility Law, see Almeida (2000), Nascimento and Debus (2000), Tavares et al. (1999), Kopits, Jimenéz, and Manoel (2000), World Bank (2001).

12. This assertion has been made by the *Economist*, Nov. 19, 2001.

References

Abrucio, Fernando Luiz. 1998. *Os Barões da Federação: O Poder dos Governadores no Brasil Pós-Autoritário*. São Paulo: Universidade de São Paulo.

Afonso, José Roberto, and Luiz de Mello. 2000. "Brazil: An Evolving Federation." Paper prepared for IMF/FAD Seminar on Decentralization, Nov. 20–21, Washington, D.C.

Almeida, Mansueto. 2000. "Fiscal Decentralization in Brazil: Good Design and Bad Implementation." Unpublished paper, MIT.

Ames, Barry. 1995. "Electoral Rules, Constituency Pressures, and Pork Barrel: Bases of Voting in the Brazilian Congress." *Journal of Politics* 57(2):324–343.

Ames, Barry. 2001. *The Deadlock of Democracy in Brazil*. Ann Arbor: University of Michigan Press.

Arretche, Marta, and Jonathan Rodden. 2001. "Legislative Bargaining and Distributive Politics in Brazil: An Empirical Approach." Unpublished paper, MIT.

Banco Central do Brasil. 2001. *Boletim das Finanças Estaduais e Municipais*. Brasília.

Bevilaqua, Afonso. 2000. "State Government Bailouts in Brazil." Discussion paper 421, Department of Economics, PUC-Rio.

BNDES. 2000. "Guerra fiscal: Competição tributária our corrida ao fundo do tacho?" *Informe-SF* 4 (Jan.).

Carey, John M., and Gina Yannitell Reinhardt. 2001. "Coalition Brokers or Breakers: Brazilian Governors and Legislative Voting." Paper presented at the conference, "Brazilian Political Institutions in Comparative Perspective," Centre for Brazilian Studies, St. Anthony's College, Oxford University, May 28–29.

Dillinger, William. 1997. *Brazil's State Debt Crisis: Lessons Learned*. Washington, D.C.: World Bank.

Dillinger, William, and Steven Webb. 1999. "Fiscal Management in Federal Democracies: Argentina and Brazil." Policy research working Paper 2121. Washington, D.C.: World Bank.

Faria, Laura Viere. 1996. "On Central Bank Independence for Brazil." In Carlos Geraldo Langoni, James Ferrer, and Marcio Ronci, eds., *The Quest for Monetary Stability*. Rio de Janeiro: Getulio Vargas Foundation.

Figueiredo, Argelina Cheibub, and Fernando Limongi. 2000. "Presidential Power, Legislative Organization, and Party Behavior in Brazil." *Comparative Politics* 32(2): 151–170.

Gomez, Eduardo. 2000. "Brazil: A Political Economy of Federalism and Sub-national Debt Workouts." Unpublished paper, RAND.

Inman, Robert, and Daniel Rubinfeld. 1997. "The Political Economy of Federalism." In Dennis Mueller, ed., *Perspectives on Public Choice*. Cambridge: Cambridge University Press.

Kopits, George, Juan Pable Jiménez, and Alvaro Manoel. 2000. "Responsabilidad fiscal a nivel subnacional: Argentina y Brasil." Unpublished paper, IMF.

Mainwaring, Scott. 1991. "Politicians, Parties and Electoral Systems: Brazil in Comparative Perspective." *Comparative Politics* 24:21–43.

Mainwaring, Scott. 1992. "Brazilian Party Underdevelopment in Comparative Perspective." *Political Science Quarterly* 107(4):677–707.

Mainwaring, Scott, and David Samuels. 2001. "Federalism, Constraints on the Central Government, and Economic Reform in Democratic Brazil." Unpublished paper, University of Minnesota.

Melo, Marcu. 2000. "Institutional Obstacles to Market Reforms? The Politics of Tax Reform in Brazil." Paper presented at the Twenty-Second Congress of the Latin American Studies Association, Miami.

Mora, Mônica, and Ricardo Varsano. 2000. "Fiscal Decentralization and Subnational Fiscal Autonomy in Brazil: Some Facts in the Nineties." Unpublished paper, IPEA, Rio de Janeiro.

Nascimento, Edson Ronaldo, and Ilvo Debus. 2000. "Entendendo a Lei de Responsabilidade Fiscal." *Lei Complementar* 101/2000.

Oliviera, João do Carmo. 1998. "Financial Crises of Subnational Governments in Brazil." Unpublished paper, World Bank.

Rigolon, Francisco, and Fabio Giambiagi. 1998. "Renegociação das dívidas estaduais: um novo regemi fiscal ou a repitição de uma antiga história?" Unpublished paper, BNDES.

Rodden, Jonathan, and Susan Rose-Ackerman. 1997. "Does Federalism Preserve Markets?" *Virginia Law Review* 83(7):1521–1572.

Samuels, David. 2000. "The Gubernatorial Coattails Effect: Federalism and Congressional Elections in Brazil." *Journal of Politics* 62(1):240–253.

Samuels, David. 2002. *Ambassadors of the States: Political Ambition, Federalism, and Congressional Politics in Brazil*. Forthcoming. Cambridge: Cambridge University Press.

Samuels, David, and Richard Snyder. 2001. "The Value of a Vote: Malapportionment in Comparative Perspective." *British Journal of Political Science* 31:651–671.

Shah, Anwar. 1991. *The New Fiscal Federalism in Brazil*. Washington, D.C.: World Bank.

Shah, Anwar. 1999. "Incentives to Cultivate a Party Vote in Candidate-Centric Electoral Systems: Evidence from Brazil." *Comparative Political Studies* 32(4):487–518.

Shankar, Raja, and Anwar Shah. 2000. "Bridging the Economic Divide within Nations: A Scorecard on the Performance of Regional Policies in Reducing Regional Income Disparities." Unpublished paper, World Bank.

Sola, Lourdes, Christopher Garman, and Moises Marques. 2000. "Central Banking Reform and Overcoming the Moral Hazard Problem: The Case of Brazil." Paper presented at the Twenty-Second Congress of the Latin American Studies Association, Miami.

Souza, Celina. 1996. "Redemocratization and Decentralization in Brazil: The Strength of the Member States." *Development and Change* 27:529–555.

Stepan, Alfred. 1999. "Federalism and Democracy: Beyond the U.S. Model." *Journal of Democracy* 10:19–33.

Tavares, Martus Antonio Rodrigues, Alvaro Manoel, José Roberto Afonso, and Selene Peres Nunes. 1999. "Principles and Rules in Public Finances: The Proposal of the Fiscal Responsibility Law in Brazil." Paper presented at CEPAL Regional Seminar on Fiscal Policy, Brasília, Jan.

Varsano, Ricardo. 2001. "Brazil: Tax Reform and the 'Fiscal War' in the Federation." *Federations* 1(1):1–11.

Werlang, Sérgio Ribero da Costa, and Armínio Fraga Neto. 1992. "Os Bancos Estaduais e o Descontrole Fiscal: Alguns Apectos." Working Paper 203, Escola de Pòs-Graduação em Economia da Fundação Getúlioi Vargas.

World Bank. 2001. "Issues in Brazilian Federalism." Report of the Brazil Country Management Unit.

8

The Challenge of Fiscal Discipline in the Indian States

William J. McCarten

India is de facto a decentralized federal democracy of 1 billion inhabitants and twenty-five states that embraces a great deal of ethnic, linguistic, and cultural diversity. More than half of general government expenditures are undertaken by state and local governments. It also has many attributes of a highly centralized country, including a quasi-federal constitution, a high concentration of effective taxing powers at the central level, a highly regulated financial market dominated by centrally owned financial institutions, and significant parts of its economy still subject to central directives. Much ingenuity has been devoted to the business of resolving these apparent contradictions and making Indian fiscal federalism work in practice. But this same ingenuity has deprived India of some potential benefits of pure federalism, such as sole accountability of each level of government for its fiscal performance.[1] Despite the existence of hierarchical federal structures capable of imposing hard budget constraints, lines of authority and accountability have become blurred across levels of government, resulting in a softening of budget constraints or in state-level expectations that their budget constraints might soften. In turn, institutions and policies, which have softened budget constraints or created expectations of softening, have complicated macroeconomic management, distorted state-level debt financing decisions, encouraged states to make bad intertemporal budget choices, and contributed to major distortions in subnational public expenditure composition. Fortunately, a few important steps have recently been taken by the states to achieve greater fiscal consolidation and by the center to reduce the risk of moral hazard exposure.

This case study examines the institutions and incentive mechanisms that influence budget outcomes at the state level and reviews the power of mechanisms of correction when soft budget constraints become a major fiscal problem. These mechanisms are the hierarchical mechanism of central oversight and control of state debt and deficit financing, credit market incentives, political checks on deficit financing and populist politics through electoral processes, the potential role of capitalization effects on land markets, and the interstate competitive effects of fiscal regime performance in attracting or discouraging investment. The case study seeks to identify the most important constitutional features and market characteristics that influence subnational deficit financing and debt management in India, as well as the informal rules of the game of intergovernmental fiscal relations.

8.1 Description and Overview of Indian Federalism

Upon independence, India's political leaders inherited a badly fractured society and an economy that had stagnated during the previous fifty years of colonial rule. They resolved to create a centralized, federal constitution both to ensure the cohesiveness of a vast country and build a system of government that would act as an engine of economic growth and development. The framers of India's 1950 constitution divided the powers of government into three lists: a union or central list, a states list, and a concurrent list of shared jurisdictional assignments. In addition to the usual powers over matters related to interstate commerce, the institutions of macroeconomic policy, and defense, all residual powers are placed on the union list. The central or union government has wide power to intervene in state affairs and exercise supervisory power over the states. Matters relating to land rights, public health and sanitation, agriculture, agricultural education, irrigation and water use, roads, and local government are placed on the *states List*. Matters relating to population control and family planning, education, minor ports, electricity, and trade and supply of certain basic agricultural commodities have been placed on the *concurrent list*. States incur about 87 percent of total expenditure on social services and 59 percent of expenditures on economic services, embracing both current and capital account activities. Significantly, the responsibility for economic and social planning was made a concurrent subject. But at least during the period from 1950 to 1991, state planning units functioned primarily as the agents of the central planning authority.

In an effort to prevent intergovernmental jurisdictional disputes, the constitution divided most taxing powers between the center and the states without overlap. These unique assignments have inhibited the states from broadening their tax bases in an efficient manner to meet increasing expenditure responsibilities for infrastructure and social spending. The unique assignments have also undermined the scope for cooperative and tax harmonization initiatives that have developed in other federal countries. The states were given the power to levy a broad-based sales tax, but the tax room intended for the states by this provision has been partially preempted by the authority given to the center to impose excises on almost any commodity.

8.1.1 Revenue Sources

Indian states raise less than half of their financial requirements from their own resources. States' own tax yields have been a relatively constant 5.7 percent of GDP over the period 1995 to 2000 despite tremendous untapped opportunities for improvements in state tax policy and administration. Out of expenditure amounting to 16 percent of GDP in recent years, the states' own revenues financed only the equivalent of 7 to 8 percent of GDP, the remaining 8 to 9 percent being financed through transfers from the central government budget or debt financing organized by the central government. Thus, the central government is responsible for the financing of 55 percent of states' spending. States account for approximately 58 percent of the combined center and state expenditures net of state interest and central transfers. The average performance in states' own revenue generation masks wide disparities among the states. For example, Gujarat manages to mobilize own tax and nontax revenues equivalent to 76 percent of its current account expenditures; for Uttar Pradesh and Bihar, the corresponding percentages are 36 percent and 35 percent, respectively. Effective tax effort varies considerably across states, from a high of 12 percent of state national product in Tamil Nadu to a low of 6 percent in Uttar Pradesh and 5 percent in Bihar among major states. Cost recovery, particularly in power, irrigation, and water resources use, meets less than one-third of break-even costs for noncommercial users. The local government or third-tier tax to GDP ratio is estimated to be just about 1 percent, compared to about 7.5 percent for the central taxes and 8.5 percent for the state-level taxes.

8.1.2 Fiscal Federal Relations in the Era of Planning

Formal economic planning, begun in 1950 shortly after independence, greatly augmented the central government's effective powers of command and control over state governments and the private economy. Under the leadership of its first prime minister, Jawaharlal Nehru, India committed itself to ownership and control of what the fabian socialists evocatively termed "the commanding heights" of the economy. From 1950 until 1991, the system of federal transfers, together with other instruments of central planning such as exchange controls, investment licensing (which enabled the central government to influence the regional distribution of investment), and tight control over lending policies of financial institutions, enabled the center to exercise a strong centripetal influence over state government finances. These instruments and a commitment to planning of private and public investment discouraged states and local governments from developing economic policies of their own and nurtured a political culture of dependence at the state level.

The process of harmonization of state policy priorities and the national development strategy is a by-product of central approval of the size and composition of annual state plans and state utilization of centrally sponsored scheme resources. The center is cash rich relative to its expenditure responsibilities. It has used transfer instruments such as matching grants and spending conditions on block grants to influence the expenditure outcomes of states, which are revenue poor but rich in expenditure mandates. During the era of formal planning, the paramount goals of the system of federal transfers were to encourage states to act as the agent of plan-led economic growth and provide an effective channel to fuel this growth with ever-increasing domestic savings. Reliance on voluntary absorption of domestic savings, largely generated in the farm sector, appeared to be an eminently sensible strategy for incremental resource mobilization, given the difficulty of taxing farmers directly under the best of conditions and the relatively low real interest rates prevailing prior to the onset of liberalization. High public sector borrowing by the states was judged to be sustainable, provided that lent funds were invested efficiently in infrastructure projects or social spending with high social rates of return. Transfers formulas were rules based and reasonably stable rather than ad hoc.

Until the mid-1980s this mechanism largely achieved its purpose. Public sector investment rose from 4 percent of GDP in the early 1950s to approximately 12 percent in the 1980s, of which state level investment accounts for more than half. The system of fiscal relations functioned adequately as long as financial repression permitted deficit financing with loans that bore low positive real interest rates,[2] the supply of highly subsidized services such as power to agricultural users was limited, and the "license raj" system required Government of India approval of all private investments and virtually ensured that all states would retain their existing proportional shares of private investment from period to period.

Market liberalization reforms swept away much of this system. In particular, the investment license raj was abolished, giving the states more de facto economic autonomy. Beginning in the late 1980s, the private sector overtook the public sector as the engine of growth.[3] The interstate competition to attract private investment began to over-shadow public sector investment as a determinant of state-level economic growth. But during the 1990s, the economic liberalization process suffered from a fundamental imbalance. Progress has been slow in implementing capital market, banking, and pension reforms, although progress in banking reform began to speed up in 2000.[4] In principle, the newly found autonomy of states and local governments should provide them with opportunities to design expenditure and revenue policies better tailored to local needs and conditions. But the loosening of central control of state public finances in an economy with incomplete financial sector reform increased the risk that many states would make the wrong adjustment choices and employ innovative financing instruments purely in an effort to escape from hard budget constraints. To some extent, this has already happened, and even when the central government has acted to push the onus of paying for pop-ulist policies back onto the states, it appears to have taken most states by surprise.

Reform of state finances has assumed greater significance for macro-economic management as the fiscal deficit of state governments has reached unsustainable levels. Current account deficits have emerged in most states since 1986–1987 and have led implicitly to the diversion of central transfers to the states intended for capital projects to service the interest expenses of states. As shown in figure 8.1, the gross fiscal deficit to GDP ratio of all state governments rose to a high of 4.2 percent in 1998–1999, the highest recorded in Indian fiscal history so far. The fiscal performance of individual states varied widely over the 1990s, with the most marked deterioration coming in some of the poorer states. (See also table 8.5). In Uttar Pradesh, the fiscal deficit rose from 4.5 percent of GSDP in 1993–1994 to 8.6 percent in 1997–1998; in Bihar, from 4.0 to 6.2 percent; in Orissa from 5.7 to 6.3 percent. In 1998–1999, the states' fiscal deficit worsened to 4.2 percent, as the central government's gen-erous wage settlement influenced the wage bills of overstaffed states

Percentage of GDP

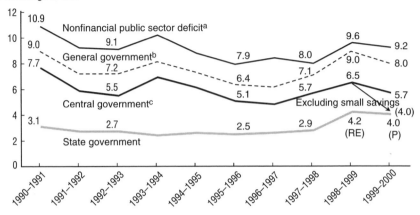

Figure 8.1
Public sector deficits, 1990–2000, excluding disinvestments revenues.
[a]Includes general government deficit, oil pool balance, and market-financed central public enterprise deficit (on-lending from central government to central public enterprises is netted out).
[b]The fiscal deficit = central fiscal deficit (excluding divestment revenues), state government deficit, excludes net lending from the center to states.
[c]The 1998–1999 figures are provisional (adjusted for actual tax returns and expenditures).
Source: Budget Documents, RBI Bulletins, RBI Annual Report (1998–1999), Staff Estimates.

Table 8.1
Financing of all states' fiscal deficit (percent of GDP)

	1990–1991	1994–1995	1995–1996	1996–1997	1997–1998	1998–1999 (RE)	VC 1999–2000 (BE)
Fiscal deficit	3.2	2.6	2.5	2.7	2.9	4.2	4.0
Financing							
Loans from center	1.7	1.3	1.1	1.2	1.5	1.8	1.9
Market term loans	0.5	0.4	0.5	0.5	0.5	0.6	0.5
Other (PFs, reserves, and deposits)	1.0	0.9	0.9	1.0	0.8	1.8	1.6
Revenue deficit	0.8	0.6	0.6	1.1	1.0	2.2	2.2

Source: RBI Annual Report 1998/99, Supplement to RBI Bulletin on Finances of State Governments, CSO, World Bank staff estimates.
Notes: GDP numbers are at the 1993–1994 base. For 1998–1999 GDP, revised estimates (July 1999) have been used.

administrations. Financing these large deficits has meant increased borrowings from the central government and the issuance of guarantees by the states for the borrowing of state-owned public enterprises.

Decentralization at the local level has also raised issues of financial accountability and control. Prior to 1992, local government in India did not have a recognized constitutional identity. While the legal status of urban local governments has now been raised, they continue to exercise only such taxing and expenditures responsibilities as were devolved to them by their respective state governments. Urban governments lack adequate revenue resources to carry out their mandates and suffer from fragmentation of responsibilities. Urban infrastructure in major centers is overburdened to the point where it is deterring new private investment. In general, cost recovery for services that could be sold is very weak. Potentially efficient forms of urban taxation, such as property taxation and user charges, have not been buoyant revenue generators.

Rather than raise user fees to finance the expansion of services, municipalities have looked to loans at concessional terms from centrally controlled lending institutions or have entirely abdicated their responsibilities to state agencies.

To generalize, while the commitment to formal planning and plan-led growth achieved a high degree of formal harmonization between the center and the states in matters of public expenditure, a lack of mutual trust and understanding has prevented the most rudimentary coordination in the area of indirect taxation, resulting in a highly inefficient and distortionary indirect tax system. The 1990s witnessed a burgeoning of centrifugal forces. State fiscal positions deteriorated in part because states pursued populist policies and took advantage of loosening central controls to explore ways to circumvent hard budget constraints.

8.1.3   Fiscal Transfers

There are four components or channels to the fiscal transfer system with implied associated hierarchical controls.

Finance Commission Transfers
State governments account for almost 57 percent of general government expenditures but only 35 percent of revenues. To cope with the resulting shortfall, the constitution stipulates that a Finance

Commission be established every five years to devolve to the states parts of the proceeds of some taxes assigned to the center for reasons of efficiency and administrative ease. Rules for making transfer awards have varied from commission to commission, so that a set of firm principles to guide incoming commissioners has not evolved. Minor debt relief has been extended periodically by the center to states on the recommendations of successive Finance Commissions, but as shown in table 8.2, when the quantum of debt relief is normalized by the state domestic product of the year in which it was granted, the trend is clearly one of decreased relative commitment to central debt forgiveness over time.

Over the course of the 1970s and 1980s, finance commissions expressed sympathy with the argument that the mismatch between state development mandates and inadequate instruments of taxation required greater tax share awards and special block grant awards defined in absolute rupee terms for deficit gap filling. In response, central finances were destabilized as the center sought to raise its own tax revenues or borrow in order to comply with Finance Commission awards and finance increasing proportions of state expenditures. Whereas the tax shares were allocated to states on the basis of objective criteria such as population and disparities in per capita state income, block grants have been allocated to states on the basis of their projected gap on the nonplan account between projected revenues and projected expenditures for a five-year period. Using these projections, the commission makes recommendations for tax devolution and grants-in-aid as required by the constitution to achieve a hypothetical balance or surplus on the nonplan current account.

Table 8.2
Debt forgiveness by finance commissions

Finance commission	Year of report	Rs billion	GDP billions	% of GDP
Sixth	1974	19.7	667	2.95
Seventh	1979	21.6	1,025	2.11
Eighth	1984	22.9	2,223	1.03
Ninth	1989	9.8	4,357	0.22
Tenth	1995	5.0	10,672	0.05
Eleventh	2000	34.0	20,050	0.17

Source: Table 19.5 H.L. Bhatia, Public Finance. Report of Tenth Finance Commission, Report of the Eleventh Finance Commission.

This gap-filling methodology has been a major contributor to the softening of originally hard budget constraints of the states by encouraging them to slip from current account surpluses into deficit positions. Indeed, knowledge of this projection methodology by state budget makers may have had perverse consequences according to Gurumurthi (1995). He contends that "with a view to maximizing their share in the central transfers, it is not unusual to see states tending to incur a large amount of expenditure in the base year prior to the constitution of a Finance Commission" (35). Even if state budgeting behavior is not as strategic as Gurumurthi alleges, the gap-filling approach is likely to discourage states from running current account surpluses. New econometric research on the determinants of states' own tax efforts also indicates that increases in grants from the central government to the states have reduced the efficiency of tax collections by states and that the poorer states, which benefit most from the gap-filling approach, are the least efficient in tax collection. R. Jha et al. (1999) model the determinants of tax effort by major states and find that the higher the ratio of central grants in total expenditures of any government, the lower is its tax effort.

Some recent commissions have adopted formal methodologies for measuring the divergence in fiscal capacity in objective terms and allocating devolved resources among the states so as to compensate for these divergences. This approach was partially adopted by the Ninth Finance Commission. If adopted comprehensively, a by-product of this approach is that the tax devolution awards would be invariant to actual tax collections, thus removing the disincentive for states with low tax effort outcomes to achieve improvements. This approach is also attractive because it can address vertical and horizontal imbalances with a single policy instrument.

The Tenth Finance Commission sought to reform the incentive of the transfer system by recommending a phased reduction of general grants-in-aid, which had previously been used to fill revenue gaps between current revenues and expenditures, and two new incentive schemes for debt relief of principal owed to the center—one tied to improvement in fiscal performance in the current account and a matching debt relief scheme tied to the amount of state public enterprises divestment proceeds used to retire state debt.

These two debt-reduction schemes might have been expected to provide a powerful incentive for the states to adjust, but in practice the actual fiscal benefits realized by the states from these schemes have been meager. Little privatization of state-owned enterprises has occurred since the release of the Tenth Finance Commission's report, in part because of the political power of state employees, who resist privatization.

Successive Finance Commissions established a tradition of unconditional debt forgiveness. The sixth, seventh and eighth commissions gave substantial debt relief to the most indebted states in the proportion of their indebtedness relative to the size of their economies.

Planning Commission Transfers
The second channel is provided by the Planning Commission (PC), which has a mandate to coordinate the development plans of the center and the states. At its inception, the commission was enjoined to reduce poverty and work to minimize inequalities in income, status, facilities, and opportunities among individuals and groups. The states were responsible for preparing their own plans. However, these were assessed and adjudicated by the Planning Commission in terms of national objectives and norms before financial support of a state plan is secured. Most transfers awarded by the Planning Commission to the larger states are block transfers, composed of loans (70 percent) and grants (30 percent). The center also on-lends bilateral and multilateral agency lending at the same terms as for regular plan assistance.

In practice, the Planning Commission has substantial executive authority in determining public sector investment programs, especially by the states. Most significant, in the case of the states, it has the final word on allocating plan assistance, which for most states provides the bulk of the debt financing and grants needed to implement their investment programs. These transfers are used to finance the state infrastructure investments and new current account programs during the five-year life of a plan. Each state is guaranteed a quantum of financing, tied to the size of its state plan, which is a mixture of grants, loans, and access to centrally guaranteed funding from financial institutions. The provision of central financing for the wage components of new programs for the first five years from inception has also created a bias for expansion of programs and ballooning of state civil services.

Each year, the states bilaterally negotiate the size of their own plans with the Planning Commission. At this time, the limits are set on state borrowing from all sources, including the central government, domestic financial institutions, additional central assistance for externally aided projects, and projected small savings on-lending. Historical borrowing records of individual states and other economic indicators are taken into account, but formal debt sustainability analysis has not been an ingredient in the process.

A formula based largely on population and deviations in per capita income among the states provides a transparent foundation for most grant and debt financing. However, despite the great reliance on formula-based transfers, the annual bilateral negotiations between the Planning Commission and individual states introduce an element of nontransparency into state debt financing and encourage states to pursue fiscal policies leading to moral hazard problems. Much discretion remains at the margin for the Planning Commission to augment the grant resources of individual states. It does not publicize the rationale for its decisions or its assessment of state debt and deficit sustainability. The process of setting debt ceilings for individual states does not appear to take into account dynamic sustainability considerations, such as the growth rate of real state income.

Conditional Grant Transfers

The third channel for transfer is conditional matching grants (usually covering between 50 to 80 percent of costs) for shared-cost programs for centrally sponsored schemes (CSS), which are intended to ensure that the center can influence state priorities so as to achieve national policy goals. Examples of such programs include primary education expansion programs, child nutrition programs, public works, and poverty alleviation schemes. The mushrooming of centrally sponsored or shared-cost schemes designed and monitored by the central government has increased state dependency on central resources to finance marginal expenditures. In 1995–1996 there were 182 CSS being supported with central funding equivalent to 1.3 percent of GDP. The vast number of such schemes, their high administrative overhead costs, and rigid eligibility criteria have undermined effectiveness and distorted state priorities. The center intends to streamline the CSS system and convert most of the programs into block grants, but little progress has been made in this initiative to date.[5] One reason for the lack of progress is that the new block funding offered to the states as a quid pro quo is less generous than existing funding.

Deficit Financing

The fourth channel is deficit financing, most of it provided with an implicit central guarantee. In recent years, about 38 percent of the aggregate fiscal deficit of all states has been financed with net loans from the center. This is a dramatic decline from a 50 percent contribution in 1991–1992, reflecting the increased burden of repaying past loan principal. Most of the remaining components in deficit financing are controlled directly or indirectly by the central government.

Market borrowings, which are resources from captive sources of finance, are state-issued bonds placed with banks—as part of the statutory liquidity ratios (SLR) requirements that these institutions must meet—insurance companies, and nongovernment pension and provident funds. The central government allocates the SLR securities among states, while states initiate other forms of borrowing. The central bank assumes responsibility for marketing or assigning the agreed debt obligations of individual states to financial institutions. Prior to liberalization, as much as one-third of the gross fiscal deficit of the central government was monetized (Srinivasan 1993). As recently as early 1993, the SLR was 37.75 percent, representing a substantial amount of financial sector repression. But during the early to mid-1990s, financial repression was eased, and the government established an enabling environment for market-based pricing of new capital issues. The SLR was reduced in stages to free private sector asset space in the portfolios of financial institutions lending. Real interest rates on government securities rose sharply. The SLR is currently 25 percent of deposits. The states also receive debt financing from various unfunded or weakly funded provident, pension, and insurance funds for civil servants and public enterprise employees. The central government passes on funds that it borrows on behalf of the states at its average cost of funds. These costs have been rising with financial liberalization.

As a final instrument to control subnational borrowing, states since 1985 have been required to clear their overdraft positions with the RBI within ten days or lose checking privileges with the RBI. This threat has provided some fiscal discipline with respect to short-term spending controls and management of arrears, but it has not fostered hard budget constraints in the sense of preventing states from adopting unsustainable expenditure and debt financing policies.

8.1.4 Logic and Problems of the System

The logic of the fiscal transfer and debt financing system assumed that states would run current (revenue) account surpluses, or at least current nonplan surpluses, so that borrowed resources used to finance deficits would fund only productive capital account investments. Such a strategy for financing capital outlays would be financially viable if all capital expenditures yielded net cash flows sufficient to cover amortized principal and interest obligations. Weak cost recovery in power, water, and irrigation by the states implies inefficient use of these resources and increasing infrastructure supply scarcity and use of borrowing to finance current expenditures. As shown in figure 8.2, even in the mid-1980s, the states collectively exhibited a decreased capacity to maintain levels of investment expenditure, while their interest expense obligations began to rise. Interest has risen from approximately 14 percent of states' own revenue plus share of central taxes in 1980–1981 to approximately 25 percent of this revenue aggregate by 1996–1997. By contrast, capital expenditures by the states, exclusive of net lending, declined from approximately 31 percent of states' own revenue plus transferred tax shares in 1980–1981 to approximately 17 percent of the same revenue aggregate in 1996–1997. Investment in power, irrigation, roads, and urban infrastructure and rural water has stagnated. Expenditures for the operation and maintenance of capital assets used in each of these sectors have declined, while explicit and implicit subsidies for power, transport, and irrigation have increased. Concurrently, a policy failure to levy and collect adequate user charges on social and economic services and to operate public utilities on a cost recovery basis has led to a relative decline in state nontax revenues and increased subsidization of state utilities. Although an overall crisis in

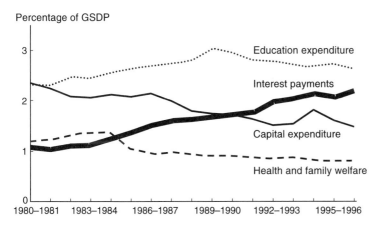

Figure 8.2
Key components of state governments' expenditure. *Source*: RBI

state finances leading to default may not be imminent in most states, a quiet crisis of expenditure composition has emerged.

Overstaffing in response to populist demands and adoption of wage parity with the center by most states during the 1980s has contributed to dwindling capital expenditure. Consequently, public investment at the state level has fallen far short of plan intentions, and the resultant productivity of capital is low. As state resource constraints hardened during the late 1980s and early 1990s, states maintained or increased their real expenditures on wages and salaries and on subsidies, while reducing expenditures on socially productive capital and maintenance and permitting expenditures on basic health and primary education to stagnate. With financial liberalization, interest rates increased and interest payments absorbed an increasingly large share of state resources. Gradually but perceptibly, many states found themselves increasingly unable to play their intended role in India's development.

The scatter diagram in figure 8.3 below shows a measure of state debt service ability in a preliberalization base year, 1990–1991 on the horizontal axis and the same measure six years later on the vertical axis.

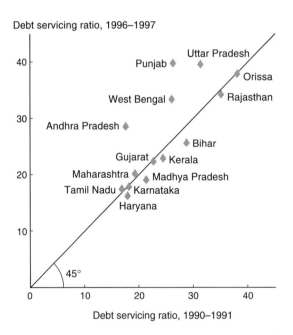

Figure 8.3
Debt servicing ratio (DSR) as a percentage of discretionary revenue.

Points above the 45 percent line imply a deterioration in debt service ability; points below indicate an improvement in the second period. The diagram thus provides relative positions of states at two points in time and a notion of movement. The numerator of the ratio is gross interest paid and amortization of principal. The denominator is own tax revenue plus own nontax revenue and devolved tax shares. Grants from the Planning Commission and shared-cost grants have been excluded from the base because these funds are earmarked for other purposes. The diagram shows clearly that all states did not react in the same manner to the new policy environment and that the system permitted the marked deterioration in debt servicing ability of at least four states to go unchecked until the late 1990s.

Once key supports for the old planning system, such as low real interest rates and the licenses raj vanished, the internal logic of the system began to collapse. As more of the interregional investment patterns came to be determined by market forces, poorer states appeared to be attracting proportionately less investment because of their deficient infrastructure endowments. Unfortunately, there was a major recognition lag on the part of state-level policymakers and their advisers in appreciating that the macroeconomic structure of India had changed fundamentally and that the states needed new financing strategies for the era of economic liberalization.

8.2 Incentives and Channels of the Soft Budget Constraint

The fiscal transfer system that has evolved to deal with vertical fiscal imbalances within the federation has a number of characteristics that work against fiscal correction by the states: (1) provision of debt financing to states by financial institutions on uniform terms regardless of the degree of state creditworthiness; (2) a large vertical fiscal imbalance that tends to erode the "Wicksellian connection" or link between expenditures in a state and tax burdens on state residents; (3) weak or nonexistent linkage between loan disbursement from the Planning Commission for state capital projects and actual capital infrastructure expenditures by the states; (4) a built-in incentive to establish new programs on the current account because such programs qualify for loan and grant financing from the Planning Commission for the first five years from inception; and (5) the fragmenting and priority-distorting impacts of the large number of conditional shared-cost grant schemes, each with its own eligibility criteria. Some states have exploited these design flaws by taking opportunistic approaches to maximizing transfers without addressing their fundamental fiscal problems. Finally, without mandates to undertake macroeconomic management, subnational governments may be more prone than their national counterpart to fiscal irresponsibility.

The plan-nonplan distinction and associated central financing support restrictions have led to duplication and waste and adversely affected state finances (Kurian 1999). Mixing loans and grants in a fixed proportion regardless of the varying mixes across states in the composition of capital and current account expenditures for state projects and programs encourage the slower-growth states to assume an inappropriate mix of debt and taxes. Prior to 1969, loans and grants were awarded to states after a project-by-project assessment. The 1969 adoption of the 70 percent loan–30 percent grant financing proportionality reflected the then reasonable assumption that 30 percent of plan expenditures would be allocated to current account activities, while the remaining 70 percent would be assigned to fund productive capital expenditures. By contrast, the plans of most states now typically allocate between 70 percent to 80 percent of social spending and from 35 percent to 50 percent of economic spending to current account activities.

States and municipalities are likely to assume that the consequences of a potential default will not be catastrophic because partial bailout will be arranged by either the creditors or a senior level of government. These expectations of bailouts by states and their agencies have encouraged Indian states to adopt high-risk deficit financing strategies. In India, a major direct default has yet to occur, but indirect defaults by urban development authorities, which are controlled by state governments, have occurred to center infrastructure investment banks, and bills owed by states to centrally owned electric power grids sometimes go unpaid.

High levels of power tariff subsidization for farmers have produced massive losses for state electricity boards (SEB) and fostered overdraft positions that have been difficult for many states to clear. For a long time, large subsidies from the states to their electricity utilities (estimated to be equivalent to 1.5 percent of GDP) masked the deterioration in electricity board finances. The awareness that state governments are prepared to extend a regime of soft budget constraints led to lax bill collection by SEBs, widespread power theft, and nonpayment of the bills that SEBs owe to creditors. Near-bankrupt SEBs have been "chronic defaulters in honoring their payment obligations to their suppliers—the coal mines, the power stations of the Center which sell power to the state boards and the Indian Railways" (Dhawan 1997). Even in the late 1980s, power was available to many farmers for only four hours per day. In this way, soft budget constraints and associated subsidization have led to binding supply constraints that retard growth. Ironically, the soft budget constraints bring about real opportunity cost prices for rural electricity that are many times higher than the cost recovery prices for SEB energy under proper management regimes. Removal of state power subsidies and other subsidized central inputs would also discourage overexploitation of groundwater.

8.2.1 Institutional Deficiencies of State Budgeting Processes

The state budget-making model is a system of investment-led budgeting with weak checks on recurrent costs, no mechanisms to force trade-offs among programs within departments, and little medium-term perspective.[6] The budget is a single document presented to the state assembly, but the process is essentially dualistic. Budget preparation typically involves incremental increases for existing programs and the addition of new programs. New programs on the current account may be classified as plan. Plan expenditures, including wages, will then qualify for partial central funding for five years from inception once they have been sanctioned by the Planning Commission as part of the national plan. All budgets are divided into plan and nonplan components, as required by central guidelines. Plan spending consists of new projects plus their running costs until the plan period is over, and running costs are then transferred to the nonplan account of the budget for funding against states' own revenue resources and devolved shared taxes.

The link between policy, planning, and budgeting has been weak at the state level, partly because of dependence on the center for policy initiatives. Aggregate financial discipline of the budget process is weak, and hard expenditure targets are almost nonexistent, as evidenced by the tradition of having up to three supplementary budgets. Supplementary budgets undermine the usefulness of initial budget targets (Premchand 1999). There is little managerial autonomy and no reward for improved cost-effectiveness. An inadequate expenditure management framework embodied in the structure of the Indian planning process creates perverse budgeting incentives for the states. The budgeting process does not evaluate the incremental recurrent costs of planned projects or encourage departments to make trade-offs between alternative current and capital use of funds. The status quo approach leads to delayed implementation, cost overruns, and low social rates of return on public investment.

8.2.2 Reverse Spillover in Subnational Government Wage Determination

India maintains a tradition of establishing pay commissions every ten years to advise the central government on the determination of public service compensation. The recommendations of such commissions are applicable only to the employees of the central government. Nevertheless, their recommendations have a major influence, by the demonstration effect, on subsequent pay awards by state governments and state public enterprises. The Fifth Pay Commission (FPC), which reported in 1997, recommended an upward adjustment of about 30 percent in the average rate of central government compensation and a 30 percent reduction in employment levels over ten years. But the government of India, secure in the knowledge that its own wage bill did not bulk very large in overall general government expenditure commitments, chose to enhance the award of the Pay Commission by providing a pay award of approximately 35 percent and ignore the recommendations on rightsizing. By contrast, state governments in India have much more employment-intensive public commitments (such as education, health services, and public works) than does the center. The wage bill of state governments are typically much larger in relation to their GSDPs, in the range of 5 to 8 percent, so that an increase of 35 percent would amount to an incremental expenditure commitment of 1.8 to 2.8 percentage points of GSDP.

8.2.3 Institutions of the Soft Budget Constraint

Small Saving Accounts On-Lending
The small savings mechanism, related to the automatic on-lending of 100 percent of net deposits in centrally controlled postal saving accounts to the state where the deposits are made, is an important avenue of partial escape from hard budget constraints. When net deposits exceed budgeted targets, state deficit slippages occur, aided by supplementary budgeting. Such an escape is not in the long-term

best interests of states, particularly the ones experiencing the most fiscal stress. The relative access to these funds among states is not tied to creditworthiness, relative economic growth performance, or any indicator of fiscal performance. The quantum of this source of financing exceeded budgeted predictions in the late 1990s. The high transaction costs of assembling these funds leads the union government to charge a relatively high interest rate (14 percent in 1998–1999) on funds on-lent to the state where the savings are derived. This high-cost financing is often supported by state savings incentives to depositors. It has grown recently to be equivalent to 1.6 percent of GDP (1999–2000), far outstripping the financing contribution of market loans at 0.6 percent of GDP.[7] In 1998–1999 small savings and provident fund accruals unexpectedly increased and the receipts net of repayments exceeded Rs 330 billion as compared to the initially projected level of Rs 216 billion. The relative success of the poorer states, such as Bihar and West Bengal, in mobilizing small saving account deposits within their jurisdiction has softened their budget constraints while burdening them with high-cost debt (Venkitaramanan 1999). This outcome is explained in part by the lack of other convenient outlets for savings in the poorer states, such as Bihar, and the use of state-sponsored incentive schemes, such as lotteries and emoluments for small savings promoters, by other states such as Punjab and West Bengal.

State Guarantees and Other Contingent Liabilities
The issue of the contingent liabilities of states has assumed heightened importance since 1994–1995, when borrowings by state-owned public enterprises were removed from coverage under the ceiling established for states' market and SLR borrowings. Prior to 1994–1995, state enterprises were given separate borrowing allocations each year as part of state-specific global ceilings for SLR and market borrowings. Their SLR qualification status permitted state-controlled enterprises to mobilize funds at relatively low rates of interest. At the same time, the allocation of a specific limit on the amount that could be raised meant there was some control on the extent to which state governments could issue guarantees. Subsequently, guarantees have become a convenient means for states to circumvent the ceiling on the quantum of their market borrowings. Each state is now free to permit its state public enterprises to borrow as much as they can in the domestic market. The rising deficits on revenue account have preempted financial resources from investment projects. Therefore, the growing need for infra-

structure and public investment inspired state governments to issue guarantees to mobilize resources through bond issues and discouraged lenders and credit rating agencies from assessing project-specific risks. Some states have used bonds financed through special-purpose vehicles or corporations with little or no credit records but with borrowing guarantees from state governments to raise debt financing for direct budgetary support.

The outstanding guarantees increased from 3 percent of GDP in 1992 to Rs 796 billion or 5.0 percent of GDP by September 1998. The growth in guarantees particularly since 1995 has been significant; the annual growth rate between March 1995 and September 1998 was 13.1 percent, whereas the growth in debt during the same period was 7.5 percent. The value of these contingent liabilities may rise quickly if state governments respond to the demand for increased infrastructure investment by encouraging more "build-own-transfers," which often require guarantees to the private sector, and off-budget financing by state infrastructure agencies, without making adequate policy provision for project-specific cost recovery.

The other significant issue associated with state guarantees is the rationale of extending guarantees by the states for the borrowings of its public enterprises, especially SEBs, which are incurring large losses. Attracting private sector investment for power generation projects in the absence of tariff reform requires granting rate of return guarantees by many states with counterguarantees extended by the government of India. In the case of foreign investors, the guarantees implicitly involve the assumption of foreign exchange risk. Past guarantee issuance for SEBs and other public enterprises has become an obstacle to reform because when a state-owned SEB is privatized, the state government has to bear the up-front cost of reforms. If the SEB has raised a large amount of loans guaranteed by the state government, the cost of unwinding these commitments as part of privatization is formidable. There is a lot of variation across states in issuing these liabilities. As a percentage of GSDP, they range from 4 percent in Utar Pradesh to 14.4 percent in Punjab.

There are also many other potential implicit contingent liabilities falling on the states such as underfunded pension and provident fund obligations, arrears of state enterprises, and cleanup cost of the liabilities of public enterprises to be privatized.

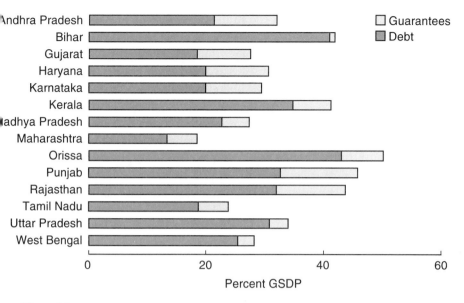

Figure 8.4
Outstanding debt and guarantees of the 14 major states in India, 1997/98.

8.3   Potential Control Mechanisms

Attempts to maintain fiscal discipline in the Indian federation have relied heavily on hierarchical oversight and control, but this mechanism has not been used effectively since the liberalization of economic life began in 1991. This section reviews those attempts, and then discusses the problems and prospects of discipline based on capital markets, political accountability, and land markets.

8.3.1   *Hierarchical Controls and Intergovernmental Fiscal Rules*

Coalitions government at the center in the mid-1990s often gave the impression that they intended to acquiesce or ignore states' efforts to maneuver past the hard budget constraints being watched over by officials of the Planning Commission, the Finance Ministry, and the central bank. Although subsequent policies articulated at the end of the decade, such as the intention to recover any funds lost through counterguarantees called against the states, the center's weak signaling of it commitment to hard constraint may have encouraged financially imprudent and intertemporally inconsistent policies by some states.

Under Article 293 (3) of the Indian constitution, any borrowing by state governments requires prior concurrence of the center whenever there are any loans outstanding from the latter. Because all states are in debt to the center, unrestricted power to borrow is effectively blocked. The states are also prohibited from borrowing abroad with the exception of loans from multilateral investment banks intermediated by the central government. According to Rao (1999), "In actual practice, the Planning Commission in consultation with the Union Finance Minister and the Reserve Bank of India (RBI), simply determines the total quantum of states' borrowing and allocates each state's share." In this way, borrowing from noncentral creditors is intended to be effectively controlled by the center. But at least two channels exist to enable the states to break through the protective defenses of the hard budget constraint: uncontrolled increases in small saving borrowings due to greater than expected net deposits, and taking borrowing off budget with state guarantees for borrowing by state-controlled special-purpose vehicles.

States have managed to finance large components of their own and their municipalities' capital budgeting needs for such projects as major irrigation systems, power projects, and roads by off-budget borrowing with guarantees.

The strain placed on state finances by mounting state debt, populist subsidies, and rising wage bills generates intense bargaining by the states to secure more resources from the center as well as central initiatives to foster economic adjustments by the states. The officially sanctioned forums for such bargaining are the annual bilateral discussions between a state and either the Planning Commission or the Finance Ministry of India. Failure to achieve the desired accommodation has often resulted in bargaining by press release, with the states appealing directly to their constituencies for support in the ongoing dialogue. State leaders make direct appeals to their political allies in the central government for more financial resources. In response, central political leaders, mindful of the center's own mounting debt and the strong tradition of rule-based formulas for resources sharing, have been cautious about requests for more financial resources or in using hierarchical controls to impose adjustment on the states. The center is encouraging voluntary state adjustment and consensus building for joint actions likely to improve state finances, such as adoption of value-added taxes by the states and self-imposed limits on the level of guarantees.

8.3.2   Capital Markets

The absence of any correlation between state creditworthiness and risk premiums on interest rates borne by subnational governments in India has prevented the emergence of a market-based fiscal discipline regime for states.[8] Currently, any state that successfully executes a fiscal correction will not receive an immediate reward from the financial community; based on experience, it might even expect to incur penalties in the form of diminished resource transfers from the center. But substantial additional liberalization of the Indian debt market for state government securities will be required before it can be looked to in performing an effective fiscal surveillance and policing role. A by-product of efficient market debt intermediation, where it can be created, will be a more effective screening out of projects with low internal rates of return, in the case of special-purpose debt, and timely market signaling of fiscal loosening, in the case of general obligation debt.

States obtain credit ratings for the public enterprise bonds that they guarantee in support of major irrigation and power projects. Two important local credit rating agencies, CRISIL and ICRA, have taken note of the deteriorating finances of a number of states by marginally reducing credit rating. For example, Maharashtra's rating was reduced by one grade in the light of its mounting debt and increasing wage bill obligations early in 1999. In January 2000, CRISIL, the largest credit rating agency, issued a general credit warning that "ratings for state-government backed instruments are likely to come under pressure due to worsening financial conditions and lack of any effort to improve fiscal situation in the states."[9] The agency foresees a systemic deterioration in the credit profile of the states that may lead to revision of their ratings in the absence of comprehensive fiscal and structural reforms.

But some market signals under current immature conditions are often confusing to the states. In 1999, the Reserve Bank of India began to encourage states to auction their debt issues directly to the market, with an initial limit set at 35 percent of market borrowings. In 1999, Punjab, a state experiencing sharply deteriorating finances due to aggressive pursuit of populist policies, used this new borrowing route to auction a small issues of Rs 600 million. This issue was fully subscribed, and the average yield on the issue was 12.39 percent versus 12.5 percent for the current yield on SLR placements. Hence, a state with a sharply deteriorating fiscal performance achieved a lower-than-average return, which suggests that purchasers of debt issues are uninformed of the financial position of states or expect a central bailout.

The secondary debt market in India remains underdeveloped, particularly the short-term money market, and state debt issues are not rediscounted or repriced to reflect fiscal performance and implicit risk of default. Risk management systems are weak in the secondary market as a whole. Fine pricing of assets is difficult and credit ratings crude. Banking and insurance remain nationalized industries. Although the government appears to be serious about lowering its stake in banks to below 51 percent, its effective control on the bank's functioning might continue. Public sector bankers have little incentive to conduct comprehensive risk assessments of loan proposals, particularly when they are made to subnational government agencies with an implicit government guarantee. This retarded area of reform, in combination with large general government fiscal deficits, has kept interest rates high and discouraged the development of mature secondary markets in government debt, which might encourage market-based fiscal discipline.

Creditworthiness has not been the chief criterion for lending to municipalities or urban development authorities. Municipal agencies that have not met their obligations to national development banks often hope to use political channels and processes to mitigate the negative consequences of weak fiscal performance and avert default. When municipal borrowing is undertaken by development authorities with limited local oversight or from creditors such as nationalized infrastructure development banks, accountability and debt servicing commitments are difficult to maintain. Under these conditions, public servants are lending in effect to other public servants. The market agents needed to achieve market-based fiscal discipline—creditors seeking a high risk-adjusted rate of return, borrowers seeking the best loan terms, and accountable local executive agencies—are nowhere to be found.

8.3.3 The Political Mechanism: Democratic Institutions and Fiscal Discipline

Indian state governments, like their national counterparts, are democratically elected on the basis of first-past-the-post competitions or the plurality rule. Elections are constitutionally required every five years. Until very recently, state governments that were unable to maintain the confidence of the state legislatures were often dismissed by centrally—appointed state governors on the advice of the central cabinet. Such dismissals under Article 356 of the constitution have usually been followed by a period of administrative rule by the governor known as President's Rule. Elected governments have also been superseded by President's Rule for failure to maintain a constitutionally required standard of law and order. From 1967 to 1991, President's Rule was invoked seventy-eight times and affected almost all states. However, the incidence of state government dismissals appears to have decreased recently under the influence of a 1995 Supreme Court ruling requiring the central authorities to provide the President and the public with a detailed set of reasons for such action.[10]

Party discipline is maintained by tight state party control over constituency nominations. The mediating role of state legislators in solving the problems of and delivering benefits to their constituencies varies greatly from state to state. State-level cabinets are more involved in economic decisions than at the national level, particularly under coalition governments. India was characterized by one-party domination at both the center and state levels from independence until the 1970s. As long as the Congress party held office at the center and in most of the states, differences over policy, including economic management, could be mediated informally within the dominant party (Hardgrave and Kochanek 1993). With the loss of one-party hegemony, center-state policy disputes are increasingly bargained in public forums including the Conference of Chief Ministers, the National Development Council, and, of course, the mass media.

The 1990s were a period of coalition or minority government at the center. Consensus politics has inhibited New Delhi from playing a strong leadership role in bringing about structural reforms at the state level. During the 1990s, the center made little headway in implementing microeconomic structural reforms in collaboration with the states to augment the gains achieved from its unilateral macroeconomic reforms.

The period since 1970 has witnessed the growth of regional parties at the state level and the fragmentation of parties of both the left and right, leading to coalition politics as the norm at the state level by the early 1980s. Political coalitions are not stable at the state level in many states. The combination of coalition governments losing their majority before the completion of their five-year constitutional term and the possibility that state governments would be dismissed by the central government has fostered a short-term time horizon among elected governments. In the 1980s and 1990s, there was a strong anti-incumbency trend and a lack of likelihood that chief ministers would be reelected or return to office after an election defeat.

These relatively short mandates mean that political leader have short-term time horizons when in office. Rather than competing for the support of the median voter, state politicians often strive to solidify the support of their main support group. State-level political leaders endeavor to maintain a stable core voting block defined in sectarian, caste, or occupational terms. When they attain office, these political leaders have rewarded their supporters with public sector jobs and highly subsidized, lower-priced services, including electric power and university fees, once they attain office. Leaders who lose power but maintain such a core constituency have a reasonable probability of return to office in some future coalition.

Dutta (1997), in an important empirical study of political instability and coalition government at the state level, examined fiscal polices pursued by majority and coalition governments in fifteen major states for a twenty-five-year period. Using an econometric model and pooled data from many states and periods, he found that unstable coalition state governments have a significantly higher proportion of current account (noncapital) expenditures relative to state domestic product and a significantly lower proportion of current account surplus to state domestic product than other state governments. Hence, the statistical evidence for the period he reviews indicates some evidence that unstable coalition governments are guilty of a greater level of fiscal indiscipline. He argues in the Indian context that "if political power alternates rapidly and randomly between competing political parties or groups of parties then each government will follow myopic policies since its assigns a low probability" to being reelected.

The late S. Guhan, a former state finance secretary, eloquently described the implication of short tenures for state governments: "The implications for governance of this degree of instability are serious. State governments, or their Chief Minister, with a time-horizon of two to three years cannot be expected to have deep commitment to long-term development or even an involvement in medium-term issues during their uneasy and limited tenure, they will be forced to politicize and interfere with the administration in order to survive; and tempted to make hay while the sun shines" (Guhan 1995).

Most state governments have pursued populist social policies, particularly with respect to the provision of power and irrigation services to farmers. Throughout the 1970s and 1980s, the states expanded investments in physical infrastructure (power, roads, irrigation, ports, roads) and provision of social services, but without establishing mechanisms for cost recovery and for maintaining these assets in the long run. Prices charged for power, water, irrigation, and other services declined to levels equivalent to a small fraction of production costs and are at the origin of extremely large implicit and explicit subsidies estimated at 7 percent of GDP for "nonmerit" goods.

The success of the development strategy pursued by the center from 1960 to approximately 1986 in propagating the spread of green revolution agricultural technology built a large constituency of stakeholders among farmers for increased rural electrification coverage and expansion of irrigation with little or no cost recovery. The irrigation potential nearly tripled from the beginning of the First Plan to the end of the Seventh Plan (Vaidyanathan 1994). In their efforts to encourage the spread of the green revolution and increased agricultural productivity, most states heavily subsidized inputs used by farmers, including surface irrigation and electricity. Indeed, some states, such as Tamil Nadu and Punjab, give free electricity to farmers. These policies appeared sustainable during the 1960s and 1970s, when rural electrification covered fewer than half of the villages and farm use of electricity to power tubewell irrigation was not the norm. But as shown in Figure 8.5, by 1995 fully 89 percent of all villages in India were electrified versus only 33 percent in 1970. Increased use of electricity by

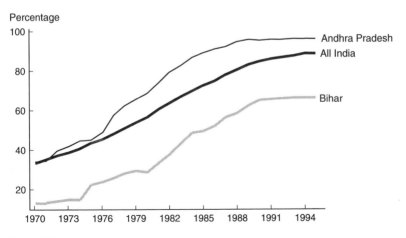

Figure 8.5
Percentage of electrified villages. *Source*: Fan, Hazell, and Thorat (1998).

farmers, coupled with low agricultural power tariffs and widespread power theft, created financial stress for SEBs.

The nexus among nationally administered prices, subsidization of agricultural inputs, and softening budget constrains makes it difficult to unravel parts of the state system of subsidization with piecemeal reforms. One subsidized group will resist reform unless others forfeit their subsidies as well. For example, farmers employing tubewell technology with highly subsidized power oppose higher tariff rates on the grounds of horizontal equity. They point to the relatively more generous subsidization of farmers receiving surface irrigation. There is a complex interconnection among low administrative pricing policies at the central level with implicit taxation of agricultural commodities, high rates of subsidization for farmers at the state level, and concessional financing to the states by the center. Over time, a soft budget loop has grown up connecting the state finances, the household economies of farms, and the central government. Unraveling such a system through agricultural pricing and input subsidization rate reform would create major differential losses among stakeholders unless there were very close coordination within a state across departments and even between center and state policies.

8.3.4   Land Markets and the Capitalization Impacts of State Fiscal Strategies

State governments have tried to contribute to farmer prosperity and indirectly to higher land rents and property values with their support for underpriced irrigation and power services. States, which have the constitutional power to tax both agricultural land and agricultural income, have been disinclined to do so and prefer to let the revenue yields of land taxes dwindle away. To generate their own revenue, the states have relied primarily on indirect tax system such as stamp duties, market fees, and interstate sales tax. Many of these taxes are regressive and often capricious in their incidence. Most state taxes fall on consumption or occasionally back on farmers through hidden taxes, such as on market fees, associated with the marketing of agricultural produce. Market fees are likely to be shifted backward to farmers, falling disproportionately on smaller farmers in remote areas. Such groups, unlikely to be politically powerful, may suffer capitalization impacts on the value of their land. Because of this approach to revenue generation, rural property owners do not expect that higher state government spending will lead to higher direct taxes on land or associated capitalization impacts on the price of land. But extreme underpricing has led to a lack of conservation and effective use on the demand side and rationing, particularly for power, on the supply side.

From independence until the century's close, the government of India retained colonial wartime legislation on rent controls. During the 1980s, judicial decisions linked property tax liabilities in all urban areas to the fair rents authorized under rent controls regardless of whether a property is rented or used by the owner. Rent control has led to low levels of building maintenance, and the link between controlled rents and property valuation undermined the abilities of local governments to raise revenue from property taxation. Hence, property owners do not perceive an automatic link between mounting municipal or state debt and future tax liabilities that will be borne by land. Accordingly, local land markets are unlikely to discipline local borrowing in the near to medium term.

The relative efficiency of state fiscal systems in providing adequate public infrastructure relative to tax burdens may be a potent force in influencing interstate investment decisions and provide an increasing influential check on fiscal laxity. Competition for investment is likely to become increasingly important in India and encourage better fiscal management over the medium term. This process, which can be interpreted as interstate capital migration induced by state fiscal performance or a capital Tiebout effect, holds out the prospect of improving the fiscal performance and public service delivery in states that are active participants endeavoring to attract substantial domestic and foreign private investment. But it may not be an effective incentive for states at the tail end of the fiscal benefit rank order.

8.3.5 Why the Problem Is Persistent, and What Should be Done

Past indifference by the center to the size of small saving borrowing, the growth of contingent liabilities, and issues of debt sustainability has weakened the regime of subnational macroeconomic control for general government finances. In the narrow rule-based sense, the central government attempts to impose hard budget constraints on the states in the form of restrictions on access to market credit for deficit financing. However, a lack of market-based fiscal discipline implies that there are no price (e.g., interest rate risk premia) or quantity (e.g., credit rationing) signals to deter states that borrow too much relative to their growth prospects and debt servicing capacities. A corollary is that there are no obvious rewards for prudent fiscal management. Individual state borrowing ceilings have not been determined with reference to state-specific debt sustainability analysis, such that borrowing ceilings have done little to stop the growth of state debt to state domestic product ratios.

In the absence of improved efforts at raising their own tax revenues, most state governments are likely to continue their dependence on high-cost small savings to fund their increasing deficits. Future policy toward small savings will be a very important element in the evolution of states' fiscal deficits. The government of India (GOI) has begun to adjust interest rate paid to depositors on small savings account more frequently in the light of rates in other markets. The GOI has also increased the spread between the deposit interest rate and the onlending rate by 1/2 a percentage point in recognition of the high administrative costs borne by the GOI in managing these deposits. Moreover, some recent signs indicate that national policymakers want to initiate more substantive reform of the system of fiscal federalism. For example, the terms of reference of the Eleventh Finance Commission explicitly enjoin it to "review the state of the Finances of the Union and the States and suggest ways and means to . . . restore budgetary balance and maintain macroeconomic stability" (Srivastava and Sen 1999), whereas previous finance commissions were discouraged from examining transfers other than their own. The official Ninth Plan (1999) has acknowledged many of the structural weaknesses of the current fiscal federal system. Under the theme of cooperative federalism, it proposes to move with the states to a more flexible approach to transfer design and the coordination of development strategies. It acknowledges that "fixation of unrealistic Plan size which does not materialize, has affected the credibility of the whole planning exercise" and proposes to remove the bias on favor of large plans by delinking the size of the plan from the level of central assistance to the states.

Measures that would discourage fiscal indiscipline by the states include rejection of the gap-filling methodology by finance commissions, basing future tax share devolutions on differences in fiscal capacity to be measured in ways that are invariant to actual tax collections, and adoption of a no-bailout commitment by the central government, or at least a commitment that any partial bailout is contingent on significant adjustment by the benefiting state. Reforming the small savings system might be accomplished by breaking the automatic link between where the funds are deposited and where they are lent and perhaps introducing state-level fiscal performance criteria into future allocation decisions.

The center has also responded to accumulating arrears of state public enterprises with defensive measures designed to harden budget constraints. Since 1997, outstanding arrears of SEBs to Coal India and the centrally owned power grid corporations have been deducted against the normal central assistance from the Planning Commission, up to a maximum of 15 percent of such assistance for each state. An Indian committee on state guarantee consisting of state representatives and central bank advisers has recently suggested ceilings on the use of guarantees by states. The committee's report has suggested linking guarantees to the size of state economies, their revenues, or the consolidated fund itself and that the ratio of incremental guarantees to incremental debt should be kept constant or reduced. Gujarat and Andhra Pradesh have established a ceiling for the amount of limits for contingent liabilities.

New institutional frameworks are also needed for state budget design, expenditure management, and state debt management. One urgent priority for the states, and perhaps the central government, is to adopt a much more comprehensive approach to debt management that would embrace the macroeconomic implications of aggregate state debt and deficits, determination of debt ceilings, and assessment of appropriate limits on contingent debt liabilities associated with the debt of PE and guaranteed for private participation in infrastructure financing.

Mature credit markets and a more transparent political oversight process would improve subnational fiscal policy policing and better differentiate performance differences among the states. Indeed, the strong constitutional hierarchical mechanisms may discourage the other correction mechanisms such as strong electoral or credit market oversight from operating. The adoption of Musgrave's notion of pure federalism with sole accountability would likely strengthen land market capitalization and electoral impacts. Another alternative to sole accountability is the cooperative or negotiated approach to debt control practiced in Australia. Under this approach, the subnational governments are actively involved in formulating macroeconomic objectives, agreeing on global deficit targets for general government, and then determining the financial requirements of individual states. But the much larger number of Indian than Australian states and the absence in India of a long-standing tradition of forging wide national consensus for fiscal corrections suggests that it would be difficult to graft the Australian approach on to the Indian federal polity.

8.3.6 Recent Developments

Indian fiscal federal arrangements appear to be at the crossroads. The theoretical literature on design of incentives related to intergovernmental transfers as summarized by Bird (1999) indicates that there are essentially only two broad frameworks: a bargaining situation between principals, in this case a bilateral process, or a principal agent framework where a dominant central government establishes, either unilaterally or after consultation, a uniform framework for transfer design. Indian federalism might be entering a new era characterized by bilateral bargaining between the center and individual states intended to achieve state fiscal adjustment with renewed growth. The bilateral approach has the potential to take center-state relation in a far different direction from the multilateral or symmetrical approach to negotiating new center-state agreements envisaged by the advocates of cooperative federalism. Alternatively, a general dissatisfaction with the status quo may be the prelude to a more far-reaching review and overhaul of the entire system with a concentration on reform of Planning Commission transfer incentives to improve fiscal performance and foster a more balanced national growth.

During 1999 and 2000, central policymakers, appreciative of the need to provide clearer and tangible reward signals for states that embarked on fiscal reforms as a counterweight to the existing disincentives, set out to craft stronger mechanisms of fiscal correction for states experiencing the greatest fiscal stress. The center's initial response was to offer memorandums of understanding (MOUs), negotiated between the center and individual target states, under which a state agreed to implement a customized program of fiscal adjustment measures in return for medium-term loans and cash advances of future pledged funding. This approach clearly fell within the bilateral bargain framework. The first round of MOUs with the fiscally stressed states of necessity had an ad hoc quality and lacked transparency. Its impact on fiscal performance has yet to be assessed. The terms and conditions of the loans and cash advances were not publicized. Many commentators on this first-round process have stressed that in order to have real legitimacy, conditionality-based support by the center for the adjustment reforms of individual states should be transparent, with state residents and financial markets being able to learn about the term. Individual states have objected that bilateral bargaining enhances the position of those states with the most bargain power in relation to the center. There is also a danger that by using the instrument of new loan funds to generate incentives for adjustment, the center has only provided resources that are nonrecurring and can be used to postpone adjustment.

In a separate initiative, the government of India wrote to the sitting Eleventh Finance Commission near the end of its term, requiring it to "evolve a monitorable fiscal reform programme to accompany [its] grants-in-aid." Therefore, the supplementary report of the Eleventh Finance Commission is intended to be the legitimizing instrument for a new round of bargained conditionalities within a more transparent principal agent framework, with the release of otherwise devolved grants against achievement of fiscal consolidation targets or the adoption of measures of adjustment. The MOU process linked to broad conditionalities or a similar approach might also be established to determine the way in which discretionary funds are allocated by the Planning Commission.[11]

8.4   Conclusion

A quasi-federal constitution provides India with hierarchical control to foster the maintenance of hard budget constraints, but many other aspects of the fiscal federal system, as they operated during the 1990s, have encouraged states to explore soft budget tactics. The traditional mechanisms for curbing excessive debt accumulation, such as capital market risk premia, electoral disapproval, capital Tiebout effects, and capitalization of debt and future tax burdens on privately held asset prices, have not provided significant impetus to fiscal correction. However, India's system of intergovernmental transfers has remained basically sound, and it continues to provide a relatively transparent, predictable, and rule-based framework. By subjecting state borrowings to central government approval and precluding states' access to financing from either external markets or their own banks (of which there are none), India's fiscal federal arrangements have succeeded in imposing a relatively hard budget constraint. India has been spared the moral hazards and macroeconomic crises witnessed in several federated states of Latin America. While many states have seen rising debt-to-state GDP ratios, the overall ratio of total state debt to national GDP has been relatively stable at around 20 percent for the past decade. And the fiscal deterioration at the state level has been reflected primarily in a worsening composition of expenditure, with salaries, subsidies, and interest payments crowding out nonwage operations and management costs and capital spending.

Nevertheless, the Indian case demonstrates that the hierarchical mechanism is often awkward and fraught with difficulties. The stylized facts of this case study include high levels of vertical fiscal imbalance and a variety of inadequate marginal incentives, leading to moral hazard challenges and the expectations by some states during the 1990s that they might manage to shift much of the onus of adjustment to the center. For the most part, these expectations have not been validated by the center. Over the short run, states have sought ways around hierarchical oversight even when hard budget constraints have not been breached intertemporally. Hierarchical control has fended off the worst forms of opportunism, but they have not been obvious enough or omnipresent enough to induce prudent budget making by states. Political fragmentation, coalition governments at the center, and governments of short duration at the state level have made coordinating politics between the center and the states difficult and reduced the center's effective will to curtail populist policies by the states. This has led to difficulties, but hierarchical controls, even if enforced in a cautious or halfhearted manner, have prevented unfettered state access to credit. The domestic capital market has failed to send strong signals or act as an early warning system, both because most of the market consists of captive financial institutions and during the period under review, the market may have believed that there was an implicit guarantee.

The Indian case suggests that hierarchical institutions alone are not an optimal mechanism for policing subnational finances. Past use of paternalistic forms of oversight, of which President's Rule is the most extreme, has encouraged state governments to adopt short time horizons. Paternalistic oversight strengthened lenders in the belief that should state fiscal problems appear intractable, a paternalistic central government will step into the shoes of state governments and provide adequate financial resources to resolve the problem.

Whether the way forward in India will be a new bilateralism or a principal agent rule setting with aspects of conditionality for highly indebted states, some features of the Australian approach, such as a more timely dissemination of information on states' finances, perhaps institutionalized with the support of state-level fiscal responsibility legislation and consultations on macroeconomic outlooks, are worth exploring.

Liberalization of economic markets and decentralization have made India ripe for more institutional reforms, including those needed to strengthen hard budget constraints and make their implication more tangibly visible to state politicians. Dissatisfaction with the status quo is growing. But broad-based tax reform, financial markets liberalization, and banking sector liberalization have lagged far behind liberalization of the market for goods. Much additional reform in these subjects will be required to foster creditworthiness and more mature markets for state debt before the market will be able to send strong signals to state cabinets. If institutional and policy regime changes succeed in dispelling the notion that future budget constraints for states and municipalities might soften, subnational government is likely to become both more accountable and more effective in meeting society's public needs. Although debt obligations for most states are manageable with reasonable programs, efforts to date at fiscal correction have not been equal to the challenge.

Acknowledgments

The views expressed in this chapter are mine and do not necessarily reflect those of the World Bank or the Asian Development Bank. My former colleagues Shahrokh Fardoust, Edgardo Favora, Kanishka Ghoshal, Rajni Khanna, Balabaskar Naidu, V.J. Ravishankar, Mike Stevens, Fahrettin Yagci, Roberto Zagha, and Farah Zahir have assisted generously in the production and review of this chapter, although I remain solely responsible for the judgments expressed here. I also owe debts to Roy Bahl, Amaresh Bagchi, and Patricia Reynolds for their comments and to the late S. Guhan for being my initial guide to Indian federalism. The sponsorship of the World Bank's decentralization thematic group is gratefully acknowledged.

Notes

1. Pure federalism is defined by Musgrave (1959) as the case where state governments possess full autonomy.

2. John Williamson and Molly Mahar (1998) judge that India moved from full financial repression in 1973 to partial repression by 1996 for interest rates and credit controls.

3. Gross fixed capital formation (GFCF) for India rose from 17 percent in 1970–1971 to 26.3 percent in 1995–1996. An investigation of the sectoral composition of GFCF shows that the private corporate sector's contribution grew from 2.4 percent of GDP to 9.1 percent over this period. Public sector capital formation also grew from 6.5 percent of GDP to peak in 1986–1987 at 11.7 percent of GDP and then dwindled to 7.9 percent in 1995–1996.

4. For example, during 2000, the GOI gave "in-principle" approval to two public banks for dilution of the government's shareholding to 33 percent by mobilizing fresh capital through public issues and cleared a uniform voluntary retirement scheme for the banking sector, removing a major hurdle to bank restructuring, particularly that of weak banks.

5. According to the text of the Ninth Plan, "In principle, the CSS should be confined to schemes of an inter-State character, matters impinging on national security, selected national priority where Central supervision is essential for effective implementation and multi-State externally financed projects where Central Co-ordination is necessary for operation reasons. Except for such schemes, all other schemes should be transferred to the States along with the corresponding funds." Para 6.10 Planning Commission (1999) *Ninth Plan*.

6. This section draws on Stevens (1999).

7. Reserve Bank of India, 1999, Bulletin, Appendix III, S222.

8. Market-based fiscal discipline is the proposition that yields on government bonds are tightly correlated with indicators of insolvency risk and that increasing yield spreads discipline to subnational governments by encouraging them to undertake fiscal corrections.

9. Business Standard (2000): "Crisil sees state governments finances going further downhill".

10. Some commentators, notably Lijphart (1999), allege that, "in practice President's Rule was been used mainly by the central government to remove state governments controlled by other parties and to call new state elections in the hope of winning these" (190).

11. "The Centre should attach conditionalities on the development funds that it gives to the states, [according to] Planning Commission member, Montek Singh Ahluwalia. [H]e said that the central aid to the states for development purposes should go with conditionalities so that the reforms process gains momentum at the state-level" *Financial Express*, Nov. 23, 2000.

References

Bhatia, H. L. 1994. *Public Finance*. 18th ed. New Delhi: Vikas.

Bird, Richard. 1999. "Threading the Fiscal Labyrinth: Some Issues in Fiscal Decentralization." In Joel Slemrod, ed., *Tax Policy in the Real World*. Cambridge: Cambridge University Press.

Breton, Albert. 1996. *Competitive Government*. Cambridge: Cambridge University Press.

Business Standard. 2000 "Crisil Sees State Governments' Finances Going Further Downhill." Report of Jan. 7. Mumbai.

Chelliah, Raja J. 1999. "Issues Before the Eleventh Finance Commission." Seminar on issues before the Eleventh Finance Commission, New Delhi.

Dhawan, B. D. 1997. "Latent Threats to Irrigated Agriculture." In M. Desai Bhupat, ed., *Agricultural Development Paradigm for the Ninth Plan under New Economic Environment.* New Delhi: Oxford University Press.

Dutta, Bhashkar. 1997. "Coalition Governments and Policy Distortions: The Indian Experience." In Parthasarasthi Shome, ed., *Fiscal Policy, Public Policy and Governance.* New Delhi: Centax Publications.

Fan, Shenggen, Peter Hazell, and Sukhadeo Thorat. 1998. "Government Spending, Growth and Poverty: An Analysis of Interlinkages in Rural India." International Food Policy Research Institute Discussion Paper No. 33.

Guhan, S. 1995. "Center and State in the Reform Process." In Robert Cassen and Vijay Joshi, eds., *India: The Future of Economic Reform.* New Delhi: Oxford University Press.

Gurumurthi, S. 1995. *Fiscal Federalism in India.* New Delhi: Vikas Publishing House.

Hardgrave, Robert L., Jr., and Stanley A. Kochanek. 1993. *India: Government and Politics in a Developing Nation.* Fort Worth Tex.: Harcourt Brace Jovanovich.

Jha, Raghbendra, Puneet Chitkara, Somnath Chatterjee, and M. S. Mohanty. 1999. "Tax Efficiency in Selected Indian States." *Empirical Economics* 24 (4).

Kurian, N. J. 1999. "Need for Restructuring of Government Finances: Center and States." Seminar on issues before the Eleventh Finance Commission, New Delhi.

Lakdawala, D. K. 1987. *Eighth Finance Commission's Recommendation: Center State Budgetary Transfers.* New Delhi: Oxford University Press.

Lijphart, A. 1999. *Patterns of Democracy.* New Haven, CT: Yale University Press.

Mathur, Om Prakash. 1999. *India: The Challenge of Urban Governance.* New Delhi: National Institute of Public Finance and Policy.

Musgrave, Richard. 1957. *The Theory of Public Finance.* New York: McGraw-Hill.

Planning Commission. 1999. *Ninth Plan.* http://www.nic.in/ninthplan/.

Premchand, A. 1999. "Issues before the Eleventh Finance Commission." Mimeo. New Delhi.

Rao, M. Govinda. 1998. "India: Intergovernmental Fiscal Relations in a Planned Economy." In Richard M. Bird and François Vaillancourt, eds., *Fiscal Decentralization in Developing Countries.* Cambridge: Cambridge University Press.

Rao, M. Govinda. 1999. "Role of Sub-national government in the Process of Fiscal Reform in India." In Ric Shand, ed., *Economic Liberalization in South Asia.* New Delhi: Macmillan.

Reserve Bank of India, 1999. *Report of the Technical Committee on State Government Guarantees.* Mumbai: Reserve Bank of India.

Srinivasan, T. N. 1993. "Indian Economic Reform Background, Rationale and Next Steps." Mimeo. New Haven.

Srivastava, D. K., and Tapas K. Sen. 1999. "Issues before the Eleventh Finance Commission." Seminar on issues before the Eleventh Finance Commission, New Delhi.

Stevens, Mike. 1999. "Back to Office Report: India." Mimeo. Washington, D.C.

Vaidyanathan, A. 1994. "Performance of Indian Agriculture since Independence." In Kaushik Basu, ed., *Agrarian Questions.* New Delhi: Oxford University Press.

Venkitaramanan, S. 1999. "A Long Haul to Reform." *Hindu*, Feb. 15.

Williamson, John, and Molly Mahar. 1998. "A Survey of Financial Liberalization." Essays in International Finance. Department of Economics, Princeton University.

World Bank. 1996. *India: Five Years of Stabilization and Reform and the Challenges Ahead.* Washington D.C.: World Bank.

World Bank. 1997. *India: Sustaining Rapid Economic Growth.* Washington, D.C.: World Bank.

IV

Newly Decentralizing Countries in Transition

9

Soft-Budget Constraints and Local Government in China

Jing Jin and Heng-fu Zou

A significant feature of China's economic reform since 1978 is the devolution of the central government's control over the economy to subnational governments. The fiscal system is decentralized among five levels of government—national, provincial, municipal, county, and township governments—which are broadly categorized into center, provincial, and local governments (all subprovincial governments). This chapter mainly focuses on soft budget constraints in the relationship between the central government and the provinces. The term *local* refers to the levels below provinces and *subnational* to the levels below the center unless otherwise specified.

China's subsidy, taxation, credit, and administrative pricing systems are all subject to soft budget constraints. Prior to 1994 under the Chinese fiscal regime, the collection of all taxes and profits followed the prereform pattern: local government collections were remitted to the center and then transferred back to the provinces according to expenditure needs approved by the center. Policymakers in the central government decided what type of revenues should be collected and how these revenues were to be reallocated for national and local public good provisions. Most expenditures at subnational levels were financed by central transfers and complemented by a few self-retained local tax receipts. The prereform fiscal system resulted in a fundamental lack of incentives and efficiency, which became the major concern of the central authorities. In the 1980s, a series of reforms were implemented to revamp the fiscal relations between the central and subnational governments. Although incentives to spur tax collection efforts by local governments were successful to a certain extent, they also reduced the share of revenues passed on to the central government.[1] Before the 1994 tax system reform, the central government's share of total revenue declined from 44 percent in 1978 to 23 percent in 1993, while the total subnational revenue share increased from roughly 56 percent to 77 percent during same period. At the same time, the consolidated government revenue share in GDP also shrank, from 47 percent in 1978 to 13 percent in 1993. Although fiscal decentralization in the 1980s shifted more resources to local governments in terms of increased share in total revenues, the shrinking pie also considerably reduced the budgetary resources allocated at the provincial level (table 9.1).

Throughout the 1980s, the central government's inability to cut spending to stay within declining revenue created persistent budget deficits that contributed to mounting inflationary pressures. At the same time, subnational governments faced greatly expanded expenditure responsibilities stemming from obligations imposed by national policy (Wong 1991). As the central government responded to fiscal pressure by attempting to devolve expenditure responsibilities to lower levels of government, it left provincial governments starved for revenues. Apart from the intensified bargaining between central and local governments over the sharing schemes, fiscal pressures created by the contract system of the 1980s led to undesirable responses by subnational governments. Examples include the diversion of resources from budgetary to extrabudgetary channels, the duplication of industries to capture revenues that formerly flowed to the national treasury, generous tax concessions to local state-owned enterprises (SOEs) under their own jurisdictions, and expanded local bank lending to these SOEs. All of these measures circumvented the central government's efforts to impose hard budget constraints and weakened overall financial discipline.

As the country moved toward economic federalism with the fiscal decentralization coincident with a continuous decline of government revenue as a percentage of national income in the fiscal sphere, the unitary political system was also transformed and decentralized. Although the central bureaucratic hierarchy continued to select, assign, and promote top provincial cadres (Huang 1996), since 1983, bureau-level officials (e.g., the heads of provincial fiscal bureaus and the managers of provincial branches of national banks) have been selected by provincial governments and appointed by the corresponding level of the People's Congress. No central approval is required. Driven by common economic interests and the pressure to seek growth, the most important measure of their political performance, the directors of fiscal and banking agencies tend to "stand where they sit" rather than

Central and provincial government revenue shares in total revenue and GDP

Year	Tax revenue (without SOE remittance) (billion yuan)	Revenue from enterprises (Profit remittance, billion yuan)[a]	Total revenue (billion yuan)	Central tax revenue (billion yuan)	Total central revenue (billion yuan)	Subnational revenue (billion yuan)	Share of total central revenue in total revenue (%)	Share of subnational revenue in total revenue (%)	GDP (billion yuan)	Total government revenue as a percentage in GDP (%)
1978	113.2	57.2	170.4	17.6	74.8	95.6	43.9	56.1	362.4	47.0
1979	114.6	49.5	164.1	23.1	72.6	91.5	44.2	55.8	403.8	40.6
1980	116	43.5	159.4	28.4	71.9	87.5	45.1	54.9	451.8	35.3
1981	117.6	35.4	153	31.1	66.5	86.5	43.5	56.5	486.2	31.5
1982	121.2	29.6	150.8	34.7	64.3	86.5	42.6	57.4	529.5	28.5
1983	136.7	24.1	160.8	49	73.1	87.7	45.5	54.5	593.5	27.1
1984	164.3	27.7	191.9	66.5	94.2	97.7	49.1	50.9	717.1	26.8
1985	200.5	4.4	204.9	77	81.4	123.5	39.7	60.3	896.4	22.9
1986	212.2	4.2	216.4	77.8	82	134.4	37.9	62.1	1,020.2	21.2
1987	219.9	4.3	224.2	73.6	77.9	146.3	34.7	65.3	1,196.3	18.7
1988	235.7	5.1	240.7	77.4	82.5	158.2	34.3	65.7	1,492.8	16.1
1989	266.5	6.4	272.9	82.3	88.7	184.2	32.5	67.5	1,690.9	16.1
1990	293.7	7.8	301.5	99.2	107	194.5	35.5	64.5	1,854.8	16.3
1991	314.9	7.5	322.4	93.8	101.3	221.1	31.4	68.6	2,161.8	14.9
1992	348.3	6	354.4	98	104	250.4	29.3	70.7	2,663.8	13.3
1993	434.9	4.9	439.8	95.8	100.7	339.1	22.9	77.1	3,463.4	12.7
1994[b]	521.8		521.8	290.7	290.7	231.1	55.7	44.3	4,675.9	11.2
1995	624.2		624.3	325.7	325.7	298.6	52.2	47.8	5,847.8	10.7
1996	740.8		740.7	366.1	366.1	374.6	49.4	50.6	6,788.4	10.9
1997	865.1		865.1	422.7	422.7	442.4	48.9	51.1	7,446.3	11.6
1998	987.6		987.6	489.2	489.2	498.4	49.5	50.5	7,939.6	12.4

Sources: China Statistical Yearbook (1999); *China Government Finance Yearbook* (various issues).

[a]Before 1984, a considerable amount of central revenue came from SOEs' profit remittance, which exclusively went to the central treasury. Since 1984, the profit remittance had been increasingly replaced by enterprises income tax. Profit remittance from SOEs remained as a residual category until 1993 before it terminated.

[b]Tax assignment system reform introduced. Data after 1994 are not compatible with those before 1994.

delegate to their central line administrators. As a result, the former hierarchical management has been considerably weakened and increasingly transformed into horizontal administration featured by a highly fragmented economy. The central authority's attempt to strengthen the hierarchical management by strengthening personnel management at the level of provincial party secretaries and governors thus may not necessarily be able to penetrate the horizontal alignment coalitions increasingly shaped by common interests and contiguity at the subnational level. According to Yang (1997), the heads of faster-growing provinces now tend to be promoted more quickly than otherwise would be the case. Bo (1996) also finds that provincial leaders of more populous and richer provinces are more likely to be promoted than those in less populous and less developed ones.

This chapter outlines some major economic and administrative mechanisms that undermine the central government's endeavor to harden the budget constraint on provincial governments. Section 9.1 describes briefly the evolution of China's intergovernmental fiscal relations in the postreform period, section 9.2 presents the major channels of soft budget constraints on provincial governments, and section 9.3 sets out the conclusions.

9.1 Evolution of Intergovernmental Fiscal Relations, 1980s–1990s

9.1.1 1980–1993: Fiscal Contract System (Tax-Sharing System)

In 1980, the centralized fiscal regime was replaced with the fiscal contract system whereby each level of government contracted with the next level up to meet certain revenue and expenditure targets. Central and subnational governments shared the revenue proportionately or in the form of a fixed quota plus a percentage share. At the same time, subnational governments were required to finance their own expenditures through self-generated and shared revenues, a step in the direction of hardening the budget constraint on local governments.

Unlike other countries where taxes are collected by the central government and then allocated to subnational governments, local authorities in China collected all tax revenues and remitted a portion to higher levels of government. The amount submitted to the central coffers depended on provincial receipts and the sharing formula between the center and provinces. Given such a highly decentralized revenue collection system, the center had to resort to various instruments to ensure revenue remittance from local authorities. These instruments in turn led to perverse reactions from the provinces, which always found ways to retain more revenues through their relaxed revenue collection for and the negotiations with the center regarding shared revenue.

From 1980 through the early 1990s, four revenue-sharing systems were employed, with many variations. Until the tax system reform in 1994, six different contract types were in use between the central government and provinces, with many more at the subprovincial level (table 9.2) (also see World Bank 1993 and Bahl and Wallich 1992).

Type A: Incremental contract Based on 1987 revenues, the provincial retention rate of all tax revenues ranged from 28 percent to 80 percent, while local remittance the center needed was to increase from 3.5 percent to 6.5 percent (contracted growth rate) on an annual basis. Tax revenues in excess of the stipulated growth rates were retained entirely by provinces.

Type B: Basic proportional sharing A fixed proportion of all revenues was remitted to the center.

Type C: Proportional sharing and incremental sharing A certain proportion of the actual revenue collection of the previous year was retained, and then a different (usually higher) proportion of revenues was retained for the incremental amount in excess of the total revenues for the previous year.

Type D: Remittance incremental contract A specific nominal amount was transferred to the center in the initial year; in subsequent years, the remitted amount increased at a contracted rate (9 percent for Guangdong province and 7 percent for Hunan province).

Type E: Fixed remittance A specific nominal amount was transferred to the center with no annual adjustments.

Type F: Fixed subsidy Deficit provinces received fixed subsidies.[2]

Two crucial features survived every change in revenue-sharing systems. First, central fixed revenues were not subject to revenue sharing, so whatever was designated as central revenues left the pool of revenues to which revenue-sharing formulas were applied.[3] Second, enterprise income, both remitted profits and direct tax revenues (after 1984), was still divided among governments according to their administrative subordination—state-owned enterprises subordinated to the central, provincial, and local governments, respectively.

Table 9.2
Revenue-sharing system between the central and provincial governments, 1988–1992

	Type A — Incremental contract		Type B — Basic proportional sharing	Type C — Proportional sharing and incremental sharing		Type D — Remittance incremental contract		Type E — Fixed Remittance	Type F — Fixed Subsidy
	Contracted growth rate (%)		Retention rate (%)	Proportion	Incremental sharing	Remittance (100 million)	Incremental contract (%)	(100 million yuan)	
Beijing	4.00	50.00							
Hebei	4.50	70.00							
Liaoning	3.50	58.30							
Shenyang	4.00	30.30							
Haerbin	5.00	45.00							
Jiangsu	5.00	41.00							
Zhejiang (exl. Ningpo)	6.50	61.50							
Ningpo	5.30	27.90							
Henan	5.00	80.00							
Chongqing[a]	4.00	33.50							
Tianjin			46.50						
Shanxi			87.60						
An Hui			77.50						
Da Lian				27.70	27.30				
Qingdao				16.00	34.00				
Wuhan[a]				17.00	25.00				
Guangdong						14.10	9.00		
Hunan						8.00	7.00		

Shanghai	105.00	
Heilongjiang	2.90	
Shangdong (exl. Qingdao)	4.90	
Hubei (exl. Wuhan)		1.22
Ji Lin		1.07
Sichuan (exl. Chongqing)		1.79
Jiangxi		0.50
Sha'anxi		1.20
Gansu		1.30
Fujian		0.50
Inner Mongolia		18.40
Guangxi		6.10
Tibet		9.00
Ningxia		5.30
Xinjiang		15.30
Guizhou		7.40
Yunan		6.70
Qinghai		6.60
Hainan		1.40

Source: Ministry of Finance, P.R. China. Also see Bahl and Wallich (1992), World Bank (1993).
[a]After the cities of Wuhan and Chongqing were treated differently from Hubei and Sichuan provinces, the provinces changed from net providers to the state to net recipients of subsidies from the state.

9.1.2   Problems of the Fiscal Contract System

Declining Central Revenue as a Percentage of Total Revenue
The decentralized nature of tax collection by local governments meant that the central government lacked effective supervision of tax collections and remittances by provincial governments. Consequently, local governments avoided sharing revenues with the center through various means. For example, if the total revenue collected by Jiangsu provincial government was within the total amount of the previous year (took taking 1987 as the base year) plus a 5 percent increase, Jiangsu provincial government could retain 41 percent of the total revenue collected. Any amount exceeding the total increased revenue can be retained by the provincial government. Frequently, tax revenues stagnated for years, limiting the amount for sharing with the center. This phenomenon was prevalent among the provinces under contracts A, B, and C. Assuming some growth in taxes accruing to the provinces by transferring budgetary revenue to extrabudgetary items or allowing generous tax recessions to local enterprises so that benefits could be accrued within the enterprises under the jurisdiction of subnational governments, the center's share would decrease.

In other cases, tax remitted to the center was fixed in nominal terms for many years, and growth was retained by the province. Guangdong, one of the fastest-growing economies in China, is a case at point. Its remittance was fixed at 1.4 billion yuan for many years. Not until 1988 was the remittance incremental contract implemented (table 9.2), under which its remittance was set at an annual increase of 9 percent, with 1987 as the base year. By 1993, its remittance increased to 2.4 billion yuan, barely 7 percent of its total 34.7 billion revenue.

With the power of tax collection, provincial governments acted strategically to escape sharing their revenues with the center, which resulted in a decline of central revenue share in relation to that of the local government in total revenue (table 9.1). Tax generation in such a fiscal system tends to be inelastic with respect to GDP and procyclical. In a rapidly growing economy with fiscal contracts containing a large fixed component, the rate of increase in tax revenues would be less than that of income growth. Tax policy thus becomes a procyclical mechanism that exacerbates economic fluctuations instead of moderating them (Agarwala 1992). When government expenditure increases in line with GDP, the deficit is likely to expand as a consequence.

Extrabudgetary Fund

The rapid growth of extrabudgetary revenues was a striking feature of tax reform during the 1980s. By 1992, the size of such revenue was almost equal to state revenue and accrued mostly to state-owned enterprises and their supervisory agencies (see section 9.2). Richer provinces could raise extrabudgetary funds more easily than poorer ones.

Regional Disparity

The fiscal contract system led to an increasing regional disparity. Provinces with enormous economic potential such as Guangdong accumulated a substantial and growing revenue base by retaining most of the incremental revenues within the province through a contract system that, in fact, favored better-off provinces with more bargaining power, and for some other provinces, moving revenues to extrabudgetary funds without sharing with the center. This shift in financial flows from the early 1980s, where central government received more from the provinces with surpluses than it paid out in transfers and grants (Ahmad 1997), handcuffs the central government in stabilizing the economy and bridging horizontal imbalances.

Administrative Decentralization

The transition from a vertical hierarchy to horizontal administration began with Mao's decentralization of state enterprise ownership among the central, provincial, and county governments and local communes during the 1970s (Sachs, Woo, and Yang 2000). During the 1980s, the central authorities gave subnational governments the power to nominate and assign most provincial officials. Before 1983, the Cadre that dominated the Chinese Communist party appointed and promoted officials two levels down, as evidenced by the fact that the the the Department of Organization (DOO) under the Central Committee of the CCP managed this process. Since 1983, the central government has been less involved in supervising provincial-level appointments, making the appointment system only "one level down." Directors of fiscal agencies and tax bureaus are now determined by provincial governments and their party committees (Huang 1996). This new decentralized organization includes managers of local branches of state banks (a point that will be elaborated later).

In combination with fiscal decentralization, provincial governments now have the wherewithal and authority to circumvent central plans and policies in favor of regional priorities. Although provincial fiscal agencies and tax bureaus were subject to the hierarchical (professional) instructions of the Ministry of Finance at the center, they are, in fact, under the leadership of their respective provincial governments. The new mechanism has problems of its own: "The shortcoming of the two-level downward system was excessive centralization and unwieldiness; the problem with the one-level system was that it encouraged nepotism and localism because it concentrated too many appointment decisions locally" (Manion 1985).

9.1.3 1994–Present: Dual Track System of Tax Assignments Together with the Contract System

The central government introduced the tax assignment system in 1994 to strengthen the central government's ability to achieve macroeconomic stabilization, regional equalization, and efficient public goods provisions. At the same time, the reform introduced more rigorous budget constraints on local governments.

The objectives of the reform package were fourfold: (1) to simplify and rationalize the tax structure by reducing tax types, tax rates, unifying the tax burden on taxpayers, and reducing exemptions; (2) raise the revenue-to-GDP ratio; (3) raise the central-to-total revenues ratio; and (4) put central-local revenue sharing on a more transparent, objective basis by shifting the negotiated sharing of general revenues to a tax assignment system.

Under the new system, taxes were reassigned between the central and local governments as follows:

• Taxes exclusive to the central government: Tariff duties, income taxes of state-owned enterprises (SOEs) under the jurisdiction of the central government, consumption taxes, import-related consumption taxes, and taxes imposed on banks, nonbank financial institutions and insurance companies, and taxes on railroads

• Taxes exclusive to provincial governments: Sales taxes (provided that sales taxes applicable to banks and railroads would be payable to the central government), income taxes from SOEs under the jurisdiction of provincial governments and collectively owned enterprises, and personal income taxes

• Shared taxes: The value-added tax (VAT) (at the fixed rate of 75 percent for the central government, and 25 percent for local governments), stamp duties on securities transactions, taxes on natural resources, and other taxes

In order to implement this tax assignment system and ensure the effective collection of the central government's portion of revenues, the central and provincial tax collection bureaus were to be separated. Once separation was fully implemented, the central and provincial governments were to collect their own exclusive taxes. The shared taxes were to be levied and collected by the central tax bureau and then shared between the central and provincial governments.

This new tax assignment system met with unprecedented resistance from provincial authorities, and significant concessions by the central government were obtained (for details, see Wang 1997). As a compromise, the revised scheme would ensure provincial interests of fait accompli with the new assignments applied only to the incremental receipts (with 1993 as the base year).

The revenue-sharing contracts negotiated under the old system were allowed to remain effective at the same time. The provinces were still supposed to remit a specified amount of locally collected revenues to, or receive a certain amount of subsidies from, the central government. In practice, after the provinces share taxes with the center under the new rule effective since 1994, they have had to "hand over remittances to or receive subsidies from the center according to the old revenue-sharing contracts. In the end, no one knew what constituted real central revenue or local revenue" (Wang 1997).

The de facto dual track system that combined tax assignment with the contract regime thus limited the ability of the central government to harden budget constraints on local governments. Moreover, a policy to ensure the provincial revenue level in 1993 triggered sudden inflated receipts in their 1993 reported budgetary revenues.[4] Provinces that tried to underreport their revenues in order to avoid sharing with the center in the previous fiscal contract system now faced the opposite problem. More 1993 budgetary revenues also meant more return transfers the provinces could receive from the center. In 1993, the actual total subnational revenues increased by 88.8 billion within a single year, from 250.3 billion yuan in 1992 to 339.1 billion yuan, which was 28.3 percent higher than the budgeted amount and 39.9 percent higher than the previous year.[5] The Ministry of Finance agreed to top up the reported 1993 revenues of provinces with one proviso: if the province's revenue growth rate of 1994 was not parallel to that of 1993, the 1993 base amount would be subjected to readjustment according to the lower growth rate of 1994, and the extra transfers for 1993 would be deducted from the transfers for 1994.

The implementation of the new tax system increased central revenues from 95.8 billion yuan in 1993 to 290.7 billion yuan in 1994 and correspondingly raised the central share in total revenues from 22 percent in 1993 to 55.7 percent in 1994, and decreased aggregated provincial revenues from 339.1 billion yuan in 1993 to 231.1 billion yuan in 1994 (table 9.1). According to the deal between the central and provincial authorities, the reduced amount was to be topped up by central return transfers. Therefore, in 1994, the central expenditure was 4,14.4 billion yuan (including transfers), although the budgetary spending at the discretion of central government was only 175.4 billion yuan. Transfers from the center to provinces soared from 54.5 billion yuan in 1993 to 238.9 billion yuan in 1994, among which roughly 180 billion was the return transfers from the center to top up to their 1993 revenue level.[6]

After all these adjustments, the redistribution of revenues did not improve. The central government's revenues continued to experience a decline (52.2 percent in 1995, 49.4 percent in 1996, and 48.9 percent in 1997)[7] because local government tax revenues from the agricultural tax, individual income tax, and business tax increased at a faster pace than central government tax revenues from the VAT, certain customs tariffs, and consumption taxes. In addition, the central government increased export VAT rebates and reduced customs tariffs in order to encourage exports and technology imports and attract foreign direct investment.

9.2   Forms of the Soft Budget Constraint

The fiscal year in China follows the calendar year. State budgets are prepared every September, and the National Budget Department of the MOF collects the spending plans and revenue estimates from ministries and agencies of the central and provincial governments. The aggregated budget prepared by the MOF (for central and aggregated subnational governments combined) is then submitted to the State Council. After the State Council approves the budget, the draft budget is sent to the National People's Congress (NPC), usually by March of the next year, for final approval, when the processing budget has already been executed for three months. Pursuant to the budget law effective January 1, 1995, the NPC reviews and approves the budget for the central government. The budget law also lays out rules and procedures for the review and approval by the corresponding people's congresses of the corresponding local governments' budgets. In practice, the review and approval of subnational budgets follow the approval of the budget by NPC at the superior level. Only after the aggregated national budget is approved can the NPC at the provincial level start to review the aggregated provincial budget. The auditing of the national budget by the National Auditing Office is carried out in June of the next year.

Prior to 1994, budget deficits were financed through a combination of credits from the People's Bank of China (PBC) and domestic and international borrowing as debt revenues. The new budget law (effective January 1, 1995) states in its first chapter that budgets at all levels of government shall be balanced. Chapter 10 of the same law stipulates that any violation of the balanced budget approved by the legal process would result in administrative prosecution against parties directly responsible. The government now finances its budget deficits only through domestic and international borrowings, and such borrowing is no longer counted as debt revenues in the state budget.

9.2.1   Legacies of 1994 Fiscal Reform and Central-Provincial Bargaining

One way for subnational governments to balance their budgets each year is by increasing transfers from the center through grant allocations and revenue bargaining. Fiscal redistribution by earmarked grants occurs through an ad hoc case-by-case process, which is often poorly targeted and provides grants too small to meet basic needs in poorer regions. Also, the arbitrary nature of central grant allocations has led to extensive negotiations and rent seeking by local authorities, tying up valuable administrative resources.

Under the contract system of the 1980s and early 1990s, transfers were obtained by local authorities through negotiating or renegotiating the contracted rates and periods under each sharing method. Remittance revenues were subject to adjustment and resulted in a default by subnational governments. For example, in 1991, in response to the regional flood in some eastern areas (Hua Dong region), the central government waived or reduced the required remittances from the affected provinces (Gao 1993). The budget constraint suffered a considerable discount during the bargaining process between the center and provinces.

The fragmented data released by the Chinese government after 1994 provide little information on the outcomes in the post–fiscal reform period. Hence, a quantitative assessment not possible at present. However, several facts have indicated the difficulties of hardening budget constraints on subnational governments.

Transfers

Tax assignment reform implemented in 1994 fixed transfers to ensure the fait accompli of provincial revenue in 1993. This left the central authorities with little revenue to narrow regional disparity. From 1995 to 1997, the annual transfers averaged only 3 billion yuan, which was unlikely to contribute to horizontal balance. Bargaining for central transfers increased among poorer provinces when the allocations of grants remained arbitrary in nature and the introduction of a formula-based transfer scheme lagged behind.

Revenue Assignments

The 1994 reform redefined the fiscal relations only between the center and provinces. It authorized provinces to define the intergovernmental fiscal relations between provinces and their localities. When provinces reshaped their fiscal relations with the localities, they followed the central government's suit by assigning themselves the most stable and biggest chunk of revenues. As a result, local fiscal difficulties were exacerbated, and deficits further devolved down along the hierarchy. This reform therefore lacks any way to ensure the fiscal capacity of local governments to deliver their public good provisions.

Expenditure Assignments

The 1994 reform focused on only the revenue side as manifested by the emphasis on raising the two ratios (total government revenue as a percentage in GDP and central government revenue as a percentage in total government revenue) without clarifying and adjusting expenditure responsibilities among levels of government. Although the central government specified that framework provincial budgets should follow, such guidance consists solely of some general principles "Budget Law," 1994). In addition, expenditure pressure has increased at the provincial level, partly due to the centralization efforts in revenue and partly due to the increasing spending mandated by the central authority.[8] Like the central government in the 1980s, provinces now attempt to devolve expenditure responsibilities to lower levels. Without local government elections to restrain subnational governments' excessive taxing power, some of the expenditures are ultimately devolved to the individuals in the forms of proliferated charges, fees, and fines.

Tax Administration

In the prereform era before 1994, tax policies could not be implemented as intended because tax collection was manipulated by the subnational governments to act strategically with the center in prioritizing their needs. As a consequence, the central government may not have full control over its tax bases and marginal tax rates because tax administration in China became ruled by negotiation rather than law (Vehorn and Ahmad 1997).

The structure of tax administration was overhauled during 1994, when the system was split into a central administration responsible for the collection of central and shared taxes and a parallel provincial (or local) tax administration for local taxes. In September 1993, when the State Council officially approved the reform plan, to be effective on January 1, 1994, only three months were left for the preparation. The tax bureaus could not be split before the new rules came into effect (Wang 1997).

Although the central government reserves sole authority over tax bases and rates, this administrative arrangement tends to encourage better collection effort for taxes retained at the subnational level but relatively less effort for taxes that are transferred upward. The central authorities believed that the continued decline of central revenue share in total revenue after 1994 was partially attributed to such implementation bias of subnational tax administration. As shown in table 9.3, the increase in provincial taxes was by far outpaced that of central taxes, in particular for personal income tax and other charges. Consequently, the share of central tax in total revenue declined, as did the aggregate central revenue share in total government revenue.

Although the 1994 tax system reform is a substantial move toward tax assignments, lagged reforms in other areas forbid the central government from hardening the budget constraints on provinces. For example, the ownership and the income tax of SOEs are still defined by the enterprises' jurisdictional subordination. As a result, SOEs continue to be the arenas where the budget constraints on lower

Table 9.3
Selected central and provincial tax shares in total government tax revenue, 1994–1997

Central revenue in each year	Revenue at central level (billion yuan)	Share in total revenue (%)	VAT (billion yuan)	Share in total revenue (%)	Central SOE income tax (billion yuan)	Share in total revenue (%)	Consumption tax (billion yuan)	Share in total revenue (%)
1994	290.7	55.7	172.8	33.1	38.9	7.5	48.7	9.3
1995	325.7	52.2	194.8	31.2	48.3	7.7	54.1	8.7
1996	366.1	49.4	222	30	51.2	6.9	62	8.4
1997	422.7	48.9	246	28.5	35.6	4.1	67.9	7.9
Average annual growth rate	**13.3**		**12.5**		**11.7**		**-3.3**	

Provincial revenue in each year	Revenue at local level (billion yuan)	Share in total revenue (%)	Business tax (billion yuan)	Share in total revenue (%)	Local SOE income tax (billion yuan)	Share in total revenue (%)	Personal income tax (billion yuan)	Share in total revenue (%)	Other charges (billion yuan)	Share in total revenue (%)
1994	231.2	44.3	64.7	12.4	19.3	3.7	7.3	1.4	27.1	5.2
1995	298.6	47.8	82.8	13.3	23.2	3.7	13.1	2.1	45.1	7.2
1996	374.7	50.6	100.6	13.6	25.7	3.5	19.3	2.6	63.3	8.6
1997	442.4	51.2	116.1	13.4	37	4.3	26	3	80.2	9.3
Average annual growth rate	**24.2**		**21.5**		**24.2**		**52.8**		**43.5**	

Source: Liu (1999).

levels of government are softened (center to provinces, provinces to localities).

9.2.2 Subsidies

Subnational governments in China pay huge subsidies to SOEs for their losses resulting from market or price distortions. With direct owner-ship of SOEs, subnational governments can subsidize their respective loss-making enterprises and list such financial transactions as negative revenues in their budgets. Less explicit forms of subsidies are debt for-giveness and reduced or refunded government taxes and charges.

Between 1985 and 1995, total subsidies declined from 50.7 billion yuan to 32.8 billion. Their share in total expenditure (including SOE subsidies) dropped from 20 percent in 1985 to 4.6 percent in 1995 (figure 9.1). Such a significantly diminished role of subsidies may be largely attributed to a comparatively rapid increase in total expenditure when subsidies remained around their 1985 level. In practice, a portion of the government assistance to SOEs covers the operational inefficiencies of these enterprises (Lall and Hofman 1995).

At the same time, SOEs are obligated to employ redundant workers and bear the cost of related services, such as housing, health care, child care, schooling, and pensions. Many SOEs share the spending respon-sibilities of local governments and have become conduits for central-local financial transfers. As Steinfeld (1999) explains, SOEs are continually exposed to intervention by local state agencies, empowered

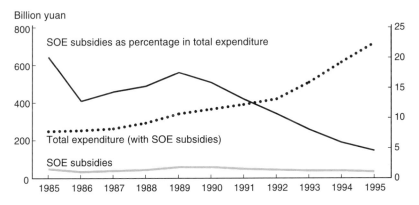

Figure 9.1
Subsidies to loss-making enterprises as percent of total expenditures. *Source*: Finance Yearbook of China (1997).

by the very policies of governmental decentralization that were intended to undermine command planning. Meanwhile, profit contracts—arrangements intended to rationalize the relationship between firm and state—fail to protect the firm from the state yet encourage the firm to overproduce and overexpand. Overproduction is then fostered by soft credit, capital made available through a banking system that was supposed to be the linchpin of market reform. On top of all that, new accounting standards, intended to permit managers the kind of autonomy that would encourage market behavior, make the misapplication of funds or outright decapitalization of the firm even easier.

9.2.3   Credit Plan and Borrowing from Commercial Banks

Prior to the economic reforms in China, the credit plan, together with the cash plan, the central government budget, and the foreign exchange plan, represented the financial side of the physical plan. Although plans are still drafted, their significance has steadily diminished since 1978. The reestablishment of the banking system in the early reform period (1978–1994) led to the independent operation of the People's Construction Bank of China (renamed China Construction Bank, CCB) and the Bank of China (BOC), which were subordinates under MOF and PBC, respectively, before the reform. At the same time, the Agricultural Bank of China (ABC) was established to take over the PBC's rural banking business. By 1994, there were three policy banks,[9] four state commercial banks,[10] four universal banks,[11] and a number of other local commercial banks and nonbank financial institutions.

The Credit Plan
The annual credit plan,[12] which was formulated by the PBC, in consultation with the MOF and State Planning Commission (renamed the State Development and Planning Commission, SDPC), took into account the need for investment in fixed capital and working capital, as well as PBC's direct financing of the government's deficit.[13] Ultimately, the credit plan was approved by the State Council and implemented by the PBC's provincial and local branches and, later, through a set of credit quotas for each specialized and universal bank. As banks have been transformed into financing institutions, local governments have gained a powerful influence over the administration of bank lending through the appointment of regional bank leaders. Apart from these formal controls, local governments retain intangible influences

that banks ignore at their own peril. For example, the supply of water and electricity, housing, recruitment of bank employees, and schooling of children all are potentially under the influence of local governments (Huang 1996). These relationships further undermine central control over subnational governments and possibly lead to corruption. "Contiguity brings personalism to relationships, and personalism is the enemy of arm's length relationships" (Tanzi 1995). Local governments thus gained substantial control over the credit supply, which has become a source of soft budget constraints of local governments and SOEs, as well as inflation (Qian and Rolland 1998).

The commercialization of banks has enhanced the profit motives of lending operations, merging the economic interests of banks with those of the local governments, both of which want to develop industries with high accounting profits (Huang 1996). Thus, the developmental urges of banks are now similar to those of the local industrial bureaus. This convergence of incentives means that it is harder for the central government to achieve its industrial policy goal through the credit plans. Moreover, although the formal power over credit creation rests with the headquarters of the PBC (and ultimately with the State Council), the operational autonomy granted to the local bank branches attenuates this central power. Bank branches are motivated to create credits on their own by converting deposits into loans (Bowles and White 1993).

The credit plan also allocates preferential interest rates to some regions and sectors. In addition to making direct contributions to the capital of the bank, the MOF provides indirect support to the bank through interest subsidies allocated each year in the annual budget of the government to the projects receiving loans from the bank. These subsidies are intended to further the government's economic development policies by enabling borrowers to obtain loans at interest rates below commercial rates (World Bank 1993).

Local officials' easy influence on the pattern of overlending combined with underpricing of loans contributed to the excessive expansion of banks' credit and a mounting number of bad and nonperforming loans. Even frequent interest rate changes could not curb the situation, partly because the soft budget constraints on SOEs make them unresponsive to the cost of borrowing. In fact, the impact of interest rate changes was felt much more on household savings than on bank lending (Mehran, Quintyn, Nordman, and Laurens 1996). According to a statement by the governor of the PBC, Dai Xianglong, the share of nonperforming loans in the portfolios of the four largest state-owned banks increased to 25 percent by the end of 1997. "Ultimately the borrowers of nonperforming loans may default, requiring the lender to absorb the loss, drawing on either reserves or its own capital" (Lardy 1998). In 1998, the MOF issued 270 billion yuan in government bonds to recapitalize these state-owned banks. Such capital rejection injections are an indirect measure of the center's bailout to local governments.

Following the commercialization of the banking system,[14] China's State Development Bank was established on March 17, 1994, replacing the PCBC as the policy-oriented bank fostering economic development through long-term financing for policy-oriented and related projects in accordance with the government's development plan and industrial policies. More specifically, its mission is to extend loans to policy-oriented medium- and large-scale construction, technological transformation, and related projects for key state infrastructure facilities, basic industries, and pillar industries.

According to China's 1994 budget law, local governments are forbidden to borrow on the capital market. However, local enterprises (which provide public services) can and do borrow from banks and on the capital market despite their dependence on government subsidies of various kinds, which often makes them de facto government agencies. Given the still limited direct and indirect transfers from the center to provinces, such borrowing from local commercial banks by enterprises (under the jurisdiction of local governments) actually finances much subnational spending. This in turn creates contingent liabilities for local governments and, given the lack of transparency, is less easily controlled than explicit government borrowing.

Although the central government reserved credit resources such as bank loans and capital market access for use only by state-approved projects and it strengthened the traditional investment plan and approval mechanism, local authorities still maintained considerable latitude in securing and deploying financial resources. For example, subnational government maintained the power to approve investment projects below 50 million yuan (projects above 50 million yuan require approval by SDPC) and technical transformation or technology promotion projects below 30 million yuan (projects above 30 million yuan require approval by the State Economic and Trade). These projects can be funded by commercial and indirect borrowing. These rules have resulted in redundant investment of medium- and small-sized invest-

ment projects directly under the jurisdiction of subnational governments. Moreover, in the fiscal system before 1994, the product tax
and business tax were both exclusively assigned to the subnational
government, leading to the expansion of capital construction, particularly those industries (e.g., tobacco and alcohol) that generate high
revenue from the product tax and business tax.

Chinese funding statistics are separated into five categories: budget,
domestic credit, foreign capital, own funds ("self-raised," retained, or
extrabudgetary funds), and, more recently, other sources, like stocks
and bonds (World Bank 1995). Investment in aggregate and individual
projects relies on a combination of funding sources, and the portfolio
of sources has been changing over time. The nature of budget finance
of enterprise investments has changed from direct capital grants to an
annual lump-sum allocation to the capital construction fund, managed
by SDPC. Budgetary financing for investment has declined in local
budgets, and consequently recourse to alternative finance sources has
become more common (World Bank 1993). As the share of budgetary
funds fell, investments increasingly were financed by nonbudgetary
sources (foreign capital, domestic credit, and other) in the second half
of the 1980s, with an increasing reliance on own funds in the early
1990s. The share of self-raised funds increased substantially from 32
percent in 1985 to 43 percent in 1995, and the share of foreign capital
increased from 7 percent in 1985 to 15 percent in 1995 (figures 9.2 and
9.3). By 1991, the amount of nonbudgetary financial resources used for
local projects equaled central projects and largely exceeded the investment on central projects by 1995 (figure 9.4). The domestic credit level
reached 22 percent in 1990 and increased modestly to 23 percent in
1995.

9.2.4   Indirect Borrowing and Foreign Borrowing

Indirect Borrowing
Provincial and local governments undertake indirect borrowing mainly
by creating dummy financial companies that are able to borrow and
provide resources for local government expenditures. Another method
of indirect borrowing has been through a buildup of arrears, as well as
IOUs on the procurement of agricultural products (Ahmad 1997).

Thus, soft budget constraints are reflected in the proliferation of
trust and investment companies (TICs) and securities houses under
the jurisdictions of provincial and local governments. According to

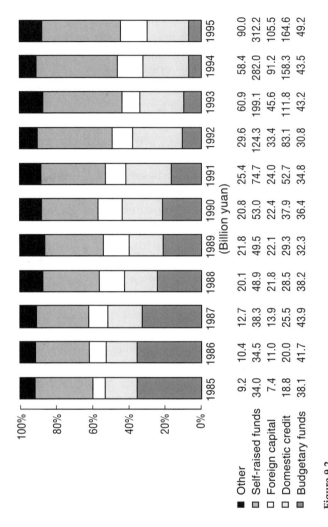

Figure 9.2
Source of funds. *Source:* China Statistical Yearbook (1996).

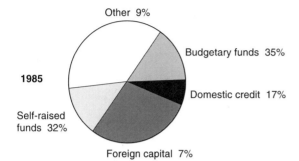

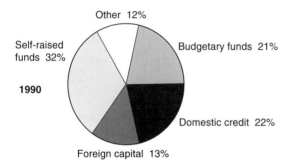

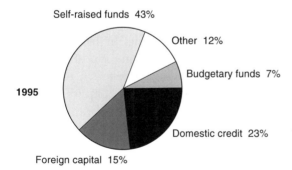

Figure 9.3
Sources of funds. *Source*: China Statistical Yearbook (1996).

Billion yuan

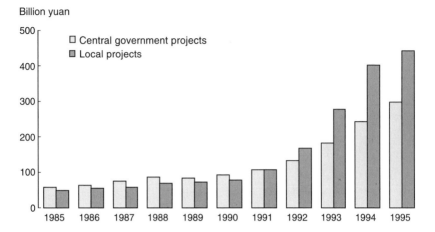

Figure 9.4
Investment of nonbudgetary resources. *Source*: China Statistical Yearbook (1996).

Mehran, Quintyn, Nordman, and Laurens (1996), TICs receive government and enterprise trust deposits or entrusted deposits. The larger companies also underwrite and broker securities. Most TICs were established by the four state-owned specialized banks, while other banks, the MOF, and some municipalities also own TICs. Banks initially established these TICs to circumvent the credit quotas, but most TICs have been increasingly engaged in the banking business, taking household deposits, and granting working capital loans. In the late 1980s, as many as 365 TICs were operating throughout China. A portion of these TICs are engaged in international business and referred to as international trust and investment companies (ITICs). Some of them are involved in external borrowing.

External Borrowing
SDPC authorizes and establishes quotas for external debt. The State Administration of Foreign Exchange (SAFE) monitors and regulates compliance with these quotas for external borrowing through a registration process. Under the budget law, local governments are not allowed to incur foreign indebtedness unless otherwise permitted by law. However, external borrowing by the central and local government-owned financial institutions has been managed by a "window" management system, under which the issuance of debt requires a quota from the SDPC and an approval from SAFE. This system of

quotas and approvals favors a limited number of predesignated window companies. The window management system is being replaced by a credit management system, whereby the quotas and approvals will be granted to central and local government-owned enterprises and financial institutions (including leasing companies) on the basis of their demonstrated capacity to repay the borrowings, their freestanding creditworthiness, and China's balance-of-payments situation. Unless otherwise stated by the central government in the relevant debt issuance documents or other official PRC documents, borrowings by these entities are not guaranteed by any direct or indirect credit support from the central government. Most of these local window financial institutions are TICs controlled by local governments. Before Guangdong International Trust and Investment Company (GITIC) went bankrupt in the first half of 1999, other local financial institutions enjoying the same treatment included Fujian ITIC, Tianjin ITIC, Shanghai ITIC, Dalian ITIC, Shangdong ITIC, and Shenzhen ITIC. By the end of 1998, the external debt of domestic financial institutions (including central agencies) was $41.99 billion, accounting for 28.8 percent of China's total external debt.[15] With the bankruptcy of GITIC, the first since the economic reform, the central government took a step forward in hardening budget constraint on subnational governments by refusing to bail out GITIC. Should financial difficulties emerge on a large scale among these ITICs, it is not clear whether the central government will join forces with provincial authorities to bail them out.

9.2.5 Tax Incentive Policies

Tax incentive policies are widely adopted by developing countries to attract foreign direct investment or serve their industrial policy (e.g., increase infrastructure investment and high- and new-technology investment). One of the most salient features of China's tax incentive policies is its strong discrimination against domestic investors in favor of foreign investors and its regional and industry preferences (World Bank 1999).[16] In addition to general fiscal incentives, the application of these tax incentives, especially the exemptions and reductions of corporate income tax, can be more generous within the special economic zones (SEZs), coastal open economic zones, economic and technology development zones (EDTZs), and high- and new-technology development zones.[17] These policies sparked keen competition among subnational governments for the right to establish such special economic zones, which adversely affected the central government. First, subnational governments' offer of ever-greater tax relief reduced government revenues. Second, the establishment of unauthorized SEZs weakened the ability of the central government to set and control macroeconomic policy.

Only four cities—Shenzhen, Xiamen, Zhuhai, and Shantou—were opened as SEZs in 1980. In 1984, fourteen more coastal cities were opened to foreign investment as ETDZs, allowing them to grant SEZ-like incentives. Through the 1990s, special zones extended to all coastal provinces, which were authorized to give tax incentives or attractive commercial terms to foreign investors. Special incentives for developing projects in the interior were also created, especially for provincial capital cities (Rosen 1999). Yang (1997) reported 111 development zones in 1991 (only 27 of which were centrally approved), 1,951 by September 1992, and as many as 8,700 by mid-1993.

9.2.6 Extrabudgetary Funds

Although public finance has been centrally controlled since 1949, certain revenues and expenditures of SOEs, local governments, agencies of the central government, and certain public institutions have historically been excluded from the state budget. These extrabudgetary revenues and expenditures are subject to varying degrees of control and regulation by the central government.

Since 1980, a devolution of expenditures from central to local governments, down to the township level, has led to a rapid increase in local expenditures, particularly administrative costs, health, education, and scientific research expenditures. The decentralization of expenditures over the reform period can be attributed to the following shifts: (1) a new emphasis on functions traditionally administered at local levels, such as social expenditures; (2) increases in administrative expenses and wages (largely due to the rapid increase in the number of civil servants at local level), which fell more heavily on local governments; and (3) sharp rises in locally administered but centrally set price subsidies. The local own-tax sources of revenues have not kept pace with rising expenditures, and local governments have become increasingly dependent on their extrabudgetary funds to perform their functions. In 1992, for example, the total extrabudgetary funds at both the central and subnational levels represented 46 percent of total expenditures, whereas extrabudgetary funds financed 41 percent of local expenditure and 54 percent of central expenditure (figure 9.5).

Extrabudgetary funds fall under three broad institutional categories: (1) extrabudgetary funds of local fiscal bureaus, including surcharges on taxes set by local governments (e.g., agricultural surcharges); (2) extrabudgetary funds of administrative agencies and institutions (nonprofit agencies, *shi ye dan wei*), including highway maintenance and other cost-recovery fees, market, and other fees, collected by government units; and (3) extrabudgetary funds of SOEs, including earmarked funds for the technical transformation and major maintenance funds (e.g., depreciation funds), retained profits, and short-term loans for circulation purposes (i.e., working capital). Foreign investment and international loans are sometimes included in this category. Before 1992, about 80 percent of these funds were owned by the enterprise sector (figure 9.6).[18]

Initially, the explicit objective of extrabudgetary transactions was to allow increased flexibility. They were also supposed to change the structure of incentives to help revitalize SOEs, speed up growth, and in general improve incentives for government units.

The increasing use of price subsidies and SOE subsidies during the second half of the 1980s pushed more pressing expenditures off the budget. This allowed a rapid growth of extrabudgetary funds, which became a particularly striking feature of the tax reform period of the 1980s (figure 9.7). A combination of reform initiatives (e.g., the profit-retention schemes, enterprise retention of depreciation funds, and the

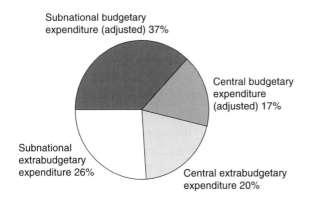

Figure 9.5
Composition of total expenditure, 1992. *Source*: Finance Yearbook of China (1997).

Billion yuan

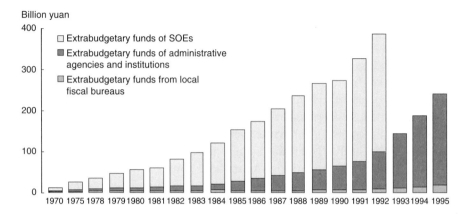

Figure 9.6
Composition of extrabudgetary revenue. *Source*: Finance Yearbook of China (1997).

Billion yuan

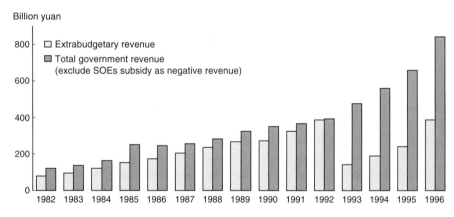

Figure 9.7
Extrabudgetary revenue as a percentage of total government revenue. *Source*: Finance
Yearbook of China (1997).

deduction of pretax amortization before tax payments, which transferred resources from the government to the enterprise sector) gave the
SOEs more autonomy but at the same time reduced fiscal control over
resources. Starting in 1993, extrabudgetary funds of SOEs were abolished, which then led to a substantial increase of extrabudgetary funds
in the other two categories (see figure 9.6). In 1996, for example,
the aggregated extrabudgetary revenue of central administrations
increased by nearly 200 percent and that of the provincial governments
increased by 41 percent.[19]

Extrabudgetary funds together with local government self-raised funds (all off the budget) are used in ways that supplement the budget: to finance fixed-asset investment, major maintenance, bonuses and welfare payments, administrative expenditures, expenditures in the social sectors, transfers and taxes paid to the central government, increases in working capital, and other earmarked programs (figure 9.8).[20]

From the second half of 1980s to the first half of the 1990s, the extrabudgetary funds became the central government's major concern. Since provinces are required to report extrabudgetary revenues only in very broad aggregated categories and there are no requirements for them to report their extrabudgetary expenditures to the MOF, the central authority lacked any effective instruments to monitor the funds. Although MOF resorted to restricting the number of banking accounts, that is, requiring all extrabudgetary funds be deposited into the specific fiscal accounts with each extrabudgetary fund having one bank account, this measure actually made the fiscal departments rely on the banking sector for the surveillance. Nonetheless, the banking sector was experiencing a substantial decentralization under which each bank was urged to depend on its own funding resources. As branches of different banks at localities started to solicit more clients, they were more than happy to offer shelter for extrabudgetary funds, among which a

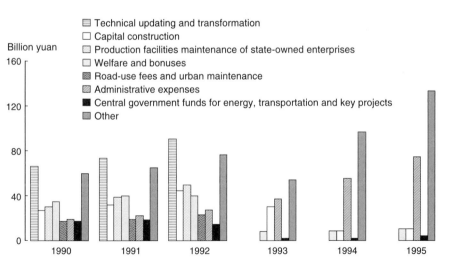

Figure 9.8
Extrabudgetary expenditures. *Source*: Finance Yearbook of China (1997).

portion came from local fiscal departments.[21] As a result, one agency could end up with several accounts for one kind of extrabudgetary fund.

The growth of extrabudgetary funds has undermined control over the scale of total government expenditures by enabling growth-oriented local governments to spend more freely outside the purview of central budgetary control. Local governments have tended to spend virtually all the revenues generated from ad hoc off-budget fiscal levies (Lall and Hofman 1995). In 1996, the twenty-ninth decree of the State Council brought thirteen extrabudgetary funds, totaling 150 billion yuan, under the supervision of the MOF (Ding 1997). According to the decree, all revenues generated from these funds are to be remitted to the treasury, and their expenditure is subjected to financial management by the MOF based on the proposed plans drafted by line administrations. The income from these extrabudgetary funds is to be earmarked for specific projects and not used for any other purposes or to balance the budgets. The decree further stated that similar measures would be introduced as the government sees fit.

Although the policy measures introduced in 1993 and 1996 shrank the extrabudgetary funds statistically, with high investment demand and limited financing, extrabudgetary funds have remained, proliferating at all levels of government. For local governments, which control most of these funds, they have become an important financing source. The proliferation of extrabudgetary funds has blurred the distinction among budgetary priorities and weakened the budgetary control mechanisms essential to a well-functioning fiscal system.

9.3   Conclusion

During the fiscal reform of the 1980s and 1990s, local governments in China responded to tightening budget constraints in ways that undermine desired fiscal discipline by (1) expanding the local tax base at the cost of the central government; (2) turning budgetary into extrabudgetary funds and tapping enterprises' extrabudgetary funds for government purposes; (3) pushing expenditures into extrabudget items, sometimes financed by indirect local borrowing, which placed additional demands on local banks and strains macroeconomic stability; (4) raising funds through internal and external borrowings; and (5) extending tax preferential policies by lavishly establishing SEZs. In addition, local governments have reduced effective tax rates on enterprise profits below the statutory rate by enterprise profit contracts. They have offered tax concessions to enterprises that affect the size of taxable income, to the detriment of tax buoyancy—for instance, by manipulating the rules for pretax repayment of investment loans. And because the resource-strapped local governments depend on local enterprises for their revenues, they are tempted into inefficient regional competition and local protectionism made possible by gaps in competition regulations.

The reform introduced in 1994 continues to meet significant resistance at the local level. The premise that taxes belong to the central government unless specifically assigned to the localities is not accepted at the local level. The goals of uniformity and transparency were compromised at the outset when the central government set the transfer rule based on the assurance of the status quo distribution in 1993.

In addition, the reform's effectiveness on hardening the budget constraints on provinces is undermined when (1) expenditure assignments are not clarified between levels of governments and provinces can always pass on expenditure responsibilities to the lower levels, (2) provinces are allowed to define the fiscal relations with localities and have the opportunity to squeeze most of the revenues (left by the center) for themselves, and (3) local officials are not restrained by any form of institutionalized local political participation so that they can pass their deficits on to local residents.

A shift to the tax assignment system by itself cannot harden budget constraints. The highly fragmented authoritarian arrangement still features the ownership of enterprises by local governments that have strong links to financial intermediaries. Thus, local governments enjoy both a soft budget constraint and autonomy in lending decisions, which enables them to resort to SOEs for both delivery of public services and debt financing. Soft budgets are thus incurred for both the SOEs and local governments. At the same time, SOEs treat tax liabilities lightly in an environment where the local finance bureaus play the double role of tax collector and owner and in a situation where taxes are frequently contracted rather than assessed. Budgetary financing of SOE investment is still virtually free; repayment ratios of the banks are extremely low or repayments are canceled out against tax obligation. This works to the detriment of banking sector stability.

The separation of policy and commercial lending is not enough by itself to foster commercialization of the banking sector. Specialized banks are still subject to lending quotas, are obliged to provide working capital loans to SOEs, can lend only for government-approved projects, and finance SDB through the compulsory purchase of its bonds. Banks cannot operate on a commercial basis until project-specific credit allocation has been eliminated. A hard budget constraint on local governments and SOEs cannot be established until local governments and the banking sector are separated and distributed ownership is phased out.

In the past twenty years, tax preferential policies played a significant role in attracting foreign direct investment to facilitate the economic reform agenda in China. However, the lavish adoption of such a policy by subnational governments without the approval of the center largely undermined fiscal discipline and negatively affected the industrial restructuring and regional development agenda set by the central government. The tax system reform should also address this issue by cleaning up the SEZs and tax preferential policies.

Notes

1. Unlike the previous system, reform in the 1980s allowed provincial authorities to retain all or a proportion of the tax collected after sharing with the center.

2. Bahl and Wallich (1992).

3. Examples are income taxes from railways, coal mining, and the petroleum and airline industries, as well as income taxes of banks, insurance companies, and other organizations.

4. Most of which clustered in the last three months of the year after the central government promulgated the tax reform plan in September 1993 (Wang 1997).

5. Ma Hong and Sun Shangqing quoted in Wang (1997).

6. *Finance Yearbook of China* (1997). All revenue and expenditure figures exclude debt.

7. *Finance Yearbook of China* (1998).

8. For example, the Agricultural Law, Education Law, and Science and Technology Law all put forward that subnational governments' spending in these areas shall increase at a higher rate than that of the government's current revenue.

9. State Development Bank of China (renamed the China Development Bank, CDB), Agricultural Development Bank of China, and Export and Import Bank of China.

10. Industrial and Commercial Bank of China, Agricultural Bank of China, Bank of China, and People's Construction Bank of China.

11. Bank of Communications, China International Trust and Investment Corportation (CITIC)'s Industrial Bank, China Everbright Bank, and Hua Xia Bank.

12. See World Bank (1993).

13. World Bank (1990).

14. The five specialized banks: Bank of China, Construction Bank of China, Industrial and Commercial Bank of China, Agriculture Bank of China, and the Bank of Communications.

15. Ministry of Finance.

16. For detailed information about tax exemptions and reductions, see World Bank (1999, 21–25).

17. Besides the widely applied income tax holidays, the reduction in corporate income tax rate is also substantial; whereas the corporate income tax rate is 33 percent, many activities and regions enjoy reduced tax rates of between 15 and 24 percent. In addition, many investment projects in those regions and activities are exempted from the 17 percent import tariffs on imports of equipment and raw materials. Export-oriented enterprises in the special economic zones and the economic technological development zones where the enterprise income tax has already been reduced to 15 percent would be taxed at 10 percent (World Bank 1999).

18. Since 1993, the extrabudgetary funds of SOEs are categorized not as extrabudgetary funds but as enterprises' own fund.

19. *Finance Yearbook of China* (1997).

20. Data on extrabudgetary revenues have been collected since 1952, but data on extrabudgetary expenditures were not recorded until 1982.

21. Some of the local fiscal agencies moved their budgetary fund to extrabudgetary accounts.

References

Agarwala, Pamgopal. 1992. *China: Reforming Intergovernmental Fiscal Relations.* discussion paper 178, Washington, D.C.

Ahmad, Ehtisham. 1997. "China." In Teresa Ter-Minassian, ed., *Fiscal Federalism in Theory and Practice*. Washington, D.C.: International Monetary Fund.

Bahl, Roy, and Christine Wallich. 1992. "Intergovernmental Fiscal Relations in China." Research working paper 863, Development Research Group, World Bank.

Bo, Zhiyue. 1996. "Economic Performance and Political Mobility: Chinese Provincial Leaders." *Journal of Contemporary China* 5(12):135–154.

Bowles, Paul, and Cordon White. 1993. *The Political Economy of China's Financial Reforms*. Boulder, Colo.: Westview Press.

"Budget Law of the People's Republic of China." 1994. Beijing.

China Development Bank. 1999. *Prospectus Supplement*. New York.

China Statistical Yearbook. Various issues.

Ding, Xianjue. 1997. "Renzhen guanche luoshi guowuYuan 'Jueding' jingshen, qieshi jiaqiang yusuanwai zijin guanli" [Implementing the decision by the State Council, strengthening the financial management of extrabudgetary fund]." Paper presented at Fiscal Reform and Development Seminar, Beijing.

Finance Yearbook of China. Various issues.

Gao, Qiang. 1993. "Problems Remained in China's Intergovernmental Fiscal Relations, Tax Assignment System and Prospects for Future Reform." In Ministry of Finance and International Monetary Fund, eds., *China: Intergovernmental Fiscal Relations*. Beijing: China Economics Press.

Huang, Yasheng. 1996. "Central-Local Relations in China during the Reform Era: The Economic and institutional Dimensions." *World Development* 24(4):655–672.

Lall, Rajiv, and Bert Hofman. 1995. "Decentralization and the Government Deficit in China." In Jayanta Roy, ed., *Macroeconomic Management and Fiscal Decentralization*. Washington, D.C.: World Bank Institute of the World Bank.

Lardy, Nicholas. 1998. "China and the Asian Contagion." *Foreign Affairs* 77(4):78–88.

Liu, Zongli. 1995. "Guanyu dangqian he jinhou yige shiqi de caizheng gongzou" [Fiscal works at the present and in the near future]. *Caizheng* [Public Finance], no. 8:2–7.

Liu, Zhongli. 1999. *Exploring Problems of Public Finance in China* [Zhongguo caizheng wenti yanjiu]. China Finance and Economics Press.

Manion, Melanie. 1985. "The Cadre Management System, Post Mao: The Appointment, Promotion, Transfer and Removal of Party and State Leaders." *China Quarterly* 102 (June):203–233.

Mehran, Hassanali, Marc Quintyn, Tom Nordman, and Bernard Laurens. 1996. *Monetary and Exchange System Reforms in China: An Experiment in Gradualism*. Washington, D.C.: International Monetary Fund.

Qian, Yingyi, and Gerard Roland. 1998. "Federalism and the Soft Budget Constraint." *American Economic Review* 88(5):1143–1162.

Rosen, Daniel H. 1999. *Behind the Open Door: Foreign Enterprises in the Chinese Market Place*. IIE.

Sachs, Jeffery, Wing Thye Woo, and Xiaokai Yang. 2000. "Economic Reforms and Constitutional Transition." *Annals of Economics and Finance* 1:435–491.

Steinfeld, Edward. 1999. *Forging Reform in China: The Fate of State-Owned Industry*. Cambridge: Cambridge University Press.

Tanzi, Vito. 1995. "Fiscal Federalism and Decentralization: A Review of Some Efficiency and Macroeconomic Aspects." In Michael Bruno and Boris Pleskovic, eds., *Annual Bank Conference on Development Economics*. Washington, D.C.: World Bank.

Vehorn, Charles, and Ehtisham Ahmad. 1997. "Tax Administration," In Teresa Ter-Minassian, ed., *Fiscal Federalism in Theory and Practice*. Washington D.C.: International Monetary Fund.

Wang, Shaoguang. 1997. "China's Fiscal Reform in 1994: An Initial Assessment." *Asian Survey* (U.S.) 37:801–817.

Wang, Yongjun, and Zhihua Zhang. 1998. *Zhengfu Jian Caizheng Guanxi Jingjixue*. (Intergovernmental Fiscal Relations). Beijing: China Economic Press.

World Bank. 1990. *Financial Sector Policies and Institutional Development*. Washington, D.C.: World Bank.

World Bank. 1993. "China: Budgetary Policy and Intergovernmental Fiscal Relations." Report 11094-CHA. Washington, D.C.: World Bank.

World Bank. 1995. "China: Public Investment and Finance." Report 14540-CHA. Washington, D.C.: World Bank.

World Bank. 1999. *China: Preferential Tax Policy*. Washington, D.C.: World Bank.

Wong, Christine P. W. 1991. "Central-Local Relations in an Era of Fiscal Decline: The Paradox of Fiscal Decentralization in Post-Mao China." *China Quarterly* 128:691–715.

Yang, Dali, L. 1997. *Beyond Beijing. Liberalization and the Regions in China*. Routledge: London.

10

Creating Incentives for Fiscal Discipline in the New South Africa

Junaid Ahmad

In a recent compilation of lessons learned about decentralization, Roy Bahl (1999) highlighted three channels through which central interventions often undermine the discipline of a hard budget constraint for local governments. These are deficit grants to cover year-end deficits on local government budgets, direct central government coverage of shortfalls on specific items of expenditure, and bailouts on delinquent debt. All three channels involve direct or indirect fiscal assistance at the end of the year from central authorities. Repeated over time, such assistance can potentially create a regime of soft budgets, effectively undermining the fiscal resolve of subnational governments and the efficiency gains expected from moving government closer to communities.

In the case of South Africa, all three of the channels—deficit grants, coverage of specific expenditure shortfalls, and bailouts—have been used by the central government to provide assistance to subnational governments in both the apartheid and the present democratic eras. That South Africa, at first glance, conforms to the international experience of how hard budget constraint for subnational governments has been violated adds little new information to the vast policy literature on decentralization that has emerged over the past decade (Litvack, Ahmad, and Bird 1998). Instead, the case of South Africa provides insights into why and under what conditions the constraint of hard budgets may not be binding on any tier of government in a decentralized system. In addition, South Africa's case suggests important lessons for managing the implementation of a new intergovernmental system and how to address the issue of potential budgetary game playing between different tiers of governments during a period of policy transition.

Sections 10.1 and 10.2 summarize the evolution of the intergovernmental system in South Africa from apartheid to the democratic era.

Each section illuminates the key factors in the design of the intergovernmental system in South Africa that has created scope for a soft budget constraint at the local level. Section 10.3 provides a summary of the lessons that emerge from South Africa's experiences.

10.1 South Africa's Intergovernmental System: The Apartheid Era

The political design of apartheid—separation on the basis of race—was entrenched in South Africa's intergovernmental system. What emerged was a dual structure of subnational governments. The violation of the hard budget constraint for subnational governments was a direct result of the political underpinnings of this dual system.

10.1.1 The Intergovernmental System

For the white population,[1] the apartheid leadership developed an intergovernmental system composed of a central government at the apex, four provincial administrations under it, and within each province a tier of independent local governments. The system was highly centralized. Major sources of revenue, representing about 85 percent of the total tax collection, were assigned to the central government. These included the personal income tax, the sales tax (and later VAT), and the corporate income tax. The provinces acted as delegated administrations of the center and were dependent on central transfers for their functioning. Less than 5 percent of the expenditures implemented by the provinces were financed from own resources.

The local governments, known as white local authorities (WLA), were independent political entities. Each WLA had elected council members. In addition, WLAs were assigned revenue sources that are typical of municipal governments, including residential and commercial property taxes and user charges, and were responsible for a limited set of municipal services, such as water and electricity distribution, waste removal, and traffic control. Furthermore, each WLA was responsible for land planning and zoning regulations. Finally, WLAs could raise capital funds directly from the capital markets and even received central guarantees for their borrowings. Overall, this system of central government, provincial authorities, and local governments for white communities covered 80 percent of the land for about 20 percent of the population.

In parallel, a separate intergovernmental system was established for the black population. The black community representing 75 percent of the population was forcibly herded into ten regions covering 20 percent of the land that was basically economically barren.[2] The regions were given different levels of political and economic autonomy but as artificial regions enjoyed neither. Their survival depended on annual fiscal transfers from the central government of (white) South Africa that, at the height of the apartheid system, represented about 7 percent of GDP. As none of these homelands was creditworthy, their access to capital markets required central guarantees. The South African central government established a public financial parastatal, the Development Bank of Southern Africa, to borrow from domestic capital markets and on-lend to the homelands. The financial parastatal had the guarantee of central government.

The two parallel systems were in effect completely linked. The public finances of the "white" intergovernmental system were being used to keep the homelands operative. But this "cross-subsidy"[3] of the home-lands through direct fiscal transfers and guarantees to secure loans failed to achieve the ultimate goal of apartheid: to keep the races physically separate. The economic needs of the white communities, in particular the white local authorities, required that blacks be permitted to migrate to the urban centers temporarily to provide labor for white businesses and households in the WLAs. In practice, the migration to the urban centers of white South Africa was permanent and forced the apartheid leadership to sanction the establishment of townships as black local authorities (BLAs). These townships were developed at some distance at the peri-urban areas of the WLAs. Like their regional counterparts, the homelands, the BLAs had neither political nor economic autonomy. Black households were not allowed to own property, and by law formal and informal economic activities were banned from operating in BLAs. By definition, therefore, BLAs had no chance to develop a fiscal base. In addition, as a product of the apartheid system, the leadership of the BLAs had neither legitimacy nor accountability with communities.

To keep these BLAs operating, a system of cross-subsidies similar to the ones given to the homelands had to be developed. Fiscal transfers were provided from the central authorities through the provincial administrations along with financial guarantees. In addition, WLAs provided fiscal transfers to adjacent BLAs, financed through payroll and turnover taxes. While central transfers were designed to provide operating funds, the horizontal flow funds from WLAs to BLAs were earmarked for capital expenditures. In practice, both flows eventually financed operating expenditures of BLAs.

10.1.2 Implications for Implementing a Hard Budget Constraint

The apartheid architecture of dual intergovernmental systems opened the door to deficit grants, or year-end grants, to cover revenue shortfalls for both the homelands and the BLAs. A straightforward interpretation would suggest that the design of the cross-subsidy scheme is the primary reason for this fiscal outcome. Ad hoc and determined on an annual basis at the end of the fiscal year, the fiscal transfers were inherently prone to becoming open-ended funding mechanisms. In addition, by central design, the homelands and BLAs had no source of their own revenues and as a result were completely dependent on central funds, with no recourse to raising any local resources to meet year-end shortfalls. The central government could not expect fiscal effort by subnational governments to contribute to the financing of local expenditures. Equally important, without access to their own tax instruments, BLA leadership had little incentive to reduce spending.

But the real explanation for the deficit grants, as Abedian and Ajam (1999) point out, had little to do with the technical design of the fiscal system. Rather, the system was based on a political economy exposure that made soft budget constraints a forgone conclusion. The apartheid leadership was determined to sustain the apartheid architecture. As a result, explicit fiscal transfers and implicit financial transfers were used to sustain the dual intergovernmental system. For those charged with running the BLAs and homelands, this was an open invitation to be profligate in their expenditures with the expectations that end-of-the-year deficits would be financed. The ad hoc nature of the intergovernmental transfer system was therefore a symptom of the problem, not its cause. The political exposure of the center inherent in the apartheid design left it predictably at the mercy of the local authorities.

Not surprisingly, over the 1980s into the 1990s, central budget deficits increased gradually, reaching a height of 8 percent of GDP in 1992. If the implicit liabilities of the center were added, the deficit may well have crossed into double-digit figures.[4]

While the apartheid structure represents an example of a system that creates an extreme and aberrant set of political exposures leading to soft budget constraints, the lesson is telling. Central governments that create political expectations for which they can be held liable open their fiscal systems to abuse. No amount of technical design would have prevented the incentives of open-ended financing created by apartheid's political and economic objectives. In a more rational political system, the vulnerabilty to political exposures can be minimized with better design and management of intergovernmental systems. This is the lesson emerging from the new South Africa.

10.2 South Africa's Intergovernmental System: The New Era

The postapartheid central government has moved in progressive stages to fundamentally alter and rationalize the intergovernmental structure. Three sets of reforms have characterized this process: administrative amalgamation, fiscal and financial restructuring, and reform of the municipal delivery systems. This ambitious policy agenda has resulted in a new intergovernmental system that has become an example of best practices for many developing and transition economies in terms of both the process of implementation and the outcome. Despite its success, the reform process has also created incentives favoring soft budget constraint for subnational governments. At the provincial government level, this has been a result of both political exposure and the design of the fiscal system that links provinces and central authorities. At the local government level, the budget softness is a result more of the access to financial markets through public financial parastatals.[5] Yet, interestingly, the decentralization of economic and political responsibilities was undertaken during a period in which central government budget deficits fell from 8 percent of GDP in 1994 to less than 3 percent in 1999. South Africa's case thus provides an interesting story of how decentralization is consistent with fiscal discipline at the macrolevel in contrast to the apartheid system of central control that led to fiscal indiscipline.

10.2.1 Amalgamation

The democratic process required abolishing of racial jurisdictions, an objective achieved through redrawing of boundaries and administrative mergers. At the regional level, homelands and provincial administrations were merged to form new provinces. Similarly, at the local level, the BLAs and WLAs were unified to form nonracial local governments. These boundary demarcations and administrative mergers have resulted in a three-tiered governmental structure: central government, provincial government, and local governments.[6] The local government tier is a two-tiered system, with each province subdivided into district councils and each district council overseeing several municipalities. There are nine provinces, fifty-one districts, and over two hundred municipalities.[7] The rights of these new tiers—provinces, districts, and municipalities—have been established in the new constitution as independent tiers of government.

10.2.2 Fiscal and Financial Restructuring

Complementing the amalgamation process, South Africa's new leadership also adopted a phased approach to the fiscal and financial restructuring of the intergovernmental system. This involved a fundamental reform of the expenditure and tax assignment between different tiers of government, the fiscal transfer system, and the rules about access to capital markets.

The expenditure assignments followed to a large extent the principles of benefit spillovers and redistribution. As a result, education, health, and welfare—expenditure benefits of which are regional, if not national, in scope and the financing of which would have large redistributive implications—were assigned jointly to central and provincial governments. Services like water and electricity distribution, whose benefits are local in nature, were left as the responsibilities of local governments.

In terms of tax assignment, fiscal efficiency objectives were achieved by placing the responsibilities for the administration of corporate and personal income tax and the VAT at the central government level. Similarly, the administration and management of property taxes were assigned to local authorities. Local authorities were also assigned payroll and turnover taxes for the financing of capital expenditure in the municipal infrastructure sector.[8] The newly created provinces, like their old counterparts, however, were not given any own-source tax powers.[9]

In conjunction with the reform of the expenditure and tax assignment, government focused on rationalizing the flow of fiscal transfers between different tiers of governments. The objectives were to manage the vertical imbalance created by expenditure and revenue assignments to replace the ad hoc, inefficient, and inequitable system of transfers that characterized the apartheid system and make the system more accountable. As a result, government has introduced a new set of fiscal transfers based on clear economic principles and administered in a more transparent and accountable way (see box 10.1).

Government is now in the process of reforming the rules about access to capital markets by subnational governments. The overall policy approach is to decentralize borrowing powers to local governments. To achieve this objective, government has announced an end to the provision of central guarantees for local government borrowing from capital markets. In addition, it is legislating an act to regulate the borrowing powers of local governments. The act will specify the disclosure of information related to local government liabilities and assets and the types of revenue sources that can be pledged as collateral. In addition, it will specify the rules about municipal bankruptcy. This will include a bankruptcy process to be mediated by the judiciary rather than through a political or administrative system. The act will also specify the minimum level of delivery of essential services that will be required to be kept functioning with municipal taxes in the case of bankruptcy.[10] Finally, the act will regulate off-budget borrowing by making it illegal for municipalities to finance expenditure through municipal corporations or manipulating the financing of statutory obligations such as pension funds.[11] All of these measures, from full disclosure of assets and liabilities to bankruptcy procedures incorporated into legislation, enable central authorities to decentralize borrowing powers while significantly reducing the potential of moral hazard of ultimately inheriting local liabilities. The legislation also entrenches by law the costs that will be imposed on local authorities, in particular the elected politicians for fiscal mismanagement.

While provincial governments have the constitutional right to access capital markets, the central government has reached a policy understanding with provincial authorities that provinces will not borrow from private sources. Given that provinces do not have access to their own taxes, this policy measure is indeed necessary. Otherwise, the authority to borrow from capital markets will be taken as a signal that financial transactions of provinces are backed by central authorities.

10.2.3 Institutional Reforms

Complementing the amalgamation process and the fiscal and financial restructuring, the reform of the intergovernmental system also

Box 10.1
South Africa's fiscal transfers to local and provincial governments

---

Local Government

• A *municipal basic services grant* to enable poor residents in all local government jurisdictions to receive access to basic municipal services. The basic approach involves estimating the number of people in poverty (household income less than R800 per month in 1998 prices) and the current cost of providing basic services for each person.

• A *municipal institutions transfer* for those jurisdictions currently lacking the basic administrative capacity to raise their own revenue or lacking the basic infrastructure necessary to function as local authorities. This transfer pays for a minimum level of resources to provide and maintain basic facilities for the operation of local government (such as community centers and an office for elected officials).

A detailed description of the formula can be found in the 1997 framework document, *An Equitable Share of Nationally Raised Revenues for Local Government*. As the new system targets the poor, a number of municipalities will receive lower subsidies in the future than they previously enjoyed. A once-off transitional grant was introduced in 1998–1999 to facilitate this adjustment.

Provincial Government

The actual formula used by the Budget Council to determine each province's equitable share is based on the provinces' demographic and economic profiles. It consists of the following categories:

• Education share, based on the average size of the school-age population and the number of learners enrolled (40 percent)

• Health share, based on the proportion of the population without private health insurance and weighted in favor of women, children, and the elderly (18 percent)

• Social security component, based on the estimate of people entitled to social security grants (elderly, disabled, children) (17 percent)

• Basic share, based on each province's share of the total population of the country (9 percent)

• Backlog component, based on the distribution of capital needs as captured in the schools' register of needs, the audit of hospital facilities, and the share of rural population in each province (3 percent)

• Economic output share, based on the estimated distribution of gross geographical product (GGP) (8 percent)

• Institutional grant, divided equally among the provinces (5 percent)

Sources: Abedian and Ajam (1999).

involved implementing legislation to facilitate certain institutional reforms at the subnational level. These include the regulatory framework for privatizing and corporatizing public services, developing community delivery systems, and establishing metropolitan governments in the context of the larger cities (see box 10.2 for an example of metropolitan restructuring).

The corporatization and privatization of municipal services and the development of community delivery systems suggest that decentralizing policies is not only about regulating the political, economic, and administrative relationship between different tiers of government. It also includes the decentralization of responsibilities into the private sector and communities. The involvement of the private sector—market decentralization—and communities in the delivery and financing of services provides an additional mechanism for unbundling government, creating competition, and fostering incentives for better governance.

But in setting up the involvement of the private sector in service delivery raises the issue of regulating quasi-monopolies, especially in the infrastructure sector. While active bidding for concessions in, for example, the water and electricity distribution sectors enables the competition *for* the market, once allocated the rights, the concessionnaire does not face competition *in* the market. As a result, a regulator may be needed. South Africa faces a choice in the design of the regulatory system. It can create a centralized system of regulations with a central regulator or allow decentralized regulation to emerge. The latter may include the mandatory publication of information on performance and thus allow communities to compare between-service deliverers and create bottom-up pressure on local governments. Decentralized regulatory systems would also include the ability of the local governments to set up their regulatory system. This may be the model adopted in the water sector, while in the electricity sector, a centralized regulator is the model that has been adopted.[12]

10.2.4   Implications for a Hard Budget Constraint in the Provinces

To understand the sources of softness in the budget constraints of subnational governments in South Africa's new intergovernmental system, one needs to assess the case of the provincial middle tier separately from the situation of the local government tier. The provinces are considered first. Four factors have created the opportunity for budget games

Box 10.2
Metropolitan governance: The case of Johannesburg

With municipalities fragmented along racial and economic lines into WLAs and BLAs, the challenge for the leadership in Johannesburg was to create a unified, nonracial system of metropolitan governance. The racial boundaries of the municipalities were first reconfigured with the merger of adjacent black and white local authorities. Four new municipalities were thus created. The challenge was now to ensure that the four municipalities would address problems of externalities, economies of scale, and redistribution in the delivery of services in a coordinated manner. The political debate focused on two models of metropolitan coordination: the Toronto "megacity" model and the Minneapolis–St. Paul "risk-pooling" model. In the first approach, the municipalities would be converted into administrative wards linked through a metropolitan government that would have the fiscal and delivery responsibilities. In the second model, a leaner metropolitan government would link the four municipalities. This metro tier would inherit and pool the business taxes of the municipalities and redistribute the revenues through a formal grant system based on fiscal and poverty indicators. The pooling of the business taxes at the metropolitan level would ensure that municipalities could not enter into a beggar-thy-neighbor type of competition. The revenue sharing would also achieve a level playing field and form the basis of an "insurance pool" whereby all municipalities would receive the fiscal benefit of economic development regardless of the location of the economic activity in the metropolitan area. Johannesburg's one-city plan has adopted a third approach. It has followed the centralized, coordination of the megacity model by centralizing political authority, treasury management, and spatial planning under one central node. But the city is implementing delivery of services through economic and administrative decentralization. For goods for which some form of user charge can be levied—such as water and sanitation, waste services, and electricity production and distribution—the city has transformed its line-function delivery system into corporate bodies with different forms of private sector involvement. For goods with more public goods characteristics, such as slum upgrading, primary health, and libraries, the city is delivering the services through decentralized administrative wards run by councilors and CEOs with a multiyear budget allocated by council. While unbundling the metropolitan government into corporations and community delivery allows greater accountability, it also raises the issue of how to manage the potential problem of moral hazard—between the metro government and the corporate and community bodies and between the metro and upper-tier government—implicit in this unbundling.

Sources: Ahmad (1996); Ahmad and Inman (1998).

between the provinces and central government: constitutional mandates, ambiguity in expenditure responsibility between different tiers, lack of own taxes, and centralized labor mandates. The new constitution of South Africa places the responsibility of financing and delivering health, education, and welfare jointly in the hands of central and provincial governments. But both the constitution and policy legislation focused on the intergovernmental system are ambiguous about defining what is meant by "joint responsibilities," in particular, what aspect of this jointness is central versus provincial expenditure responsibility.

In addition, although permitted by the constitution, provinces do not have any sources of their own taxes. The responsibility for financing expenditures on health, education, and welfare lies solely in the hands of the center. In this case, central government has opted to provide grants directly to provinces. These are not provided as conditional grants linked to the delivery of the social expenditures. Instead, the grants are provided as unconditional flows, implicitly allowing the provinces the flexibility to shift funding between expenditure line items.

The lack of their own taxes in conjunction with the ambiguity in the definition and separation of the responsibilities between the center and the provinces opens the opportunity for budgetary game playing between the two tiers of government. There is scope for the provinces to pass the buck back to the center on the grounds of constitutional mandates and lack of funding opportunities. In turn, the center has a limited ability to hold provinces accountable for delivery. Without having provided any sources of revenues, the center is unable to tax the provinces to finance any shortfall and hence force the political responsibility for delivery back onto the provinces. As a result, the provinces will have limited incentive to spend efficiently, knowing fully well that they cannot be taxed or punished for nondelivery.

This scope for budgetary game playing is aggravated by South Africa's system of centralized wage bargaining, which in effect locks in the expenditure commitments of the "unconditional" grants provided by the center. In fact, 60 to 80 percent of the funds in health, education, and welfare is already spoken for in terms of personnel costs even before reaching the provinces. Without having been part of central bargaining, provinces naturally do not have the political incentive to challenge the unions (see box 10.3).

Not surprisingly, provinces began to show significant deficits within a year of being established. By 1997–1998, the total provincial budget

Box 10.3
Central collective bargaining structures

South Africa's system of intergovernmental fiscal relations was super-imposed on existing centralized public sector bargaining structures. This creates enormous tensions. While provinces ostensibly have significant control over how they allocate their budgets across sectors, the reality is that personnel costs, the largest component of provincial budgets, lie virtually outside their control. While in principle provinces have the right to hire and fire, in practice both in terms of the politics and the collective bargaining system, this is difficult for provinces to implement. The system of centralized determination of conditions of service within the public sector therefore has imposed severe rigidities on provincial budgets.

There are problems surrounding these areas:

• *Size of government*: Supernumeraries, or excess workers (concentrated in a few provinces), are estimated at 60,000. The situation is compounded by the lack of an affordable retrenchment tool. There has been a moratorium on retrenchments since 1996. Instead, government has relied on the voluntary service package, which has not been an effective retrenchment tool. There are current efforts to renegotiate this.

• *Wage bargaining*: Government negotiators are mandated by a national cabinet subcommittee. Provincial governments make extremely limited input into mandating procedures. Bargaining outcomes therefore do not necessarily reflect provincial needs and constraints. Annual increases in conditions of service appear in a separate vote on the national budget. Nevertheless, agreements may be made that impose unanticipated costs on provinces. In some cases, due to the centralized mandating procedures, provinces may not even be aware of obligations arising from collective bargaining agreements. The *Budget Review* indicates that the vote would be devolved to provinces in 2000–2001.

• *Work organization*: The Personnel Administration Standards (PAS), is used in the determination of public service remuneration and conditions of employment, effectively prescribe work organization centrally and provide rigid job descriptions and are regarded as overly prescriptive concerning promotions and employment. The minister of public service administration will soon issue a code of remuneration (CORE), which will replace the PAS. The CORE will contain sections dealing with prescripts (salary range, salary code, job weight) and guidelines (nature of job, key competencies). The prescripts will be negotiated centrally. The guidelines will be decentralized, giving departments and provinces more latitude on making appointments and promotions.

Source: Abedian and Ajam (1999).

deficit amounted to approximately 1 percent of GDP. The deficits have been financed by the use of reserves and overdraft facilities from commercial banks. The willingness of the private banks to provide overdraft facilities to provinces in the absence of their own taxes suggests that even the private sector perceived the deficits to be ultimately backed by central government. This was ultimately confirmed by central government's willingness to provide additional funds in the amount of R2.1 billion in 1997–1998 to relieve provincial budgetary pressures.[13] Interestingly, R1.5 billion of this amount was directed to provinces that had invoked section 100 of the constitution, in effect announcing a failure to perform provincial functions and entering into a financing arrangement with the center.[14]

10.2.5 Controlling the Provincial Budgets

Faced with the potential of growing deficits, central government implemented a series of hierarchical controls to manage the budgets of provincial governments. The policy measures varied. These included first a commitment to multiyear budgeting at the central level—the medium-Term expenditure framework (MTEF)—that determined the levels of resources available for intergovernmental transfers over a three- to five-year period. In addition, central government implemented direct monitoring of provincial budgets, which included indirect management of expenditure patterns at the provincial level through budgetary institutions that bring together the central ministries and their counterparts at the provincial level. Ultimately, the effect of these controls and measures was to establish a set of rules that ensure an ex post balanced budget through top-down processes.[15]

The case of South Africa clearly shows that where subnational governments do not have access to their own taxes and expenditure patterns are in effect precommitted through mechanisms like wage bargaining councils, hierarchical controls will be needed to impose budgetary discipline. Such controls are needed even more if the design of the fiscal systems offers little incentive for capital markets to play their role of allocating credit in a manner that signals the creditworthiness of the subnational governments. The limited access to revenue instruments by provinces was a signal to capital markets that provincial debt would be backed by the center.

But the case of South Africa also suggests insights into why the hierarchical controls were binding and credible. With a relatively well-developed capital market[16] and progressively open macro economy, the threat of financial flows imposed a major constraint on central government's fiscal behaviour. In 1996, a year after the first democratic elections and the appointment of the first African National Congress (ANC) finance minister, capital flight put the exchange rate into a free-fall.[17] Within weeks, the exchange rate had depreciated by 50 percent. Faced with this currency crisis, the new finance minister developed and announced a fiscal stabilization program—growth, employment, and redistribution (GEAR)—that publicly committed the government to bringing down its budget deficit along a preannounced path. Since then, the ANC government has been monitored by private markets on their commitment to this fiscal austerity plan. Indeed, one of government's key successes has been the reduction of the central government deficit to below 3 percent of GDP in fiscal year 1999–2000 from a height of 8 percent in the early 1990s. In face of this market-imposed and market-monitored plan, hierarchical controls to manage the expenditures of provincial government were perceived as credible and binding.

In addition, the dominance of one political party, the ANC, and its influence on the political process have also been perceived as providing teeth to the control of the provinces by the center. Each political party at the national level announces its candidate for premier, and then elections are held at the provincial level. The dominance of the ANC in seven of the nine provinces means that the national selection by national party members is in effect the determining choice of the premier, who then responds primarily to the central party's directives rather than to community needs. Given that ANC's national priority has it committed to the principle of fiscal stability, its political control complements its budgetary control to ensure that the hierarchical processes achieve their intended effect. But ultimately, the objective of the fiscal controls, fiscal stability, was itself a result largely of market discipline created by the open macro economy and the linkages between local and global capital markets.

A political choice—or problem of political exposure, to borrow the term from Abedian and Ajam (1999)—may be at the root of the financial crisis that emerged with the creation of the new provinces. The political negotiations for a new South Africa required the creation of a provincial tier. It allowed the rapid closure of the homelands and provided opposition parties—the Nationalist party and the Inkhata Freedom party—the political space to claim an identity for their ethnic constituencies in the new South Africa. To protect the interest of the provinces in a multitiered government, the constitution also created the Fiscal and Financial Commission (FFC) with reporting responsibilities to Parliament.[18]

Since the negotiation and adoption of the new constitution, however, there has been significant ambiguity within the political leadership of the ANC with regard to the status of provinces. Not surprisingly, the Ministry of Finance has chosen to downplay the role of the FFC, ignoring in particular the issue of provincial taxation powers recommended by the FFC. The political uncertainty is reflected around the question of whether provinces are deconcentrated or decentralized entities within the intergovernmental system. This political exposure may have left provinces in a "neither fish nor fowl" status that provided the setting for the type of budgetary games that led to the underfinancing of welfare expenditures in 1998–1999. But unlike the apartheid era, the political exposure on provinces in the postapartheid South Africa was controlled by better design of intergovernmental fiscal rules.

10.2.6 Implications for a Hard Budget Constraint in the Local Governments

The case of local governments is quite different from that of provinces. The sheer number of municipalities—originally over 800 and currently amalgamated to about 300—suggests that central authorities will not be able to rely on hierarchical controls as the primary mechanism of oversight and management. Instead, government has relied on imposing accountability and fiscal discipline through various diversified channels.

First, at the political level, communities can directly elect their representatives. Second, the electoral process has been strengthened by ensuring that local authorities have access to their own tax instruments, including commercial and residential property taxes. Third, local authorities have access to well-defined and funded recurrent and capital grants programs.[19] Fourth, legislation will enable local authorities to access capital markets directly with clear rules on information disclosure and a judiciary-based bankruptcy process. Fifth, land markets for the commercial and industrial properties as well as the upper-income households are working well enough to impose competition between the large cities. Sixth, a new financial management system is being introduced across all local authorities and will provide

public information on the fiscal and financial state of each local authority on a quarterly basis.

Jointly, these mechanisms ensure that communities (electoral
processes and reactions to adjustments to tax rates), markets (through
land markets and allocation of credit), and central processes (fiscal
transfers systems, financial management requirements, and information disclosure) have limited the ability of local authorities to engage
in unsustainable fiscal expansion. Not surprisingly, local authorities,
unlike the case of provinces, have not been able to make the center
liable for local expenditure, and capital markets have been less reluctant to provide them bridging finance to balance budgets.

10.2.7   Potential Problems

There are potentially three windows within the fabric of the intergovernmental system that may offer a scope for local governments to pass
on their liabilities to upper-tier governments: problems of metropolitan size, public financial intermediaries, and political exposure.

Metropolitan Size
Through the amalgamation process, national legislation has mandated
the creation of metropolitan governments. Popularly known as mega-
cities, of which the top six represent about 40 percent of GDP, there is
a potential of a "too-big-to-fail" syndrome. The assumption here is that
during a financial crisis, metropolitan governments will be bailed out
because of the potential macro implications of their collapse. This
potential problem is, however, partly being addressed by promoting
the economic decentralization of cities. In other words, cities are being
encouraged to decentralize municipal services into business corporations, preferably with private sector participation. This decentralization
of economic services into the private sector would put the management
of infrastructure into the bankruptcy laws of the private sector. In
addition, private participation would bring in equity finance with
the added benefit that private financiers would have an incentive to
monitor debt. Finally, private participation has the potential of crowding private sector competition into the municipal infrastructure sector.

While the economic decentralization model would assist bringing in
private sector discipline and competition in the financing and delivery
of infrastructure, this approach would be applicable for goods only in
a contestable market. The pure local public goods, such as libraries and

community facilities, would fall outside this approach. In this case, the metropolitan governments, in particular Johannesburg, are looking at the model of community decentralization. The city is being carved out into ward zones, with ward councilors and an administrative CEO who will be given a fixed sum of resources annually through a transparent budgeting system and to be spent through community participation in the ward structure. Thus, hierarchical control of the ward administration through the budgetary system by the metro tier will be complemented by bottom-up control through community participation in the ward structure.

The financial sector in South Africa may also provide a mechanism to help central government by establishing a buffer between the local and upper tiers of governments. In particular, discussions are being undertaken by the private sector to establish municipal bond insurance. In case of a default by a municipality, the bond insurers guarantee the timely payment of interest and principal in accordance with the issuer's original payment schedule. The insurance agency will work with the issuer to address financial problems and thereby minimize its own losses. As in the U.S. market where over 40 percent of the municipal bonds are insured, the insurance guarantee is generally irrevocable, and the instruments are guaranteed for the life of the bond, regardless of what may happen to the insurer. To reduce their exposure, the insurance agencies will diversify their risks by reinsuring with specialized agencies. In the case of South Africa, several international reinsurance agencies are entering the local capital market.

Public Financial Parastatals

International evidence has often suggested that the presence of financial paratatals offers an off-budget mechanism for central authorities to finance public liabilities. In particular, during a time of financial crisis, it may be politically convenient to seek off-budget mechanisms to "hide" the problem in the expectation that a resolution to the crisis is forthcoming if the problem can temporarily be financed. International experience also suggests that such public sector intermediation runs the risk of displacing private capital and dampening the role of capital markets in the allocation of credit.

South Africa retained the Development Bank of Southern Africa, the financial parastatal used to fund the homelands, and converted it to a municipal infrastructure bank. Intended to finance the smaller municipalities that would not be able to access the capital markets, the bank also started financing the country's large cities. In the case of Johannesburg, the bank increased its lending to the city precisely when the private capital markets were pulling out of Johannesburg as a result of its economic mismanagement. Whether this intervention by the financial parastatal delayed the ultimate restructuring of the city (see box 10.2) and whether this was done with the sanction of central government will be difficult to prove directly. But it clearly showed the potential that public intermediation has in terms of providing a back door to soft budget constraint.

In South Africa, three factors can potentially limit the negative impact of public financial intermediation. First, the presence of private actors in the capital market provides a political lobby force that will limit the encroachment of public intermediation. On the other hand, the same political lobby group will not hesitate to shed private risk onto public books and use a financial parastatal for this purpose, a problem that suggests that a clean separation of roles for public and private financial institutions in the financing of public or quasi-public goods is difficult to achieve in practice. A preferable option may be to avoid public financial institutions (see box 10.4).

The second factor is the independence of the reserve or central bank. This independence in effect ensures that debt of local authorities will be difficult to monetize. International experience, especially the cases of Argentina, Brazil, and China, suggests that public debt of subnational governments is often monetized where the central bank is under the political control of the government and subnational governments have access to subnational public parastatals. In Argentina, for example, the provinces were using their subnational public banks to finance the provincial deficits knowing that the central bank would use its powers to support subnational public paraststals. In the case of South Africa, the tradition of independent reserve bank has been preserved through the country's massive political change in the past decade. The credit goes to the political authorities for having learned from international experience the value of preserving an independent central bank. But the presence of a relatively well-developed capital market also ensured a political force capable of lobbying for the independence of the central bank. Ultimately, the threat of capital flight, as experienced in 1995, remains a strong constraint on the ability of political leadership to reduce the independence of the reserve bank. The latter was entrenched in the constitution. In addition, during the constitutional talks, and this is the third factor, the ANC rejected the

Box 10.4
Evolution of capital markets and decentralization of borrowing powers

In countries without a domestic capital market, it may be preferable to have central fiscal transfers (e.g., from central borrowing from international sources) provide resources to subnational governments while policy efforts focus on developing a private commercial banking system. This approach avoids the creation of public financial intermediaries, keeps the fiscal and financial sectors separate, and can offer a better starting point for a municipal finance system. As the private banking system establishes itself, long-term finance can be provided through centrally funded discount facilities. These facilities stretch the terms of commercial bank lending to municipalities but take on only the maturity risk. Commercial banks retain the credit risk for their retail lending, thus preserving the separation of risks between the public and private sectors. Colombia offers lessons for designing discount facilities. The need for discount facilities will disappear as capital markets emerge with financial instruments offering long-term finance. And as long as the fiscal system is well designed, subnational governments will be able to secure longer maturities. Still, for fiscally weak municipalities, the fiscal transfer system will remain an important vehicle for accessing funds. In more developed capital markets, private credit rating agencies and bond insurance agencies offer a market-based mechanism for monitoring and regulating subnational borrowing. These institutions in turn require public sector regulation.

Source: Ahmad (1999).

establishment of provincial banks but opted for direct subnational borrowing from capital markets.

Political Exposure
The problem of political exposure may also be a potential problem in the case of local governments. In designing the new intergovernmental system, central authority has clarified the rules of the game in the new fiscal regime for the local governments. But the local governments have inherited the backlog of the past system in two specific ways. First, there is a vast difference in the service delivery between whites and blacks—the legacy of apartheid. Second, in legislating an amalgamation process to create new local government structures, the financial liabilities of the old system—debt owed to the private sector—have now been inherited by the new local governments. These new authorities are questioning the appropriateness of financing from a local tax

base, the restructuring process, the backlog, and the old liabilities for which the new political leaders feel that they are not accountable.

Central authorities have reacted to this problem of political exposure through several channels. The first response has been political. The central political leadership took the decision early on in the reform strategy that the financing of the restructuring process and the backlog of services would be done jointly by all three tiers of government. In effect, this created a political statement that if the responsibilities of the backlog could not be so easily transferred to the center, liabilities of local governments would meet the same fate in the future. This political approach, of course, was fully compatible with and driven to a large part by the macro stance of lowering deficits.

In addition, however, central authorities have made a portion of the implicit political exposure an explicit part of the budget. The capital grants for local authorities are meant precisely for subsidizing the local governments' efforts to redress the service inequities. Similarly, government is in the process of implementing a restructuring grant for the large cities to support their reform process.[20] The commitment to macro deficit targets has forced government to reduce the level of support on the restructuring grants. As a result, the grants have been targeted to the largest of the cities where the failure to reform quickly would have the largest negative externalities on the economy. More important, by placing a portion of the political exposure directly onto the budget, the government has constrained the fiscal threat of the political liability by pushing it onto the formal budget process.

10.3 Lessons

South Africa's experience so far suggests that a framework of a hard budget constraint in a multitiered government cannot be imposed through one specific channel; such a magic bullet is elusive. Instead, a systemic policy approach in which hierarchical regulatory controls, fiscal tools, markets, and community accountability all are needed to provide the right incentives for each tier of government to be held accountable for their management of economic affairs.

In South Africa, the multiyear budgeting, explicit commitment to macro fiscal targets, and financial management regulations form the core of the hierarchical systems. Jointly, these systems show how much money is available from the center and to which tier of government. The money is also delivered very transparently to each tier through a system of fiscal transfer that is legislated and formula based. It limits the scope for ad hoc bargaining and manipulation of resources. In addition, local governments have access to their own tax instruments, which means that at the margin, this tier of government can be held responsible for its own expenditure decisions.

Clearly the power to tax forces local governments to take into account the impact on economic nodes and households. In South Africa, the ability of capital owners to shift locations of firms between the large cities, or shift capital out of the country, and the willingness of communities and households to pay, or withhold payment, are examples of how the taxing power of governments creates a dynamic interface with business and households. This interface is lacking at the provincial level, which is solely dependent on fiscal transfers.

The design of the fiscal transfers can also take advantage of community control of public officials. First, the municipal capital grants are allocated through local governments. Second, these grants are used to finance projects that are designed and implemented by communities. Not only does this process increase the sustainability of the specific projects, it enhances the interface between local authorities and communities.

In addition, the design of the hierarchical systems and the fiscal tools will shape the interface between the public and private sector. In the case of capital markets, fiscal policy design has influenced capital market responses to provinces and local governments very differently. In the case of the former, capital markets have provided funds most probably under the assumption that the center will be liable. In the case of local authorities, creditors have been more cautious, sensing that local governments are ultimately liable for their borrowings. The different response of the capital markets to the two different tiers of government was not a sign of market imperfection but rather a market response to different fiscal policy. Similarly, how governments ultimately design the regulatory framework for private sector participation in infrastructure financing and provision will determine whether the power of private sector competition can be used to minimize the fiscal exposure of government and whether private sector competition can help enforce hard budget constraints. A weak regulatory regime or one that is susceptible to capture or political interference may result in weak private sector participation or one that leaves government vulnerable to implicit contingencies (Litvack, Ahmad, and Bird 1998).

Ultimately, the design of the intergovernmental system will provide policymakers with the scope to take advantage of the checks and balances offered by the judicious interface of hierarchical controls, fiscal instruments, markets, and electoral systems.

South Africa's experience suggests in particular that any policy assumption that in developing or transition economies with potentially imperfect markets and nascent democratic regimes, hierarchical controls must play a more dominant role (or in a neat framework of policy sequencing, initially a more dominant role), may need to be qualified. The issue of who guards the guardians in a hierarchical system is an equally legitimate policy issue, as is the concern for market imperfection or slow-responding electoral systems, whose existence is used as a reason for relying on hierarchical systems of control in the first place. In fact, given the imperfection of each of these channels, the simultaneous use of all may enable a more synergetic system to emerge. At the least, it diversifies the risk of central government of having to rely on one policy instrument.

The case of South Africa suggests that global financial markets in conjunction with local markets offer an important constraint on central authorities' decision making and make hierarchical systems more credible and binding. Similarly, the separation of powers within the public sector is itself another mechanism for signaling the commitment and credibility of hierarchical rules. South Africa's independent judiciary and independent reserve bank are, for example, enabling policymakers to support the decentralization of borrowing powers.

In this context, the particular role of local financial markets and how policy fosters their development and integration into global capital markets is emerging in South Africa as an important component of enabling a more effective and accountable decentralized system of governance. The South African case suggests therefore that the policy issue of how to foster an independent and private capital market system is at the core of establishing a hard budget constraint for a multitiered system of government. This chapter suggests that countries may well be advised to avoid creating public financial institutions, especially subregional banks. In addition, the South African case suggests that the design of fiscal decentralization will determine the effectiveness of a capital market response to local government creditworthiness. Finally, the chapter suggests that to avoid unplanned liabilities for the central government, fiscal decentralization should precede financial decentralization.

However well a policy is designed, its Achilles' heel will remain its vulnerability to political economy exposures. The apartheid context and the financing of the dual government structure are extreme examples of this problem. But South Africa's new intergovernmental system also shows this vulnerability. In terms of fiscal and financial strength, this system is hour-glass in shape: a strong center and a local tier, with a constrained provincial middle. But it is through the provinces that welfare, health, and education are financed and delivered. The weak fiscal, financial, and regulatory powers of the provinces are a result of the evolving political economy in which the central political forces have reduced the role of a middle tier in South Africa. Yet the constitution provides provinces more decentralized powers. This contrast between the original intent of the constitution and their implementation in practice has created the space for the type of budgetary games that characterized central-provincial fiscal relations during the 1995–1997 period. The center responded by imposing strong hierarchical rules and used the dominance of the ANC as a political party to keep the provinces in tow. Whether this top-down control is tenable in the long run remains to be seen. Currently, there is talk of converting the grants into more conditional grants (greater hierarchical control) and selectively devolving some of the functions to the district council or metropolitan level (enabling greater control by local authorities). Ultimately, however, as long as the political decision about the role of the provinces remains uncertain, there will be a problem of political economy exposure.

An important element of imposing hard budget constraints is setting the tone or the rules of the game during a transition period. Central government was quick to respond to the currency crisis with a fiscal plan and has remained committed to the macro targets of the plan. Even during periods of macro economic recessions when a Keynesian type of expansion may have been warranted, central authorities maintained their fiscal posture. Similarly, central government was quick to address the issue of provincial deficits with state-of-the-art fiscal control measures. In terms of local government, central government announced the stoppage of guarantees for local borrowing and has been even more forceful in regulating and even closing subnational financial parastatals. With all of these measures, central government has slowly but surely gained credibility in the market that it will sustain its fiscal program and expect the same from subnational tiers. This disciplined approach was essential in a transition economy to signal to subnational governments that the bailout regime of the apartheid era is indeed over. South African policymakers were quite cognizant that how governments intervene in the short run can break the trends from the past and set the expectations for the medium term.

South Africa's intergovernmental system continues to evolve and change quickly. These changes are fundamental in nature, with political, economic, fiscal, and financial decentralization happening simultaneously. Yet in spite of these rapid changes and during the process of decentralization, the country has significantly improved its macro fiscal and monetary conditions. While the reasons for this success are manifold, one key determinant has been the central government's ability to impose to a large degree a hard budget constraint on subnational governments. It was achieved by the judicious use of hierarchical controls, markets, and electoral voice, with each channel providing a check and balance on the other. Ultimately, this synergetic use of the different channels is perhaps the lesson that South Africa offers other countries to avoid the so-called dangers of decentralization.

Acknowledgments

This chapter benefited from comments and suggestions made by Gunnar Eskeland.

Notes

1. Differences between white and black areas were not the only ones; apartheid also imposed differences between the Indian and Coloured population. For expositional economy, this chapter focuses on the differences between the black and white population only.

2. These regions were known as homelands and independent countries.

3. In fact, as Swilling, Humpries, and Subhane (1991) point out, the apartheid system was a tax on the black community to keep the apartheid system alive and resulted in a redistribution from the low-income black households to high-income white households. For an elaboration of the latter point, see Wildasin (1993).

4. One must add with cynicism that the deficit was perhaps controlled ultimately by "investing" in "police and security" as a form of hierarchical control.

5. The new constitution of South Africa has established three independent tiers of government: central, provincial, and local. Unlike many other constitutions, such as the U.S. and Indian, the local tier in South Africa is not a creation of the regional or provincial level of government. This independence has a lot of implications for the design of intergovernmental fiscal systems. It avoids the tension between the second and third tier of governments as economic forces, such as urbanization and technological change,

progressively make the local tier economically and politically a more important level of government. India is a good example of how decentralization policies are difficult to implement, as states are reluctant to support the decentralization of powers to local bodies. The latter are under the legal and constitutional mandate of the former. While this chapter is not the place to address this important issue, from the point of view of hard budget constraints, the independence between the two tiers reduces the potential budgetary game playing and contingent liabilities that may be possible.

6. The local government white paper provides a description of the different phases of this process.

7. Six of the district councils are in fact metropolitan governments overseeing administrative wards. Where the districts oversee a group of smaller municipalities, the allocation of power between the two tiers has not yet been finalized. This chapter does not discuss the budgetary game playing and fiscal liability exposure that are possible between the two tiers. But the principles about soft budget constraints that emerge from the discussion about the fiscal relations between the center and the province apply.

8. While good fiscal practice would suggest that these two taxes are not best suited for financing infrastructure, in reality they are imposing limited inefficiencies in the fiscal system. Both the rates of the turnover and payroll have been kept very low (less than 0.5 percent) and are determined centrally for the country as a whole. Finally, they are levied at the metropolitan and district levels rather than the municipal level. These factors limit the potential sources of inefficiencies, including the cascading effects of turnover taxes, "race to the bottom", and spatial dislocations. In addition, the taxes are set by the center and are in effect a transfer. See Bahl and Solomon (1999).

9. As argued later in this chapter, this policy decision is an important source of the soft budget constraint incentive that provincial governments face.

10. Without this clause, central government may face the problem of time inconsistency, thus reducing the credibility of policy measures ex ante.

11. See Ahmad (1998).

12. As elaborated later in this chapter, the choice and credibility of the regulatory institution are important determinants in a decentralized system that includes market decentralization of whether a soft budget regime exists for subnational governments. A failure of the regulatory body because of either regulatory capture by the agents to be regulated or political interference by central government can leave central government with subnational liabilities.

13. A significant portion of the payment was for pension and welfare grants. This specific expenditure has been at the center of court cases levied by individuals who have not received their welfare grants. The court has passed judgment that ultimately the center is responsible for this payment despite the fact that the constitution broadly defines this expenditure as the joint responsibility of the center and the provinces. This expenditure responsibility best defines the ambiguity underpinning the concurrence list of the constitution.

14. Abedian and Ajam (1999) point out that the application of section 100 for two of the provinces (Eastern Cape and Kwa-Zulu Natal) did not raise much debate in the media or within the public at large. They suggest that this is an indication of how the mechanisms of political accountability are weak in new democracies. It may also be argued that it is well accepted that provinces are fiscally dependent on the center and that no one, including markets, was surprised at the use of section 100.

15. An important caveat needs to be raised. While budgets determined on a multiyear approach reduce the possibility of discretion on a year-to-year basis, several experts have suggested that the fact that vertical allocation is left to the political process reintroduces the discretionary element, albeit over a slightly longer basis. A potential approach to minimize this potential is to fix the vertical percentages in a fiscal act.

16. South Africa is unique in Africa, and also relative to its stage of economic development, in having a relatively well-developed private financial system. In addition to a well-developed commercial and merchant banking system, it has particularly strong contractual savings institutions—private insurance companies and pension funds. In fact, assets of insurance companies and pension funds correspond to 80 percent of GNP—higher than in United States and Canada—and South Africa has the highest level of insurance premium relative to GNP in the world (Vittas 1994). Local capital markets have long-term money that can be invested in municipalities and cities.

17. Until then, the ANC had appointed a technocrat from the private sector to the position of the minister of finance.

18. For greater detail on the operations of the FFC, see Ahmad (1998).

19. In particular, the Consolidated Municipal Infrastructure Grant is the primary capital grants system through which central government finances the funding of municipal infrastructure through local government and community participation.

20. As the discussion in the main text suggests, this grant has been wrongly described as a "Johannesburg bailout." While Johannesburg was the first city to receive the grant, the motivation was based fully on addressing the problem of removing the backlog.

References

Abedian, I., and Ajam, T. 1999. "Multi-Tiered Governments and Hard-Budget Constraint: The Case of South Africa." Draft paper, World Bank Country Office.

Ahmad, Junaid. 1996. "Structure of Urban Governance in South African Cities." *International Taxation and Public Finance*, 3(2):193–213.

Ahmad, Junaid. 1998. "South Africa: An Intergovernmental System in Transition." In Richard Bird and François Vaillancourt (eds.) *Fiscal Decentralization in Developing Countries*. Cambridge: Cambridge University Press.

Ahmad, Junaid. 1999. "Decentralizing Borrowing Powers" *PREM Notes*, no. 15, Jan.

Ahmad, Junaid, and Robert Inman. 1998. "One City: A Proposal for Capetown." Policy brief. World Bank.

Bahl, Roy. 1999. "Implementation Rules for Fiscal Decentralization." *Working Paper*, Georgia State University. no. 10.

Bahl, Roy, and David Solomon. 1999. "Turnover and Payroll Taxes." Draft note.

Lall, Rajiv, and Bert Hofman. 1995. "Decentralization and Government Deficits in China." In Jayanta Roy, ed., *Macroeconomic Management and Fiscal Decentralization*. Washington, D.C.: World Bank.

Litvack, Jennie, Junaid Ahmad, and Richard Bird. 1998. "Rethinking Decentralization in Developing Countries." Washington, D.C.: World Bank, Poverty Reduction and Economic Management Network.

Republic of South Africa. 1999. Local Government White Paper, Pretoria, South Africa.

Swilling, Mark, Richard Humpries, and Khehla Subhane. 1991. *Apartheid City in Transition*. Cape Town: Oxford University Press.

Vittas, Dimitri. 1994. "Contractual Saving in South Africa." Working Paper Draft. Washington, D.C.: World Bank.

Wildasin, David. 1993. "Local Finance of Urban Infrastructure in South Africa." AF1EI Working Paper, World Bank, Washington D.C.

11 Systemic Soft Budget Constraints in Ukraine

Sean O'Connell and
Deborah Wetzel

An important question for transition economies, and especially Ukraine, is what the proper degree of decentralization is within a changing financial and economic culture, macroeconomic, and political system. Although the benefits associated with fiscal decentralization are well documented, they assume a number of important conditions, such as the autonomy and accountability of lower levels of government. It is important in the case of Ukraine that decentralization be considered with care because of the already difficult nature of the market transition process. The continued year-to-year decline in real revenues and budget shortfalls has resulted in a high level of distrust between the different levels of government. Unfortunately, during the near decade of Ukraine's independent existence, these levels of government have shown more alacrity in undermining one another's fiscal and political authority than they have for constructively working together to bring the country out of its economic malaise.

Ukraine has not yet successfully put into place mechanisms for implementing a hard budget constraint. Indeed, the system creates incentives in almost every realm for soft budget constraints. In such a context, the lack of hard budget constraints cannot be attributed to a specific policy failure or the lack of a single mechanism. Rather it is a systemic failure. This chapter is organized around three channels that influence budget constraints: section 11.1 focuses on the intergovernmental system, section 11.2 assesses the political realm, and section 11.3 considers capital markets for subnational entities. In each of these areas, few of the conditions that promote hard budget constraints are in place.

11.1   The System of Intergovernmental Finance and its Implications for Budget Constraints

Ukraine's population, land area, and degree of urbanization are similar to those of France and Italy. Its population is about 52 million people, and its area covers 579,000 square meters. Some 71 percent of the population live in urban areas (World Bank 1999). By population and land area, it is larger than most other transition and European countries. At $1,200 1996 dollars per capita, its GNP per capita is considerably smaller than that of its European neighbors.

Ukraine operates under a unitary system of government, although it has some characteristics of a federal state. In addition to the central government, there are 27 regional, or *oblast*-level, governments (including the Autonomous Republic of Crimea and the cities of Kiev and Sevastapol, which have oblast status), 490 *rayon* district governments, some 447 municipalities, and a large number of settlements and villages. The average size of these different administrative layers varies considerably. Oblasts have populations that range from 0.9 million (Chernivetsk) to 5.1 million (Donetsk). The size of *rayons* typically ranges between 100,000 and 300,000, whereas the size of cities and large towns can be as high as 2.6 million (Kiev). In contrast, settlements and villages typically range in population between 500 and 2,500 people.

As seen in table 11.1, activity at the subnational level is an important component of the Ukrainian economy. In 1998, revenues provided to local governments were 14.4 percent of GDP,[1] whereas total consolidated budgetary revenues in 1998 were 35.9 percent of GDP.[2] With the exception of 1995, total local revenues (including shared taxes and transfers) as a share of total consolidated government revenues have remained stable at 40 percent.

In 1998, local expenditures on a cash basis were recorded as 14.5 percent of GDP, or 38.1 percent of total consolidated government expenditures. The data on a cash basis suggest local government deficits are minimal, relative to a deficit of about 2.0 percent of GDP for the consolidated government; however, this neglects expenditure commitments made but not yet paid out. Consideration of local expenditures based on commitments rather than a cash basis significantly increases the overall imbalances between revenues and expenditures at the local level. The consequent arrears are symptomatic of soft budget constraints at the very foundation of the system.

Table 11.1
Consolidated government and local expenditures (percent of GDP)

	1993	1994	1995	1996	1997	1998
Consolidated revenues	42.8	43.4	37.9	37.1	38.3	35.9
Local revenues[a]	17.6	17.3	18.0	14.9	15.5	14.4
Consolidated expenditures	71.0	53.6	44.9	39.9	44.9	38.0
Local expenditures[b]	16.0	17.0	17.9	14.9	15.4	14.5
Consolidated cash deficit	−28.1	−10.2	−7.0	−2.8	−6.5	−3.0
State arrears[c]	N.A.	N.A.	0.8	0.6	0.4	N.A.
Local arrears[a,c]	N.A.	N.A.	2.3	3.3	0.0	N.A.
Pension arrears[a,c]	N.A.	N.A.	0.1	1.3	0.2	N.A.
Total arrears[c]	N.A.	N.A.	3.2	5.2	0.5	N.A.
Consolidated commitment deficit	N.A.	N.A.	−10.1	−8.0	−7.1	N.A.
GDP (nominal millions of hyrvna)	1,483	12,038	54,516	81,519	93,365	103,869
Local revenues/total Consolidated revenues	41.1	39.8	47.5	40.2	40.5	40.1
Local expenditures/total Consolidated expenditures	22.5	31.7	39.8	37.3	34.4	38.1
Local expenditures and arrears/total expenditures and arrears	N.A.	N.A.	44.8	45.5	34.9	N.A.

Source: World Bank (1999, 9).
Note: Consolidated figures include the pension fund, but exclude state and local enterprises.
[a]Local revenues include transfers and shared taxes from the state budget.
[b]Expenditures include transfers to state budget from local budget. Local revenues and local expenditures include consolidated information from the *oblast* level and below, so all levels excluding the central government. Note that the data may exclude extrabudgetary, off-budget, and special funds at lower levels of government.
[c]Arrears include nonpayment of wages, benefits, and goods and services as recognized by the Ministry of Finance.

Figure 11.1 gives an indication of both the magnitude and distribution of arrears among levels of government and shows that most arrears are accumulated at the local level. At the end of 1997, total stocks of operational arrears amounted to HRN6.9 billion, about 7 percent of GDP. Of these, HRN4.3 billion, or almost 60 percent, are accumulated at the local level. Although the outstanding stock of arrears began to decline toward the end of 1997, there are indications that local government arrears rose again in 1998. Complete data on arrears for 1998 are not yet available; however, it is estimated that at the end of 1998, budget arrears and pension arrears were HRN1.97

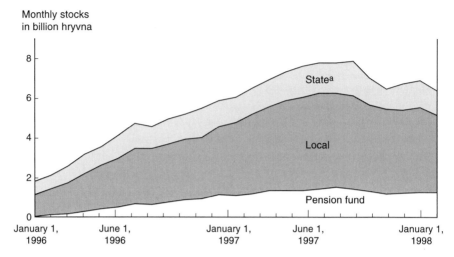

Figure 11.1
Total operational arrears 1996–1997. *Note*: "state" refers to central government. *Source*:
Ministry of Finance.

Table 11.2
Subnational arrears as a percentage of total expenditures committed, 1995–1998

	1995	1996	1997	1998
Education	17	31	21	24
Health	14	28	17	21
Social Protection	4	39	32	32
Culture	10	23	18	20
Communal services	N.A.	N.A.	N.A.	15

Source: World Bank (1999, 12).

billion and 0.96 billion, respectively. One estimate is that total arrears,
which includes public enterprises (for which the government is not
formally liable), at the end of 1998 amounted to 8.5 billion HRN or
about 8 percent of GDP (World Bank 1999, 13).

Arrears in social protection are largest, followed by those in education, and health. Table 11.2 shows arrears as a percentage of total
expenditures committed at the local level in these sectors between 1995
and 1998. Although not as significant a problem as in 1996, arrears in
these sectors are significant, with between one-fifth and one-third of
committed expenditures not being paid. No matter what the sector,
expenditure commitments on wages are those with the highest share
of arrears.

The magnitude of arrears at the local government level reflects in part an imbalance between mandated expenditures at local levels and the capacity of local government to finance such expenditures. It also reflects the squeezing of deficits through the system—from the central government, to local governments, and onward to companies, wage earners, and other parts of the economy. In effect, arrears are a form of forced borrowing (without interest) from other parts of the economy. An additional factor behind the buildup in arrears is that barter has become an increasingly common method of transaction at local levels of government, leaving governments with little cash for payment purposes. Indeed, with the use of mutual offsets, localities have a positive incentive to build up arrears that can later be offset against revenues owed by the center. Such transactions tend to reinforce soft budget constraints rather than discourage them.

11.1.1 Expenditure Assignments

One of the factors generating arrears and poor fiscal discipline is the unclear assignment of expenditure responsibilities. For local governments to exercise discipline over their expenditures, it is important that there be clarity with respect to the roles and responsibilities that different levels of government are expected to provide. In Ukraine, there is a range of issues that imply lack of certainty over which level of government is supposed to do what.

The current legal foundations of the intergovernmental system leave a great deal of ambiguity regarding not only what level of government is responsible for carrying out what service, but also what the functions of the executive and legislative branches at each level should be. The centerpiece of legal foundations for intergovernmental finance in Ukraine is the country's constitution, which establishes the territorial division of Ukraine and includes provisions for local state administrations and local self-government and for independently elected regional legislatures. The constitution emphasizes that rayon and oblast councils may be considered as local government bodies only when they represent and follow common interests of territorial communities in villages, towns, and cities. Otherwise, they act as deconcentrated agents of the center.

Provisions for decentralized government in Ukraine are further specified in the Law on Local Self-Government and other laws, including the Law on the Budget System and System of Taxation and the Law on Local Taxes and Duties. Many of these laws must still be amended to comply with the constitution. Specifics of intergovernmental finance for a given fiscal year, most notably allocation of shared taxes and equalization transfers, are provided by the annual Law on State Budget of Ukraine. Tax laws, and in particular laws on VAT and profit tax, and the real estate tax also include important provisions for intergovernmental public finance.

In the system established by these laws, the various relationships (between executive and legislative branches, between the center and subnational units, and between state administration and local self-government) are peculiarly interwoven. The system is one of deconcentrated state executive power with full vertical subordination, plus a three-layer system of mutually independent legislatures. The latter are relatively strong at the top level and much less significant at lower levels. The existing legislation does not state clearly the roles and responsibilities of the executive bodies that represent the state administration and the local representatives that represent self-governing bodies. In addition, the legislation offers no procedures to resolve competence issues over shared responsibilities. This confusion has produced a number of constitutional conflicts—for example, the controversy over roles and division of responsibilities between the head of council of city of Kiev, who assumed executive functions according to the Law on Local Self-Government, and the head of the city's state administration appointed by the president.

The ambiguity in the legal framework manifests itself even more when it comes to determining the specifics of expenditure assignments. Legislative arrangements are not clear on which level of government is meant to provide what service. Each level of government has some authority to act in each given sector, and in recent years many functions have been passed down to local governments. In theory, oblasts and rayons are meant to provide services only on a delegated basis when it has been agreed by either the state or subordinate governments that a "common interest" must be served. In practice, the data (table 11.3) indicate that the bulk of expenditures occur at the oblast and rayon levels. For example, most health and social protection expenditures take place at these levels. A different set of expenditure division problems arises at the sub-oblast level. Between oblasts, rayons, villages, and settlements, there is a lot of confusion over who should pay for communal services. These issues are complicated by the issue of divestiture of enterprise social assets to rayon and municipal governments. Local governments have been asked to take over social services

Table 11.3
Composition of local expenditures by type of expenditure and level of government, 1997 (percent)

	Oblast consolidated	Oblasts	Oblast-level cities	Rayons	Cities under rayon authority	Settlements	Villages
Social-cultural total	53.1	38.1	55.1	65.0	66.8	75.6	80.1
O/w: Education	26.1	12.1	28.1	31.9	58.8	64.9	62.4
O/w: Health	24.5	23.4	25.2	30.1	6.0	7.9	11.8
O/w: Culture	2.5	2.6	1.8	3.0	2.0	2.8	5.9
Social protection	26.0	25.6	29.5	28.0	10.2	4.2	1.3
National economy, communal services	4.9	4.7	6.5	1.8	14.8	9.3	1.0
Administration	1.9	0.2	2.5	0.4	4.4	7.2	16.0
Transfers to state	5.6	16.7	0	0	0	0	0
Budget loans	1.0	2.3	0.1	1.0	0	0	0.1
Other	3.9	5.5	3.7	2.9	2.3	2.1	1.0
Total	100	100	100	100	100	100	100
Memo:							
Capital Investment	3.6	6.8	2.6	1.1	1.6	1.7	0.5
Share of government Level in total subnational expenditures	—	34	37	21	2	2	4

Source: World Bank (1999, 32).

previously provided by state companies, but without any increase in resources.

In addition to the existing lack of clarity, the legislation allows the possibility for functions to be delegated downward or upward. For example, if a village finds that it cannot or does not want to take on responsibility for a specific item, it can delegate the function, along with the transfer meant to finance it, to the rayon. Cities can also join together and delegate functions upward. This allows for the possibility for changing assignments over time and across the country depending on the desires of the localities. No specifics are provided in the legislation as to procedures for delegation upward or downward.

Finally, there is a serious mismatch between fiscal responsibilities and the authority of local governments to reduce or increase expenditure commitments. Local governments may have responsibility for delivering services, but they do not control key variables such as wages, prices, and hiring decisions. There are a number of laws regulating wages, social payments to the population under social assistance programs, and detailing individual functions and expenditures of local governments. Other laws and bylaws detail or define responsibilities of local government for setting prices and tariffs for housing and communal services and authorize local governments to establish minimum normatives and volumes of budget financing for communally owned educational institutions. At the same time, other laws may regulate salary levels to be paid, benefits and privileges to be provided, and items that have a direct influence on the provision of services at the local level. In effect, localities—though nominally autonomous— are limited in their decision-making authority. The only mitigating factor is that enforcement of legislation and standards is relatively weak.

All in all, some of the key conditions for hard budget constraints that relate to expenditures are not met in Ukraine. First, there is little clarity in the legislation about what level of government is meant to provide what service and, even at the same level (center, oblast, rayon, village), which part of the government (state administration versus local representatives) is responsible for which activities. This makes it easy for local governments to exercise discretion in the services they choose to provide and makes imposition of fiscal discipline a much more difficult task.[3]

A second condition is that local governments be in a position to control their expenditure commitments and exercise decision-making authority. Many decisions are imposed on local governments from above, and a local government's ability to make independent decisions in order to meet its responsibilities effectively and efficiently is often limited.

Finally, to some degree, soft budget constraints have been institutionalized by inconsistencies in the system. Many of the services local governments are required to provide are constitutionally mandated or have significant externalities and redistributive implications. For example, Article 53 of the constitution mandates free secondary education and Article 49 free medical services. However, the responsibility of providing these services is left to subnational levels of government that often have insufficient resources to finance all of the mandated functions. This contradiction leads to a standard argument between lower levels of government and the center: local governments provide services that they are unable to finance because they are mandated to do so by the constitution. This leads to a large accumulation of arrears, particularly for wages and pensions. At the same time, the legacy of the communist state is such that even if they go unpaid, individuals and companies continue to work or provide services, under the assumption that eventually the center will provide sufficient resources to pay off back wages, back pensions, and the like. Given the political clout of some groups (especially coal miners), this is not a mistaken assumption. As a result, soft budget constraints are a fundamental part of the current system.

11.1.2   Revenue Assignments and Transfers

The conditions necessary for hard budget constraints to be effective also concern the sources of revenue for local governments. To the extent that a local government can push financing of local services on to another level of government, it will promote a softer constraint because the locality will have to bear less of the political burden of the taxation. Autonomy over local tax rates (referred to as own taxes) is also important because local governments are then more likely to be held accountable for how resources are used. An objective method for allocating transfers is also important for the stability and predictability of the system. Table 11.1 indicates that in 1998, local revenues constituted 14.4 percent of GDP and about 40 percent of total consolidated revenues. As in many other countries, however, it is necessary to examine quite closely what falls under the rubric of local revenues.

Table 11.4 shows the decomposition of revenues for subnational or local governments between 1993 and 1998. Local governments rely on a number of sources of revenues, but they have little control over most of these. The bulk of local revenues come from shared taxes, in which both the rate and base of the tax, as well as the rate of sharing, is determined by the center. In 1993, such taxes provided some 83 percent of local revenues. In 1998, the share of such taxes was 68 percent of total local revenues. Regulated taxes consist of four of the key tax bases in the country: the value-added tax (VAT), the corporate income tax (CIT), the personal income tax (PIT), and the excise tax. In the early years of the transition, the central government regulated the amount of tax revenue transferred to each oblast by determining the share it would

Table 11.4
Composition of Subnational Revenues 1993–1997 (percent of total subnational revenue)

	1993	1994	1995	1996	1997	1998[a]
Regulated taxes	83	80	77	74	65	68
Value-added tax	33	21	31	29	—	—
Corporate income tax	34	46	36	33	39	42
Personal income tax	10	10	9	11	22	26
Excise tax	5	3	1	1	3	—
Fixed taxes and fees and other	7	6	10	14	14	15
Trade tax	0	0	0	0	0	0
Forestry fees	0	0	0	0	0	0
State duty	0	0	0	1	1	1
Fees and other nontax duties	3	2	2	3	3	3
Water fees	0	0	0	0	0	0
Vehicle tax	0	0	1	1	1	1
Excess consumption fees	1	0	0	1	0	0
Privatization	0	0	1	2	1	1
Land fees	3	2	5	5	7	8
Other funding	0	1	0	1	1	1
Local taxes and fees	N.A.	0	1	2	2	3
Total revenues without funds from other budgets:	90	86	88	90	83	86
Total funds from state budget	10	14	12	10	17	14
Subventions from state budget	0	8	4	6	14	14
Short-term loans from state budget	9	1	2	4	0	0
Mutual settlements from state budget	1	5	6		3	
Total revenues including funds from other budgets	100	100	100	100	100	100

Source: Ministry of Finance and Treasury.
[a]Excludes revenue from extrabudgetary funds.

get of each of the taxes.[4] While this was convenient for the central government, it was not very transparent; it was not always clear on what grounds some regions were given higher shares than others. By 1996, the system was altered so that sharing rates for all shared taxes other than the VAT were uniform across oblasts. Different sharing rates for the VAT were maintained as a regulating mechanism. In 1998, these arrangements were changed further: local-level governments were assigned 100 percent of the revenue from the CIT and the PIT, and revenues from VAT and excise taxes went to the central government. In the 1999 budget, the government returned to regulating taxes, with different oblasts receiving different shares of the PIT, CIT, and excise tax—a move back to a much more discretionary system.

Fixed taxes and fees and other form a second category of revenue sources. These are taxes, fees, and charges assigned to local governments, although the bases and rates of the taxes and fees are determined by the central government. This category includes some taxes (trade tax and vehicle tax), some fees (forestry fee, water fee and land fees), and other nontax sources of income such as funds from privatization. As a source of revenues these so-called own taxes and fees increased from 7 percent of total revenue in 1993 to 15 percent in 1998. Most of these taxes and fees bring in very little revenue; the increase in recent years is largely attributable to an increase in land taxes.

What the public finance literature typically refers to as "own revenues"—revenues over which local governments have some degree of control over either the rate and the base—are seen here under the category of local taxes and fees. Some sixteen local taxes and fees, over which local governments can control the rate or the base, have been provided to the local governments in Ukraine. These taxes include items such as the dog tax, tax on advertisements, and tax on gambling. These taxes are administratively costly but provide little in the way of revenue. As seen in table 11.4, they provide only 3 percent of local government revenues and do not even amount to 0.5 percent of GDP. The main share of local taxes comes from a small tax charged to non-state-funded enterprises based on the number employed at a firm (53 percent of total local taxes). All budgetary and state-subsidized firms are exempt from this tax. The other main local taxes are hotel fees (5 percent), market fees (25 percent), and kiosk licensing fees (8 percent).

Recent experience with revenue implementation has highlighted the increasing role played by both tax offsets (noncash forms of tax payment) and tax arrears. Tax offsets as a share of the total tax take have on average increased fivefold since 1995 (see table 11.5). The share differs considerably among regions, but the pattern of increasing use of tax offsets is consistent across all oblasts. These offsets are at least in part the result of a cash crunch at lower levels of government brought on by the country's overall fiscal crisis. While such offsets are frequently a convenient means for settling obligations, they also create difficulties for budgetary management. To the extent that tax receipts are in kind, it reduces the flexibility and liquidity of the government receiving the in-kind payment and complicates budgetary management fiscal crises. This increase in offsets takes place in the context of the dramatic increase in arrears at all levels of government. In 1998,

Table 11.5
Tax offsets in total tax intake (percent)

	1995	1996	1997	1998
Republic of Crimea	3.4%	15.4%	28.5%	22.3%
Vinnytzka	0.2	13.9	37.5	32.6
Volynska	0.9	11.8	18.3	23.9
Dnipropetrovska	7.4	32.0	45.2	27.0
Donetzka	4.3	28.0	30.3	27.5
Zhytomirska	0.7	19.2	30.1	30.2
Zakarpatska	2.0	16.3	11.6	17.7
Zaporizka	5.5	15.6	18.8	17.4
Ivano-Frankivska	4.8	38.9	43.4	50.5
Kyivska	3.6	23.9	26.5	20.0
Kirovogradska	1.9	19.9	43.0	45.7
Luhanska	9.0	34.8	44.0	31.4
Lvivska	3.1	21.9	25.0	20.2
Mykolayivska	8.2	28.5	36.1	43.0
Odeska	0.6	9.9	13.2	11.1
Poltavska	9.3	33.0	52.0	44.1
Rivnenska	4.5	26.4	32.9	40.8
Sumska	7.8	32.3	43.4	28.2
Ternopylska	2.8	22.1	40.0	44.7
Kharkivska	17.2	48.6	48.4	42.2
Khersonska	3.3	26.0	50.5	51.9
Khmelnytzka	3.0	29.1	33.4	43.6
Cherkasska	0.4	13.5	31.7	27.9
Chernivetzka	5.7	25.3	37.3	44.1
Chernihivska	2.3	12.5	29.6	20.7
Kyiv	1.5	37.2	19.9	14.8
Sevastopol	4.3	20.8	25.7	24.1
Total	5.2	28.4	33.1	27.7

Source: Ministry of Finance.

accumulated tax arrears more than quadrupled in nominal terms. Both tax offsets and tax arrears are also closely tied to the issuing of *veksels*, which allow local governments to issue paper in order to procure services and reduce tax arrears at the same time.

In addition to the large amount of resources provided to local governments through tax sharing, localities also receive receive an important share of their revenues through subventions and subsidies. In recent years, between 10 and 17 percent of local government resources have been provided in the form of transfers. There is little clarity in how transfers are allocated. There is no formula-based system, and for the most part, transfers are allocated on an ad hoc basis as part of the annual process of budget negotiation. The system has been plagued by a tendency to overestimate revenue forecasts and subsequently to sequester transfers midway through the year. For example, in 1998, just 77 percent of planned transfers were given to local governments. Moreover, there was extremely wide variation among oblasts in terms of their receipt of transfers as a percentage of the budget plan. Oblasts such as Zhitomir, Sevastopol, Ternopil, and Khmelnytsk all received 100 percent or more of planned transfers. By contrast, Kiev oblast, Lviv, and Odesa received 35 percent or less. It appears that most transfers were directed at the neediest oblasts.

Neither the system of local revenues nor the system of transfers has any of the characteristics typically found to help strengthen hard budget constraints. The large majority of revenues come to local governments through either shared taxes or transfers. Typically, the revenues provided are insufficient to cover the mandatory responsibilities, and even the allocation of the budgeted amounts is highly uncertain. Localities have little authority over the tax rates or base of any of their significant sources of revenue. They also have little incentive to increase their own revenues because in doing so, they typically experience a reduction in transfers. Transfers are allocated on an arbitrary basis, and although there has been discussion of introducing a system of formula-based transfers, this has not yet occurred.[5] As a result, transfers often go to the neediest (which provides an incentive to overspend) or the most politically powerful.

Typically, borrowing from banks and the issuing of debt would be treated not as a revenue item but rather as a financing item. These items appear to play a small role in local government budgets, although their role has been increasing. According to the budgetary data, only in 1997 did they make up even 1 percent of local government sources of finance. The system for subnational borrowing and its implications for budget constraints will be discussed further.

In sum, the system of intergovernmental finance and the hierarchical relations between levels of government that it creates tend to promote soft budget constraints. Constitutionally mandated services, unclear expenditure assignments, and unpredictable transfers put localities in a position where they have every incentive to spend on the assumption that they will receive resources from somewhere. Each year, the central government says it will clear arrears, and each year they continue to grow. The system of tax sharing of revenues and transfers gives them no incentive to increase local own revenues, since other transfers will then be reduced. In its transition from a command to a market economy, many of the key fiscal mechanisms for supporting hard budget constraints are still to be implemented. In part, this relates to fundamental political uncertainties over the nature of the new regime.

11.2   Political Mechanisms and Their Influence on Budget Constraints

A fundamental premise that underlies much thinking on decentralization and its benefits is that local citizens will be in a position to hold their local governments accountable for their actions through the political process. Through either voice (the press, election outcomes) or exit (leaving a community), citizens have a mechanism for expressing their views on the effectiveness of the local government in carrying out its functions. In this section, we consider the extent to which the existing political institutions in Ukraine allow citizens to hold their local governments accountable and whether there is an incentive to do so. Despite close to ten years of transition, many of the political mechanisms that help to support hard budget constraints are not yet in place in Ukraine.

11.2.1   Access to Information

Most Ukrainian citizens can understand or find out without difficulty how their local government is organized, who is technically in charge of specific decisions, how budget resources are collected, and how much is allocated among different categories. Many Ukrainian cities and oblasts regularly publish their budgets and city council decisions in local newspapers for the benefit of the regional population. Despite these positive factors, Ukrainian citizens have access to little or no accurate information, authority, or even incentives to monitor and control their local government officials. Moreover, even if they had such information and influence, there are strong systemic disincentives to act through political or any other available channels against local officials.

Although local citizens have access to some information, they have virtually no access to information on how, when, and why important decisions such as expenditure allocations were made. Because of the ad hoc system of transfers and the lack of any tender or audit requirements, most budget implementation is determined in closed-door negotiations inside and between oblasts and municipal governments. The negotiation process for limited available funds between the oblasts and municipalities is especially adversarial, with both sides employing zero-sum-game strategies. The result is that important decisions are made beyond the public eye, and citizens are excluded from local government. Moreover, in the few cases where citizens try to participate, they find themselves at a severe disadvantage since they do not have the financial or political means to participate in the negotiation process.

The negotiations-based system leaves little data for monitoring and expost analysis of the budget process. In addition, the often arbitrary and unpredictable nature of the central government handling of the budget, such as sequestration of transfers, implies that local governments can effectively argue that any movement away from expenditure plans was the result of actions from above. With little monitoring and virtually no audits, both skepticism and distrust toward local government pervade the population of Ukraine. The result is little transparency in local government and insignificant participation.

Numerous interviews and media surveys indicate that even if citizens had irrefutable evidence that their local government representative had defrauded his constituents, they still would not act for fear of reprisal. The widely held belief that local government representatives may have illicit connections is deeply embedded in the Ukrainian psychology. This combines with the other elements of the system to create circumstances in which there are few mechanisms for gaining accurate information and little or no incentive to take an active role in monitoring local government.

11.2.2   Accountability

A key issue for implementing hard budget constraints is that of accountability. To whom are the different levels of government responsible? The current structure of intergovernmental finance in Ukraine incorporates two competing types of accountability. The first is vertical accountability, in which lower levels of executive government bodies are held accountable to higher levels all the way up to the president. The second is accountability in which legislatures are held accountable to the citizens and voters who have elected them. In Ukraine, the struggle between accountability to higher levels of government and accountability to citizens and voters reflects larger issues of the evolution of Ukraine's government as a presidential versus a parliamentary government.

Under item 10, Article 106 of the constitution, heads of the local state administrations are appointed by the prime minister of Ukraine and dismissed by the president of Ukraine. In practice, the oblast governor, his political apparatus, and oblast administration and department heads are entirely subordinated and dependent on the president and may be removed at any time by presidential order. The one exception to presidential authority in the oblast administration is the oblast council, which is directly elected in a first-past-the-post vote by the local population.

Although the oblast council nominally possesses a significant amount of authority over oblast activities, in reality the council is typically a weak partner. The council is legally the controlling entity for forming the budget. However, the oblast financial administration, which is controlled by the president through its double subordination to the Ministry of Finance and the oblast governor, controls implementation of the budget. In the current circumstances of persistent budget shortfalls, the oblast financial office decides not only which budget programs are fulfilled and which are not, but also which are fulfilled in cash and which fulfilled in either barter or through mutual debt cancellations. Because a large part of the oblast's budget is fulfilled in noncash outlays, real authority resides with the financial administration office and thus remains accountable to the president. A similar situation holds at the rayon level.

At the municipal level, however, the mayor is directly elected to a four-year term by majority vote of the city population in a first-past-the-post system. At the same time, elections are held for the city council. Because the mayor and city council are directly elected, they are much more attentive to their constituents' demands, and the two generally tend to have a collegial relationship, as opposed to the adversarial relationship that typically develops between the oblast governor and the oblast council. At the municipal level, there is intense pressure for the two sides to work together to give the impression that they are providing for the citizens' needs because dissatisfied electorates can and do take advantage of their one opportunity to take part in local government by voting out unpopular municipal governments.

Municipal governments are legislatively protected from central government interference. Article 20 of the Law on Local Self-Government establishes strict separation of power between the central authority and the municipal authority and states that mayors and city councils are accountable only to their constituents. Article 26 (subsections 10, 14, and 16) establishes that the removal of the mayor or a deputy of a local government council (rada) can be done only by the decision of a majority vote of the city council. While this legislation protects municipal governments from political reprisal arising after conflicts with the oblast during budget negotiations and implementation, there are exceptions. Two exceptions to the rule are when the Verkhovna Rada (national parliament) convenes in a special session to vote, and votes in the affirmative, on removing a city head or when a higher court decision finds a violation of national law or the constitution, which mandates the removal of the municipal authority in violation of the law. Many consider that since the court system is heavily influenced by the presidential administration, the president can and does remove mayors overly antagonistic to his regime through biased court decisions. For example, the removal of Mayor Hurlitz in Odessa in 1998 and subsequent replacement with a strong supporter of the president is thought to have been influenced from above.

Despite the mechanisms and pressures for accountability to their local constituents, the oblast continues to have extraordinary influence over the activities of municipalities. In practice, municipalities are heavily influenced and held accountable to the oblast government. Because of its role in the budget process, the oblast acts as a controller and monitor of municipal spending. At the same time, because the oblast also controls the bulk of revenues flowing to the municipal authorities, it possesses an undue amount of influence over the governance of municipal entities. This enables it to punish or reward cities based on its actions and loyalty to the center. Although there is no formal central government veto power over local government fiscal decisions, in practice, the oblast authority has a de facto veto over municipal fiscal decisions. This veto power is so ingrained into the political system in Ukraine that municipalities typically do not make any important fiscal decision independent of receiving the oblast's opinion first. However, the central government and its agents face little incentive to look out for the interests of the local governments and in fact have a greater incentive to push problems down to the local level.

11.2.3 Evolving Democratic Practices

Democratic political practices are evolving in Ukraine, although they are not yet institutionally strong enough to contribute to a hard budget constraint. For example, with the exception of the Communist party, there is no party label or discipline that carries any weight. Ukraine has over seventy-five political parties, few with strong economic programs. This combined with constantly changing political alliances and ever fragmenting coalitions makes Ukraine's political landscape one of the most chaotic in the transition countries. To some degree, this negates the importance of political parties. For example, the president is not affiliated with any party. At the local level, the Communist party does have some influence, although other party names are generally a non-factor, and many candidates are unaffiliated.

In terms of campaign finance, there is no formal campaign to finance at the oblast level because the governor is appointed rather than elected. However, the governorship of an oblast is a powerful position, and the lobbying for the post is fierce. There are no formal criteria setting out who may be nominated, and in general, the process lacks transparency. One obvious criterion has emerged in recent years: the ability of the governor to deliver votes to the president during the presidential elections.

Municipal heads, municipal councils, and rayon and oblast councils are all voter-elected positions. During elections, some public financing is provided to qualified candidates; however, the real value of these resources is low. The Law on Elections of Local Government Deputies and Mayors restricts the maximum amount a candidate may spend on his or her candidacy to fifty times the nontaxed minimum wage. This implies restricting expenditures to approximately $1,125. In theory, free time is provided equally to all candidates on both radio and television. In reality, the stronger regional interest groups can usually guarantee that their candidate receives a disproportionate share of airtime. In addition, special interest groups, often set up by the candidates themselves, frequently set up special funds; they are usually not legally related to the elections but are used to finance elections campaigns. The result is that candidates are largely funded with contributions from specific sources and interest groups with little transparency or accountability over how the funds are used.

11.2.4   Exit

An additional way for citizens to demonstrate preferences and in some sense hold governments accountable is through exit, or relocation to another community. However, in Ukraine, as in other countries of the former Soviet Union, the system of the *propiska*, or permit that authorizes residency in a community, is a legacy that largely precludes relocation as an option.

The urbanization of Ukraine took its lead from Soviet-style industrialization. Seven decades of industrialization policies emphasizing heavy industry and one-company towns have left a legacy of profound misallocation of capital and human resources. However, many of the past professional and residential choices cannot be sustained under market conditions. For the system of public finance, these misallocations imply a double burden: such a heavily distorted economy does not provide an adequate tax base for the public sector and at the same time requires massive subsidies to households lacking access to market sources of income. Such a mismatch is especially felt at the lowest levels of government and in the most economically weak regions of Ukraine.

However, the ability of Ukrainian citizens to exit or relocate to another community or town is restricted. The propiska and a work book, which records hours worked, are both necessary documents for receipt of most social benefits. Despite the fact that greater mobility of the population is a means of easing some of Ukraine's most urgent fiscal problems, generally mobility remains highly restricted. With social benefits tied to the propiska and work book, relocation often implies losing access to social benefits and presents a great disincentive. Hence, exit as an option for indicating preferences is highly limited in Ukraine.

Political mechanisms and their implications for accountability play a critical role in helping to support hard budget constraints. While political and democratic practices have taken great strides since

Ukraine's independence, they are not yet sufficiently mature to play a strong role in supporting hard budget constraints. If anything, these mechanisms often create incentives that weaken hard budget constraints. Fundamental issues of accountability remain unresolved in Ukraine and contribute to adversarial relations between branches of government (the executive and parliament) and levels of government (oblasts, rayons, and municipalities). They also contribute to unclear rules of the game and promote the discretionary nature of the system in the political realm as well as in the fiscal realm. In such an environment, it is exceedingly difficult for citizens to get accurate information on government decision making and to hold governments (at all levels) accountable. At the same time, citizens are limited in their ability to make use of exit. While citizens can and do make use of elections to express their views on current governments, in general most of the incentives within the system do not encourage accountability. This carries over to the realm of capital markets and local government borrowing, the third mechanism for supporting hard budget constraints.

11.3 Subnational Borrowing and Hard Budget Constraint Failure

It is generally accepted that since most local governments provide services that require substantial up-front investment and because these services provide a stream of future benefits over a long period, it is appropriate to finance them through borrowing to spread the cost of the assets over time. Both the Law on Local Government and the 1991 Law on the Budget System give local governments the authority to borrow directly and issue debt.[6] However, the regulatory framework for such borrowing has remained limited, and there are few institutional mechanisms that help to maintain a hard budget constraint. After briefly considering the regulatory framework for subnational borrowing, this section focuses on specific aspects of the Ukrainian capital markets to develop a broader picture of why a hard budget constraint fails to apply in Ukraine. It addresses local government loans from higher levels of government, then the issue of *veksels* by local governments, and, finally, the Odessa municipality bond default.

11.3.1 The Regulatory Framework for Subnational Borrowing

Ukraine does not have a well-established legal and regulatory framework for subnational borrowing.[7] Subnational governments (SNGs) have access to three types of borrowing: borrowing from higher levels of government, borrowing from commercial banks, and issuing bonds. Borrowing from higher levels of government is undertaken without any clear guidelines for determining how to allocate such loans, and frequently they are converted to subventions at year end. Borrowing from commercial banks is limited to oblasts and medium-size cities for liquidity purposes and for short maturities, often with the lender bank being the depository of the borrower's cash accounts. Finally, SNGs have not been successful with bond issuances, either based on volume issued or the experience of issued bonds (see the discussion of the Odessa bond issue below). The reasons for the anemic bond issuance are varied, but include high rates of inflation, lack of creditworthiness, and lack of available capital. Overall, the current legal framework does not offer the predictability and reliability necessary to reinforce hard budget constraints.

The source of borrowing authorization for SNGs is contained in Article 70 of the Law on Local Self-Government in Ukraine and in the Law on Securities and the Stock Exchange (Articles 3 and 11) (see box 11.1). The Law on Local Self-Government deals with all forms of debt, while the Law on Securities and the Stock Exchange deals only with debt issued in the form of securities, that is, bonds.

This provision is the legislative authorization for borrowing for all forms of debt. The details of good subnational debt legislation (types

Box 11.1
Article 70: Participation of Local Self-Government Bodies in Financial and Credit Relations

---

1. The council, or—on the council's decision—other local self-government bodies may issue, in accordance with legislation, local loans, lotteries and securities, may obtain loans from other budgets to cover temporary cash imbalance, to be settled by the end of the budget year, and may also receive credit from banking institutions.

2. Local self-government bodies may create, within the limits of legislation, communal banks and other financial and credit institutions, may act as guarantor of credits of enterprises, institutions and organizations which are the communal property of the corresponding territorial communities, may place their proper funds into banks of other subjects of the property right, and may receive interest, in accordance with the Law, and include this interest in the revenue part of the corresponding local budget.

of debt, method of securing such debt, remedies on default) are completely absent from the law. Article 11 of the Law on Securities and the Stock Exchange governs the authority to issue bonds. The absence of sufficiently descriptive procedures for issuance of securities is a substantial defect of this law.

Neither of these laws addresses the practice of the issuance of bills of exchange, that is, *veksels*. Although they are symptomatic of the problems of expenditure and revenue assignments discussed above, veksels are another example of an additional source of debt authority (and a soft budget constraint) that produces confusion. The current rules for issuing veksels approved by Joint Decree of the Cabinet of Ministers and National Bank No. 528 dated September 1992 state that only "businesses" are allowed to issue veksels and be acceptors, endorsers, or guarantors. However, Ministers Decree No. 1440, dated September 15, 1998, allows oblasts to issue veksels in connection with electricity through the end of 1998. The national treasury guarantees such veksels. There also appears to be a lack of consensus regarding regulatory jurisdiction over the use of veksels.

Pursuant to a presidential decree adopted as a result of the Odessa default in June 1998 and Regulation 48 of the Securities and the Stock Market Commission as amended by Regulation 91, all subnational borrowing must be approved by the minister of finance. Yet there is no explicit statement that the central government will not bail out a local government that cannot repay loans or debt issues, nor is their any clear elaboration of procedures for obtaining authorization. It is also not yet clear which department in the Ministry of Finance will carry out this function.

Neither the Law on Local Self-Government nor the Law on Securities and the Stock Exchange contains any provision relating to the type of security a subnational government may pledge to the payment of its debt. There is an existing Law on Pledge that is functional and essentially adequate to provide for securitizing debt. However, the law has developed relatively recently, and there is little experience with the judicial recognition and enforcement of these security rights on a timely basis. In addition, various issues have been raised with regard to its provisions. For example, the registration of pledges of security or collateral in the state registry is permissive but clearly states that any pledgee who registers a pledge will have the claim recognized prior to nonregistered pledges. However, there is no unified registration system in Ukraine, making it very difficult, if not impossible, to carry out due diligence on existing pledges. The pledge may be registered in the location of the pledgor, the pledgee, or the property.

There is little experience in Ukraine in judicially enforcing financial obligations against defaulting subnational issuers of debt. Even in the Odessa situation, neither the Securities and Stock Market Commission nor the city courts are aware of any pending litigation, although letters of complaint have been received by both the commission and the Ministry of Finance. There is an apparent absence of clear-cut negative consequences resulting from default.

One reason for the absence of the judicial remedial enforcement may be a requirement that a plaintiff in a financial reclamation lawsuit deposit an amount equal to 5 percent of the value of the lawsuit in hryvnya in order to commence legislation. This could be a substantial deterrent to creditors seeking legal recourse. For example, in the Odessa situation, initiation of a legal claim by nonresident debt holders would require a deposit of approximately $1 million local currency. Given the potential length of litigation and the potential for devaluation, this is a substantial cost even to a successful plaintiff and obviously discourages enforcement of claims. Experience on foreclosing against specific property is also limited and varied. There are cumbersome and lengthy procedural requirements to liquidate collateral. An additional issue regarding enforcement relates to the lack of clarity of title for local government property. The title to much property remains unclear and is still in the process of devolving from the state or being privatized.

With respect to monitoring and disclosure, there is no requirement that local governments receive independent audits, nor is there any effective audit for the full financial status of a subnational government. The Control Inspection Service (CRU) does monitor local governments, but its focus is on uncovering criminal wrongdoing rather than providing a source of regular financial accountability by auditing the financial performance of local governments. There is also a perception among some local officials that CRU audits may have been used for political ends in some instances. There does not appear to be any monitoring of the financial viability of subnational governments or their compliance with debt payment requirements.

There is, however, a resolution by the State Committee on Securities and Exchange that sets forth the disclosure requirements for issuing local bonds. These requirements are designed to reflect material and relevant information about a local government. Much of the required information is appropriate; however, there is no requirement for continuing disclosure for the period the bonds are outstanding. Furthermore, the SCSE does not appear to have any enforcement or remedial powers to deal with noncompliance, and existing prospectuses are very weak. Finally, there is no any legislation dealing with the insolvency of local governments. The recent draft Law on Bankruptcy is applicable only to corporate entities, not local governments.

Overall, the legislation relating to subnational borrowing in Ukraine does little to help reinforce a hard budget constraint. Local governments are authorized to borrow, but there is little or nothing said about processes, collateral, disclosure, and monitoring. Indeed, only in the wake of the Odessa bond default in June 1998 did the government begin to issue statements requiring the registration and approval of all subnational borrowing and statements that such borrowing would not be guaranteed by the central government. Even with the existence of such decrees and the regulations, implementation and enforcement are weak. As we shall see, when the rules of the game are weak and poorly enforced, there is ample opportunity for the softening of budget constraints.

11.3.2 Borrowing from Higher Levels of Government

Due to the weakness of private capital markets in Ukraine for subnational borrowing, loans from higher levels of government are the most widespread form of borrowing that local governments use. Unfortunately, these loans make a direct contribution to the persistence of soft budget constraints in Ukraine.

The process for intergovernmental loans in Ukraine is not one that resembles true loan finance at all. The 1991 Law on the Budget System and the 1995 draft revision of this same law indicate that intergovernmental loans may be given only to subnational governments (oblasts, rayons, and, municipalities) that are experiencing budget shortfalls or cash shortages. In the Ukrainian context of scarce liquid funds and compressed budgets, virtually every subnational body is eligible for these loans. Near-universal eligibility and correspondingly insufficient funds result in a high level of discretion in allocating the loans. Since the loans are applied for on the basis of need rather than on quality of projects and creditworthiness, local governments have every incentive to spend. In addition, loans are made on the basis of 100 percent upfront disbursement and at zero interest. Combined with a practice of turning unpaid loans into subventions, this creates a system whereby loans from higher levels of government are more frequently taken to be part of the system of grants than as a financial obligation.

National statistics on the absolute level of disbursed loans from higher levels to lower levels of government are not centrally recorded and hence unavailable. However, national statistics on the outstanding balances of intergovernmental loans are recorded. In general, most of the *oblasts* apply for and receive intergovernmental loans during the fiscal year from the Ministry of Finance, especially in the first half of the fiscal year, before oblasts budgets have been agreed on.[8] Since the Ministry of Finance has a direct relationship with the oblast financial offices, it has greater control on their repayment rates. This generally results in a lower percentage of unpaid balances for oblasts. Table 11.6 presents the aggregate percentage of the budget that unpaid balances on loans constituted for each level of government. Unpaid balances vary both across regions and by levels of government. On average, unpaid balances are larger at the lowest levels of local government.

In addition to undermining implementation of a hard budget constraint, the moral hazard in the system contributes to the persistence of soft budget constraints over time. Loan funds acquired from higher levels of government on the grounds of need encourage local governments to focus on lobbying and "demonstrating need" as opposed to focusing on local government creditworthiness and ability to repay, not to mention the quality of the project being supported. The focus on lobbying for loans at zero interest from higher levels of government has also served to weaken capital markets generally and eclipse any development of medium- or long-term markets for municipal finance.

Intergovernmental loans are just one of the systemic factors contributing to hard budget constraints failure in Ukraine. The next section considers the issuance of local government veksels or bills of exchange as an instrument that offers another means of getting around a hard budget constraint.

11.3.3 Veksels

A Ukrainian veksel or bill of exchange is legally a form of short-term borrowing widely used by both the public and private sectors in Ukraine. Technically, veksels are promissory notes, issued in accordance with procedures laid down for bills of exchange and promissory notes in the 1930 Geneva Conventions and the Joint Decree of the

Table 11.6
Aggregate percentage of the budget that unpaid balances on intergovernmental loans constituted for each level of government, 1997

Oblasts	Oblast	Cities under Oblasts	Rayons	Cities Not under Oblasts	Settlements	Villages
Crimea	0%	6%	0%	9%	8%	16%
Vinnytzka	0	0	0	1	3	4
Volynska	0	3	0	3	4	5
Dnipropetrovska	0	4	3	3	1	3
Donetzka	1	6	6	8	12	22
Zhitomirska	0	0	0	2	5	2
Zakarpatska	0	0	0	0	0	0
Zaporizka	1	2	0	1	2	5
Ivano-Frankivska	0	0	0	0	0	0
Kyivska	0	0	0	1	24	29
Kirovogradska	0	2	1	0	0	0
Luhanska	0	2	2	13	5	6
Lvivska	0	0	0	2	2	4
Mykolayivska	0	2	1	0	0	8
Odeska	0	0	0	19	20	33
Poltovska	0	1	4	5	12	16
Rivenska	0	2	0	7	4	3
Sumska	0	0	0	1	13	12
Ternopylska	0	23	8	18	11	24
Kharkivska	0	0	0	10	11	8
Khersonska	0	0	0	9	14	20
Khmelnytzka	0	0	0	0	1	4
Cherksasska	0	0	0	0	0	0
Chernivetzka	0	17	7	8	14	16
Cherniwivska	0	0	1	8	22	20
Kyiv	0	0	0	0	0	0
Sevastopol	1	0	0	23	0	15
Total	0	3	1	6	8	11

Source: Ministry of Finance, Treasury Department, Ukraine and Barents Group; see World Bank 1999, p. 69.

Cabinet of Ministers and National Bank No. 528 dated September 1992. In practice, veksel transactions are more a combination of mutual cancellation of debts among enterprises and offsetting arrangements that help localities finance expenditures and enterprises to reduce tax arrears.

In 1998, local governments, primarily oblasts and municipalities, became particularly dependent on issuing veksels to finance planned budget expenditures and collect tax arrears. Table 11.7 sets out the 1998

Table 11.7
Selected itemized tax receipts of the state budget of Ukraine, 1998

Type of Tax Collection (HRN000)	Total	Mutual debt settlements	Veksels	Receipts Through Bank transfers (cash)	% of total collected from mutual Tax settlement	% of total collected in veksels	% of total collected in bank transfers
Profit tax on state enterprises and state organizations	2,365,000	734,409	871,623	758,712	31%	37%	32%
Profit tax on communal enterprises and communal organizations	167,669	41,468	42,417	83,783	25	25	50
Profit tax on enterprises with foreign investments (private)	206,012	3,344	7,143	195,524	2	3	95
Profit tax on foreign legal entities	16,793	0	323	16,469	0	2	98
Profit tax on banking organizations	263,612	7,284	10,423	245,904	3	4	93
Profit tax on collective owned enterprises	1,616,530	295,590	816,477	504,462	18	51	31
Profit tax on joint ventures	2,437	2,437	2,822	38,201	6	6	88
Profit tax on private enterprises	144,260	6,259	8,741	129,259	4	6	90
Profit taxes on other organizations	823,365	161,790	88,424	661,782	9	11	80
Total profit taxes on enterprises	5,928,185	1,177,657	1,858,881	2,891,646	20	31	49
Total income and profit tax	9,504,560	1,359,240	1,978,779	6,166,440	21	14	35
Total tax collections	19,035,160	3,262,584	2,965,659	12,806,916	17	16	67

Source: State Tax Administration of Ukraine, compiled and collected by Lucan Way; see World Bank (1999, 81).

Ukraine State Tax Administration (STA) itemized tax receipt data and reveals the extent to which local governments depend on veksels. In 1998, over 31 percent of all local government tax collections on enterprise profits, the primary source of local government tax revenues in that year, were collected in the form of veksels. Additionally, total income and profit tax receipts and total state tax collections show significant dependence on veksels as well, with 21 percent and 16 percent collected in veksels, respectively.

Table 11.7 also indicates that local government veksels are primarily received and redeemed by state, communal, and collective enterprises (unambiguously nonprivate organizations), which also generate the largest amount of profit tax liabilities (nearly twice that of private and other similar organizations). The hard budget constraint failure in this process is systemic. On average, only one-third of state, communal, and collective enterprises' profit tax is paid in cash, with the remainder paid in veksels or mutual tax settlements. Since payment in veksels is a noncash payment, and an overvalued payment, state and other budget-funded government agencies pay their tax liabilities with lower real value obligations while retiring debt at the nominal veksel price. This amounts to an indirect and hidden subsidy by the state and local governments to state and other government-funded agencies and a failure to impose fiscal discipline on enterprises that would most likely in the absence of such transactions have to be declared insolvent.

Local government veksels have some fundamental characteristics that influence how they are used. Veksels are nontransferable (e.g., they cannot be discounted or traded), are issued at full nominal value, and are only redeemable against tax arrears to local government budgets. Enterprises thus redeem the majority of local government veksels against profit taxes.[9] More important, the combination of these factors necessitates a complex method, in fact illegal, for conducting most local government veksel transactions. Box 11.2 provides an example of how a veksel transaction is typically conducted. This example demonstrates the hard budget constraint failure that resulted from the local government veksel transaction. The oblast recognized the expenditure at full par value of the veksel, whereas the true value of the service provided was half that amount. This implies that oblast expenditures are overvalued and that a hidden liability is passed on in the form of decreased services to local government citizens.

Because a veksel can be issued only at full nominal price, a method for discounting the veksels must be found; otherwise, they would not

Box 11.2
A local government *veksel* transaction

In early January 1999 a *vodokanal* (water utility) in a regional Ukraine oblast found that it needed a significant amount of benzene as part of the normal process of conducting repairs on water systems damaged during winter. Without repairs, the local government would lose access to running water. The vodokanal informed the oblast administration and oblast financial offices of the situation and urgently requested transfer of the funds planned in the 1999 oblast budget for the vodokanal's repair and maintenance. The oblast did not have free funds available and informed the vodokanal it would have to finance the benzene with oblast-issued veksels instead. The vodokanal bore the responsibility of finding the seller and arranging the transaction.

In order to conduct the transaction, the vodokanal hired a local financial firm that had expertise in this type of *veksel* transaction. A trader at the financial firm agreed to conduct the transaction and immediately began calling different enterprises to find one interested in the transactions. The trader had to find an enterprise possessing several important characteristics. First, the enterprise had to possess on hand a sufficiently low grade of benzene that it was realistically willing to trade it in a veksel transaction. Second, it had to have either a "partner" enterprise with which it could conduct the transaction or significant debt to a third-party firm with accumulated tax arrears that was willing to participate in the transaction to cancel its debts for tax relief. This is generally recognized as a difficult task. In this case, the trader found an enterprise (call it firm A), with benzene it was willing to trade in a veksel transaction that had an appropriate partner enterprise—call it partner firm B. The trader then had to find or set up an intermediary or envelope enterprise, which it did with the assistance of a local commercial bank specializing in this activity. The envelope enterprise was an enterprise set up for the specific purpose of buying the benzene from firm A at a small nominal profit and then selling it on paper to the partner enterprise at a large profit margin.

Firm A accordingly sold its benzene to the envelope firm at 75 kopecks per liter, for 5 kopecks over its acquiring cost of 70 kopecks. The envelope firm in turn sold the benzene to partner firm B for HRN1.45 per liter, at a substantial paper profit. Partner firm B then sold the benzene to the vodokanal for HRN1.50 per liter and received the oblast veksel order as payment. To finish the deal, the accountants for both partner firm B and the vodokanal went to the oblast financial offices and registered the transaction, with partner firm B's tax arrears subsequently written off equal to the value of the transaction.

be accepted. Furthermore, since veksels are officially nondiscountable and nontransferable but taxable, a direct transaction with veksels is highly undesirable. This is because a straight nominal value to tax relief swap veksels transaction would not only imply equal cash value for the veksel, but also produce a profit tax liability on the redeeming enterprise. In order to incorporate the true value of the veksel into the transaction, the redeeming enterprise would have to charge a higher price on the service. The enterprise would then be liable to pay that profit tax liability in cash, but it would not have made any cash in the transaction itself, with a double impact on its cash flow. Therefore an illegal, open and close, enterprise is required and, as this analysis suggests, is tacitly tolerated by the local governments. This results in a culture of tolerance toward illegal activity that benefits the local government.

Veksels reflect an example of innovation on the part of local governments in response to capital market illiquidity, unpredictable transfers, ever-increasing arrears, and nontransparency. Local governments use them because the issuance of these notes allows some delivery of services and collection of tax arrears, when there could quite easily be none. Local governments have become increasingly dependent on veksels as budgets have become increasingly tight in Ukraine. However, they also serve to create yet another vicious circle in Ukraine where the budget-funded enterprise needs more and more funds to cover expenses, which have been only partially covered through veksel financing and result in larger and larger estimates on funds demanded from the budget. The secondary result is an incentive to maintain arrears, caused by the same instrument meant to lower them.

11.3.4   The Odessa Municipal Bond Default

The 1998 Odessa default, in which Odessa defaulted on HRN91.5 million, has been one of the most important events symbolizing systemic problems in the development of local government capital markets in Ukraine. To its credit, the central government has to date not directly bailed out the Odessa municipality, and the losses have been borne by investors in the bond issue. At the same time, the Odessa story highlights how the system of intergovernmental finance, politics, and weak regulation of capital markets contributes to soft budget constraints.

At the time of their issue, the Odessa bonds appeared attractive to speculators for a number of reasons. Leading up to the bond issue, the city made public its plans to fund capital investments that would have rapid turnover and carry high short-term yields: funding of the construction of parking places, toll highways, a municipal taxi fleet, and other activities with high turnover and a short payback period. The issue was short term—one year—with a 50 percent annual return, significantly higher than the 30 percent effective yearly return available on sovereign debt. The bonds were also available in a wide range of nominal values and freely transferable. As a result, the issue was fully subscribed, with heavy participation by foreign investors.

All proceeds from the bond issue were initially transferred to an independent account of the city budget held at the city's authorized bank, Porta-Franco Bank, which was also given responsibility for all financial transactions for channeling bond repayments. The implementing agency for investing the proceeds of the bond issue was the Odessa Municipal Mortgage Fund for Economic Development (OMMFED).[10] OMMFED was empowered to spend the bond proceeds according to city-directed projects and also in short-term securities in order to generate a stream of payments to repay the loan.

On May 1, 1998, the first day of the payback period, HRN2 million of the total HRN91 million to be retired came due, but no funds were transferred from the city to retire the bonds.[11] Thus, Odessa technically defaulted on the first day of the repayment period. On May 11, OMMFED transferred HRN250,000 to the city budget, which was in turn transferred to the Porta-Franco Bank and used to pay off Odessa private citizens' debt only.[12] After May 11, no more funds were transferred from OMMFED or the city budget to retire the remaining HRN90,750,000 debt. To date, this amount remains fully in default.

Odessa, like all other Ukrainian cities, is heavily influenced by the overall system of intergovernmental finance. Transfers from the state level accounted for 51 percent of Odessa's municipality revenue in 1996 (down from 90 percent in 1993).[13] Shared taxes fluctuated dramatically, and lengthy delays in the transmission of transfers were (and still are) common. Tax offsets, barter, and other forms of noncash payment to the city budget (veksels chief among them) constitute a large share of municipal revenues. Own revenues remained relatively small.

At the same time, compulsory and mandated expenditure accounted for roughly 35 percent of Odessa's total expenditures in 1996 and 1997. At the same time, protected expenditures increased to approximately 44 percent of all expenditures in 1997. Although mandatory and protected expenditures do overlap, the resulting restrictions combined with noncash payments severely limit cash flow and rule out anything more than a minor level of debt for local governments in Ukraine. At the time of the debt issuance, Odessa's current deficit on a cash basis was 5 percent of the budget. However, outstanding payables for the municipality net of receivables amounted to 22 percent of the budget at the time.

Prior to and during the bond sale period, Odessa did an impressive job marketing itself to foreign investors as an economic success story with substantial potential in industry, tourism, and trade. Odessa also had an influential, charismatic mayor, international recognition as a port city, and a well-diversified tax base by Ukrainian standards. In fact, in February 1998, the international rating agency Fitch IBCA rated Odessa senior debt at B+. Somewhat surprisingly, this rating was higher than the published rating on sovereign debt at the time: Moody's B2.

Despite the issue's full subscription, it is not easy, even with the benefit of hindsight, to understand how a reasonable investor could have rated the Odessa bonds creditworthy and invested in them.[14] Debt service on the one-year bond issue clearly represented over 50 percent of the 1997 planned revenue of the Odessa city budget.[15] Ninety-one percent of the Odessa issue was sold from June 12 to June 15, and therefore 91 percent would need to be retired in the same time period 1998. This was an extreme case of a balloon maturity, a sudden increase in debt servicing, which obligated Odessa to retire debt representing almost half of its entire 1998 projected budget in less than one week.[16] Additionally, the issue was scheduled for repayment during the corresponding May–June 1998 period, which meant that municipal planning for repayment would be difficult.[17] The budget process in Ukraine for municipalities is often not completed by May. Therefore, the repayment period would likely begin before Odessa's budget for 1998 would be agreed with the oblast.

World and domestic financial markets tightened significantly by the end of October of the same year. Despite the deterioration of world financial markets, the Odessa city council issued a public announcement on November 6, 1997, authorizing and putting forward a second series of debt issues totaling HRN500 million in both national and foreign currencies.[18] City property and taxes, in contrast to the first bond issue, were identified as collateral for the second proposed bond issue. The second series of bond issues was abandoned after the markets showed a clear lack of demand, and a formal prospectus and contract with a fiscal agency to implement the bond issue were never signed. Activity on the secondary markets for the first series of Odessa bonds sharply declined at this time as well.

The financial management of the bond proceeds by OMMFED appears questionable and has been the subject of an internal criminal examination by state authorities. For much of the first month of its activity, OMMFED concentrated on short-term contract selling of the bond proceeds into the Ukrainian interbank market. The quick investment projects did not receive funding from OMMFED in some cases until August. OMMFED's holding of funds initially in short-term securities until they were finally invested in capital investments was highly loss making. Average effective annual return on short-term securities investments equaled only half the cost of the funds—approximately 25 percent.[19]

Additionally, the Odessa city financial office's supervision of OMMFED's management and investments was apparently weak. Odessa municipal documents up to February 11, 1998, analyzing the investment projects from the bond issue show the use of funds (table 11.8).

The remaining HRN20,423,776 of the proceeds of the bond issue are not referred to in the city's analysis. The allocation of funds was largely ineffective. Not only were none of the projects completed in time, but none has received sufficient funding to be completed at all. The most extreme example is the city's highly touted municipal parking garage project, which, according to the city budget office, needs a further HRN15 million to be completed. Given the current situation raising the needed funds for completion, the parking lot's construction will be virtually impossible. The unfinished garage, already beginning to dilapidate, sits unfinished and empty next to the city's largest and most famous bazaar, generating no income.

Table 11.8
Expected use of Odessa bond proceeds (in HRN)

Housing construction	18,078,000
Parking lot construction	11,298,224
Construction of a whole sale market	5,600,000
Construction of city Univermag department store	5,600,000
Total	40,576,224

Source: Odessa Municipality.

Little progress has been made in resolving the default. The state does not implicitly or explicitly guarantee local debt issues. As of the end of July 1998, the state made clear that it has no intention of stepping in to bail out Odessa. It has been clear to Odessa for some time now that it will have to repay its debt on its own.

Although the default was the result of financial mismanagement, the municipality maintains that the default was due to a force majeure situation arising from the removal of Odessa's mayor by the government of Ukraine shortly before the bond's maturity. This remains the municipality's reasoning for not paying the bond debt. They maintain that it is either the debt of a previously discredited administration, and hence not their fault, or that, alternatively, by forcing the removal of the administration, the central government became responsible for paying the debt. In neither case does the municipality recognize its financial responsibility for the bond issue. The default remains legally unacknowledged by the Odessa municipality, even to foreign bondholders.

Security for the bonds was local property, however, and the Odessa City Property Fund—the agency responsible for selling municipal property in Odessa—is on record as stating that given Odessa's current political difficulties, the transfer or sale of any city real estate is not foreseen in the near future. To sell sufficient municipal property to cover the loan, the city would have to sell off an unprecedented large value of municipal property. Furthermore, market recognition of Odessa's desperate situation means that municipal assets could be sold only at fire sale prices. The Odessa City Property Fund, like all other state property funds in Ukraine, is highly resistant to selling property at discounted prices. It is highly unlikely that the sale of municipal assets will contribute to paying off a significant portion of the Odessa bonds.

Given the lack of legislation on municipal insolvency and weak enforcement, foreign investors have had no success in pursuing workout procedures that would cover at least part of their losses. Some domestic repayments were made, but the mechanisms were not formal.

To the extent that investors have had to take the loss and were not bailed out by the central government, the case of Odessa shows at least one positive sign with respect to hard budget constraints. Nevertheless, it is not certain what the central government's reaction would have been had it not been experiencing its own fiscal crisis; it did not have the resources to bail out Odessa even if it had wanted to. Nevertheless, Odessa's ability to avoid accountability, the weakness of the legal framework that does exist, and the lack of progress in resolving the issue do not bode well for Ukraine's capital market development.

11.4   Conclusion

The Ukraine case is illustrative of the fact that difficulties in maintaining hard budget constraints apply to highly centralized countries as well as to more federal decentralized countries. Indeed, in Ukraine, the lack of hard budget constraints cannot be attributed to a single policy or channel, but rather is the result of systemic factors in many realms. There is no doubt that the transition from a central command economy to a market-driven economy is highly complex and challenging. Yet current circumstances in Ukraine suggest that elements critical to a successful market economy, including some degree of fiscal stability and budget constraints, continue to be lost in the fray as the country's political and economic systems develop. This chapter has examined three key mechanisms that influence the government's ability to impose a hard budget constraint and finds that each mechanism tends to support soft rather than hard budget constraints.

The system of intergovernmental finance continues to be unclear and predictable and lacks most of the features that might help to maintain hard budget constraints. The assignment of expenditures functions is so general that in some areas, it causes confusion over which level of government is to perform what function. In addition, many important social and redistributive functions that are better performed at the national level have been allocated to local governments. When there are disagreements among levels, there is no mechanism for resolution of differences. Local governments have little in the way of own revenues, and only a marginal part of their revenue comes from residence-based taxation. The bulk of their resources comes in the form of shared taxes and transfers. Shared taxes are split based on percentages set out yearly in the budget law, and these percentages vary dramatically from year to year, causing instability and unpredictability. For the most part, transfers are determined in a discretionary way based on both need and negotiation skills. Mismatches between expenditure and revenue assignments have created large vertical imbalances that manifest themselves in arrears. The system as it is currently structured gives localities every incentive to spend and increase arrears and little incentive to raise local revenues. All of these characteristics lend themselves to soft budget constraints.

In the political realm, although citizens have access to some information, decision making at all levels of government is most frequently inaccessible, and citizens have few mechanisms for holding their governments accountable on a day-to-day basis. The structure of government is such that even determining who is accountable for what can be difficult. Regional governors and rayon heads, as well as bodies that are part of the state administration, report upward to the president. The legislatures at each level of government are in theory accountable to their electorate. In practice, however, these legislatures are frequently subordinated and subject to control from above. There are few authorities that practice independent oversight. In terms of party politics, there is little in the way of party discipline, and the political scene remains generally chaotic. Of the over seventy-five parties that currently exist in Ukraine, few have proposals that place a high priority on economic efficiency. Given limited internal mobility, few citizens are in a position to vote with their feet.

Finally, capital markets generally, and subnational borrowing in particular, have few of the features that have played a role in strengthening hard budget constraints in other countries. The legislative and supervisory framework is weak, with implementation even weaker. There is no explicit legislation that states that the central government will not bail out local government debts. In addition, monitoring and oversight are limited, and there is no legislation that addresses insolvency or debt work-outs for local governments. All of these factors combined have led to the creation of instruments, such as veksels, that encourage soft budget constraints and create disincentives for addressing problems with arrears and noncash payment.

The case of the Odessa municipality default illustrates how many of these factors came into play in one of Ukraine's largest issuances of municipal bonds. While the central government did not bail out Odessa, the default demonstrates the links between the intergovernmental finance, political, and capital market spheres and suggests that many fronts will need to be addressed in order to support an effective subnational capital market.

These combined characteristics create an environment for the worst manifestations of opportunism. Extensive mandates and weak revenue autonomy lead to heavily constrained and inflexible local expenditures. Until recently, local governments had de facto borrowing autonomy. The center tries to use hierarchical authority to control the spending of subnational governments, yet it does not have the ability to micromanage its expenditures or borrowing. This leads to a degree of central government dominance in the system that is inconsistent with the requirements for capital market, land market, or electoral discipline. This dominance is also ineffective and creates a situation in which the central government allows localities to solve their financial problems creatively. At best, creditors and citizens receive their due payments in either discounted form, such as veksels, or through payment in kind, in lieu of salary arrears. Such allowance for creativity in solving budget constraints in whatever form possible, no matter how complex or how negative, wreaks havoc with discipline through the entire system. The situation will likely improve only with more effective central government management and rules that can be implemented and enforced.

Notes

1. Local revenues in table 11.2 include those raised at the center and allocated to local governments through shared taxes.

2. Consolidated figures include the pension fund but exclude state and local enterprises.

3. In spring 1999, a budget code was presented to parliament that included a much more specific set of expenditure assignments. The code was eventually passed and signed by the president in August 2001.

4. See Martinez-Vasquez, McClure, and Wallace (1995) for further detail on regulated and other local taxes in the early years of the transition.

5. In 2001, the government introduced a formula-based transfer system for the allocation of resources to the oblasts, using expenditure needs and revenues capacity as key criteria. In 2002 this formula was revised to incorporate allocation of transfers from the central government to both the oblasts and rayons. The use of a formula-based system has improved the predictability of transfer flows significantly but will require fine tuning over the coming years.

6. In Ukrainian legislation, balanced local government budgets are required; however, borrowing is classified as a revenue item rather than a financing item in local government accounts. Thus, local government accounts may be "balanced" at the same time as local governments borrow.

7. This section draws heavily on DeAngelis (1998).

8. This actually results in an even larger level of the subnational loans being written off through loan reclassification. It is common for subsidized oblasts to negotiate a reclassification for loans from Ministry of Finance to subsidies. It would be far more effective to promote good governance by disbursing these funds as grants in the first place. This would increase transparency.

9. The remaining local tax collections that constitute the major sources of local government tax revenues naturally lend themselves to payments in barter.

10. Appointed implementing agency by the mayor of Odessa, at the time, Edward Hurlitz, on July 24, 1997.

11. Of the first HRN2 million matured, roughly HRN1.3 million was due to the Ukrainian savings bank Sberbank and HRN7 million was due to individual entities and private citizens.

12. The next due bond payment, to Ukrinbank for HRN150,000, was not due until May 20, 1998. All bond payments made were made on May 11, 1998, by the following process: OMMFED transferred money to the city budget, the municipality then transferred the money to the Porta-Franco Bank, which redeemed the bonds. On May 11, HRN250,000 was transferred to the Porta-Franco Bank and apparently used to pay off the face value of private citizens' debt who held a total value of HRN363,165 of matured bond debt.

13. All Odessa municipal finance data were acquired from the Odessa municipality financial offices.

14. According to the Odessa municipality financial department documents, approximately 78 percent of the Odessa bonds were purchased by nonresidents.

15. This was the first debt issue by Odessa. Therefore, investors had no debt servicing history to judge. However, they could have easily projected an expected ratio of debt service to total revenue for Odessa in fiscal 1998. It would not have been difficult to consider Odessa's revenue growth from 1996 to 1997 (10 percent) and use this as base for 1998 revenue. Conservative estimates, that is, excluding revenue generated from the investment of the short-term bond issue, place projected debt service ratios at .44 for equal revenue growth from 1997 to 1998, .40 for doubled revenue growth, and .37 for tripled revenue growth. Even a best-case scenario of tripled revenue growth, highly unlikely, implies an extremely heavy debt service ratio.

16. Municipal budgets are negotiated between city financial office and the oblast government financial offices after the oblast concludes budget negotiations with the Ministry of Finance. Often budget plans for cities are not settled until midyear. Cities begin spending before they know their budget and then adjust expenditures when the budget is settled. This would have made it very difficult for Odessa to organize in the budget a reserve fund to retire the debt over its payback period, which in any case it did not do.

17. HRN83 million of the debt servicing came due in the last week of the repayment period from June 12 to June 15. Realistically, the only way Odessa could have successfully prepared to service this balloon debt would have been to prepare a sinking fund to retire the maturing bonds, which it did not do.

18. Since this figure represents nearly three times the entire Odessa budget, it is interesting to consider the financial reasoning of those issuing the decision and if they employed similar reasoning in their bond issue.

19. This was the approximate average of eighty-three short-term deposit transactions conducted by OMMFED with different investments in short-term securities and deposits at Ukrainian banks.

References

DeAngelis, Michael. 1998. "The Legal and Regulatory Framework for Ukrainian Subnational Borrowing." Background paper. Washington, D.C.: World Bank. Europe and Central Asia Region. Processed.

Martinez-Vazquez, Jorge, Charles McLure, Jr., and Sally Wallace. 1995. "Subnational Fiscal Decentralization in Ukraine." In Richard Bird et al. eds., *Decentralization of the Socialist State: Intergovernmental Finance in Transition Economies*. Washington, D.C.: World Bank.

World Bank. 1999. "Intergovernmental Finance in Ukraine: An Agenda for Reform." Washington, D.C.: World Bank, Europe and Central Asia Region. Processed.

12 Strengthening Hard Budget Constraints in Hungary

Deborah Wetzel and
Anita Papp

As is the case in most of the countries of Eastern Europe and the former Soviet Union, the system of intergovernmental finance in Hungary has undergone radical change since the early 1990s. The move from a centralized, government-controlled economy toward one that is more decentralized and driven by market forces poses particular challenges for maintaining hard budget constraints. The roles and responsibilities of different levels of government are in flux, and new institutions are evolving. All of this occurs in the context of important political changes.

The case of Hungary demonstrates that despite the intensity of such a transition, steps can be made to strengthen and maintain a hard budget constraint among different levels of government. Not all measures and aspects of the system contribute to hard budget constraints (indeed, some do just the opposite), but on balance, the Hungarian system has developed some noteworthy mechanisms for ensuring that most of the liabilities of the local levels of government are not passed up to the center. Perhaps of greatest importance in this area is the legislation established in 1996 on municipal debt adjustments. Three key channels that influence hard budget constraints are considered here: (1) the system of intergovernmental finance and the degree to which it encourages or discourages hard budget constraints, (2) the political incentive structure in Hungary and how it influences the actions of localities, and (3) the system of capital markets and the critical role its evolution has played in strengthening hard budget constraints in Hungary. Given the embryonic nature of land markets and the property tax, a fourth potential channel of land markets is not addressed.

12.1   The System of Intergovernmental Finance and Its Impact on Budget Constraints

It has been almost a decade since Hungary began to transform its system of intergovernmental finance, and much has been accomplished in putting sound foundations in place. Although the system of intergovernmental relationships has made great progress, some key features nevertheless imply that local governments do not face a strict hard budget constraint. In what follows, the main features of the intergovernmental system are reviewed, including the structure of government, expenditure assignments, the system of transfers, and budgetary processes.

12.1.1   The Structure of Government

Hungary is a relatively small country with a population of 10 million people, has a unitary government system with nineteen counties, twenty-three cities with county rank, and about 3,200 local (municipal) governments.[1] The constitution and the 1990 Law on Local Self Government establish that the basic rights of all local governments, regardless of size, are equal. This was a major step in the restoration of democracy in Hungary. However, the current legislation sets the stage for very fragmented activities with many small local governments required to provide a broad range of services. The average size of Hungary's municipalities (including Budapest) is 3,249 people, and over half of Hungary's municipalities have a population below 1,000.

The evolving legislation has tried to address issues of fragmentation and efficient service delivery through the role of the intermediate levels of government (the counties and regions). As a reaction to their dominant role in the system prior to transition, the role of counties was greatly minimized by the 1990 Law on Local Self Government. In 1996 the government adopted the Act on Regional Development and Physical Planning, which aims to create a new balance between the central and local governments through the development of new subnational decision-making units that will elaborate regional development plans and priorities. Development councils for larger regions have been formed on a voluntary basis, and these councils are expected to become more formalized over the next five years.

Local governments have also been encouraged to create municipal associations in order to provide services more efficiently. There are now over 200 such associations operating in Hungary (Hegedus and Peteri 1997). Act 135 on the associations and cooperation of local governments has the objective of improving the quality of public services. While several forms of association are recognized by the act, none are recognized as entities with the authority to dispose of their own resources, or to become the direct independent recipient of budgetary funds, or to be held accountable as an entity.

12.1.2   Expenditure Responsibilities

There has been a considerable decline in Hungarian public expenditure as a share of GDP since the early1990s, reflecting both efforts at stabilization and a more general shift in the role of government. Total general government expenditures as a share of GDP fell from 60.7 percent in 1994 to an estimated 45.3 percent in 1998. Of these, local expenditures fell from 17.4 percent of GDP in 1994 to 12.7 percent of GDP in 1998. As a share of total general government expenditure, however, the local government share has remained stable at about 22 percent of total expenditures.

The Law on Local Government defines a wide range of local government functions. Ten functions are mandatory: provision of potable water, kindergartens, primary education and daily child care, health care, welfare services, public lighting, local roads, cemeteries, and protecting the rights of national ethnic minorities. Other potential local services include urban development; protection of the built and natural environment; housing; water management; sewage; local public transportation; public cleansing; fire service; public safety; participation in energy supply; provision of public (cultural) places; subsidies to culture, art, and sports; and support to develop a healthy way of life among the community. The list of potential services to provide at the local level is very broad; even the ten mandatory functions imply considerable responsibilities.

The use of potential responsibilities, intended to promote flexibility, leaves a degree of ambiguity in the system that promotes a lack of clarity and contributes to softer budget constraints. Typically, communities try to carry out as many functions as they can because they are the basis for receiving budgetary transfers. The option of passing a voluntary responsibility to a higher (usually the county) level most frequently occurs when a community is not able to meet the costs of providing that service. The knowledge that services can be passed up may lead to less emphasis on efficient delivery and meeting budgets than when local governments have specific responsibilities that they must carry out. It thus acts to soften the budget constraint. In addition, a system in which local governments may choose to provide a service or not each year generally leads to instability in service provision and may discourage investment in the provision of a given service. It also suggests that some functions may be assigned to local governments that are too small too carry out the responsibility efficiently.

Local governments are accorded substantial responsibilities, but they are not always given autonomy over decision making in these areas. A wide range of laws and other sectoral legislation has an impact on local government activity (Pal-Kovacs 1998). For example, the Act on Public Education (1993) clearly separates the tasks assigned to county governments and precisely defines the institutional and professional requirements of implementation, thus imposing many measures on local governments. The act specifies that full operational expenses are not covered by the state budget and that the institution's own income is part of financing. At the same time, it specifies that the normatives (allocations of resources for service provision) of the state budget cannot be less than 80 percent of total expenses paid for public expenditure on education by local governments two years earlier. This does not promote local government autonomy or assist the rationalization of expenditure.

Another example is Act 114 on Health Care. This act specifies that patients are eligible for health care in a place that can be approached by the use of "regular public transportation." It also defines quite carefully the professional requirements and the division of labor among various workers and which tasks are to be financed out of the central budget. The basis of financing is the capacity utilization agreement, which decides how much assistance the owners and maintainers of the institutions are entitled to from the Health Insurance Fund, although each year this tends to come down to negotiation. The appendix of the act defines the evolution of hospital beds for the five coming years. Generally, the spirit of this act is that the local governments perform the role of owner of the infrastructure but have little role in decision making beyond that.[2]

The large number of sectoral laws that affect local governments and the annual budget laws generally have an important influence on local government autonomy that is not entirely in keeping with the Law on Local Government. Although the Law on Local Government legislates a large degree of autonomy to municipalities in service delivery and standards, both sectoral laws and the annual budget laws constrain that autonomy in practice by defining many of the specific terms and conditions under which localities must operate. In general, this undermines an effective system of intergovernmental finance and hard budget constraints because it separates decision-making authority from accountability and makes local governments less responsible for their decisions and their performance.

12.1.3   Revenue Assignments

As seen in table 12.1, the total revenues of local governments in Hungary fell from about 16 percent of GDP in 1993 and 1994 to 12.0 percent of GDP in 1998. In 1998, local authorities raised about 10 percent of their total revenue in local taxes. While this share is much greater than it used to be (it increased significantly after the fiscal stabilization of 1994–1995), it is still only a small portion of total local government revenues when compared with transfers. Local taxes include

Table 12.1
Local government accounts, 1993–1998 (% of GDP)

	1993	1994	1995	1996	1997	1998
Total revenues	16.1	15.9	13.6	13.0	12.8	12.0
Own current revenues	3.0	2.8	2.6	3.0	3.3	2.9
Revenue sharing with central government	1.4	1.5	1.7	1.6	1.7	1.9
Transfers from central government	7.7	7.3	5.7	5.0	4.3	4.2
Transfers from other public sector	2.8	2.9	2.4	2.4	2.4	2.2
Capital revenues	0.7	0.9	0.8	0.6	0.6	0.5
Other revenues	0.5	0.5	0.4	0.4	0.5	0.3
Total expenditures	17.2	17.4	13.9	13.0	13.1	12.7
Current expenditures	13.5	13.7	11.5	10.9	10.5	10.2
Capital expenditures	3.1	3.3	2.4	2.1	2.6	2.4
Other expenditures	0.6	0.4	0.0	0.0	0.0	0.1
Balance	−1.1	−1.5	−0.3	0.0	−0.3	−0.7
Net financing	0.5	1.0	0.2	0.3	0.3	0.4
Privatization revenues	0.2	0.3	0.5	0.7	1.0	0.5
Net borrowing	0.3	0.7	−0.2	−0.4	−0.7	−0.1
Residual	−0.6	−0.5	−0.1	0.3	0.0	−0.3
Memo item: Borrowing/borrowing cap (in %)	117	167	81	27	19	30

Source: Ministry of Finance.

taxes on business, property, tourism and the communal tax that are entirely within municipal discretion. In the case of these taxes, local governments can decide whether to levy the tax at all. They are also able to set the tax rates within given limits and are responsible for assessment and collection. In addition, municipalities receive a portion of shared taxes.

While in 1997, 81 percent of municipalities made use of at least one local tax, most localities do not employ the full range of tax instruments (or the maximum rates) at their disposal (Davey and Peteri 1998, 76). There are a number of possible explanations for this. First, given that national tax rates in Hungary remain relatively high, mayors are reluctant to add an additional tax burden because the political costs may be perceived as excessive. Second, local governments have garnered revenues through privatization and the selling off of assets, and this has reduced the need to assess taxes directly. However, the pool of salable assets is rapidly diminishing, and such a strategy is not sustainable. Finally, many of the incentives in the system of intergovernmental finance tend to encourage local governments to search for sources of finance from higher levels of government in the form of grants rather than bear the cost of imposing new or higher local taxes. This reliance on revenues other than local taxes tends to encourage local governments to be less careful with the use of resources because they do not bear the political brunt of having to raise the revenues for the financing of services.

12.1.4 *The System of Transfers*

Although the magnitude of transfers has declined over time (in both nominal and real terms), transfers still provide over two-thirds of local government resources (see table 12.1). In addition to the shared revenues (which constitute 12 percent of intergovernmental transfers in 1998), table 12.2 sets out the four principal mechanisms for transfers in Hungary: normative grants (45 percent of total), earmarked operating grants (39 percent), investment grants (8 percent), and deficit grants (1 percent). Overall the system of transfers in Hungary is one of the most advanced in the transition economies. Most of it is formula based, and there are some important mechanisms for correction of transfer amounts. However, the system is also highly complicated, promotes grantsmanship, deficit grants in particular, and tends to discourage a hard budget constraint.

Table 12.2
1998 budgeted intergovernmental transfers (HUF million)

Shared taxes	
Personal income tax	93,500
Vehicle tax	8,500
Tax on land rent	1,000
Shared revenues total	103,000
Normative grants	
Normative subsidies from central budget	369,633
Normatives total	369,633
Earmarked operating grants	
Subsidies to theaters	4,770
Subsidies for local fire protection	11,600
Other subsidies (centralized appropriations)	37,822
Supplementary grants to central public education	6,507
Funds from social security	190,900
Funds from EBFs	19,000
Funds from budgetary (chapters) institutions	8,000
Budgetary supplements and refunds	1,000
Earmarked operating grants totals	279,599
Investment grants	
Addressed and targeted subsidies	43,000
Accumulation revenues within the state budget	9,000
Investment grants with regional equalization	9,000
Decentralized targeted oriented grant	4,300
Investment grants Total	65,300
Deficit grants	
Deficit grant (ONHIKI)	7,200
Deficit grants total	7,200
Total grants	824,732

Source: Compiled from Ministry of Finance Documents. See Fox (1998).

Shared Taxes

Local governments receive percentages of the personal income tax (PIT) and vehicle and property transactions taxes, representing a budgeted Ft103 billion in 1998, or about one-sixth of local revenues.[3] Sharing of the PIT provides about 85 percent of total derivation-based revenues, or Ft89 billion in 1998. These derivation-based PIT revenues represent half of the 40 percent of national PIT revenues earmarked for local governments.[4] Local governments receive 50 percent of the nationally established motor vehicle tax and all of any additional revenues if they choose to impose a motor vehicle tax surcharge. Also, county administrative offices collect a tax on land and property transactions. Thirty percent is remitted to the municipality of origin, 35 percent stays with the county office to finance administrative expenses, and the remaining 35 percent is placed in a pool and provided to counties on a per capita basis.

The PIT distribution is made more equal by guaranteeing local governments a minimum per capita amount. In 1998, villages were assured of at least Ft8,000 per person and towns of at least Ft9,800 per person. The minimum amount has escalated rapidly in recent years and is expected to cost Ft33.34 billion in 1998, up from Ft9.9 billion in 1996. The minimum PIT distribution combined with the needs-based normatives described below provide a significant equalization component to the overall transfer system.

Normative Grants

Local governments and counties receive grants based on the value of a series of normatives.[5] Most of the revenue from normatives goes to towns and villages, but about Ft9.5 billion goes to the counties. The normatives effectively create a complicated formula-based grant structure, linked mostly to expenditure needs. The total amount of normative-based revenue going to a local governments is calculated by adding the amount to be received from each of the approximately fifty normatives.[6] The revenue provided according to the normatives is generally not earmarked and may be spent for any purpose that the recipient government deems appropriate. However, local governments' expenditure flexibility is often less than it appears, because delivery of many services is mandatory, and mandates and standards in other laws effectively prescribe certain expenditures.[7]

There are at least twenty-six education normatives, usually based on the number of students.[8] For example, Ft67,000 is provided for each kindergarten student and Ft96,000 for each secondary student in grades 11 through 13. In some cases, normatives are designed to provide incentives, as when a greater amount is given for nonresident students to encourage local governments to cooperate in service delivery. The Ministry of Culture and Education recognizes that the values are not based on an analysis of actual costs, but the normatives are set to cover education wages, or about two-thirds of total education costs. Cost estimates provided by local governments suggest that the normative values are sufficient to finance about 50 percent of kindergarten costs and about 80 percent of high school costs. There are also seven pupil-based education grants for ethnic schools and programs. The ethnic normatives differ from others in that the moneys are earmarked for specific purposes.[9]

Nine social welfare normatives are used. Beginning in 1998, the largest social welfare normative was split because of a concern that the range of social welfare programs was not being adequately provided. Basic social services for the general population are linked to three normatives, two of which are calculated using total population. Combined, these provide about 20 percent of the revenues from the social welfare normatives.

The other major normative is also provided on a per capita basis, with the amount transferred to local governments varying between Ft2,500 and Ft12,500 per person. The specific amount given depends on the extent of unemployment, percentage of the population that is paying PIT, and percentage of the population that is under age eighteen and over sixty. The intent is to provide greater funding to municipalities that have larger social welfare responsibilities, though in a recent analysis of spending patterns, the Ministry of Social Welfare found no relationship between program expenditures and factors in the formula. Beneficiary-based normatives are also used for social welfare purposes. Five types of beneficiaries are identified: homes for the elderly, homeless, disabled, and orphaned and for rehabilitation purposes.

Budgeting for normative grants begins with agreement between the government, parliament, and local governments on the total amount of normative grants to be distributed. In the fall prior to the budget year, as part of the national budget planning process, local governments provide estimates on the expected number of beneficiaries and the other factors that go into calculating the normative grants. The totals of these estimates are used to set average amounts (the normatives' values) that are the basis for the distribution across governments. Then the normative values are used to calculate the amount that each local government is to receive. The local governments do not learn the amount they are to get until March of the year the money is to be provided. Payments based on these calculations are regarded as preliminary, and the actual normative payments are determined after the number of beneficiaries is determined at year end. Local governments are paid additional amounts if they underestimated the number of beneficiaries and must repay excessive amounts if they overestimated beneficiaries. Interest is charged if the difference between the total estimated and total actual amount exceeds 5 percent. The State Audit

Office inspects some municipalities to determine if the counts given by schools and other sources are accurate. A final reconciliation based on the audits can result in additional payments to local governments or a return of money if there were overpayments.[10]

Earmarked Operating Grants

Funds from a number of grants are earmarked for operating purposes. These include annual grants for theaters and fire protection and the ethnic normatives. In addition, a series of grants termed *centralized appropriations*, totaling Ft37.8 billion in 1998, are given for earmarked purposes.[11] The specific purposes often vary by year. In 1998 these grants were made for children's programs (Ft9.5 billion), teachers' education (Ft3.5 billion), textbooks (Ft1.6 billion), severance pay for employees (Ft1.5 billion), subsidies for public utility user fees (Ft3.4 billion), public utility investment (Ft2.5 billion), and old age protection (Ft5.1 billion). Sectoral ministries also have revenues to finance delivery of specific operational programs, and some of these funds are granted to municipalities. In the budget accounts, these are termed *funds from budgetary institutions*. The total value of these programs is expected to be Ft8 billion in 1998. The grants from centralized appropriations and funds from budgetary institutions are normally provided directly through sectoral ministries and often have considerable flexibility for making the specific allocations of these grants.

Extrabudgetary funds provide operating revenues for earmarked purposes. The largest of these is the social security fund, which is used to finance health services, including those provided through municipalities. Much of the revenue is distributed as reimbursement for the costs of service delivery. The labor fund, the second largest, assists municipalities in financing unemployment insurance benefits for people whose initial unemployment benefits have expired.

Investment Grants

Investment grants are made to finance specific projects that normally are selected through competitive bidding processes.[12] The funds are generally earmarked, since they are intended for specific projects. The projects often involve implementation across several years, so the grantors frequently make multiyear commitments. Since local governments sometimes are unable to provide their cost share, the funds remain unused in about 10 percent of the cases where investment grants are made.

Four categories of investment grants are made directly through the central government budget. Other grants may be made through the centralized appropriations described above. For example, in 1998, an appropriation was budgeted to provide funding for sewer systems in Budapest and the twenty-two county rights cities.

Addressed and targeted grants are the largest categories of investment grants. Projects financed through these grants are estimated to comprise 60 percent of all local investments. Addressed grants generally provide 100 percent funding and are made for large projects with significant spillover benefits. The projects are selected by the parliament, normally after recommendations from the Ministry of Interior and the sectoral ministries.

Targeted grants are usually for smaller projects with lower spillovers and are matching grants with an average of 50 to 60 percent national and 40 to 50 percent local financing. The grant component is increased 10 percent if the grantee is a municipal association. Between 1993 and 1995, the percentage paid by the national government varied by type of project, from 90 percent for clean water projects to 30 percent for projects such as improving primary school classrooms.[13]

Priority areas for targeted grants are set in the annual budget law. The major priorities for 1998 were solid waste management, rehabilitation of dilapidated primary schools, medical equipment, and sewage and water systems that are linked together. Project applications are reviewed by the Regional Public Administration Service offices (TAKISZ), the Ministry of Interior, and the sectoral ministries. All municipalities are entitled to apply for targeted grants, and applications that meet all criteria are automatically approved, though funding may not be available.

Sectoral ministries and extrabudgetary funds make grants for investments in the same manner as they do for operational purposes. These revenues are termed *accumulation revenues* within the state budget in the financial accounts and are expected to total Ft9 billion in 1998, down from Ft10 billion in 1997. The extrabudgetary funds and sectoral ministries each have priority areas established by parliament, but each has considerable flexibility in making the grants. Local governments and nongovernment entities can apply for grants through these programs. Some programs require that a minimum percentage of the grants be made to local governments. For example, the Water Fund must provide 65 percent of its grants to local governments.

Three extrabudgetary funds make grants to local governments: the Environmental Protection, Road, and Water Management Funds.[14]

Two additional grant programs are administered through the County Regional Development Councils recently formed in anticipation of European Union accession. The regional councils are not local government bodies, though the councils include local government officials in addition to private sector representatives and others. These grant programs allow some investment funds to be allocated based on regional rather than national priorities. Grants from both programs must be made in accordance with the counties' development plans. The first program, regional equalization grants, is targeted for distressed and less developed municipalities.[15] The subsidy is 10 percent greater if the grantee is a municipal association. The second program, regional development targeted appropriations, is available for all purposes and for both local governments and nongovernment entities. Either grants or recurrent subsidies can be given. The grants are made with the requirement that at least 20 percent of the funding comes from the local governments, though there is no explicit mechanism for ensuring that local governments meet their commitments. The Regional Development Councils normally provide grants of under Ft200 million, and these programs are seen as being given in place of smaller targeted grants. Larger grants still must be obtained through the addressed and targeted programs. This financing dichotomy may provide incentives to increase or decrease the size of projects, depending on which structure offers the best terms and easiest access to grants.

In general, investment grants are poorly coordinated because of the huge volume of applications and large number of granting agencies. Municipalities often bid for every possible grant, with the hope of being successful on an acceptable share.[16] As a result, each municipality often applies for multiple grants for the same project and for grants for many different projects. There are many incentives for municipalities to bid for numerous grants. Uncertainty about the overall grant system encourages local governments to apply for funding, since they worry that financing will not be available later. All of the schools or other institutions in the same municipality may apply for the same grant program. Municipalities are not prohibited from simultaneously applying for and receiving grants for the same project through many of the programs described. For example, water and sewer projects can obtain funding through the addressed, targeted environmental protection, water fund, and regional grant programs, and possibly through others.

The large number of applications means that most grant programs have applications for much more financing than is available.[17] Further, the volume of applications precludes comprehensive reviews of projects by the granting agencies. In fact, projects are seldom evaluated in terms of their economic viability. Factors such as whether the local government appears able to finance its share of the cost play a much greater role in the decision process than does project quality, although the fungibility of resources means there is little information in a local government's apparent financial capacity. All of these considerations increase the chance that decisions are based on grantsmanship and political criteria. Small communities are disadvantaged the most because they do not have the resources to compete for as many projects.

Poor coordination results in four problems. First, project selection is likely to be suboptimal for allocations across sectors and choices of specific projects. Second, some projects have received grants totaling more than 100 percent of their cost. The quality of projects proposed by local governments can be seriously diminished since there is little incentive to select optimal projects when the entire cost is borne externally. Third, conflicts between agencies can result in project work commencing but the project never being completed as some sources of finance fail to materialize. The different granting sources may make financing available on inconsistent schedules, particularly for multiyear projects. Finally, significant administrative burdens are created for both local governments and the national government.

A resolution (Resolution 263 of 1997) was adopted to allow more effective coordination of the resources managed by the ministries and the extrabudgetary funds. The resolution also allows the treasury to monitor disbursements of grant funds from the different sources.[18] The system for implementing the resolution has not been fully developed as yet, and the resolution is best characterized as laying out an objective. The expectation is for a single tender to be issued for all projects of the same type. Local governments will apply once to the institution where the largest grant is being requested. The evaluation process for all prospective grants for each project is to occur simultaneously, with the institution receiving the proposal being responsible for coordination with other potential grantors. Presumably this will allow better overall targeting of investment funds, and reduce the possibility for excessive grants. However, at this point, ministries have different willingnesses to cooperate in the disbursement of grants, with some wanting an improved process and others wanting to maintain their independent ability to influence the grant-making process. While the resolution is a step in the right direction, it is insufficient to achieve optimal project selection, design, and implementation.

Deficit Grants

Deficit grants are provided to assist local governments that have deficits through no fault of their own or local governments that go bankrupt. The total value of these grants is budgeted to be Ft7 billion in 1998, up slightly from the 1997 level. During the year, the aggregate value of deficit grants can be increased using unspent funds from the addressed and targeted grant programs. The demand for these grants has been steadily increasing; in 1999, one-third of all localities applied for deficit grants.

To determine which local governments qualify for the grants, parliament has established a series of criteria: (1) municipalities must levy local taxes (in practice, this seems to be interpreted as meaning the business tax), (2) capital expenditures must be less than capital revenues (presumably to ensure that current revenues are not being used to finance investments), (3) there must be no financial deposits with a duration of three months or more, and (4) the grants are made only to assist governments in covering mandatory tasks.

Applications for deficit grants are to be made to the TAKISZ offices by April 30 and September 30 of the year in which the grant is to be made. The TAKISZ offices analyze the applications to determine whether the local governments qualify. The findings are reported to the Ministries of Finance and Interior, which make a joint decision on whether a grant should be made and for how much. The joint decision is then presented to parliament for review.

These deficit grants provide perhaps the most specific disincentives to a hard budget constraint in the system, because local governments can increase their grant revenues through behavioral changes. Local governments have an incentive to raise less of their own revenues and increase expenditures on mandatory services since deficit grants may potentially fill any gap. As a result, even local governments that appear to be in relatively good financial condition are able to apply for and receive deficit grants. Certain revenues can be shifted from covering mandatory to nonmandatory expenditures, and deposits can be held for periods just short of three months. The grant received by a municipality can depend heavily on its grantsmanship skills.

12.1.5 Budget Management and Execution

Since 1996–1997, the government has made substantial efforts to improve budgetary management and execution by improving transparency, identifying contingent liabilities of different parts of the government, and strengthening audit procedures (Polockova-Brixi, Papp, and Schick 1999). The government has strengthened the role and competency of the Ministry of Finance and established a modern state treasury. The treasury is responsible for budget execution at all levels of government, making payments from a single government account, controlling ex ante payments against budget appropriations, and recording them in a general ledger. This has greatly improved the efficiency of budget management.

In addition, the central government has been expanding its budget management system. The state budget proposal makes provisions for the main sources of potential financing pressure on the central government, and the official three-year forecast includes expected outlays on contingent government liabilities. The State Debt Management Office reports the full list of state guarantees from a comprehensive database of public liabilities and reviews the terms of guarantee contracts. The Ministry of Finance submits to parliament reports on the potential cost of both newly considered and existing programs of contingent government support. The State Audit Office is authorized to review government activities under both direct spending and contingent support programs, the adequacy of budgetary provisions and reserve funds with respect to risk exposure, and the management of contingent as well as direct explicit liabilities. The government has put in place both regulatory and enforcement mechanisms to minimize fiscal risks from local governments.

In general, the central government's efforts to improve budgetary management and especially to identify and monitor potential fiscal liabilities have been important in strengthening the hard budget constraint. Such measures help to expose existing liabilities and clarify who will undertake the responsibility for meeting those liabilities.

12.1.6 Implications of the System for Hard Budget Constraints

The system of intergovernmental finance in Hungary presents a mixed set of incentives for localities in terms of hard budget constraints. Numerous responsibilities are given to local governments as either mandatory or voluntary functions, and yet frequently fundamental decision making with respect to key management issues such as salaries and staffing remains with the center. This is particularly important in the social sectors of health, education, and social welfare. Given the small size of most local governments, many services are provided at a scale that is not economically efficient. Expenditure assignment therefore does not match the appropriate level for service delivery. Addressing this issue through the use of voluntary assignments gives localities an incentive to try to carry out functions that they are ill equipped to carry out and leads to losses that are eventually passed up to higher levels of government.

Local governments also face few incentives to increase their own resource taxes. They have access to a property, business, and communal taxes, but they make small use of these. So although the nature of local taxes is such that it largely taxes only local residents, because localities are not responsible for raising the bulk of their revenues through local taxes, the link between raising local revenues and using local resources effectively is weak.

While a good portion of the transfers received by local governments are based on a specific formula, overall the system of transfers is quite complex and administratively burdensome. The nature of the system is such that it encourages localities to spend extraordinary amounts of time documenting information for the normatives or sending out applications for the wide range of available grants. In the current system, a premium is placed on grantsmanship skills because transfers are the marginal source of revenue for most communities. Deficit grants in particular create a set of incentives that discourage a hard budget constraint. The deficit grant system is based on gap filling, and localities are squarely in a position to alter their behavior in ways that will improve their possibility of receiving deficit grants. Deficit grants, perhaps more than any other part of the system, weaken hard budget constraints and the ever-increasing number of applications for these grants testifies to their popularity.

Although most of the above factors tend to push in the direction of soft budget constraints, at the same time, the government has put in place some oversight mechanisms that help to encourage hard budget constraints. The allocation of resources based on the normatives has a corrective mechanism that is used regularly, with local governments returning resources in some cases or receiving resources in others. The strengthened treasury, audit, and budget management practices have helped to improve budget management. Finally, the specific identification of the liabilities of different levels of government and their regulation has made a critical difference in hardening budget constraints. Before turning to this, the next section considers how the changing political environment influences local government behavior.

12.2 Political Incentive Structures and Their Influence on Budget Constraints

A fundamental premise that underlies much thinking on decentralization and its benefits is that local citizens will be in a position to hold their local governments accountable for their actions through the political process. Through either exit (leaving a community) or voice (the press, election outcomes), citizens have a mechanism for expressing their views on the effectiveness of the local government in carrying out its functions. In this section, we consider the extent to which the existing political mechanisms in Hungary allow citizens to hold their local governments accountable and whether there is an incentive to do so. In Hungary, as in many other transition economies, a political evolution is occurring hand in hand with economic transformation. Strengthened democratic processes and evolving political mechanisms work both for and against hard budget constraints, but on balance it appears that these political mechanisms work in favor of strengthening the budget constraint.

12.2.1 The Balance of Power Between the Center and the Local Governments

In Hungary, as in many other countries of Eastern Europe and the former Soviet Union, decentralization of authority takes on a particular importance as a symbol of both new-found democracy and a backlash to the old regime. When communities were given the authority to create self-governing entities, Hungary's 1,500 local governments quickly blossomed into 3,200. Remnants of the old regime, such as the county structures, were quickly dispossessed of real authority.

This large number of small communities has two important implications for the balance of power among different levels of government and its role in the evolution of hard budget constraints. First, the large number of small local governments, their emphasis on self-determination, and the fragmentation that this implies have weakened the political strength of these communities. Although a range of local government associations exists, they often have difficulties agreeing on agendas and have not yet been able to come together to create any significant political force that would be able to offset the authority of the center. The small size of most governments also minimizes the "too-big-to-fail" phenomenon that often leads to central government bailouts. In such an environment, the potential for local capture is much less significant.

Second, the center, in terms of both the prime minister and the national legislature, plays a strong leadership role in determining and following through on agendas. While both the prime minister's office and the legislature see further reform of the intergovernmental system as a priority, there is little direct representation of local interests in either body. General considerations of what is politically sustainable are taken into account by these central bodies. For example, in the ongoing discussion of how to deal with regional policy and strengthening the intermediate levels of government, the center has hesitated to impose a new administrative structure from above, as has been recently done in Poland. Instead, the center is pursuing a gradual program in which these regional structures are more likely to evolve with the support of local governments. However, the balance of political authority remains with the central government, and local governments are not yet well organized or strong enough to present a serious obstacle to the center branches of government.

12.2.2 Information and Incentives to Monitor

An important criterion for effective accountability is for local citizens to have the necessary information and incentive to monitor their governments. In general, local citizens have good information to monitor the budget process. Proposed budgets are published in local gazettes and discussed thoroughly at city councils. But access to information does not extend as far as information on the contracts for public service delivery and pricing of services that local governments contract out. Information on public contracts is hard to obtain in Hungary. With only a few exceptions, local officials take the position that contracts by public entities with private companies are not public records, and therefore citizens do not have a right to obtain such documents. Nevertheless, Hungarian law appears to have stronger public access standards than western Europe. The constitution (Article 61) specifies that everyone has a right to information of public interest. Under the Hungarian Law on the Protection of Personal Data and Accessibility of Data of Public Interest (Act LXIII of 1992), the authorities are required to grant access for anyone to data of public interest unless the data are specifically restricted by law. Data of public interest are broadly defined to include "any information under processing by an authority performing state or local government functions or other public duties, except for personal data" (Art. 2, section 3). Hungary also has a Business Secrets Law, which protects "any fact information, solution or data connected to economic activities, the secrecy of which is in the reasonable interest of the entitled party." Hungarian Law does not set forth the relationship between the Accessibility of Data and the Business Secrets Law.

Unwillingness to provide information on public contracts seems to be based on a combination of European civil law distinctions between public and private matters, reactions to the invasiveness of the communist regimes, and a common view that private companies will be damaged by public disclosure of critical business data. Maintenance of the secrecy of public contracts is common in western Europe as well as in other central European countries, although there has been a strong trend toward allowing increased access.

As is the case with public contracts, submissions used for public price setting are not public record. For example the information submitted to the Ministry of Transport, Communication and Water Management, which is used to set water rates for some 45 percent of the country, are not accessible under current practice. Furthermore, the information used to justify local tariff subsidies for hundreds of water districts is not accessible. Without such information, it is impossible for local governments to make informed price setting decisions and develop expertise in the appropriate pricing of public services. It also implies that there is little or no accountability with respect to appropriate pricing (Baar 1999).

Difficulties in getting this information may result from the fact that given the configuration of intergovernmental finance discussed above, there is little incentive on fiscal grounds to monitor local governments and hold them accountable. Since most resources and many critical decisions in terms of staffing and standards are made at the center, local governments are in a strong position to deflect the efforts of citizens to monitor and obtain information about the center. Without a strong degree of autonomy, local governments are in a position to argue that much of what they do is determined by central government actions.

12.2.3   *Evolving Democratic Practices Lend Themselves to Strong Accountability*

While the balance of power between the central and local governments favors the center and incentives for gathering information and monitoring remain relatively weak, evolving democratic processes have created a strong degree of accountability at the local level.

One element of this is the acceptance of alternating political power and the smooth transfer of power between parties with opposing viewpoints. At the central level, Hungary is one of the transition countries that has managed to implement alternance among political parties. After many years of the Free Democratic Socialists, a new government coalition of the Young Democrat Hungarian Civic Party and the Agrarian Smallholders was elected in the spring of 1998. Such a transition of power is significant for local governments in that it signals the possibility for a change in power without automatic political destabilization. Democratic processes are strong enough to bear intense competition among parties at the central level, and this is also reflected in the keen political competition at the local level. This intense competition means that opposition parties closely scrutinize the activities of the group in power.

Local governments are elected and city councils are based on proportional representation. Typically, the focus of attention is on the individual mayor and the substance of his or her activities rather than on a strong allegiance to party. Indeed, there is a relatively weak connection between party activities at the national level and those at the local level. Local councils have the authority to remove mayors for demonstrated wrongdoing, and this has been done in a number of cases. The intense competition among parties at the local level creates an important system of checks and balances, which creates an environment in which local governments are routinely held up to scrutiny and held accountable for their actions.

Thus, although there are weaknesses in both the availability of information and the fiscal incentives to monitor, there are strong political incentives that create an environment in which local governments are closely scrutinized and held accountable for their actions. Overall, the existing political mechanisms have helped to improve oversight and strengthen the hard budget constraint.

12.3   Subnational Borrowing and Its Regulation

Since the beginning of the transition, Hungary's financial sector has undergone a profound transformation with a movement toward a private market-oriented financial system. These changes and regulatory developments have had an important influence on Hungarian capital markets as a whole, but they also have played an important role in clarifying subnational liabilities and regulating subnational debt. These evolving capital market institutions have played a critical role in strengthening the hard budget constraint that local governments face. In addition, it appears that they have led to rather conservative borrowing behavior on the part of local governments.

12.3.1   The Evolution of Capital Markets

The regulation of banking, capital markets, and insurance has evolved considerably since 1989, when financial markets were opened to foreign joint ventures and smaller private banks.[19] The 1991 Banking Act established the State Banking Supervision Agency. The 1991 National Deposit Insurance Act provided insurance coverage for individual deposits up to Ft1 million. The 1995 privatization law eliminated the required minimum public shareholding in banks, and between 1994 and 1997, both private and foreign ownership in the domestic banking sector increased considerably. In 1996, the Consolidated State and Financial Capital Market Supervision Agency was established for banking and capital market operations.

The outcome of these changes has been the development of an increasingly open and competitive financial sector. Short-term spreads have fallen, and the maximum maturity of government bonds has increased from three to seven years. Public debt as a share of GDP has fallen, as has the government's share in total credit demand. In 1998, the combined assets of the Hungarian banking sector reached 66 percent of GDP, while the total assets of the insurance industry amounted to 4 percent of GDP and those of the mutual and pension funds accounted for 5 percent of GDP. Stock market capitalization is now about 30 percent of GDP, although much of this is due to privatization rather than the issuance of new shares. Bond issues by private enterprises remain low, reaching only 0.2 percent of GDP. These changes in the system herald an increasing pool of resources that local governments could potentially tap.

12.3.2 Subnational Borrowing and Regulation

Prior to 1995, local governments relied more heavily on borrowing than has been the case since that time (see table 12.1). During the 1990–1995 period, regulation of subnational borrowing was relatively limited. The 1990 Law on Local Government stated that central government will not assume responsibility for local debt. Through 1995, no limits were placed on long- or short-term local government borrowing. Authorization to borrow was provided entirely by the city, and local governments could borrow for whatever purpose and at whatever terms the city council approved. The only additional regulation during this period was that revenues derived from the central government (shared revenue, transfer payments, normative grants, infrastructure grants) could not be used for loan repayment.

In 1994–1995, several problems with subnational debt began to materialize (Jokay 1999). Municipalities began to borrow long term to cover short-term current deficits. Many borrowed for nonessential, nonpublic purposes. Debt began to be rolled over from year to year, and in some localities late payments began to appear. In this environment, debtors and creditors began to lobby the national government for bailouts and for the government to assume an implicit guarantee for mandatory public functions. A series of impending defaults in early 1995 raised critical questions of how to reorganize and reschedule local debt and maintain critical public services without the central government's assuming responsibility.

Debt Service Limits
Beginning in March 1995, a series of new laws and regulations were put in place that had a fundamental impact on municipal access to capital markets. In March 1995, a decree was issued to place limits on new debt service.[20] The debt service limit states that annual debt service on obligations beyond one year in maturity can be only 70 percent of locally generated revenues net of the portion of locally generated funds used for operational expenses. Only local taxes, fees, business income, and the like can be used for debt service. Resources from one-time asset sales are excluded from debt service. In addition, cash flows are not

counted as debt, but all lease obligations, guarantees, bond issues, and bank loans are included if they are over one year. Finally, the legislation prohibits debt and debt guarantees secured only by collateral. Debt can be secured only by a freely available cash flow.

In the short run, these limits suggest a dramatic scaling back of municipal borrowing given the limited amount of own source revenues. This is borne out in practice. As seen in table 12.1, net borrowing of local governments shifted from 0.7 percent of GDP in 1997 to –0.2 percent in 1995 and dropped further to –0.7 percent in 1997. In 1994, local borrowing represented 167 percent of what the cap would have been had it been in place in 1994. In 1995, local borrowing fell to 81 percent of the cap and then dropped even further to only 19 percent of the cap in 1997. While the debt service limits in part led to a dramatic reduction in borrowing in the short run, they create positive incentives for the increased collection of local revenues and reductions in operational expenses. They also promote better cost accounting.

The Municipal Bankruptcy Law

Hungary is the first country in the region to put in place legislation regulating local government insolvency and bankruptcy. Act XXV of 1996 on Municipal Debt Adjustment has several objectives. The foremost is to prevent and preempt municipal defaults. In addition, the legislation aims to provide a clear administrative procedure for creditors to follow in the event of insolvency and to provide reorganization and workout procedures for the municipality. The legislation makes clear again that the central government will not guarantee local borrowing and specifies that sovereign guarantees require an act of parliament and are specifically limited by the budget law. The law also sets out an approach that will ensure the provision of mandatory services even during periods of insolvency or workout.

The political consensus necessary to put such a law in place resulted from the period of dramatic fiscal instability in 1994–1995. Parliamentary parties on both the opposition and the government side agreed that municipal borrowing posed a potential risk to the central budget. There was also an agreement that in order to achieve a balanced budget, there should be a mechanism to maintain fiscal discipline. Two views existed in the parliament: (1) a centralist view that intended to incorporate local governments into the treasury system and access to capital markets would be subject to a central approval process and (2) a liberal approach that stated that consequences for bad economic decisions should be taken up locally. The latter approach contained a message not only for the municipalities but for the banking sector as well. After the costly waves of bank consolidations in 1993–1994, it was a statement addressed to OTP, the biggest creditor of the municipal sector, that no further rescues from the state could be expected.

The Socialists, as the majority coalition party, were not in the position to advocate the first solution, as they would have been accused of recentralizing government. The Free Democrats, the minority coalition party, never supported the first solution. Hence, when the law was submitted to parliament as a solution for fiscal risk generated at the local level, the ruling party coalition could easily ensure a two-thirds majority. Nonetheless, opposition members of parliament also voted in favor of the law for the general understanding of the need for fiscal stability. Thus, there were no significant debates concerning the law.

The process of debt adjustment starts the day a petition request arrives at court (see figure 12.1).[21] The process can be started by either the municipality or the creditor if the municipality meets one of the following conditions:

• The municipality or its agency has not paid a certain invoice or has not responded to a call for payment from a creditor not required to give an invoice and has not disputed or paid the invoice within sixty days of presentation.

• The municipality or its agency has not paid a debt it recognized within sixty days of the due date.

• The municipality or its agency has not paid an obligation called for by a binding court decree.

• The municipality or its agency has not paid an obligation called for by a previous binding bankruptcy court decree.

If the court determines that one of the above conditions holds, it will issue a decision to commence the debt adjustment process and publish the decree in the Enterprise Registry (the publication date is the official start of the process). The decision to begin the process will also correspond to the appointment of a financial trustee. The mayor of the municipality must ensure that the notification of creditors also appears within the Enterprise Registry and at least two national daily newspapers within fifteen days. The mayor must inform the county chief administrator, the budget and administrative office, the municipality's bank, and all the financial institutions serving the budgetary agencies

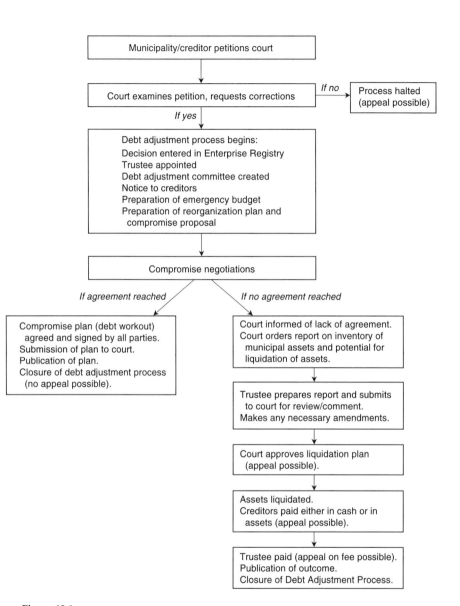

Figure 12.1
The debt adjustment process.

of the municipality, the applicable tax, customs, social security, and health insurance office.

After the beginning of the process, all debts come due, even those that are not current. Creditors have sixty days to file a claim against the locality. If they do not do so, they may not enforce a lien or take collection action against the municipality until two years have passed since the completion of the adjustment process in accordance with the court's settlement decree. At the same time, all foreclosures, collections, and lien enforcements cease. Once the process begins, municipalities are not allowed to assume additional debt, cannot establish enterprises, cannot purchase ownership interests in enterprises, and cannot service debt assumed prior to the petition for debt adjustment except for those specifically stated in the crisis management plan.

The financial trustee basically takes on the job of monitoring the business operations of the municipality, ensuring the provision of mandated public services, implementing the emergency budget, and briefing both creditors and government agencies of progress. An interesting provision of the law is that within ninety days of the commencement of the process, the financial trustee may petition the relevant court to annul contracts signed by the municipality up to a year before the filing of the adjustment petition. Contracts and obligations signed by the municipality that the trustee considers to be unduly disadvantageous to the municipality or unduly disadvantageous to a third party fall into this category (although an affected party may file a complaint in response).

In addition to the trustee, a debt adjustment committee is formed with the following members: mayor, notary clerk, chairman of the finance committee, and an additional city council member. With the exception of the mandatory local services specified in paragraph 10 of the Law of Local Government, the debt adjustment committee has full authority to decide on all issues. A draft resolution containing the emergency budget must be submitted thirty days after the commencement of the debt adjustment process.

After the emergency budget has been accepted, the financial trustee and debt adjustment committee prepare a reorganization program and proposal for compromise (debt workout) that forms the basis for negotiations with creditors. If the municipality fails to prepare these proposals within 150 days, the creditors can propose their own alternative. Both the reorganization plan and the compromise proposal are distributed to the local council and to all creditors, who are invited to compromise (debt workout) negotiations. If more than half of the creditors having claims (representing at least two-thirds of the value of the claims) can come to agreement with the municipality on a compromise, then the compromise can be accepted. Disputed claims (and their value) are treated separately. The compromise agreement must be set out in writing and include the proposal for compromise accepted by the creditors; methods of execution and control; methods of satisfying the creditors; possible adjustments of deadlines, remission, or canceling of liabilities, and all those considered essential to restore or maintain the solvency of the local municipality; and confirmation of the compromise by the creditors and the local municipality. If the agreement meets the requirements of the act, the court finishes the debt adjustment procedure and orders the decision to be published in the Enterprise Registry. There is no right of appeal.

When no compromise can be reached, the court moves to the process of asset liquidation. Liabilities are paid initially out of the emergency draft budget, and in the meantime, the financial trustee works out a plan for performance of mandatory functions, identifies which assets are needed to perform these functions, and submits this report to the court, the municipality, and all the creditors for their comment. After issuance a court decree, the financial trustee must within thirty days list the claims of creditors according to their order of priority, and within sixty days must try public liquidation of the municipal assets available for debt adjustment at the highest possible price on the market. Within thirty days after the deadline, the financial trustee will make a proposal splitting the assets among the creditors. Creditor claims can be satisfied by money or by transferring the unsold assets to the creditors, according to the priority of and proportion of the creditors' claims. The order of the priority among creditors is set out as follows:

1. Regular personnel remuneration, including severance payment due to dislocation for public service

2. Claims ensured by collateral, mortgage up to the value of the pledged property provided the property was pledged six months before the debt adjustment procedure started (if there is more than one lien on the same property, order of performance is defined by the Civil Code)

3. Claims of the government related to a previous settlement for debt adjustment, repayable subsidies, and other central budget subsidies

4. Social security debts, taxes

5. Other liabilities

The financial trustee must report immediately to the court when the job is done. The court will finish the procedure by decision, and no appeal can be lodged against this decision. At the same time, the court will relieve the financial trustee from his job and set his fee. Finally, the closing of the debt adjustment procedure is published in the Enterprise Registry.

Since the Municipal Debt Adjustment Law came into force, there have been nine municipal bankruptcy cases, two of them still under way. The immediate cause of the bankruptcies includes investment in a failed business activity, guarantees issued without knowledge of the council, and local public investment programs (linked with gas supplies) beyond the financial capacity of the municipality. No cases have occurred because of current operations of municipalities, reflecting the role of deficit grants in preventing such cases. (World Bank 1999a, 5). Typically the size of the communities was under 10,000 citizens, and although the size of the loans involved was small relative to the Hungarian capital market (Ft100 million or $400,000), the amount was typically large compared to the size of the locality's budget. In all of these cases, a compromise agreement was found and implemented. In some cases, these agreements relied on selling off the business asset under consideration; in others, terms of repayment were stretched out over time. In no case did the central government provide assistance.

Regulation of Securities

Bond issues by local governments are authorized in Law Decree 28 of 1982, and the issuance and trading of local government bonds is regulated by Act CXI on Securities, Capital Market and on the Stock Exchange. This sets information disclosure and audit requirements for localities. Local government borrowings (both bonds and loans), as well as guarantees and other contingent liabilities, are recorded ex post by the Local Government Department of the Ministry of Finance as part of the yearly submission of budget execution. Public bond issues are also registered with and must be authorized by the Supervision Commission, which was established under Act CXII of 1996 on Credit Institutions and Financial Undertakings.

For public offerings, issuers are required to disclose information on their financial and income position and operations, through both annual reports and audits (Annex IV of Act CXI specifies the information that must be disclosed in the prospectus). Issuers are required to ensure the inspection of their annual reports by investors and at the same time send the annual report to the Supervision Commission. Local governments are also required to publish in a daily newspaper and in the exchange journal all information directly or indirectly affecting the value or return of the securities.

Supervision of local debt issues is under the authority of the Supervision Commission, but with a relatively limited number of local bond issues, the commission's experience is limited. To date, it has focused on ensuring that issuance procedures have been met and that supporting documentation is within the law. There is little activity on the part of ratings agencies or other institutions that might assess local government creditworthiness.

The legislation also covers audit. All county governments, cities with county rights, the capital city and its districts, and any city with annual expenditure above Ft100 million or that would like to borrow are required to have an annual audited balance sheet. An increasing number of localities are thus required to have an independent audit each year. The State Audit office may at any time audit a locality, but given the State Audit Office's limited capacity, only a small number of localities out of the total can be audited each year. In addition, the State Audit Office carries out thematic audits in which it focuses on a particular issue across a sample of local governments.

12.3.3 Implications for Hard Budget Constraints

Municipal borrowing in Hungary had never been substantial, but the effect of implementation of the above measures is effectively to reduce local government borrowing by half.[22] The legislation states clearly that the central government will not bail out local authorities and has backed this up by staying out of municipal bankruptcy negotiations and workouts. The detailed procedures and processes set out by the above legislation have several implications.

First, localities are limited in the sources of funds they can use to repay debt, which places a strong constraint on borrowing as long as own revenue resources remain low. This provides an incentive for local governments to make an effort to raise own resources. In turn, the greater use of own revenues is also likely to have the effect of increasing accountability because citizens want to be sure that their taxes are used well.

Second, the detailed processes and procedures set out for municipal debt adjustment lay out a clear picture that in one way or another, the locality will ultimately be responsible for repayment of the outstanding debt. Localities are thus offered a conditional bailout in which they get a break on immediate payment of the debt if they choose to cooperate and develop workout agreements. Alternatively, they may choose not to cooperate in discussions with creditors, but in this case they will be subject to asset liquidation. Either way the measures taken are formalized as court decisions and given special oversight. Localities seem to have a clear incentive to cooperate, since forced asset liquidation may yield little for the locality. All of the existing bankruptcies have been resolved either prior to compromise negotiations or through such negotiations.

An interesting aspect of the law in the context of transition economies is the reliance on an independent court system for implementation. In Hungary, independence is granted to courts, judges, and prosecutors by the constitution. The 66/1997 Act on Organization and Management of Courts and 67/1997 Act on the Legal Status and Remuneration of Judges regulates the mechanisms that ensure that independence. Judges are appointed by the president of Hungary based on the proposals of the National Council of Justice, an independent, professional, self-governing body of selected judges. Judges' appointment is open-ended, except the head of the supreme court and that of the regional high courts who is appointed for six years. In practice, courts and judges seem to be fairly independent. Although corruption occurs, it is not widespread due at least in part to the fact that among civil servants, employees of the court are fairly well paid. Although they are legally civil servants, there is a separate wage table and adjustment scale for them. The general professional quality of the courts requires some improvement, and processing of cases is usually slow. Corruption is usually linked to achieving faster processing and finalization of cases. The lengthy time required for successful completion of court action has created an incentive for local governments and creditors to come to an agreed workout plan rather than work their differences out in the courts.

The Municipal Bankruptcy Code also has a feature that may have special significance in transition countries. Given their new-found autonomy after years of dominance from above, the imposition of a trustee to manage a local affairs has a psychological cost that may be stronger than in localities in other nontransition economies. Localities have only recently had some degree of autonomy restored (however limited by the center), and the loss of this autonomy and self-determination is not something that most cities would currently take lightly. Both local governments and local councils treat issues that would risk this autonomy with great attention. Localities are likely to err on the conservative side with respect to determining what they can borrow.

Finally, these regulations have also strengthened disclosure, supervision, and oversight, thus increasing transparency and reducing the potential that a locality will be able to borrow significantly more than it can afford. In addition, central oversight on the part of the Supervision Commission prevents localities from going overboard.

In sum, the measures and regulations that have been undertaken with respect to subnational borrowing and municipal debt adjustment provide strong institutional mechanisms supporting hard budget constraints. Bankruptcies that have occurred have for the most part been resolved relatively quickly and to date without recurrence. To some degree, the effectiveness of these mechanisms can be seen in the greater conservatism that localities are demonstrating with respect to taking on new debt. Indeed, local debt remains well below the thresholds set out by the cap. It will be of great interest to see whether these mechanisms maintain their effectiveness as local borrowing increases, as it is likely to do on the coming years.

12.4   Conclusion

This chapter has examined three mechanisms that can strengthen or undermine hard budget constraints. On balance, the system of intergovernmental finance discourages hard budget constraints in a number of ways. By leaving some expenditure assignments uncertain, it affords localities the opportunity to overspend and then off-load to others functions that are not financially sustainable. There is little or no link between taxation and the services provided, given the small amount of own revenues. Most important, the system of grants, and especially deficit grants, gives localities very strong incentives to spend and very weak incentives to tax. In addition, the incentives created by the system of transfers imply that little or no emphasis is placed on cost-effectiveness and accountability for mandatory services (which can be bailed out by a deficit grant), whereas other voluntary functions must be cost-effective (they are subject to the municipal debt adjustment act).

The political mechanism of political accountability tends to strengthen hard budget constraints. The potential for local capture is limited, and given the large number and small size of localities, they are unable to convince the central government to provide bailouts. As pressures from below mounted for bailouts, the central government quickly put together a range of legislation that would hold local governments to payment of their liabilities. Finally, the intense competition among parties at the local level means that governments are constantly under scrutiny by the opposition and are held to a high degree of accountability.

The mechanism of regulation of subnational borrowing strongly supports the maintenance of hard budget constraints. It makes it clear that the central government will not take on the liabilities of local governments, and the government has followed through on this in practice. The legislation promotes transparency and accountability and sets out clear rules and procedures for dealing with bankruptcy within a community, which are implemented through the use of a trustee and overseen by the courts.

It is impossible to know exactly what weight each of these mechanisms carries. In the current environment, it seems that factors supporting hard budget constraints outweigh those that undermine them. The effectiveness of the system as a whole can be diminished only by those parts of the system that create the wrong incentives. Certainly it seems clear that before considering borrowing, localities go to great extremes to receive transfers from the central government. A soft budget constraint with respect to mandatory services (through deficit grants) combined with a hard budget constraint on other services does influence spending decisions and allocations.

Overall, however, the Hungarian case demonstrates that hierarchical arrangements can be effectively used to mitigate the worst manifestations of the soft budget constraint problem. The basic incentives set out by the system (allocation of responsibilities, limited local revenue autonomy, and grants) are not ideal for encouraging market-based hard budget constraints. In addition, land, capital, and even political markets (elections) are not yet strong enough to play the disciplining role that they do in some advanced industrial economies. However, the system is not overwhelmed by soft budgets because of the hierarchical constraints that have been put into place.

Institutional mechanisms have been developed that ensure that localities will ultimately be held accountable for any opportunism they engage in. The Municipal Debt Adjustment Law makes it clear that there will be no bailouts by the central government and that local governments are responsible for their own debts. In placing the process in the hands of an independent court system and in the hands of trustees, the government loses some discretion but strongly sends a signal of the seriousness of its no-bailout commitment. In addition, the government places limits on local government access to credit markets. Over time, as both credits and other markets develop and create their own disciplinary force, such controls are likely to become less necessary. Although such mechanisms help to protect against soft budget constraints and fiscal instability, they are not so blunt that voters and creditors simply see local governments as the administrative arms of the central government. While local government autonomy is limited in some parts of the system, ultimately the localities are responsible for their own actions.

The Hungarian case thus suggests a method of addressing soft budget constraints in transition economies. At early stages of decentralization, create good laws that make it very clear that local government overspending will be painful. If high levels of vertical imbalance persist, place some borrowing restrictions on local governments. Of course, the methods also rely on an independent court system and an ability to monitor and enforce rules. Over time, as markets develop and incentives in the intergovernmental finance system are improved, such restrictions may eventually be gradually reduced. Of utmost importance, however, is sending a clear signal to localities, voters, and creditors that local governments will be responsible for repayment of their own debts.

Notes

1. This section draws heavily on World Bank (1999b). For a discussion of developments of the intergovernmental finance system in the early 1990's, see Bird, Wallich, and Peteri (1995).

2. Other sectoral acts and laws that have a significant impact on local government activities are the Act on Social Administration and Social Care; the Act on Protection of Cultural Possessions, Public Library Service and Public Education; the Act on Protection against Fire; the Act on the General Rules of the Protection of the Environment, and the Act on the Shaping and Protection of the Built Environment, and the Yearly Act on the Budget.

3. Municipalities also receive 30 percent of environmental fines.

4. The other half is used for equalization purposes and is allocated based on a set of normatives discussed below.

5. This section draws heavily on Fox (1998).

6. Analysts have given different totals for the number of normatives, depending on how normatives are counted when multiple normatives are applied to a single situation.

7. Also, recipient governments can expect political pressure from advocates for each service to spend the revenues for the purposes on which the normatives are based.

8. Many of the beneficiary normatives require careful compilation. Schools must follow detailed instructions on how to calculate the number of students. Many normatives, such as the number of students in classes 9 and 10, the number in classes 11 through 13, and the number eating lunch at school, may apply to the same school, so many separate counts must be kept. One case was observed where twenty-three normatives applied to a single school. Generally these normatives are based on the average number of students each day, so daily counts (and sometimes more than once per day) must be maintained. Further, the academic year crosses two fiscal years, so schools and local governments will normally need to follow two different sets of definitions and normative values during the same academic year.

9. The normatives are generally described in Annex 3 of the budget, but each of the earmarked grants is contained in a separate annex. For example, the ethnic normatives are presented in Annex 8.

10. The State Audit Office examines normative grants in about 500 municipalities per year and performs comprehensive audits in about 40 to 50 other municipalities.

11. Accumulation revenues inside the state budget and funds from budgetary institutions are not categorized as centralized appropriations because they may also be provided to entities other than local governments.

12. In most cases, the transfer of these funds occurs as payment on the basis of invoices for actual expenditures rather than through direct transfers to local governments.

13. See Hegedüs (1996).

14. The extrabudgetary funds are financed through a variety of means. For example, the Road Fund is mostly financed with an excise tax on fuel, but the portion available for grants to municipalities (less than Ft1 billion) comes from a 25 percent share of the central government's part of the motor vehicle tax.

15. Formally, the regional development subsidies are made through the Ministry of Environment and Regional Development, and the regional equalization grants are made through the Ministry of Interior. The ministries use a scoring system (which is approved by parliament) to determine the distribution of revenues across counties and then allow the Regional Development Councils to make the specific allocations.

16. One municipality indicated that it submits as many as 1,000 applications annually, though only a small portion of these request significant resources.

17. For example, the Road Fund annually receives about 1,000 applications, of which it can fund about 150.

18. Resolution 263 also permits the treasury to ensure that debts owed to the central government are met prior to any disbursement of funds.

19. This section draws on World Bank (1999a).

20. Effective January 1996 this debt service limit was added to the Law on Local Government.

21. The following discussion is based on Charles Jokay's unofficial translation of the Act on Municipal Debt Adjustment (Law XXV of 1996) passed on March 26, 1996, by a margin of 84 to 16 percent.

22. Until the mid-1990s, Hungary's municipal debt market was dominated by the National Savings Bank, which offered short- and medium-term lending instruments to municipalities that held accounts with the bank. Since 1994 OTP's market dominance has declined, and other banks have begun to compete for market share, although the demand for municipal borrowing has declined.

References

Baar, Kenneth. 1998. "Contracting Out Municipal Services: Transparency, Procurement and Price Setting Issues—The Case of Hungary." Funded by USAID.

Bird, Richard M., Christine Wallich, and Gábor Peteri. 1995. "Financing Local Government in Hungary." In Richard Bird, Robert Ebel, and Christine Wallich, eds., *Decentralization of the Socialist State*. Washington, D.C.: World Bank.

Davey, Kenneth, and Gábor Peteri. 1988. Local Government Finances: Options for Reform. Nagykovácsi, Hungary: Pontes Ltd.

Fox, William. 1998. "Intergovernmental Finance in Hungary: Summary and Evaluation." Background paper, World Bank.

Hegedüs, József. 1996. The Subsidy System of Municipal Infrastructure Developments. Budapest: Metropolitan Research Institute.

Hegedus, Jozsef, and Gábor Peteri, eds. 1997. *The Modernization of Local Government Finances and Financial Management in Hungary*. Proceedings of a conference organized by the Metropolitan Research Institute, Budapest. Strasbourg/Paris/Washington, D.C.: Fiscal Decentralization Initiative of the Council of Europe/OECD/World Bank.

Jokay, Charles. 1999. The Hungarian System to Regulate Subnational Borrowing. Paper presented at conference, at Fiscal Decentralization in the Czech Republic, Hungary and Poland: Choices Ahead and Lessons for other Countries in the Region. USAID Conference, Prague, June 24–25.

Pal-Kovacs, Ilona. 1998. "The Legal and Regulatory Background of Fiscal Decentralization and the Characteristic Features of Its Operation in Hungary." Background paper, World Bank.

Polackova Brixi, Hanah, Anita Papp, and Allen Schick. 1999. *Hungary: Fiscal Risks and the Quality of Fiscal Adjustment*. Washington, D.C.: World Bank.

World Bank. 1999a. "Developing a Competitive Sub-National Finance Market in Hungary; Policy Issues and Challenges." Subnational development program.

World Bank. 1999b. "Intergovernmental Finance in Hungary: Continuous Progress, Continuous Change and Options for Reform." Subnational development program.

V   Conclusion

13   Lessons and Conclusions

Jonathan Rodden and
Gunnar S. Eskeland

In chapter 1, we pointed out a tension between optimistic theories of decentralization and a growing number of less promising case studies. Despite its intuitive appeal, improvements in efficiency, accountability, and governance associated with decentralization are contingent on a variety of social, cultural, and especially institutional features that are unique to each country, or perhaps even each region within countries. In particular, this book has demonstrated that fiscal and political decentralization may create incentives that soften budget constraints. The most challenging goal of this study is to explore how meaningful decentralization and hard budget constraints can go hand in hand.

The problem of soft subnational budget constraints is rooted in a commitment problem at higher levels of government. Central government commitment to a firm framework comes easily if the center is disinterested in local performance problems. However, it is more typical that the center *has* an interest, and thus is vulnerable to bailout demands (recall the fire truck analogy from chapter 1). Thus, our focus is on the underlying causes of the central government's vulnerability, as well as steps that can be taken to facilitate commitment.

Our analysis points out two rather different frameworks consistent with subnational fiscal discipline. A system might work well without hierarchical mechanisms if it is characterized by very low levels of external effects, or a central government that is either quite limited in its powers, unambitious in its goals, or in possession of strong commitment facilities. For instance, we argue that the United States has good commitment in its Constitution, history, high number of states, and low levels of externalities emanating from the constrained ambitions of the center and the large size of the states. But this book has made it quite clear that there are important differences between a country like the United States, which was never centralized, and one like Hungary, which attempts to decentralize after having a long experience with a strong, ambitious central government.

Among our case studies and beyond, a highly constrained and unambitious central government seems to be a rarity among decentralized systems—even long-established federations where reasonably autonomous subnational governments are the dominant employers and spenders in the public sector. In contrast with the United States, the German constitution reflects a much higher level of ambition when it spells out a guarantee of "equivalent living conditions" in all of the federal states. In several of the case studies, we see that such ambitions may easily result in bailouts if institutions are not carefully structured to curtail opportunism. Most of the case studies describe some combination of the fiscal, political, and financial factors—discussed in chapter 1 and formalized in chapter 2—that make the central government vulnerable to manipulation by the subnational governments and as a result unable to "just say no" and stand by it. When these factors are present, a prima facie case exists for hierarchical constraints. In fact, it is difficult to escape the conclusion that in many newly decentralizing countries, the best way to harden budget constraints, at least in the short to intermediate term, is for the central government to improve and clarify rather than abdicate its role in overseeing subnational governments. Complete central government disengagement from local fiscal affairs is neither possible nor desirable in newly decentralizing countries. However, we will add qualifications to this reaction, arguing that central involvement must be based on clear, transparent rules rather than discretion, and we will examine a variety of background and institutional conditions that might undermine or bolster the center's effectiveness in enforcing such rules and regulations.

The case studies describe many contexts—for example, small jurisdictions with limited tax autonomy and a historically strong central government—in which the center simply cannot commit to a no-bailout policy. In highly centralized countries like Norway, we have seen that the center can respond to this vulnerability by tightly regulating and monitoring subnational fiscal decisions. In this respect, one might place Norway opposite the United States as two ends of a continuum. However, Norwegian-style hierarchy is simply not plausible in vast federations like India where subnational assertions of power come about descriptively and also make sense normatively. For the majority of the cases under analysis, neither the American nor the

Norwegian solution is practical. The case studies hint that central government involvement in local public finance can be honed and made to supplement developing market mechanisms rather than obstruct their growing role. To the extent the center cannot credibly give up its powers and commit to a no-bailout policy, institutional mechanisms such as borrowing controls and monitoring have a role to play. Market discipline can grow, but only as a process of gradual central government disengagement. In each round of play, local officials and their constituents (voters, creditors, asset owners) learn about an evolving incentive framework, especially concerning the credibility of the central government's institutions. In general, however, the basic institutions that support or undermine this commitment cannot be changed overnight, and the learning process is likely to be gradual.

This chapter proceeds by providing a brief overview of the case studies in section 13.1 to place them in two dimensions: the severity of the soft budget constraint problem and the institutional framework for subnational finance. In section 13.2, we discuss systems characterized by a disengaged higher-level government that relies mostly on market mechanisms, focusing on two cases from North America. We discuss the institutional, political, and historical conditions under which such a framework can be successful. In section 13.3, we discuss hierarchical oversight and control mechanisms, examining both successful and unsuccessful attempts to impose fiscal discipline from above. Section 13.4 concludes with our assessment that in many cases of decentralization, the path toward improved fiscal discipline involves a judicious combination of nondiscretionary hierarchy and evolving market mechanisms. Section 13.5 provides concluding reflections.

13.1 A Schematic Overview of the Case Studies

To begin our review of the case studies, it is useful to ask which countries experienced the most severe and persistent manifestations of the soft budget constraint problem. Although it is by no means a perfect measure, it is helpful to compare the development of aggregate fiscal balance for the subnational sectors under examination.[1] These data are presented in figure 13.1 for the developing and transition country cases (excluding China and Ukraine, for which appropriate data were not available) and in figure 13.2 for the OECD cases. Modest subnational deficits are certainly no cause for alarm, nor are large temporary deficits brought on by unexpected shocks. Figure 13.1, however, shows

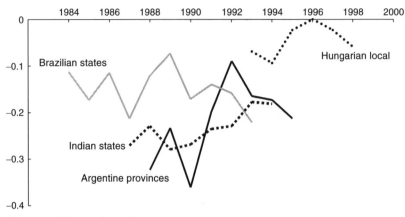

Figure 13.1
Subnational deficit as share of revenue: developing and transition country cases. *Source*:
IMF *Government Finance Statistics*.

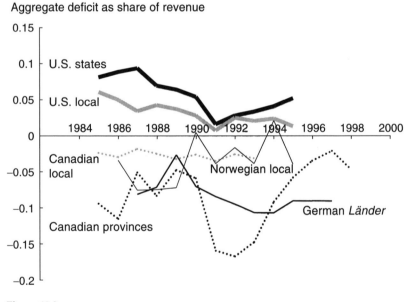

Figure 13.2
Subnational deficit as share of revenue: OECD cases. *Source*: IMF *Government Finance Statistics*.

that large aggregate deficits, ranging from 15 to over 30 percent of total revenue, have been quite persistent since the mid-1980s in the Brazilian and Indian states and Argentine provinces. These data reflect the discussions of persistent soft budget constraints in each of the corresponding case study chapters. Figure 13.2 shows that sizable and persistent subnational deficits are not limited to the developing world. Specifically, as discussed in chapter 6, the German *Länder*, particularly Bremen, Saarland, and more recently Berlin and some of the new eastern *Länder*, have faced soft budget constraints in recent years as well.

Figures 13.1 and 13.2 also suggest that some of our cases demonstrated relatively balanced budgets. Among the developing and transition countries, the balanced budgets of the Hungarian local governments stand out. As discussed in chapter 7, recent precipitous improvements in the fiscal balances, if sustained, may indicate a successful hardening of budget constraints there. Figure 13.2 shows that budgets have been balanced on average in the U.S. state sector, as well as in the local government sectors in the United States, Canada, and Norway. In each of these cases, aggregate subnational deficits have been very small as a percentage of revenue, and in the United States, surpluses and contributions to "rainy day funds" are common.

Figure 13.2 also tells an interesting story about the Canadian provinces. At the beginning of the 1990s, a recession combined with declining intergovernmental transfers put serious pressure on provincial budgets. This led to large short-term increases in provincial deficits and debt burdens. As discussed in chapter 3, the provincial governments eventually responded to pressure from creditors, voters, and asset owners by adjusting tax rates and expenditures. A similar story can be told, albeit on a smaller scale, in the United States. The U.S. states and local governments faced regional economic downturns, unexpected increases in health care costs, and cuts in federal grants in the late 1980s and early 1990s. Some states ran large deficits, and as shown in figure 13.2, the aggregate surplus declined significantly. As with the Canadian provinces, the U.S. state and local governments adjusted to these shocks on their own, and aggregate surpluses increased throughout the 1990s.

The U.S. states and Canadian provinces are the clearest examples of market discipline. The states and provinces have wide-ranging fiscal autonomy; most of their revenues come from broad-based taxes for which the bases and rates are determined locally. Moreover, they borrow in competitive capital markets, and their respective central governments place no constraints on their spending and borrowing. State and provincial politicians and their constituents have few reasons to expect bailouts; there is no history of bailouts, no clear mechanism through which local obligations might be assumed by other jurisdictions, and attempted bailouts by the federal government would risk being challenged on constitutional grounds. Persistent deficits are assumed to lower credit ratings and raise borrowing costs, resulting in political pressure to adjust when faced with adverse fiscal shocks.[2]

Such reliance on market discipline is rare, however. The other decentralized public sectors with relatively balanced budgets—the local and municipal sectors in Norway, Canada, and Hungary—apply strong hierarchical oversight. These case studies described strict rules and regulations governing local spending and borrowing decisions, imposed and enforced by the central government (in Canada, by the respective provincial governments). In each of these cases, hierarchical oversight appears to obviate the market mechanisms partially. In other words, credit markets, local voters, and asset owners play a much smaller role in disciplining local fiscal decisions.[3]

Figure 13.3 lays out the role of market and hierarchical mechanisms over the past decade in a two-by-two table. The horizontal axis represents the strength of market-type mechanisms, and the vertical axis represents the strength of hierarchical mechanisms. The table is divided into four quadrants, and the cases are displayed in the quadrant that best characterizes the strength of each type of mechanism during the last decade. The Canadian provinces and U.S. state and local governments fall into the southeast quadrant; they rely almost exclusively on markets for credit, votes, and capital and are not subject to hierarchical mechanisms (Many, but not all, U.S. states apply debt limits to municipalities, and monitoring and enforcement is varied at best). The local government sectors in Norway, Canada, and Hungary, in the northwestern quadrant, rely primarily on hierarchical mechanisms.

The remaining cases fall somewhere in the southwestern quadrant— a combination of hierarchical and market-type mechanisms that are both relatively weak. For these, the case study chapters describe significant manifestations of the soft budget constraint problem. Those cases for which deficit data were available—the federal states or provinces of Germany, India, Brazil, and Argentina—each displayed large and persistent deficits (figures 13.1 and 13.2), though Germany's are concentrated in a handful of the smallest states. The Chinese and

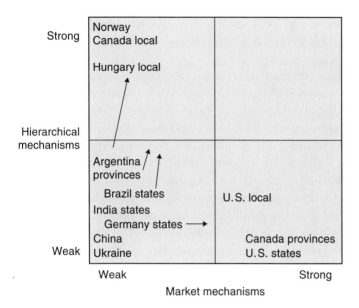

Figure 13.3
Hard budget constraint mechanisms, 1986–1999.

Ukrainian case studies also described persistent soft budget constraint problems.

The arrangement of cases in figure 13.3 is not very precise; no doubt it masks some of the subtlety and complexity of the case studies, yet it teaches some valuable lessons. Arrows indicate the direction of recent reforms described in the case studies. While both undoubtedly still face serious weaknesses, the Argentine and Brazilian case studies described some moves toward greater hierarchical oversight. The Brazilian Fiscal Responsibility Law is a particularly aggressive move in this direction. The local government sector in Hungary has moved out of the southwest quadrant by combining markets and hierarchy, but this transition has been dominated by increased hierarchical oversight. While exhibiting very little hierarchical oversight, the German *Länder* exhibit greater market oversight than the other cases in the southwest quadrant, and the case study does indicate some tentative improvements. The U.S. local government sector is placed slightly higher than the states and the Canadian provinces, reflecting that many states use some hierarchical restrictions on local governments, though local electoral competition, land markets, and credit markets clearly are important as well. These two alternative mechanisms are placed in relief in Canada, where both the provincial and local governments face relatively hard budget constraints but are governed by market and hierarchical mechanisms respectively.

The remainder of this chapter asks why countries end up in the southwestern quadrant of figure 13.3 and how they might move out of it or avoid it altogether. Sections 13.2 and 13.3 take a closer look at the institutional requirements for market and hierarchical hard budget constraint mechanisms. The emptiness of the northeastern quadrant in figure 13.3 reflects an inherent impossibility in applying both mechanisms forcefully; strong central government dominance is not compatible with strong market-like oversight. Nevertheless, we argue that it is possible to move toward the middle of figure 13.3 by shoring up nondiscretionary hierarchical mechanisms in the short run while gradually strengthening the scope of market discipline. Since the country context may limit the scope for central government disengagement and commitment, the context also sets limits for reliance on market mechanisms, even in the long term.

13.2   Market Mechanisms

The provinces and states of Canada and the United States demonstrate that hard budget constraints can be enforced without central government oversight of subnational fiscal and borrowing decisions. In fact, we have argued that local fiscal discipline will be enforced by market-like competition for capital and political support only if creditors, citizens, and asset owners believe that the central government will not be responsible for local fiscal decisions. How do such beliefs develop? A brief look at Canadian and American history suggests that the process might be slow, incremental, and sometimes painful.

In both the Canadian provinces and U.S. states, voters learned the hard way that the costs of imprudent fiscal decisions would be borne locally; they endured painful fiscal crises without receiving bailouts. The most important events in the United States took place in the 1830s and 1840s, when many of the states ran into serious debt servicing difficulties and defaulted (see English 1996; chap. 2, this volume). Despite vigorous lobbying efforts on the part of the most indebted states, no federal bailout was granted. According to one historian, taxpayers "saw how the abuse of state credit increased tax burdens at the most inopportune time and led to over-expansion, waste, extravagance, and fraud" (Ratchford 1941, 121). In chapter 3, Bird and Tassonyi describe a similar learning process in Canada, starting even in the pre-Confederation period. Like the American states, the provincial governments ran into difficulties with bond issues for railways and canals, and voters learned through a series of crises that they would ultimately pay the costs for provincial fiscal decisions. Even in the nineteenth century, voters and creditors alike learned to view the states and provinces as sovereign entities.

It is interesting to note that many of the U.S. states have self-imposed constitutional and statutory borrowing restrictions and balanced budget requirements.[4] In contrast, the restrictions imposed on local governments in Canada and the United States are hierarchical (Epple and Spatt 1986). States and provinces face restrictions imposed by themselves, or perhaps more accurately imposed by state and local voters on their representatives. The first state-level fiscal restrictions in the United States were imposed by angry voters in the 1840s after a series of costly tax increases resulting from imprudent borrowing decisions (English 1996). These restrictions were viewed favorably by credit markets and quickly spread to other states. Much more recently, similar rules have been implemented in several Canadian provinces. Following a period of persistent provincial deficits and unprecedented indebtedness, pressure from voters combined with a desire to reassure creditors led many provinces to impose fiscal restrictions on themselves. In both countries, such self-imposed restrictions demonstrate the strength of the markets for votes and credit.

What lessons for other countries can be drawn from the Canadian and American experiences? Importantly, some Canadian provinces and U.S. states had fiscal sovereignty prior to the formation of a federal union and then formed federal unions with limited ambitions and powers. When a nation with a strong central government decentralizes, the challenges are different and more daunting. As we shall argue, reliance on market discipline depends on either weakness centrally or restraint in the discretionary use of central government powers. Canada and the United States originally came about when governments for huge, sparsely populated areas formed coalitions into greater federations. The powers and ambitions of their federal governments were limited by constitutional construct, and these federal governments were also weak militarily and fiscally relative to those large areas. For the United States, the limits placed on the federal government are illustrated by the notion that residual powers—those powers and responsibilities not explicitly vested with the federation—are vested in the states. Under decentralization, the opposite idea is often in operation, as reforms proceed by suddenly assigning to lower-level governments a new list of powers and responsibilities.

A feature of the U.S. federation that has gone almost unnoticed in the fiscal literature is that—as affirmed by the Eleventh Amendment to the U.S. Constitution—states are sovereign and cannot be compelled to repay debts (English 1996).[5] Thus in the event of a state default, the federal government is not enabled in its judiciary capacity to enforce the claims of creditors. With the federal government being cleared of such responsibilities, expectations of bailouts may be reduced for two reasons. First, by not being involved in enforcement actions, the federal government avoids direct implication in inflicting pain on the state. Second, as creditors have weaker powers, the state faces less pain in a default situation, making a caring center less vulnerable. Countering these advantages, however, is the fact that the supply of credit will be less abundant since third-party enforcement is not available.

13.2.1 Fiscal Institutions

Subnational Revenue Autonomy and Vertical Fiscal Imbalances

In addition to their explicitly limited central governments, the Canadian provinces and U.S. states share a related unique feature: among subnational governments, they are (along with the Swiss cantons) the most fiscally autonomous in the world. They fund themselves primarily through broad-based taxes for which bases and rates are set without federal interference.[6] Although equalization transfers do make up a significant portion of the revenue of some of the smaller Canadian provinces, on the whole the Canadian provinces and U.S. states are much less reliant on intergovernmental transfers than the other cases examined in this book (see figure 13.4).[7]

As explained in chapter 1, high vertical fiscal imbalances certainly can represent an obstacle for market discipline. If a state's fiscal difficulty could be seen as resulting from the discretionary acts of the central government, market participants would likely look to the center rather than the subnational government for a resolution. High vertical fiscal imbalances therefore can send signals to voters, creditors, and asset owners that the higher-level government is responsible for local fiscal outcomes and obligations.

High vertical fiscal imbalances do not automatically lead to soft budget constraints. The two cases with the highest levels of transfer

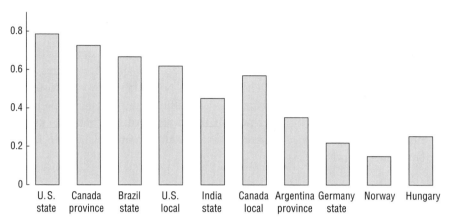

Figure 13.4
Own-source subnational revenue as percent of total subnational revenue. *Source*: Rodden (2002).

dependence in figure 13.4—Hungary and Norway—were able to achieve relatively hard budget constraints through hierarchical mechanisms. In fact, Von Hagen and Eichengreen (1996) use a large sample of monetary unions to show that high vertical imbalances typically *are* accompanied by more stringent borrowing restrictions. Rodden (2002) builds on this observation and uses a global data set to demonstrate that high levels of vertical fiscal imbalance, if accompanied by stringent hierarchical borrowing restrictions, are associated with balanced subnational budgets; the largest subnational deficits are found when high vertical imbalances combine with borrowing autonomy. The case studies of Ukraine, Brazil, India, and Argentina provide further evidence that weak hierarchical mechanisms and transfer dependence are a dangerous combination.

In practice, newly empowered state and local governments in developing countries largely depend on transfers and revenue sharing because of the challenges of devolving revenue-raising responsibilities. First, there may be a strong normative case for central government redistribution in countries with severe income inequality between regions. This redistribution can be pursued through expenditure programs such as health, education, social protection, and infrastructure—*and* these can be decentralized—if they are funded in part through transfers based on national taxation. Second, on efficiency grounds, jurisdictional tax coordination and other limitations in revenue autonomy have potential payoffs in reducing distortions to private behavior, excessive tax competition, tax exporting, and the costs of administration. As a descriptive prediction, vertical imbalances will be increasing as one decentralizes a broader domain of expenditures to small jurisdictions at low levels, unless one has either a very distorted or a regulated system of subnational taxation. Thus, transfer dependence may be a feature that is not easily disposed of, and market-type discipline is unlikely to emerge as the predominant mechanism for small jurisdictions.[8]

Rules Versus Discretion in the Design of Intergovernmental Transfers

If there is a relationship between transfer dependence and soft budget constraints, the root cause is the discretion of the central government, combined with expectations about how that discretion will be used. Even if provinces are quite self-reliant in revenue, unused taxing powers of the center may still be available and even expected to be used to provide bailouts in the future. Conversely, even when transfers are large, discretion in the disposition of these can conceivably be locked up by institutional features such as strict adherence to clear and transparent formulas or delegation to autonomous commissions.[9]

The discretion that remains at the center can be used in two ways in principle. The inclination to use it "the wrong way"—to bail out a troubled jurisdiction even when trouble is self-inflicted—can be thought of as in the Samaritan's dilemma: the invitation to manipulate the center lies in the center's vulnerability (his redistributive heart, in the case of the Samaritan). Thus, the relatively hard budget constraints of U.S. federalism might be attributed in part to the fact that the federation came about as a voluntary union with a limited mandate. The U.S. Constitution guarantees the right to "the pursuit of happiness," a modest goal compared to the "equal conditions" of the German Constitution.

That is not to say that a strong tendency toward redistribution cannot in principle be associated with hard budget constraints. The two may be compatible if the redistributive mechanism is expected not to work when problems are self-inflicted. But the principal agent model allows some redistribution to be consistent with incentives even when the center lacks information to distinguish luck from effort (fiscal effort, for instance). The requirement is that the center can commit—in the sense an insurer would be committed—not to give full coverage, so that incentives to effort remain. Thus, incentives for fiscal effort require information to distinguish exogenous shocks from self-inflicted pain, as well as commitment to refuse assistance in the case of self-inflicted pain.

Perhaps the most important lessons of the case studies about the design of transfers concern the clarity and predictability of rules that govern distribution. If one can remove the distribution of grants from the uncertainty and vote trading of the legislative process, one may also have reduced subnational expectations of bailouts and forgiveness.

But even if the rules governing intergovernmental transfers are clearly defined and adequately enforced, the rules themselves might undermine hard budget constraints, as in Germany. The constitution-ally mandated equalization system, though predictable and formulaic, has sent a message to the smallest and poorest states that fiscal indiscipline can ultimately be rewarded with increased transfers. More generally, the intergovernmental fiscal system has provided the states with weak incentives for fiscal effort. A related problem was described for the Indian system of intergovernmental transfers. While the process employed by the Finance Commission does include some clearly defined rules, perhaps its greatest weakness lies in the basic rules and procedures themselves. The Indian system has featured a gap-filling approach that discourages fiscal discipline.

The problems with transfers based on bargaining were demonstrated most clearly in the case study of Ukraine, where the intergovernmental system has been overwhelmed with rent seeking and opportunism. A history of discretionary transfers and political bargaining also clearly undermined fiscal discipline in Brazil. The ad hoc bilateral bargaining between the central government and localities under China's "fiscal contracting" system, as well as the new "dual track" system, also result in soft budget constraints for the localities. Although transfers in India appear to rely on clearly established rules, in practice the process leaves a great deal of room for discretion and bilateral negotiation.

The recommendation of limiting the center's discretion to avoid gamesmanship of subnational jurisdictions goes directly to the heart of any decentralization reform. The first big question is whether, or in what areas, the center can let go of ambitions with respect to sub-national entities and thereby sever its channels of vulnerability. The second big question is whether it can lock up its discretionary powers in a credible way, or at least increase the costs to itself of subsequently deviating from the announced framework. Most likely, any decentral-ization is half-genuine at best, meaning that scenarios exist in which the center would consider deviating from its preannounced stance. Given such scenarios, it becomes important whether the key to discretion is buried sufficiently deeply; often it is not.

Clarity of Responsibilities

Market discipline requires not only that subnational governments have the fiscal autonomy necessary to respond to adverse shocks on their own, but also an intergovernmental system that makes this sufficiently clear to citizens, asset owners, and creditors. Thus, the distribution of revenue, expenditure, and regulatory authority between levels of government should be clear and stable. In many of the cases, market discipline was undermined by the fact that tax bases overlap, and major areas of government expenditure fall into the realm of joint tasks or concurrent powers. Overlapping tax bases, uncoordinated tax administration, and a muddy distribution of spending authority led to confusion and incentives for opportunistic behavior in Brazil. In Ukraine, the basic distribution of authority between governments is poorly defined and shifting, seriously undermining accountability. In India, most public sector activities fall into the realm of concurrent powers or joint tasks for three or two levels of government, harming accountability through cost shifting.

True clarity of responsibility and accountability may, however, be more difficult in practice than in theory. National revenue may be an important funding source for redistribution and public expenditure programs such as education and health services. Decentralizing these services can be very helpful to make the services accountable to users and local citizens, but the national government is likely unable to express indifference with respect to the services delivered, even if expenditure responsibility is clearly vested in the local government. First, its role in providing funds along with its own political accountability may prevent such indifference. Second, its hand in funding gives it an instrument in acting on service delivery, and it would be imprudent (or impossible) to lock this instrument up or give it away. Thus, users and citizens may not be confused but right when directing their anger for flawed services toward both the provincial and the national capital. A provincial governor who thinks the national government will take part of the blame and pay part of the bill if she skimps on school quality may be right. Reflecting their own vulnerabilities, many national governments are unlikely to be credible if stating that reduced funding will be the response if the province should fail in reaching educational goals. These observations illustrate the challenges in establishing incentive compatibility under conditions of low development and high transfer dependence.

Local Provision of National Public Goods

Above we described a situation where the center is vulnerable to manipulation because it cares about what the subnational government is charged with providing; pressures for bailouts build if local governments are responsible for the services with national constituencies. More specifically, if subnational governments are responsible for expenditures like welfare, unemployment, and pensions, pressure turns to the central government when revenues fall short. Some of the Canadian provincial crises in the 1930s unfolded in this way because the provinces were responsible for most relief expenditures. A similar dynamic led to pressure for bailouts of state and provincial pension programs in Brazil and Argentina, and further examples are provided in the South African chapter.

Intergovernmental transfers that are deemed insufficient to cover mandated spending responsibilities have been a major part of the problem in India. The system of gap filling and occasional debt forgiveness employed by the Finance Commission can thus be seen as compensating for inadequate funding to fulfill the obligations set out for them by central planning directives. Similar problems were reported in the case studies of Argentina, Brazil, and, most severely, Ukraine.

When nations are large, this perspective is particularly important under the rather compelling case for viewing poverty alleviation as a national public good (Wane 2000). Musgrave's (1959) recommendation that redistribution is a national responsibility in effect reflects this perspective. Similarly, Sen's (1999) observation that democratic nations prevent famines hints toward a national public good as a descriptive matter. Thus, at least in democracies, national intervention can be expected when core dimensions of welfare are threatened locally, and so commitments not to intervene with bailouts or other assistance will always face certain bounds in terms of credibility.

13.2.2   Political Institutions

Political institutions are critical to the beliefs and perceptions that undermine market-type fiscal discipline. The central government's vulnerability and commitment to "say no" when pressured for bailouts depends on its organization and incentive structure. In many situations, the central government is an organization that by its very design has trouble saying no. Local officials and their constituents are aware of this and can exploit it.

Consider first the role of legislatures in democracies. When local governments are unable to pay workers, contractors, or bond holders, these groups are likely to put strong pressure on the region's representatives in the central legislature. As described in chapters 1 and 2, decision making in legislatures is often characterized by logrolling and vote trading between representatives of regions. This leads to excessive spending, as political scientists have demonstrated (Shepsle and Weingast 1984), and also may afford the representatives of fiscally troubled jurisdictions opportunities to strike bailout deals. These bailouts may represent politically rational outcomes even if costs exceed benefits for the country as a whole. Demonstrating a key proposition of Inman's formal analysis in chapter 2, the decentralized, fragmented nature of the Brazilian legislature was clearly an important structural reason for soft state-level budget constraints. In particular, the state governors have been able to trade votes and push their agendas through the Senate. On more than one occasion, logrolling in the Senate made bailouts possible, and once negotiations started, they led directly to increases in the size and scope of bailouts.

Strong Presidents and Political Parties
This problem can be mitigated if the legislative process gives authority to individuals or groups held accountable by a national constituency for the overall fiscal and economic performance of the country. Strong presidents and political party leaders can play this role. Brazil has often featured weak and fragmented political parties and presidents who were unable to command the support of partisan colleagues in the legislature. This has often made it relatively easy for the states to push for bailouts and stand in the way of key intergovernmental reforms. More recently, a president with a national coalition that derives electoral strength from its responsibility for stabilizing the economy and ending hyperinflation has been able to create incentives among legislators and even governors to support a reform agenda aimed at hardening the budget constraints of the states. The Argentine case tells a similar story about reforms made possible by partisan ties linking the president, the legislature, and provincial governors.[10]

Standing up to pressure from subnational officials, local workers, contractors, and bond holders whose payments are threatened requires a great deal of political strength, cooperation, and far-sightedness at the center. Politicians are unlikely to have this strength if their re-election chances are determined primarily by the provision of pork to their districts or bailiwicks, as in Brazil. Nor are they likely to muster this strength if the central government is a fragile coalition on the verge of collapse, as has sometimes been the case in India. In these situations, the central government's no-bailout commitment lacks motivational credibility (Shepsle 1991). Local officials and their constituents know that the central government does not have incentives to be resolute. Strengthening party discipline and leadership and enhancing the stability of political coalitions may be ways of improving motivational commitment.[11]

Delegation: An Independent Central Bank as an Example

A different kind of commitment was illustrated by Ulysses when binding himself to the mast (Shepsle 1991). A commitment has imperative credibility if the actor is unable to break the commitment even if the motivation should arise. Thus, if legislators have incentives to provide bailouts, imperative commitment to resist is obtained by removing from legislators the discretion to provide bailouts. A similar argument was made about intergovernmental transfers: they should be determined by rules rather than legislative discretion. More generally, the delegation of authority from the legislature to other bodies that are more insulated from political pressure might help strengthen the government's commitment. First, an independent central bank might be an important source of imperative commitment. Local governments, their constituents, and their creditors know that the central government *can* provide bailouts if it controls the money supply. In contrast, if monetary policy is formulated by an autonomous agency with an anti-inflation mandate, these actors know that the central government itself faces a harder budget constraint.

The Judiciary and the Predicament of Enforcing Property Rights

A contract such as a loan defines certain delineated rights and obligations, and the capacity and willingness of government to adjudicate and enforce these in general are at the heart of the rule of law. Thus, the occasions when a government representative seizes debtor assets on behalf of creditors may be important in the general incentive structure.

When government is a contracting party, legal tradition may afford government assets immunity from seizure. Government entities thus may be poorly suited as contracting partners, since the other party may be deprived of the support ordinarily available to enforce contracts. Such immunity is rather compelling in settings with imperfect separation of powers (i.e., no independent judiciary). If the sheriff would never seize the king's car on behalf of creditors, then declaring immunity of the king's assets is a useful clarification. In modern times, however, immunity can be and often is ruled out explicitly in the law and in the contract. This allows the enforcement of contracts, helping government entities such as kings, countries, and municipalities be suitable contracting partners, at least in principle.

Nevertheless, separation of powers will never be perfect, and if a contract dispute is sufficiently political, intervention from executives or legislators may help it escape or override the judicial process. This can be done in an innocent fashion without compromising the courts themselves, for instance, by paying off creditors who would otherwise go to court to have their claims serviced. Thus, when a defaulting entity (whether a state-owned company, a private company or family, or a subnational government) is bailed out, it can be seen as a maneuver that prevents a call on government, broadly defined, to enforce contracts under the law.

This call to enforce the property rights may indeed be a compelling case for political intervention, since the law may have enforcement consequences that are unacceptable politically.[12] If schools are to be closed, taxes raised, or police pensions reduced, pain is being distributed, and through adjudication and enforcement, the higher-level government is implicated in triggering the pain. Actually, if the law does not set explicit limitations for the powers given to creditors, voters could in principle lose all control over taxation and service delivery, thus all control over their jurisdiction, including private property. For these reasons, unless the law delicately sets limits to creditor rights in actions against subnational government, the process cannot be contained within an unpoliticized judicial machinery. An important aspect of the bailout is that it allows the confrontation between creditors and debtor to escape the judicial process, and thus prevents what might otherwise be an embarrassing and costly exposure of the limits to the rule of law. A bailout makes the situation go away, so the obligation to enforce property rights may no doubt contribute to bailouts in practical life.

By the same logic, bailouts might be avoided if creditors have few legal rights relative to a subnational government debtor in default *and* creditors lack political clout. As examples, both Inman (chapter 2) and English (1996) find it important for the resistance to state bailouts in the United States in the 1840s that many of the bondholders were foreigners and thus weak politically in a U.S. context.

An arrangement with weak creditor rights is found among sovereign nations, but also among the states in the United States. Against sovereign nations, third-party enforcement is either unavailable or limited and extremely costly. Similarly, in the U.S. federation, the federal government and its institutions effectively are barred from enforcing obligations of the individual states. One consequence is that the debtor is protected from the consequences of certain sanctions, and another is that the federal government is freed from the bailout pressure that might result from being implicated in such consequences. Nevertheless, this institutional arrangement is more an inheritance than something that can be recommended for adoption in general, but aspects of it may convey lessons about the bailout problem in general.

For local governments in the United States, weak creditor rights are an important part of the general framework, though in a very different arrangement. Both state law and federal law can be used in proceedings of defaulting local governments, often under a bankruptcy law and often involving a trustee acting under the supervision of the courts (McConnell and Picker 1993). One expression of weak creditor rights is that bankruptcy proceedings can be called only by the municipality, not the creditors. Interestingly, in actual U.S. practice, municipal assets are invariably left in the hands of the local government, as are important policy instruments such as expenditure programs and most taxes (a few new taxes may be authorized to service debt in an orderly way). Thus, effectively, creditors are left with very weak rights at both the municipal and the state levels. While probably having other implications both positive and negative, one interesting aspect of such weak creditor rights is that this arrangement protects the judiciary from political intervention not by building strong judiciaries (which may be difficult, particularly in a common law context) but by avoiding situations that would call for intervention. If giving creditors greater access to the tax base would violate an understanding of democracy, or if closing schools would seem to be harming children rather than the responsible parties, then these qualms could command bailouts or other political interventions in a system with less restricted creditor rights. Importantly, weak creditor rights may have costs in terms of supporting a low quantity of credit, or in terms of costly signaling by those who want to borrow, but they do appear to provide clarity as well as uncompromised enforcement institutions.

13.3 Hierarchical Mechanisms

A key observation of the previous section is that effective market discipline has many preconditions, some of which are quite difficult to achieve. This section considers the possibility that hierarchical mechanisms can fill in the gaps. It does so by first examining some cases of successful hierarchical oversight, then extracting lessons from some failures. Finally, it provides some specific lessons about how to introduce and strengthen central government rules and oversight while sowing the seeds of market discipline in developing and transition countries.

13.3.1 Successful Hierarchical Oversight

Fiscal discipline in the local government sectors of Norway, Hungary, and Canada is enforced primarily by hierarchical mechanisms, and this to some extent is also true for local government in the United States. The contrast in Canada between provinces and local government provides a useful illustration. The fiscal crises affecting the Canadian provinces in the 1930s affected the municipal governments as well. In fact, the Canadian provincial governments were responsible for funding most of the municipal-level public services, and the fiscal woes of one level therefore reflected those of the other. The provincial governments learned that they would be held responsible not only for their own debt and fiscal health, but for those of the municipalities as well. The provincial governments responded by imposing strong hierarchical controls on local spending and borrowing. The provinces now have control over the vast majority of local revenue, and local borrowing is very limited. Provincial governments regulate all aspects of local borrowing.

A similar development took place more recently in Hungary. During the early stages of the transition process, local governments began to run large and persistent deficits, some of which escalated into financial crises and demands for bailouts. Like the Canadian provinces in the 1930s, the Hungarian central government responded by implementing hierarchical controls over local spending and borrowing. The Ministry of Finance now oversees the budget process at all levels of government, controlling ex ante payments against budget appropriations. The central government regulates local government borrowing, requires balanced budgets, and enforces numerical debt service limits.

In both cases, the lower-level governments were extremely dependent on transfers, and no one could reasonably expect that local governments would adjust to adverse fiscal shocks on their own. High levels of vertical fiscal imbalance clearly presented higher-level governments with a moral hazard problem. Since they knew they would ultimately be held responsible for local burdens, they implemented top-down fiscal restrictions.

The Norwegian case tells a similar story. Local governments are highly dependent on transfers, and the central government assuages the intergovernmental moral hazard problem with strong, binding hierarchical rules. Although they are popularly elected, local governments are viewed essentially as agents of the central government. Norwegian local governments have some discretion in raising revenue, but local budgets are regulated by the central government (through the supercounty administrator), which requires operational budget balance. Loan financing for current expenditures is not allowed, and all local government borrowing must be approved by the central government.[13]

In each of these cases, hierarchical restrictions do a reasonably good job of mitigating the problem of deficit shifting, but this form of oversight is not without its costs. According to the case studies, a less severe problem of cost shifting remains. In other words, while the worst forms of moral hazard may be under control by administrative fiat, the problem is not eliminated. No matter how complex or rule based its criteria for intergovernmental transfers, it is difficult for the central government to distinguish between true local fiscal hardship and strategic information manipulation. Each of these case studies described strategic grantsmanship by local governments—attempts to hide and distort true costs and benefits in order to receive extra resources funded by other jurisdictions. Chapter Four suggests that this may be part of the explanation for the rapid growth of the public sector in Norway, so the scheme may have been less successful in containing government size than in containing fiscal deficits. This is particularly interesting in the Norwegian case since conditions may be termed extraordinarily positive for the elimination of moral hazard. There are very many municipalities, an unusual homogeneity, consensus about goals, and at both the center and locally, the belief exists that grants are used proactively to enhance discipline.

Moreover, each of these case studies expressed some concern that the dominance by the higher-level government is damaging to market oversight and more generally suppresses (some) advantages of decentralization. In Norway and Canada, lenders to local governments view the central (provincial) government as ultimately responsible for the debt, and credit markets therefore have no incentives to screen or punish for poor fiscal performance. The Canadian and Norwegian cases suggested that domination by higher-level governments provides the local governments with few incentives to be innovative or energetic, and in Norway at least, provides little scope for local democracy. The authors of each of these case studies suggested that local governments did not have strong incentives to use even their existing borrowing authority to promote local investments in schools and infrastructure.

But the costs of hierarchical oversight should not be overdrawn. Though these cases clearly demonstrate the tension between hierarchical and market-type hard budget constraint mechanisms, they also show that the two can coexist in practice. The Canadian case suggests that in spite of blunt hierarchical oversight, local fiscal decisions do affect the well-being of voters, who face some incentives to oversee local decisions. The Hungarian case displays a particularly encouraging mixture of market and hierarchical mechanisms. Much of the recent legislation strengthening central oversight is also aimed at building the elements for disengaged market mechanisms. For instance, new securities regulations introduce far-reaching information disclosure and audit requirements, which make it easier for local creditors and voters to assess local fiscal performance. The municipal bankruptcy law creates a prospect for default resolution without additional money and political intervention, though only time can tell whether the courts or political intervention will prevail. Moreover, the debt service limits themselves seem to take a clever form: local government borrowing limits are determined by a formula that provides local governments with incentives to collect more revenue and control costs. Such rules provide steeper incentives but are less redistributive if the center is credible in its commitment to them.

13.3.2   Failed Attempts at Hierarchical Oversight

In spite of some problems, hierarchical hard budget constraint mechanisms in Hungary, Canada, and Norway are deemed successful (at least
in part) because they appear to have prevented persistent deficits and
serious moral hazard problems. The same cannot be said for attempts
at hierarchical oversight in India and Brazil. The failure of market
mechanisms in these countries was described above. India has relied
on a form of hierarchical oversight for some time, while Brazil has
attempted more recently to introduce new hierarchical mechanisms in
a context of a liberal federal regime.

Forms of fiscal discipline based on markets for credit and votes have
played a very limited role in India because of the dominant role of the
central government in allocating and approving state borrowing, in
turn commanded by the limited depth of a nonpublic financial sector.
The Planning Commission, the Finance Ministry, and the central bank
are all involved in the regulation of state finances. The central government and its agencies are the primary source of credit for the states,
and all of the states are in debt to the central government. The central
government appears to have a wide range of constitutional and statutory hierarchical mechanisms at its disposal. States have several
channels for circumventing controls, including the access to and the
guaranteeing of the borrowing by state-owned enterprises. More generally, political and administrative fragmentation at the center undermines the commitment to enforce the hierarchical rules. Coordination
of the various commissions and agencies responsible for overseeing
state borrowing is also a major challenge. Perhaps even more important is the fact that in recent years, the political composition of the
central government (weak, logrolling coalitions of state-based parties)
has been poorly suited to establish discipline and enforce limits on local
borrowing. The center possesses neither the strength nor the incentives
to implement new legislation aimed at closing loopholes in the existing framework for oversight.

The story in Brazil has been quite similar. Through much of the 1980s
and 1990s, the Brazilian states faced few effective hierarchical limitations on their spending or borrowing decisions. The only restrictions
placed on the states actually had the opposite effect: by placing restrictions on states, ability to control their expenditures on public sector
wages and pensions, the center bolstered the perception that states
were unable to adjust. The central government has used the powers it

gained, however, to strengthen its authority to regulate spending and borrowing. It now has tools that were not afforded it in the constitution, instruments that in theory at least can be used to limit borrowing by states, including numerical limits on debt and prohibitions of new bond issues and of borrowing from state-owned banks. As in India, however, the effectiveness of these instruments has been undermined in practice by administrative and political fragmentation in the federal government. The most important problem with hierarchical oversight in Brazil in the past has been the key enforcement role played by the Senate, which is easily swayed by the interest of the governors. Very recently, however, the role of the Senate has been reduced, and a new set of aggressive hierarchical mechanisms has been introduced. As this book goes to press, it is too early to evaluate the Brazilian Fiscal Responsibility Law, but on paper it would appear to place serious restrictions on the Brazilian states and municipalities that are quite anomalous for a decentralized federation. Such legislation seems to move the country even further from the goal of market-based discipline. As in the past, the key to hierarchical discipline will lie in the credibility of the central government's willingness to enforce its rules during hard times.

The cases of unsuccessful hierarchical oversight suggest three related lessons. First, hierarchical oversight is not simple when subnational governments have access to a wide variety of formal and informal sources of credit. Tools for hierarchical control may be particularly restricted in federations, where the center is constitutionally constrained, at least until the point where subnational crises lend the central government a stronger hand. No matter how committed the central government may be, it can be extremely difficult to design and enforce an adequate hierarchical regime. More specifically, any regime of hierarchical fiscal discipline must focus not only on direct government borrowing, but also on borrowing through state-owned enterprises and state-owned banks. In addition to India and Brazil, evidence from China, Argentina, and even Germany suggests that central government reform efforts should attempt to enforce clear separation between the budgets of subnational governments and their public enterprises. In each of these cases, borrowing activities of (or through) subnationally owned enterprises introduced important off-budget sources of soft local government finance. As this book goes to press, it is difficult to avoid the comparison with Enron—the doomed American energy conglomerate—and the soft budget constraints created by its maze of contingent liabilities and subsidiaries. More obviously, subnational governments simply should not own banks. Fortunately, the Argentine provinces and Brazilian states have recently agreed to privatize their banks. As clearly demonstrated, an important building block in subnational government fiscal discipline is that the regulatory and supervisory power of the country's financial sector institutions—regardless of ownership—is vested in independent national institutions.

The second lesson is that hierarchical mechanisms are only as good as the strength and credibility of the central government's commitment to stand by and enforce them. The central governments of Brazil and India are in many respects arenas for the consummation of regional logrolling deals. Legislation in Brazil requires cross-region coalition building, where national parties cannot be relied on for party discipline, while legislation in India requires tricky bargains between state-based parties. Since fragmented political institutions can undermine fiscal discipline under market mechanisms as well as under hierarchical controls, this translates into a cautionary note on the extent and shape of decentralization as well.

The third lesson follows from the second: blunt hierarchical mechanisms like central government credit allocation and borrowing restrictions do not seem to work well in large, diverse federations. Large jurisdictions will assert their own powers and will likely win some battles over time to govern their own affairs. Reflecting this, political federalism is a form of government that limits the ability of central governments to intervene in the affairs of the federated units. Moreover, formal federal systems often feature constitutional provisions that protect the autonomy of the subunits, or they directly include representatives of the subunits in central government institutions—typically the upper house. In such systems, the clout of the subnational jurisdictions can undermine the success of hierarchical control mechanisms. Although the size of our sample does not allow firm conclusions, it is tempting to conclude that effective Norwegian-style hierarchical constraints are most likely to be effective in small, relatively homogeneous political entities such as Norway or a Canadian province.

13.4 Designing a Hard Budget Constraint

In the previous sections, we used the case studies to explain how different systems of fiscal decentralization work and identify key problems that undermine hard budget constraints. But we have also emphasized that one solution will not work for all cases. In fact, some "solutions" may do more harm than good under the wrong conditions. This section builds on that theme, exploring what can be done in a process of decentralization in the light of country conditions and characteristics. While a good deal of cross-national variation can be explained by historical and institutional legacies, institutions can be altered and incentives improved. In fact, fiscal crises and even large bailouts provide some of the best opportunities for institutional reform. This section concludes by bringing out some basic principles that might guide a reform agenda.

13.4.1   Can a Federation Be Flawed?

Theory concludes that autonomy in some dimension (borrowing, say) usefully can be granted to the lower levels if incentives can be structured so as to internalize external effects. The other side of the coin, however, is that hierarchical controls can be helpful if the center is unable to commit to an incentive framework that internalizes externalities—for instance, if it cannot resist calls for bailouts.[14] We have seen that the bailout problem arises when the central government is vulnerable to the effects of subnational fiscal crises *and* fiscally strong enough to execute a bailout, while too weak in terms of other regulatory or administrative instruments that could prevent subnational fiscal profligacy in advance.

Consider jurisdictions ranging along a continuum from national governments to small municipalities. At one end of the continuum, no higher-level entity (or third party in general) exists with the power to control the jurisdiction's acts ex ante. Also, no entity has the inclination (i.e., vulnerability) and fiscal powers to execute the bailout ex post. Importantly, when two neighboring jurisdictions are separated by national borders, several possible sources of external effects will typically be severed: there is little or no codependence in access to credit or in the exchange rate, political accountability is not an issue, and the obligation of judiciary enforcement is cut off. We might refer to these conditions as characterizing fiscal sovereignty. Moving along the continuum, consider a semiautonomous province within a nation. In such cases, the higher level has the fiscal powers of the lower level and then some, for instance, through its money creation powers, or simply because the power to tax originates in the coercive powers of the central government. Moving even further to small municipalities, it might be the case that the lower-level jurisdictions are highly dependent on higher levels for financing and serve primarily as conduits for the implementation of national government policies. In these cases, it seems appropriate that the ambitions and fiscal powers of higher-level governments should be matched by other powers, for instance, to regulate the activities of lower-level governments. As the center's vulnerability increases, so should its ex ante regulatory powers.

Although it seems attractive, this kind of institutional symmetry—a federal government that matches limited goals with limited powers—often does not evolve. Institutions may be described as staggered layers: some "heavy" layers are difficult to change and constitute the rules of the game, while some "lighter" ones represent the actions in each period of play.[15] In some countries, basic heavy institutions create a troubling asymmetry: a center that is weak in its regulatory authority in relation to the subnational governments may be strong fiscally and thus vulnerable to their fiscal irresponsibility. This asymmetry appears often to be a side effect of the bargains that create and maintain many large, diverse federations. Even if they start out with symmetric and quite limited powers, central governments in federations gain wide-ranging fiscal authority over time, especially in response to wars and other crises. However, the constraints of federalism—whether formal and constitutional or informal and political—often prevent the central government from amassing symmetric powers to regulate the activities (including borrowing) of the states or provinces. Whether a country maintains an explicitly federal constitution, the central government might find it difficult to regulate local fiscal behavior if it is fragmented by frequent power struggles, short-term incentives, and difficult coalition building. Not only might this situation invite strategic manipulation by the states, but the very strength of the central government's fiscal position in relation to the states often invites political manipulation by the central government. For instance, the central government might create bailout expectations by using its discretion over transfers and loans to favor its political allies.[16]

13.4.2 The Challenge of Decentralization

Figure 13.5 illustrates these issues by displaying three key dimensions of relations between governments. First, it categorizes the central government as fiscally strong or weak. Second, it asks whether the central

		Has the center credibly locked away its discretion?	The central government's ability to **regulate** subnational government is:	
			Weak	Strong
Central government is **fiscally**:	Strong	No	Bailouts and soft budget constraints	Hierarchical mechanisms
		Yes	Unconstrained decentralization	
	Weak	Not relevant	Sovereignty	

Figure 13.5
Dimensions of intergovernmental relations.

government can credibly lock up its discretionary power to provide bailouts. Third, it examines the strength of the central government to regulate the activities of lower-tier governments. In the far northeastern cells, which we have merged, the central government is strong fiscally, but these fiscal powers are matched by strong regulatory powers. The use—and the usefulness—of regulation allows us to denote this cell by the presence of *hierarchical mechanisms*. We could have used a more loaded term—*subordination*—but hierarchical instruments can be used selectively, in ways that limit decentralization without eliminating it. The most important example is when the central government's deep pockets make it vulnerable to manipulation but its regulatory capacity effectively limits the potential moral hazard problem. We have reviewed several "hierarchical" mechanisms that might be successful in this regard. In this environment, whether the central government has locked away its discretion is not important, since the subnational government does not have much power with which to manipulate the center.

Decentralization in practice often means that a country moves toward the left in the table as the freedoms and powers of subnational entities increase. Under such increased freedoms, the center's fiscal strength, combined with a variety of other factors described above, makes it vulnerable to manipulation by subnational governments.[15] A danger is that central governments will lose hierarchical instruments without giving up or credibly locking away their fiscal powers. Our case studies show that decentralization falls rather easily into the "bailout" cell, where the central government has weak control over lower-level governments while it retains the deep pockets that render it vulnerable to gamesmanship. As we have seen, it can be extremely difficult to move quickly to the cell *unconstrained decentralization*, where central discretion has been credibly locked away so that market mechanisms alone support efficient subnational behaviors. A central government with strong fiscal powers will thus find it difficult to make credible promises not to provide bailouts should emergencies arise, particularly where the central government, because of a history of state socialism, is viewed as having both wide-ranging responsibilities and a generous set of policy instruments at its disposal.

In terms of the resulting incentives for subnational governments, the cell *unconstrained decentralization* has much in common with *sovereignty*. Steps can indeed be taken to improve the center's commitment, but we have argued that full commitment will not emerge instantly in response to some institutional tinkering. For this reason, realistic acknowledgment of the center's powers, ambitions, and commitment problems is key to successful decentralization, and the framework will often include regulation and oversight quite different from what is experienced by a sovereign. A key challenge of decentralization is to move downward while to the left, but it is unlikely that countries will move directly to the lowest row of figure 13.5 other than in situations like Yugoslavia. In fact, we contend that true subnational "sovereignty" is quite rare, and an approximation is mostly likely to develop when independent entities like the American colonies cede authority to a (then) weak central government in an explicitly limited way.

Combining Markets and Hierarchy

From a centralized starting point, one cannot expect central governments to disengage or commit so quickly or completely as to make market mechanisms sufficient for fiscal discipline. Yet hierarchical credit allocation mechanisms will often be both too inflexible and too bendable; they can stand in the way of good projects and then bend to unfortunate political pressures for bad projects. Thus, central control, especially when it comes to borrowing and investment, is not likely to provide a satisfactory long-term answer to the problem of subnational fiscal discipline, especially in large, diverse federations.

How is it possible for a country to move its subnational jurisdictions away from outright subordination without softening budget constraints? Although the best strategy depends on the characteristics of the country in question and the starting point, the case studies seem to point to a general strategy resolving this dilemma. This strategy entails sustained, perhaps even increased, central government oversight in the short term, using the rules and administrative procedures that create the strongest possible incentives for voters, creditors, and asset owners to oversee local fiscal decisions in the longer term. The central government's involvement should be rule based and nondiscretionary and must enhance its own commitment and transparency. Horizontal delegation, including to independent central banks, agencies, judiciaries, and arbitrators, may be quite valuable.

Practical steps can be taken to strengthen market discipline even in the short run. Consider once again the case of Hungary. As suggested above, the new rules regulating local borrowing in Hungary, while placing real constraints on the borrowing behavior of local governments, create incentives for local governments to increase revenue efforts and cut costs. The new regulations also invite oversight from voters and creditors by forcing local governments to provide information, including by establishing accounting and auditing procedures. The most interesting innovation in Hungary is the new legislation governing local government bankruptcy. Instead of the center being pressured to respond to local fiscal crises on an ad hoc basis, this legislation points to a set of clear procedures. The most important aspect of the process is that it does not involve the central government legislators or executives; it relies on courts and arbitrators. This is as good an effort as any to signal to local governments, their voters, and their creditors that the central government will not use the public purse to resolve local fiscal crises. Such laws can help establish the precedent that the consequences of local fiscal decisions will be felt by local citizens and creditors. Political pressures for bailouts and other interventions will emerge, but a good defense lies in establishing such a standard procedure. The record from other countries (see English 1996, and chaps. 1 and 2 on the United States and Canada) indicates that the early tests are the important ones.

Can Bailouts Improve Incentives?

One should not exclude the possibility that central government oversight can be improved and market discipline encouraged, perhaps ironically, through a bailout. In some of the cases, subnational governments were highly dependent on transfers that were simply inadequate in the face of exogenous shocks produced by fluctuations in interest rates, inflation, and other factors over which they had little control. In such cases, central governments may be unable to avoid some sort of unplanned emergency transfers in the event of a subnational fiscal crisis. Also, the crisis and the bailout may allow an opportunity for negotiations and improvements in institutions that otherwise would be impossible. The main problem with unplanned emergency transfers, especially at the early stages of democratization and decentralization, is the demonstration effect; they may undermine the learning process that can eventually lead to market discipline.

But all bailouts are not created equal, and our lesson is that bailouts differ by the institutional reforms accompanying them. The Argentine case demonstrates that bailouts need not teach local governments and their constituents that profligacy pays. The central government may be able to structure a package with reforms that staves off default and alleviates the most serious hardships without creating bad incentives for the future. The fiscal pacts that have been negotiated between the central government and the provinces have not absolved provincial governments of their responsibility to repay their debts. In fact, provincial governments have been forced to deal with significant political and fiscal hardships after the debt renegotiations. The central government has an important mechanism at its disposal: it offers to collateralize transfers and channel them to the creditors of each province. This facilitates enforcement, bringing willingness to pay closer to ability to pay if the former should be lower. The cost may be that the center puts itself in the middle: it would most likely have to deviate if it should be challenged to continue sending transfers directly to creditors under a severe provincial crisis.

The Argentine and the Brazilian cases show that bailout episodes can provide important opportunities for major reform of the intergovernmental system. In federations in particular, the center's desire to enhance its regulatory powers may require concessions from subnational governments, but these often come only if the center has something to give in the way of debt renegotiation.

13.5   Concluding Reflections

As subnational governments gain new rights and responsibilities around the world, a number of things can go wrong. In many countries, decentralization is a political process driven by transitions that usher in more democratic, participatory forms of government. Actual experiences with decentralization will depend critically on institutional and political incentive structures. While these are in some respects products of lengthy processes of evolution and learning, they are also fundamentally products of human design. Opportunities for serious, purposive institutional design are rare but not entirely lacking. When they present themselves—often as the result of failure and crisis—it is useful to have some basic guiding principles.

We have examined many aspects of institutional reform, ranging from the specific design of intergovernmental transfers to the basic structure of federal constitutions. The case studies presented in this book suggest a perspective that gives nuance to many hard-held views on decentralization. One example is our assessment that continued central government regulation, while contrary to a "fundamentalist" view of decentralization, can be applied sensibly so as to allow benefits of decentralization, while addressing incentive problems that relate to the center's commitment problems. Furthermore, we have suggested that bailouts themselves can present windows of opportunity for such reform. Above all, we have stressed the importance of replacing political discretion with clear, transparent, and automatic rules and procedures.

Credibility and incentives change over time, and it follows that decentralization can deepen over time, reflecting greater trust and respect as it evolves. This deepening is also more likely to take place at higher levels of income, education, and institutional capacity, and as the rule of law, independence of the judiciary, and mechanisms for democratic participation are strengthened. One observation stands out above all others: the importance of accountability to ordinary citizens. This does not improve automatically simply because authority and resources shift from higher- to lower-level governments; it is the product of careful institutional design. Perhaps the most important but vexing hard budget constraint mechanism is an active and informed public with incentives and tools to oversee government decision making. In the long run, budget constraints are most likely to be hard, and decentralization deemed a success by scholars and citizens alike, if decentralization bolsters the accountability of governments at all levels to their citizens.

Notes

1. Fiscal deficit data are taken from IMF's database *Government Finance Statistics*, and defined as total subnational revenue (tax revenues plus grants) minus total expenditures (investment and current, including interest expenditures).

2. Evidence of a link between deficits and the electoral success of incumbents is provided by Lowry, Alt, and Ferree (1998).

3. In the case of Hungary, an important step has been taken toward the less politicized mechanisms of the marketplace with the passage of a bankruptcy procedure. It provides clarity and puts pressure on lenders to be prudent, and has worked in several instances of restructuring without bailouts.

4. Bayoumi, Goldstein, and Woglom (1995) find that the self-imposed constitutional controls reduce the interest rate for state general obligation bond issues by about half a percentage point in the U.S.

5. Ratified February 7, 1795: "The Judicial power of the United States shall not be construed to extend to any suit in law or in equity against one of the United States by Citizens of another State, or by Citizens or Subjects of any Foreign State."

6. Provincial income taxes in Canada could for most provinces be characterized as shared revenues, but the arrangement is voluntary (and not agreed to by all). Some provinces have also initiated coordination on the sales taxes.

7. Figure 13.4 displays own-source subnational revenue as a percentage of total subnational revenue. 1 − (transfers + revenue sharing)/total subnational revenue. It attempts to give a realistic comparative perspective on local fiscal autonomy by calculating the amount of revenue in each subnational sector that is raised locally. Thus, for instance, shared revenue that is legislated, collected, and redistributed by the central government is excluded.

8. An additional reason for persistent high levels of vertical fiscal imbalance is provided by Treisman (1999), who argues that central governments use transfers to pay off would-be secessionist regions, especially in ethnically divided federations.

9. The relative autonomy of the Finance Commission is one of the attractive features of India's system. An independent commission governing the distribution of grants is also a key feature of the Australian federal system.

10. See Dillinger and Webb (1999) and Jones, Sanguinetti, and Tommasi (2000).

11. The mechanisms that might create disciplined, vertically integrated political parties—like pure proportional representation with party lists compiled by the center—are likely to reduce the accountability of the center to local governments. This highlights a tension of institutional design familiar to political scientists: that between setting up incentives that promote strong accountability to local governments and their constituents, on one hand, and the internalization of externalities or resolution of cooperation problems on the other. Identifying the appropriate institutions to balance the centripetal and centrifugal forces in federal systems has been an ongoing (and unfinished) project of federalism scholars from Riker (1987) to Bednar, Eskridge, and Ferejohn (1999) to Weingast and de Figueredo (2001).

12. In Shakespeare's. *The Merchant of Venice*, the creditor is promised "a pound of flesh" (from the borrower's body) if the note were not repaid. Modern law would of course rule out and disregard such a clause (limiting creditor powers, in effect). In Shakespeare's case, it had not, and the case consequently screams for a bailout intervention.

13. In a recent development, when the mayor of Austevoll municipality "declared" bankruptcy, the minister of local governments declared, "Municipalities cannot go bankrupt." Subsequently, the supercounty administrator not only indicated where the municipality should make savings and revenue efforts, but also explained that the municipality

had been punished in grants allocation for its lack of revenue effort (*Bergens Tidende*, Oct. 5, 18, 2000).

14. For a parallel perspective from the firm, see Holmstrom and Milgrom (1994).

15. Williamson (2000), to illustrate, mentions norms and religion as forming over a century to a millennium and bureaucracy and judiciary over decades to a century. In our context of government design, the distinction would be between superlaws such as constitutions, and laws, assuming that the former can be changed less frequently than the latter, thus changing the nature of the subsequent game. In the decentralization literature, formulas for revenue sharing and grants are seen as important ways to structure the game in subsequent periods. But as we have argued, such formulas may not carry the commitment that they would need to structure future play.

16. For evidence on India, see Khemani (2001). On Brazil, see Arretche and Rodden (2001).

17. The idea that strength and discretion can represent weakness is important in game theory and also in many walks of life. In repeated prisoner's dilemma games, committing to tit-for-tat strategies can eliminate coordination problems. In public stock companies, managers' financial discretion (they are not watched very carefully) and love of their positions make them vulnerable to greenmailing. In a family, extreme wealth can make it hard to give the younger generation reasons to use their gifts well. And if you are with a strong or charming or well-connected person, you can behave stupidly since you know he or she can get you out of trouble. Becker (1974), in "The Rotten Kid Theorem" makes the point that these behavioral problems are ironed out under perfect information, and Bergstrom (1989) discusses under what special conditions this holds true. Homer, in *Iliad*, describes how Ulysses tries to solve this problem by giving up discretion and committing to a special course of action. For corporations, public accounting and audits combine attempts to reduce information asymmetries and commitment.

References

Arretche, Marta, and Jonathan Rodden. 2001. "Legislative Bargaining and Distributive Politics in Brazil: An Empirical Approach." Unpublished paper, MIT.

Bayoumi, Tamim, Morris Goldstein, and Geoffrey Woglom. 1995. "Do Credit Markets Discipline Sovereign Borrowers? Evidence from the U.S. States." *Journal of Money, Credit, and Banking* 27(4):1046–1959.

Becker, Gary. 1974. "A Theory of Social Interactions." *Journal of Political Economy* 82:1063–1094.

Bednar, Jenna, William Eskridge, and John Ferejohn. 1999. "A Political Theory of Federalism." Unpublished paper, University of Michigan.

Bergstrom, Theodore. 1989. "A Fresh Look at the Rotten Kid Theorem and Other Household Mysteries." *Journal of Political Economy* 97:1138–1159.

Dillinger, William and Steven Webb. 1999. "Fiscal Management in Federal Democracies: Argentina and Brazil." Policy Research Working Paper 2121, World Bank, Washington, D.C.

English, William. 1996. "Understanding the Costs of Sovereign Default: American State Debts in the 1840's." *American Economic Review* 86(1):259–275.

Epple, Dennis, and Chester Spatt. 1986. "State Restrictions on Local Debt: Their Role in Preventing Default." *Journal of Public Economics* 29(2):199–221.

Holmstrom, Bengt, and Paul Milgrom, 1994, "The Firm as an Incentive System." *American Economic Review* 84(4):972–991.

Jones, Jones, Mark, Pablo Sanguinetti, and Mariano Tommasi. 2000. "Politics, Institutions, and Fiscal Performance in a Federal System: An Analysis of the Argentine Provinces." *Journal of Development Economics* 61(2):305–333.

Khemani, Stuti. 2001. "Partisan Politics and Subnational Fiscal Deficits in India: What Does It Imply for the National Budget Constraint?" Unpublished paper, World Bank.

Lowry, Robert, James Alt, and Karen Ferree. 1998. "Fiscal Policy Outcomes and Electoral Accountability in the American States," *American Political Science Review* 92:4(December):759–774.

McConnell, Michael, and Randal Picker. 1993. "When Cities Go Broke: A Conceptual Introduction to Municipal Bankruptcy." *University of Chicago Law Review* 60:425, 466, 474–476.

Musgrave, Richard. 1959. *The Theory of Public Finance: A Study in Public Economy* New York: McGraw-Hill.

Ratchford, B. U. 1941. *American State Debts*. Durham, N.C.: Duke University Press.

Riker, William. 1987. *The Development of American Federalism*. Norwell, Mass.: Kluwer.

Rodden, Jonathan. 2002. "The Dilemma of Fiscal Federalism: Grants and Fiscal Performance Around the World." *American Journal of Political Science* 46(3):670–687.

Sen, Amartya. 1999. *Development as Freedom*, New York: Anchor Books.

Shepsle, Kenneth. 1991. "Discretion, Institutions and the Problem of Government Commitment." In Pierre Bourdieu and James Coleman, eds., *Social Theory for a Changing Society*. Boulder, Colo.: Westview.

Shepsle, Kenneth, and Barry Weingast. 1984. "Political Solutions to Market Problems." *American Political Science Review* 78(2):417–434.

Treisman, Daniel. 1999. *After the Deluge: Regional Crises and Political Consolidation in Russia*. Ann Arbor: University of Michigan Press.

Von Hagen, Jürgen, and Barry Eichengreen. 1996. "Federalism, Fiscal Restraints, and European Monetary Union." *American Economic Review* 86(2):134–138.

Wane, Waly. 2000. "Optimal Taxation with Poverty as a Public Good." Policy Research Working Paper, World Bank.

Weingast, Barry, and Rui de Figueredo. 2001. "Self-Enforcing Federalism." Unpublished paper, Stanford University.

Williamson, Oliver. 2000. "The New Institutional Economics: Taking Stock, Looking Ahead." *Journal of Economic Literature* 38(3):595–613.

Index